Certificate Stage

Module D

Managerial Finance

Revision Series

Feb 97

British Library Cataloguing-in-Publication Data

A catalogue record for this book is available from the British Library.

Published by AT Foulks Lynch Ltd
Number 4
The Griffin Centre
Staines Road
Feltham
Middlesex
TW14 0HS

ISBN 07483 3546 3

© AT Foulks Lynch Ltd, 1997

Acknowledgements

The past ACCA examination questions are the copyright of the Association of Chartered Certified Accountants. The answers to the questions from June 1994 onwards are the answers produced by the examiners themselves and are the copyright of the Association of Chartered Certified Accountants. The answers to the questions prior to June 1994 have been produced by AT Foulks Lynch Ltd.

We are grateful to the Chartered Institute of Management Accountants and the Institute of Chartered Accountants in England and Wales for permission to reproduce past examination questions. The answers have been prepared by AT Foulks Lynch Ltd.

CONTENTS

Examiner plus - the examiner's official answers
Further questions on this topic from the real exams with the examiner's official answers.

SECTION C – MANAGEMENT ACCOUNTING

Apportionment and absorption of costs

Examiner plus - the examiner's official answers
Further questions on this topic from the real exams with the examiner's official answers.

Budgeting and control

Examiner plus - the examiner's official answers
Further questions on this topic from the real exams with the examiner's official answers.

PREFACE

The new edition of the ACCA Revision Series published for the June and December 1997 examinations is an exciting product which incorporates 'Examiner Plus' - **all the new syllabus examinations from June 1994 up to and including December 1996 plus the Examiner's official answers.**

We have cross referenced all these questions to their topic headings in the contents pages so you can see at a glance what questions have been set on each syllabus area to date, topic by topic.

The inclusion of these questions and answers really does give students an unparalleled view of the way the new syllabus examinations are set and, even more importantly, a tremendous insight into the mind of the Examiner. The Examiner's answers are in some cases fairly lengthy and whilst the Examiner would not necessarily expect you to include all the points that his answers include, they do nevertheless give you an excellent insight into the sorts of things that the Examiner is looking for and will help you produce answers in line with the Examiner's thinking.

The Revision Series contains the following features;

- **Practice Questions and Answers -** a total bank of around 90 questions and answers

- An analysis of the past new syllabus exams - including all examinations since June 1994-providing a complete analysis of all examinations set under the New Syllabus

- Update notes which bring you up-to-date for new examinable documents and any changes to the Official Teaching Guide as at 1 December 1996

- Details of the format of the examination

- The Syllabus

- Formulae and tables where appropriate

- General Revision Guidance

- Key Revision Topics

- Examination Technique - an essential guide to ensure you approach the examinations correctly

---

CHANGES TO PAPER 8

Please note that there are three changes which affect Paper 8.

1	The management accounting examiner is changing with effect from the June 1997 examination.
2	The format of the exam is changing with effect from June 1997.
3	The syllabus is being modified with effect from December 1997.

The change in exam format and syllabus modifications are highlighted in the examination format and syllabus section on page ix, and further details are included in the updates section on page xxxiv.

The change in examiner is explained more fully in the updates section on page xxxiv and some notes from the new examiner are set out there.

---

1 EXAMINATION FORMAT AND SYLLABUS

FORMAT OF THE EXAMINATION

	Number of marks
Section A: Case study on financial management	40
Section B: One question (out of two) on financial management	20
Section C: Two questions (out of three) on management accounting	40
	100

The financial management content will account for approximately 60% of the marks and the management accounting content for the remainder.

Time allowed: 3 hours

This format will be used for the first time in June 1997. Previously, both management accounting and financial management topics were examinable in both sections A and B of the paper.

With effect from June 1997, the management accounting and financial management areas will be more clearly distinguished in the examination paper and each section will concentrate on either management accounting or financial management issues.

Introduction

Note: from December 1997, some relabelling of syllabus areas will occur to achieve a clearer distinction between Financial Management and Management Accounting, although the content of the syllabus itself will not change. See the updates section on page xxxiv for clarification of this.

Paper 8 examines two related subjects, Financial Management (weighting of 60%) and Management Accounting (weighting of 40%).

The paper builds on the overview of cost accounting from paper 3 and covers

- the application of the management accounting techniques used in planning, control and decision making and the interpretation of information available from their use

- the preparation, organisation, summarisation and presentation of management information/reports.

The paper introduces financial management areas, including

- the understanding of current practical methods used in making financial management decisions and the influence of the environment on such decisions

- the appreciation of the workings of the financial system, the evaluation of alternative sources of finance and the assessment of investment possibilities

- the communication of the consequences of financial management decisions to accountants and non-accountants.

Managerial Finance

(1)   COST AND MANAGEMENT ACCOUNTING METHODS

    (a)   Determining and allocating/apportioning costs of activities and outputs through the use of appropriate concepts, methods and techniques

        (i)   absorption, marginal and opportunity cost approaches to the accumulation of costs for specific orders (job, batch, contract) or operations (process, service)

        (ii)   activity based costing; use of cost drivers and activities.

    (b)   Consideration and application of information required in relation to

        (i)   costing of products and services
        (ii)   preparing plans
        (iii)   monitoring/controlling performance
        (iv)   decision making.

(2)   INFORMATION FOR PLANNING AND CONTROL

    (a)   Budgeting and budgetary control

        (i)   identify objectives of budgetary planning and control systems (including an introduction to behavioural influences)

        (ii)   identify/evaluate budgetary systems such as fixed and flexible, zero based and incremental, periodic and continuous

        (iii)   developing/implementing budgeting systems: functional/subsidiary and master budgets (including cash budgeting)

        (iv)   monitoring and controlling performance; calculation of variances; determination of cause of variances

        (v)   quantitative aids in budgeting; least squares regression; scatter diagram with correlation; forecasting with regression; introduction to time series and seasonality to analyse time related data.

    (b)   Standard costing

        (i)   uses and limitations of standard costing

        (ii)   determination of standards

        (iii)   identification and calculation of variances; sales variances (including quantity and mix), cost variances (including mix and yield); absorption and marginal approaches

        (iv)   identify significance and inter-relationship of variances

        (v)   relevance to business performance measurement and control.

    (c)   Cost allocation/apportionment/absorption

        (i)   absorption and marginal costing; impact on profit reporting; relevance in planning and control

        (ii)   activity based costing; use in costing of products and services; use as a planning and control device.

(3)   THE COSTING/PRICING OF PRODUCTS AND SERVICES

    (a)   Consideration and application of information requirements in relation to

        (i)   job costs
        (ii)   process costs
        (iii)   service industries
        (iv)   internal services.

(4)   MANAGEMENT OF WORKING CAPITAL

(*Note:* from December 1997 this will be relabelled as Section 6)

(a)   The nature and scope of working capital management.

(b)   The importance of effective working capital management to corporate survival.

(c)   Cash: selection of appropriate cash balances, managing cash surpluses and deficits. The nature and functions of the short term money market.

(d)   The management of debtors (including those overseas) involving credit evaluation, terms of credit, cash discounts, debt collection techniques, credit management monitoring and evaluation, factoring and invoice discounting.

(e)   Creditors: advantages and disadvantages of alternative methods of paying suppliers (including those overseas), the dangers of trading on credit.

(f)   Stock: alternative stock management systems and models including Total Quality Management (TQM), Just in Time (JIT), Economic Order Quantity (EOQ), etc.

(5)   FINANCIAL OBJECTIVES

(*Note:* from December 1997 this will be relabelled as Section 4)

(a)   The nature, purpose and scope of financial management.

(b)   The relationship between financial management, management accounting and financial accounting.

(c)   The relationship of financial objectives to organisational strategy and ethos and to other organisational objectives. The constraints/conflicts which different objectives may put upon each other.

(d)   The nature, scope and form (long term and short term) of financial objectives of different types of organisation, including not-for-profit organisations.

(e)   The roles, responsibilities and relationships of key personnel involved in and with organisations (shareholders, lenders, managers, employees, customers, suppliers, government).

(6)   FINANCIAL MANAGEMENT FRAMEWORK

(*Note:* from December 1997 this will be relabelled as Section 5)

(a)   The commercial and financial environment in which organisations operate (the nature and function of the money and capital markets including banks and other financial intermediaries, the Stock Exchange, the Alternative Investments Market and Over the Counter markets).

(b)   The economic environment in which organisations operate

  (i)   application of macro-economic theory as a basis for understanding the key economic variables affecting the business environment

  (ii)   fiscal policy, its nature, effectiveness of fiscal policy

  (iii)   money and interest rates, the role of money in the economy, the supply and demand for money

  (iv)   monetary policy, attitudes to monetary policy, problems of monetary policy

  (v)   supply-side policies, supply side problems, policies to improve supply side

  (vi)   policies towards monopolies and oligopolies, privatisation and deregulation

  (vii)   green policies; implications for management of the economy and the firm

  (viii) the significance of corporate securities (share capital, debt and preference shares) to commercial organisations and the markets in which they operate, and the influence of markets on organisations

  (ix)   the Efficient Markets Hypothesis and its relevance to decision making and to financial management practice.

(7)   SOURCES OF FINANCE

(a)   Sources and relative costs (including issue costs but not calculations of the cost of capital) of various types of finance and their suitability to different circumstances and organisations (both large and small companies, listed and unlisted) including

(i)   the nature and importance of internally generated funds

(ii)   capital markets (types of share capital, new issues, rights issues, loan capital, convertibles, warrants)

(iii)   the effect of dividend policy on financing needs

(iv)   bank finance (the various forms of short, medium and long term finance that are available, including leasing)

(v)   trade credit

(vi)   government sources: grants, regional and national aid schemes, tax incentives etc

(vii)   venture capital and financial sources particularly suited to the small company

(viii) international money and capital markets, including an introduction to international banking, and the finance of foreign trade.

(b)   Determining requirements for finance (how much, for how long, for what purpose) in relation to a client's operational and strategic objectives. The importance of the choice of capital structure to an organisation.

(c)   Calculating financial gearing and other key financial ratios and analysing their significance to the organisation.

(d)   Determining appropriate sources of finance by identifying and evaluating appropriate sources, taking into account such factors as

(i)   cost of finance including its servicing
(ii)   timing of cash payments
(iii)   effect on gearing and other ratios
(iv)   effect on the company's existing investors.

(8)   CAPITAL EXPENDITURE AND INVESTMENT

(a)   Identifying potential investment opportunities.

(b)   Appraising capital investments (domestic) for commercial and non commercial organisations through the use of appropriate methods and techniques

(i)   return on capital employed and payback

(ii)   discounting based methods, including the importance of the cost of capital to investment appraisal (but not the calculation of cost of capital)

(iii)   internal rate of return

(iv)   net present value

(v)   capital rationing (single and multi-period)

(vi)   lease or buy decisions

including the effects of taxation and inflation on investment decisions, the handling of risk and uncertainty, eg through the use of probabilities, sensitivity analysis and simulations.

2 ANALYSIS OF PAST PAPERS

Topics	J94		D94		J95		D95		J96		D96	
Investment appraisal	6 1	O ●			5 1	O O	2	●			6	O
Project financing	1	O			1	●	5	O	6	O	1 2	● ●
Economic policies/macroeconomics	2	●			1 2	● ●	2	●	2	●	2 2	● ●
Process costing	2	●	4	O					2	●			✓
Management accountants role	2	●			2	●						
Budgeting	2	●	1	O	2	●	1	O	2 4	● O	1	O	✓
Standard costing & variance analysis	3	O			2 3	● O	3	O	2	●	3	O	✓
Performance evaluation	4	O										
Management of working capital	5	O	2	●	2 5	● ●	2 1	● O	5	O	5	O
Finance markets			2	●	6	●	2 1 5	● ● O	2	●	2 2	● ●
Microeconomics - pricing			2	●			4	O				
Absorption/marginal/activity based costing			3	O	4	O			3	●	4	O	✓
Financial gearing			5	O					1	O		
Capital rationing			6	O								
Ratio analysis					6	O	6 1	O O	5	●		
Forecasting/statistical techniques					2	●	2	●	1	O		
Service department costing									3	O	2	●

Key

The number refers to the number of the question where this topic was examined in the exam.

O   This topic formed the whole or a substantial part of the question.

●   This topic formed a non-substantial part of a question.

3 GENERAL REVISION GUIDANCE

PLANNING YOUR REVISION

What is revision?

Revision is the process by which you remind yourself of the material you have studied during your course, clarify any problem areas and bring your knowledge to a state where you can retrieve it and present it in a way that will satisfy the Examiners.

Revision is not a substitute for hard work earlier in the course. The syllabus for this paper is too large to be hastily 'crammed' a week or so before the examination. You should think of your revision as the final stage in your study of any topic. It can only be effective if you have already completed earlier stages.

Ideally, you should begin your revision shortly after you begin an examination course. At the end of every week and at the end of every month, you should review the topics you have covered. If you constantly consolidate your work and integrate revision into your normal pattern of study, you should find that the final period of revision - and the examination itself - are much less daunting.

If you are reading this revision text while you are still working through your course, we strongly suggest that you begin now to review the earlier work you did for this paper. Remember, the more times you return to a topic, the more confident you will become with it.

The main purpose of this book, however, is to help you to make the best use of the last few weeks before the examination. In this section we offer some suggestions for effective planning of your final revision and discuss some revision techniques which you may find helpful.

Planning your time

Most candidates find themselves in the position where they have less time than they would like to revise, particularly if they are taking several papers at one diet. The majority of people must balance their study with conflicting demands from work, family or other commitments.

It is impossible to give hard and fast rules about the amount of revision you should do. You should aim to start your final revision at least four weeks before your examination. If you finish your course work earlier than this, you would be well advised to take full advantage of the extra time available to you. The number of hours you spend revising each week will depend on many factors, including the number of papers you are sitting. You should probably aim to do a minimum of about six to eight hours a week for each paper.

In order to make best use of the revision time that you have, it is worth spending a little of it at the planning stage. We suggest that you begin by asking yourself two questions:

- How much time do I have available for revision?
- What do I need to cover during my revision?

Once you have answered these questions, you should be able to draw up a detailed timetable. We will now consider these questions in more detail.

How much time do I have available for revision?

Many people find it helpful to work out a regular weekly pattern for their revision. We suggest you use the time planning chart provided to do this. Your aim should be to construct a timetable that is sustainable over a period of several weeks.

Time planning chart

	Monday	Tuesday	Wednesday	Thursday	Friday	Saturday	Sunday
00.00							
01.00							
02.00							
03.00							
04.00							
05.00							
06.00							
07.00							
08.00							
09.00							
10.00							
11.00							
12.00							
13.00							
14.00							
15.00							
16.00							
17.00							
18.00							
19.00							
20.00							
21.00							
22.00							
23.00							

1   First, block out all the time that is **definitely unavailable** for revision. This will include the hours when you normally sleep, the time you are at work and any other regular and clear commitments.

2   Think about **other people's claims on your time**. If you have a family, or friends whom you see regularly, you may want to discuss your plans with them. People are likely to be flexible in the demands they make on you in the run-up to your examinations, especially if they are aware that you have considered their needs as well as your own. If you consult the individuals who are affected by your plans, you may find that they are surprisingly supportive, instead of being resentful of the extra time you are spending studying.

3   Next, give some thought to the times of day when you **work most effectively**. This differs very much from individual to individual. Some people can concentrate first thing in the morning. Others work best in the early evening, or last thing at night. Some people find their day-to-day work so demanding that they are unable to do anything extra during the week, but must concentrate their study time at weekends. Mark the times when you feel you could do your best work on the

timetable. It is extremely important to acknowledge your personal preferences here. If you ignore them, you may devise a timetable that is completely unrealistic and which you will not be able to adhere to.

4   Consider your **other commitments**. Everybody has certain tasks, from doing the washing to walking the dog, that must be performed on a regular basis. These tasks may not have to be done at a particular time, but you should take them into consideration when planning your schedule. You may be able to find more convenient times to get these jobs done, or be able to persuade other people to help you with them.

5   Now mark some time for **relaxation**. If your timetable is to be sustainable, it must include some time for you to build up your reserves. If your normal week does not include any regular physical activity, make sure that you include some in your revision timetable. A couple of hours spent in a sports centre or swimming pool each week will probably enhance your ability to concentrate.

6   Your timetable should now be taking shape. You can probably see obvious study sessions emerging. It is not advisable to work for too long at any one session. Most people find that they can only really concentrate for one or two hours at a time. If your study sessions are longer than this, you should split them up.

What do I need to cover during my revision?

Most candidates are more confident about some parts of the syllabus than others. Before you begin your revision, it is important to have an overview of where your strengths and weaknesses lie.

One way to do this is to take a sheet of paper and divide it into three columns. Mark the columns:

OK   **Marginal**   **Not OK**

or use similar headings to indicate how confident you are with a topic. Then go through the syllabus (reprinted in Section 1) and list the topics under the appropriate headings. Alternatively, you could use the list of key topics in Section 5 of this book to compile your overview. You might also find it useful to skim through the introductions or summaries to the textbook or workbooks you have used in your course. These should remind you of parts of the course that you found particularly easy or difficult at the time. You could also use some of the exercises and questions in the workbooks or textbooks, or some of the questions in this book, as a diagnostic aid to discover the areas where you need to work hardest.

It is also important to be aware which areas of the syllabus are so central to the subject that they are likely to be examined in every diet, and which are more obscure, and not likely to come up so frequently. Your textbooks, workbooks and lecture notes will help you here, and section 2 of this book contains an analysis of past papers. Remember, the Examiner will be looking for broad coverage of the syllabus. There is no point in knowing one or two topics in exhaustive detail if you do so at the expense of the rest of the course.

Writing your revision timetable

You now have the information you need to write your timetable. You know how many weeks you have available, and the approximate amount of time that is available in each week.

You should stop all serious revision 48 hours before your examination. After this point, you may want to look back at your notes to refresh your memory, but you should not attempt to revise any new topics. A clear and rested brain is worth more than any extra facts you could memorise in this period.

Make one copy of this chart for each week you have available for revision.

Using your time planning chart, write in the times of your various study sessions during the week.

In the lower part of the chart, write in the topics that you will cover in each of these sessions.

Example of a revision timetable

Revision timetable Week beginning:							
	Monday	Tuesday	Wednesday	Thursday	Friday	Saturday	Sunday
Study sessions							
Topics							

Some revision techniques

There should be two elements in your revision. You must **look back** to the work you have covered in the course and **look forward** to the examination. The techniques you use should reflect these two aspects of revision.

Revision should not be boring. It is useful to try a variety of techniques. You probably already have some revision techniques of your own and you may also like to try some of the techniques suggested here, if they are new to you. However, don't waste time with methods of revision which are not effective for you.

- Go through your lecture notes, textbook or workbooks and use a highlighter pen to mark important points.

- Produce a new set of summarised notes. This can be a useful way of re-absorbing information, but you must be careful to keep your notes concise, or you may find that you are simply reproducing work you have done before. It is helpful to use a different format for your notes.

- Make a collection of key words which remind you of the essential concepts of a topic.

- Reduce your notes to a set of key facts and definitions which you must memorise. Write them on cards which you can keep with you all the time.

- When you come across areas which you were unsure about first time around, rework relevant questions in your course materials, then study the answers in great detail.

- If there are isolated topics which you feel are completely beyond you, identify exactly what it is that you cannot understand and find someone (such as a lecturer or recent graduate) who can explain these points to you.

- Practise as many exam standard questions as you can. The best way to do this is to work to time, under exam conditions. You should always resist looking at the answer until you have finished.

- If you have come to rely on a word processor in your day-to-day work, you may have got out of the habit of writing at speed. It is well worth reviving this skill before you sit down in the examination hall: it is something you will need.

- If you have a plentiful supply of relevant questions, you could use them to practise planning answers, and then compare your notes with the answers provided. This is not a substitute for writing full answers, but can be helpful additional practice.

- Go back to questions you have already worked on during the course. This time, complete them under exam conditions, paying special attention to the layout and organisation of your answers. Then compare them in detail with the suggested answers and think about the ways in which your answer differs. This is a useful way of 'fine tuning' your technique.

- During your revision period, do make a conscious effort to identify situations which illustrate concepts and ideas that may arise in the examination. These situations could come from your own work, or from reading the business pages of the quality press. This technique will give you a new perspective on your studies and could also provide material which you can use in the examination.

4 EXAMINATION TECHNIQUES

THE EXAMINATION

This section is divided into two parts. The first part considers the practicalities of sitting the examination. If you have taken other ACCA examinations recently, you may find that everything here is familiar to you. The second part discusses some examination techniques which you may find useful.

The practicalities

What to take with you

You should make sure that you have:

- your ACCA registration card
- your ACCA registration docket.

You may also take to your desk:

- pens and pencils
- a ruler and slide rule
- a calculator
- charting template and geometrical instruments
- eraser and correction fluid.

You are not allowed to take rough paper into the examination.

If you take any last-minute notes with you to the examination hall, make sure these are not on your person. You should keep notes or books in your bag or briefcase, which you will be asked to leave at the side of the examination hall.

Although most examination halls will have a clock, it is advisable to wear a watch, just in case your view is obscured.

If your calculator is solar-powered, make sure it works in artificial light. Some examination halls are not particularly well-lit. If you use a battery-powered calculator, take some spare batteries with you. For obvious reasons, you may not use a calculator which has a graphic/word display memory. Calculators with printout facilities are not allowed because they could disturb other candidates

Getting there

You should arrange to arrive at the examination hall at least half an hour before the examination is due to start. If the hall is a large one, the invigilator will start filling the hall half an hour before the starting time.

Make absolutely sure that you know how to get to the examination hall and how long it will take you. Check on parking or public transport. Leave yourself enough time so that you will not be anxious if the journey takes a little longer than you anticipated. Many people like to make a practice trip the day before their first examination.

At the examination hall

Examination halls differ greatly in size. Some only hold about ten candidates. Others can sit many hundreds of people. You may find that more than one examination is being taken at the hall at the same time, so don't panic if you hear people discussing a completely different subject from the one you have revised.

While you are waiting to go in, don't be put off by other people talking about how well, or badly, they have prepared for the examination.

You will be told when to come in to the examination hall. The desks are numbered. (Your number will be on your examination docket.) You will be asked to leave any bags at the side of the hall.

Inside the hall, the atmosphere will be extremely formal. The invigilator has certain things which he or she must tell candidates, often using a particular form of words. Listen carefully, in case there are any unexpected changes to the arrangements.

On your desk you will see a question paper and an answer booklet in which to write your answers. You will be told when to turn over the paper.

During the examination

You will have to leave your examination paper and answer booklet in the hall at the end of the examination. It is quite acceptable to write on your examination paper if it helps you to think about the questions. However, all workings should be in your answers. You may write any plans and notes in your answer booklet, as long as you cross them out afterwards.

If you require a new answer booklet, put your hand up and a supervisor will come and bring you one.

At various times during the examination, you will be told how much time you have left.

You should not need to leave the examination hall until the examination is finished. Put up your hand if you need to go to the toilet, and a supervisor will accompany you. If you feel unwell, put up your hand, and someone will come to your assistance. If you simply get up and walk out of the hall, you will not be allowed to reenter.

Before you finish, you must fill in the required information on the front of your answer booklet.

Examination techniques

Tackling Paper 8

The examination will consist of three sections. Section A, which is compulsory, will comprise a mini case study covering some aspect of financial management. This will normally contain a mixture of four or five computational and discussion questions. This section is worth 40 marks, which will not be divided equally among the questions. The case study will be designed to test the depth of your understanding of the syllabus. You will be expected to provide your own assessment of the situation and to include your reasoned opinions. You should spend about an hour and 10 minutes on this case study.

In section B, you will have to answer one out of two problem-solving questions on financial management topics. In section C, you will have to answer two out of three questions on management accounting topics. These questions will be worth 20 marks each. All questions will include a mixture of computation and discussion. You should spend about 35 minutes on each question.

Your general strategy

You should spend the first ten minutes of the examination reading the paper and deciding which questions you will do. You must divide the time you spend on questions in proportion to the marks on offer. Don't be tempted to spend more time on a question you know a lot about, or one which you find particularly difficult. If a question has more than one part, you must try to complete each part.

On every question, the first marks are the easiest to gain. Even if things go wrong with your timing and you don't have time to complete a question properly, you will probably gain some marks by making a start.

Spend the last five minutes reading through your answers and making any additions or corrections.

You may answer written questions in any order you like. Some people start with their best question, to help them relax. Another strategy is to begin with your second best question, so that you are working even more effectively when you reach the question you are most confident about.

Once you have embarked on a question, you should try to stay with it, and not let your mind stray to other questions on the paper. You can only concentrate on one thing at once. However, if you get completely stuck with a question, leave space in your answer book and return to it later.

Answering the question

All Examiners say that the most frequent reason for failure in examinations, apart from basic lack of knowledge, is candidates' unwillingness to answer the question that the Examiner has asked. A great many people include every scrap of knowledge they have on a topic, just in case it is relevant. Stick to the question and tailor your answer to what you are asked. Pay particular attention to the verbs in the question.

You should be particularly wary if you come across a question which appears to be almost identical to one which you have practised during your revision. It probably isn't! Wishful thinking makes many people see the question they would like to see on the paper, not the one that is actually there. Read a question at least twice before you begin your answer. Underline key words on the question paper, if it helps focus your mind on what is required.

If you don't understand what a question is asking, state your assumptions. Even if you do not answer in precisely the way the Examiner hoped, you may be given some credit, if your assumptions are reasonable.

Presentation

You should do everything you can to make things easy for the marker. Although you will not be marked on your handwriting, the marker will find it easier to identify the points you have made if your answers are legible. The same applies to spelling and grammar. Use blue or black ink. The marker will be using red or green.

Use the margin to clearly identify which question, or part of a question, you are answering.

Start each answer on a new page. The order in which you answer the questions does not matter, but if a question has several parts, these parts should appear in the correct order in your answer book.

If there is the slightest doubt when an answer continues on another page, indicate to the marker that he or she must turn over. It is irritating for a marker to think he or she has reached the end of an answer, only to turn the page and find that the answer continues.

Use columnar layouts for computations. This will help you to avoid mistakes, and is easier to follow.

Use headings and numbered sentences if they help to show the structure of your answer. However, don't write your answers in one-word note form.

If your answers include diagrams, don't waste time making them great works of art. Keep them clear, neat and simple. Use your rule and any templates or geometric instruments you have with you. Remember to label the axes of graphs properly. Make reference to any diagrams in the body of your text so that they form an integral part of your answer.

It is a good idea to make a rough plan of an answer before you begin to write. Do this in your answer booklet, but make sure you cross it out neatly afterwards. The marker needs to be clear whether he or she is looking at your rough notes, or the answer itself.

Computations

Before you begin a computation, you may find it helpful to jot down the stages you will go through.

It is essential to include all your workings and to indicate where they fit in to your answer. It is important that the marker can see where you got the figures in your answer from. Even if you make mistakes in your computations, you will be given credit for using a principle correctly, if it is clear from your workings and the structure of your answer.

If you spot an arithmetical error which has implications for figures later in your answer, it almost certainly is not worth spending a lot of time reworking your computation.

If you are asked to comment or make recommendations on a computation, you must do so. There are important marks to be gained here. Even if your computation contains mistakes, you may still gain marks if your reasoning is correct.

Use the layouts which you see in the answers given in this booklet and in model answers. A clear layout will help you avoid errors and will impress the marker.

Essay questions

In this paper you could be asked to write a short essay of up to about 12 marks.

You must plan an essay before you start writing. One technique is to quickly jot down any ideas which you think are relevant. Re-read the question and cross out any points in your notes which are not relevant. Then number your points. Remember to cross out your plan afterwards.

Your essay should have a clear structure. It should contain a brief introduction, a main section and a conclusion. Don't waste time by restating the question at the start of your essay.

Break your essay up into paragraphs. Use sub-headings and numbered sentences if they help show the structure of your answer.

Be concise. It is better to write a little about a lot of different points than a great deal about one or two points.

The Examiner will be looking for evidence that you have understood the syllabus and can apply your knowledge in new situations. You will also be expected to give opinions and make judgements. These should be based on reasoned and logical arguments.

Case studies

The case study asks you to apply your knowledge in a particular situation. Expect to spend up to a quarter of the time available for the question on reading and analysing the information and planning your answer.

Start by reading the questions based on the case study. Then read the case study, trying to grasp the main points. Read the case study through again and make notes of the key points. Then analyse the case and identify the relevant issues and concepts. Before you start your answer, read the questions again along with relevant parts of the case study.

If alternative answers present themselves, mention them. you may sometimes find it helpful to consider short and long term recommendations separately.

Reports, memos and other documents

Some questions ask you to present your answer in the form of a report or a memo or other document. It is important that you use the correct format - there are easy marks to be gained here. Adopt the format used in sample questions, or use the format you are familiar with in your day-to-day work, as long as it contains all the essential elements.

You should also consider the audience for any document you are writing. How much do they know about the subject? What kind of information and recommendations are required? The Examiner will be looking for evidence that you can present your ideas in an appropriate form.

5 KEY REVISION TOPICS

The aim of this section is to provide you with a checklist of key information relating to this Paper. You should use it as a reminder of topics to be revised rather than as a summary of all you need to know. Aim to revise as many topics as possible because many of the questions in the exam draw on material from more than one section of the syllabus. You will get more out of this section if you read through Section 3, General Revision Guidance first.

FINANCIAL MANAGEMENT

Paper 8 provides an introduction to financial management. The key areas are:

- purpose and objectives of financial management
- financial markets
- the economic framework
- working capital
- sources of company finance
- investment appraisal.

1 OBJECTIVES OF FINANCIAL MANAGEMENT

Possible corporate objectives include maximising profit, maximising sales, maximising profit share and survival. The primary assumed financial goal is to maximise share price which is achieved by investing in positive NPV projects. This is the main requirement of the owners (shareholders) who have invested in the business. Short-term profits can be manipulated using creative accounting techniques. Financial management as a whole involves the search for good investments, the means to finance them and finding what to do with the surplus (to incorporate dividend policy).

Objectives can be classified into primary and secondary, quantitative or qualitative, financial or strategic. Objectives for not-for-profit organisations are likely to be different from those of commercial organisations in that they will tend to focus on performance and output measures. There are numerous areas for potential conflict in trying to meet objectives, e.g. short-term objectives may conflict with long-term ones; the requirements of shareholders (return on their investment) may conflict with the objectives of managers (such as a high salary), or of employees (who want stable and highly paid employment).

2 THE FINANCIAL MARKETS

Financial markets bring together lenders and borrowers. There are two main types of markets - the money markets dealing with short-term (up to one year) finance and the capital markets dealing in long-term finance. The money markets tend to be specialised and include the inter-bank market, the discount market, and local authority money markets. The main UK capital market is the Stock Exchange, but there is also the alternative investment market (AIM) and the Oftex market.

Each market specialises in certain securities, for example, commercial paper and bills of exchange and Treasury Bills are traded on the money markets, whereas Government gilts, company shares and debentures and Eurobonds are traded on the capital markets. Markets thus provide marketability for securities.

Primary markets specialise in selling securities to investors in the first place whereas secondary markets deal in 'second-hand' securities (like the buying and selling of shares on the Stock Exchange). Markets price securities to reflect the risk-return trade-off that applies to all securities. Financial intermediaries often act to link borrowers and lenders; examples are banks, insurance companies and pension funds.

3   EFFICIENT MARKETS HYPOTHESIS

There are three main forms of this concept:

- The weak form states that share prices reflect all past information. Therefore, the only thing that will now change share prices is new information. Since new information occurs randomly between 'good news' and 'bad news', share prices should move randomly to reflect this pattern. Studies show that this is in fact the case. There is no correlation between changes in share prices from one day to another.

- The semi-strong form states that share prices reflect all publicly available information, and that any such information is quickly incorporated into the share price.

- The strong form states that share prices reflect all information whether public or not.

If financial markets are weak form efficient, technical analysis (Chartism) seems to be a pointless occupation. The same goes for fundamental analysis if the market is semi-strong; any information discovered will already be included in the share price. If the market is strong-form efficient, insider trading will not yield any abnormal returns. However, since insider trading is illegal, the implication is that it does yield abnormal returns and therefore the market is not deemed to be strong form efficient.

4   MACROECONOMIC OBJECTIVES AND POLICIES

Governments try to achieve four main economic objectives:

- full employment
- price stability
- economic growth
- positive balance of payments.

These policies can conflict; for example, in the UK, economic growth tends to increase inflation and worsen the balance of payments.

There are two main types of policy used in attempting to achieve these objectives. Firstly, monetary policy focuses on the supply of money in the economy. It seeks to regulate economic activity by changes in interest rates. This will affect the amount of borrowing which the personal and business sectors will take on by affecting the amount of interest payable. Interest rate changes are also likely to affect the exchange rate.

Fiscal policy regulates demand through Government expenditure and taxation. An increase in taxation reduces consumer disposable income and a decrease in Government spending reduces demand in the economy.

Policy based on monetary controls was in the ascendancy during the 1980s and associated with Milton Friedman and neoclassical economic theory. Fiscal policy is associated with Keynes who would presumably not be too unhappy with a 1994/95 Government deficit of £36bn given a near 2.75 million unemployment figure, which, it could be argued, is the product of classical policies pursued during the 1980s.

5   **STRATEGIC WORKING CAPITAL MANAGEMENT**

Working capital is defined as current assets less current liabilities. Strategic working capital management examines investment in current assets *vis-a-vis* investment in fixed assets on the one hand, and the financing mix of those assets as between short-term and long-term finance on the other.

Fixed assets tend to be the wealth-creating assets, the engine-room of value. They include projects, investments, machines and the like. Current assets (stock, debtors and cash) provide liquidity and act as a buffer between receipts and payments. Investment in current assets has an opportunity cost, that is, it needs to be financed. Thus firms will often look to maximise their investment in fixed assets and minimise their investment in current assets. This is profitable, but risky due to the potential lack of liquidity it creates.

Long-term finance is generally more expensive than short-term finance. Companies may, therefore, choose to finance their activities mainly through short-term finance. However, this is risky on two scores. Firstly, short-term interest rates are more volatile than long-term rates and secondly, short-term finance will need to be regularly renewed. Problems will occur if renewal is not permitted. Firms that follow an aggressive strategy of investing predominantly in fixed assets (usually due to high sales growth) financed by short-term assets are said to be overtrading.

6   **DEBTOR CREDIT CONTROL AND POLICY**

Firms must find the answers to a number of questions when deciding upon credit control and policy:

- To whom should credit be given (use references; study past history)?

- How much credit should be given (start low)?

- What discounts should be offered?

- What methods should be used to control the debt (regular statements and follow-up letters, formal procedures invoked for chasing late payers)?

Businesses should attempt to calculate the financial implications of any change in credit policy; for example, if the company wants to increase sales through giving easier credit, then the financial benefit of the extra contribution earned from the sales must be matched against the appropriate costs: these will include the opportunity cost of the higher debtor level, the cost of extra bad debts, the cost of any extra discounts given and so on.

Some companies factor their debtors by handing over the whole sales ledger; others may obtain finance using debtors as security.

7   **INVENTORY MANAGEMENT**

The main points here are:

- The rate of stock turnover (cost of sales ÷ average stock). Generally, the higher the better, but any reduction in average stock can lead to an increased risk of a stock-out.

- EOQ $= \sqrt{\frac{2cd}{h}}$ where c = order cost, d = annual demand, h = holding cost per unit. The EOQ gives the lowest cost order amount. The number of orders in any one year will, therefore, be total demand divided by the EOQ.

- Re-order level = Lead time average x daily usage. However, this will produce a stock-out if either the lead time or the average daily usage increases. Thus firms will often hold a 'safety stock' above the above minimum re-order level. This incurs extra costs (such as the opportunity cost of the investment and stock-holding cost) but saves money by reducing the risk of a stock-out.

- Just-in-time reduces stocks held and requires a close relationship with the supplier. Stock is ordered to meet an immediate order, not to be held as stock.

8   CASH AND TREASURY MANAGEMENT

There are three demands for cash (following Keynes):

- the transactions demand for daily cash requirements
- the precautionary demand for unexpected events
- the speculative demand to take advantage of any business opportunities that may arise.

(These demands can be applied to stock as well.) Cash can be planned for by drawing up cash budgets. Future deficits need finance arrangements and future surpluses can be invested in money markets.

Cash models are sometimes used to determine when cash should be invested in money markets; examples are those of Baumol and Miller-Orr.

Treasury management incorporates all aspects of cash management, such as ensuring proper procedures and security in cash handling and transfer: ensuring and arranging that sufficient finance is available for company investments; controlling foreign exchange transactions. These activities are now usually centralised to keep closer, more expert and more cost-efficient control on the financing requirements of the company.

9   LONG-TERM FINANCE - SHARE CAPITAL

This includes knowledge of both ordinary and preference shares. Ordinary share dividends (variable) and preference share interest (fixed, this interest is not tax-deductible) are paid out of profits and will, therefore, be shown as appropriations of profit rather than as business financing expenses. Ordinary shareholders are in a riskier position because they are paid after preference shareholders. They therefore require a higher return. There are many different types of preference shares including cumulative, participating and redeemable shares.

Ordinary shares are issued in a variety of ways:

- offer for sale (sale to an issuing house, such as a merchant bank)

- public issue (sale to the public arranged by the company itself)

- sale by tender (investors must apply to buy shares at an offered price)

- introduction (no new shares issued; simply enables a listing on the Stock Exchange)

- placing (placing shares in the hands of a few big financial institutions)

- issues to existing shareholders (for example, rights issues at a discount to the market price - you need to calculate the theoretical ex-rights price; scrip dividends instead of cash; stock splits to reduce share prices).

Mananananananan

The main advantages of equity finance to a company are:

- there is no fixed interest charge
- there is no requirement for redemption (usually)
- there are no issue costs for retained earnings
- shares are marketable; this encourages investors to buy.

The main disadvantages of equity finance to a company are:

- an issue of new shares may affect control

- an issue of new shares can be expensive

- equity finance is expensive; investors require a high return to compensate them for the risk (in the form of dividends and/or capital gains)

- dividends (unlike interest or debt) are not tax-deductible.

10   LONG-TERM FINANCE - DEBT

The main types of long-term company debt are debentures (secured on assets), mortgages and bank loans. In addition, there may be unsecured debt (sometimes called secondary or mezzanine debt: because it is riskier debt, investors will require a higher return). At the extreme of very high risk, unsecured debt is junk bonds: but these are not found in the UK.

Debentures and other debt can sometimes be converted into ordinary shares at terms and times prescribed by the company. The market price of such a convertible will be influenced by the value of the shares it can be converted into if conversion looks likely, or by the value of the underlying debt itself if conversion is unlikely. If conversion takes place, the amount of debt decreases and equity increases. This will reduce gearing. The effect on EPS is problematic. Although there will be extra shares, the conversion will save interest charges.

Debt also sometimes has warrants attached to it. This allows holders to purchase shares at a prescribed price at prescribed times in the future. Unlike convertibles, if warrants are exercised, the underlying debt remains. The value of the warrant depends on how likely it is to be exercised and will increase in value the more the market share price exceeds the exercise price. Because warrants and convertibles are potentially valuable options to the investor, the investor will require a lower return on the debt itself.

One of the big advantages of issuing debt for a tax-paying company is that the interest on the debt is tax deductible. This greatly reduces the cost of debt to the company and is an enticement to increase borrowing. Non-tax-paying companies may issue zero-coupon debt which pays no interest at all; the return to investors is entirely a capital gain (although an element of this is liable to be taxed as income by the Inland Revenue).

Other advantages of debt are that it is cheap to issue, and it does not affect voting rights in the company.

However, debt does bring potential disadvantages:

- interest has to be paid whether profits are made or not

- debt increases the risk of equity; in terms of whether a dividend is paid or not, and, if the company is liquidated, the fact that there is more debt to pay off before shareholders receive any final payment

- companies need to make provision for redemption of debt

- debt may bring restrictions on further borrowing, or on accounting ratios.

11   CAPITAL STRUCTURE

Financial gearing is measured by the debt/equity ratio. Gearing produces financial risk (the risk that interest has to be paid whether profits are made or not) and financial leverage (because interest is a fixed amount any percentage change in EBIT will produce a higher percentage change in EPS). Operating leverage arises from the existence of fixed costs so that EBIT fluctuates by a greater amount than any changes in sales. The 'traditional' approach to capital structure states that early levels of gearing increase company value, but as the company moves beyond an 'optimal' gearing level, the extra financial risk of the gearing reduces company value.

12   METHODS OF INVESTMENT APPRAISAL

The two non-discounting methods are payback and the accounting rate of return (ARR) or return on investment (ROI).

Payback is the number of years of cash inflows it takes to return the amount of the cash outflow.

The ROI is the average annual profit divided by the average investment (original cost + residual value)/2. Other definitions of ROI may use cash flow instead of profit, and initial investment rather than average investment.

Although both methods are simple to use and easy to understand, neither takes account of the time value of money.

The two main discounting methods are net present value (NPV) and internal rate of return (IRR). Projects with a positive NPV give a return higher than investing money at the opportunity cost (as reflected in the discount rate), and so should be accepted. The IRR of a project is that rate of interest which discounts the cash flows to an NPV of zero. The decision rule is to invest in any project with an IRR greater than the required rate of return. NPV and IRR give consistent decisions on whether to accept a project or not.   *in Absolute Terms*

However, if two projects are mutually exclusive (that is, you only want one of them), the project with the highest NPV should be chosen. Projects cannot be ranked according to IRRs because the IRR is a percentage and takes no account of scale; most of us would prefer a return of 25% on an investment of £1,000 than 100% on an investment of £1.

IRR is also more difficult to use because, for example:

- there may be more than one IRR

- the decision rule is difficult to use if the discount rate changes during the course of the project.

Finally, there is a theoretical inconsistency with IRR in that it assumes in its calculation that cash inflows can be reinvested at the project's IRR; NPV assumes that the cash inflows from all projects can be reinvested at the discount rate, which itself reflects the opportunity cost of funds.

MANAGEMENT ACCOUNTING

The Management Accounting section of the Managerial Finance syllabus covers certain key areas which are fundamental to an understanding of the topics that make up the syllabus.

These topics are:

- full absorption costing
- marginal costing
- basic decision making techniques
- cost information for planning and control
- budgetary control
- standard costing.

Full absorption and marginal costing are unlikely to be examined as separate topics as these will have been covered by earlier examinations. The concepts however, remain vital to the main body of the syllabus that you need to address.

Keep in mind the introductory sections in management accounting textbooks that detail the roles and purposes of management accounting. This whole section deals with the 'utility value' of information and the way information needs to be adapted to suit the needs of different managers and different forms of organisational structure.

In relation to questions in Section B in the examination - expect these short questions to be quite open ended, and also expect to rely on your own observations/experience of industry and commerce.

13   FULL ABSORPTION COSTING

Conventional full or total absorption costing: make sure that you are conversant with techniques of:

- allocation
- apportionment
- absorption of overhead.

The word 'allocation' can usually be prefaced by the term 'direct' or 'specific' bringing out the fact that some overhead costs are quite specific to an activity, department or cost centre. The term 'apportionment' can usually be prefaced by the word 'arbitrary' - the overhead cost item needs to be spread on a basis that is thought to be fair and equitable. Know what these methods might be, but understand the limitations of spreading any cost on a basis that requires judgement.

The term **'activity based costing'** needs to be explained and you need to be aware of the techniques that will be used by this approach and be able to compare them with conventional approaches.

The terms you need to be conversant with are:

- cost drivers
- cost pools.

Remember that this approach puts the emphasis, not on spreading costs, but on seeking out what causes the cost to be incurred or what 'drives' the cost.

A comparison between product costs produced 'conventionally' and one produced under an 'ABC' system would be useful for you to study.

14   MARGINAL COSTING

Do not lose sight of the basic distinction between full absorption and marginal costing. With full absorption costing the attempt was to charge each unit of output with a share of the fixed overheads. With marginal costing fixed costs are seen as costs of operating the business for a period of time and need to be covered by the contribution generated by each activity.

This fundamental difference will be tested in a variety of potential questions. In Paper 8 there is only a limited requirement to study decision making as this is also covered in Paper 9. However, your revision must take into account cost analysis by 'behaviour' - which costs are fixed, variable or semi-variable?

This knowledge about cost behaviour should assist you to answer questions that involve decisions about pricing, as well as those about planning.

Remember the 'marginal cost equation':

> Sales - Variable Costs   = Contribution
>
> Contribution - Fixed costs= Profit
>
> or:
>
> S-Vc=C=Fc+P

15   BASIC DECISION MAKING TECHNIQUES

Remember that decision making in Paper 8 will tend to cover some of the questions on planning and control which have decision making implications. Perhaps, as a result of plans being prepared in the budgeting process, an ad hoc decision needs to be made involving possibly the use of a scarce resource such as labour hours.

You will need to remember the work you have done in your earlier studies regarding limiting factors. Contribution per unit of limiting factor needs to be known, so if the constraint is a shortfall of labour hours, the contribution per labour hour will need to be known for each product or activity.

A further area for you to consider is that of output pricing. This topic requires you to have a basic knowledge of economics as a basis for making decisions regarding pricing.

Remember that the nature of Paper 8 is to draw on other disciplines such as economics and financial accounting as a basis for the study of managerial finance. The Examiner will be looking for you to display and apply a wide range of knowledge drawn from both past and current studies.

16   COST INFORMATION FOR PLANNING AND CONTROL

There are certain basic areas that can be examined in this field. Some examination questions will be predominantly based upon calculations and appear in Section C of the paper. However, an important part of this topic will be contained in the motivational and behavioural side of budgeting.

Make sure you understand terms like 'goal congruence', 'responsibility accounting' and 'participation', so that you can show the Examiner that you are aware that control systems will only work if the managers involved are motivated.

You also need to consider that different needs will be apparent in different businesses. The planning needs of a local authority will be different to those of a profit-orientated business, and different again to those of a charity. Examination questions may well bring out this difference.

17   BUDGETARY CONTROL

This is a major area of the syllabus. Short scenario questions may be expected in Section B and questions on it may appear at frequent intervals in Section C. It could also feature as a major component part of the Section A case study type question.

The main areas for your revision should be:

- preparation of cash budgets - detail the timings of inflows and outflows of cash, and the distinction between profit and liquidity.

- preparation of functional budgets: putting together an overall master budget with subsidiary budgets for sales, production and purchases coordinated together.

- preparation and use of flexible budgets: budget allowances will need to be set for the volume of activity planned; these allowances can then be allowed to actual volumes achieved. Questions often involve the ability to segregate semi-variable costs into fixed and variable components by using techniques such as high/low, or regression analysis.

- zero-based budgets: the applicability of these in different businesses.

- periodic and continuous budget systems.

Bear in mind that budgeting will be done differently in different businesses. Control systems will only work if the planning process is thorough and suitable to the particular business. In answering examination questions, the Examiner will require you to recognise the uses and limitations of budgetary control, and not just be concerned with your ability to manipulate figures.

18   STANDARD COSTING

You will need an ability to calculate variances, and be able to distinguish between planning and operational variances.

Make sure that you can calculate a total material cost variance and analyse it into:

- price variance, and
- usage variance: and analyse this into mix and yield variances if appropriate.

Make sure that you can calculate a total labour cost variance, and analyse it into:

- rate variance, and
- efficiency variance: and analyse this into idle time categories if appropriate.

Make sure that you can calculate a total overhead cost variance, and analyse it into:

- total fixed overhead variance, subdivided into:

    - expenditure variance
    - volume variance
    - efficiency variance

- total variable overhead variance, subdivided into:

    - expenditure variance
    - efficiency variance

- total sales variance, analysed into volume and price.

You will need to be aware of the procedures for setting cost standards and once again the motivational implications involved.

It is advisable for you to be able to calculate ratios for volume and efficiency as well as cost variances in these categories.

It will be useful if you can explain the reasons for variances and the action management might take to remedy adverse variances.

19   PRESENTATION OF MANAGEMENT INFORMATION AND REPORTS

Remember that you need to be technically competent in calculating variances and using cost and management accounting data generally. You must also be able to present your data logically and in a way that is clear to different levels of management, and in report form if required.

6 UPDATES

INTRODUCTION

Examinable documents

Every six months (on 1 July and 1 December) the ACCA publish a list of 'examinable documents' which form the basis of the legislation and accounting regulations that will be examinable at the following diet.

The ACCA Official Textbooks published in June 1996 were fully up-to-date for the examinable documents published by the Association on 1 July 1996. There are currently no examinable documents for Paper 8.

There are three changes affecting Paper 8 in 1997.

1 NEW EXAMINER

From June 1997, there is a new examiner for the management accounting section of the syllabus. The financial management examiner remains unchanged. The new management accounting examiner has issued some notes on his approach to the examination, and these are reproduced below.

Introduction

Candidates and tutors will be aware that the management accounting section of paper 8 seeks to build on the coverage of cost accounting in paper 3 Management Information.

Similarly it is further developed and extended in paper 9 Information for Control and Decision Making.

From June 1997 management accounting will be examined in a separate section of paper 8 in which there will be an element of choice.

Examination

The examination will consist of three equally weighted questions none of which will be compulsory. Any change to this policy will be announced in the Student's Newsletter.

I intend to set both computative and discursive questions in the section on management accounting. In the long run I expect marks will approximately be split equally between computative and discursive aspects. It is unlikely that candidates will avoid some quantitative aspects, equally, good marks would not be possible without the ability to engage in some discussion or analysis. This will be moderated, naturally, by any particular student's question choice.

Philosophy

I am concerned that management accounting is seen as more than a collection of techniques which can be learned and repeated. The questions will often be based on data which is set in some business context. Candidates should be prepared to apply the techniques but also to evaluate the usefulness or interpret the significance of them in a given setting or context provided. The test of good management accounting is whether it is useful to the manager and appropriate in the setting in which it is required to support management.

The Examiner is conscious of the skills to be tested at Certificate Stage, namely:

(a)   analysis and evaluation;
(b)   application of concepts and principles;
(c)   identification and definition of problems;
(d)   interpretation of results;
(e)   criticisms of solutions.

A range of different approaches will be used to examine these skills.

In many management accounting texts we often see examples which use manufacturing settings; this is after all the origins of much cost and management accounting. This examination intends to draw questions from a range of settings, both manufacturing and service industries, profit seeking and non-profit seeking environments where this is reasonably possible. This said, detailed knowledge of any particular industrial or commercial environment, beyond that intimated in the question or appreciated by any generally aware candidate would not be required.

The above should not give candidates any cause for concern, however, further detail and examples of the examining approach will be presented in a short article in the Students' Newsletter. (At the time of publication, the article referred to had not yet been published.)

2   EXAMINATION FORMAT

The format of the examination is to be amended from June 1997.

In the previous format, management accounting and financial management topics were both examinable in Section A and Section B. With effect from June 1997, the management accounting and financial management areas will be more clearly distinguished in the examination paper and each section will concentrate on either management accounting or financial management issues.

		No of marks
Section A	Case study on financial management	40
Section B	1 (out of 2) questions on financial management	20
Section C	2 (out of 3) questions on management accounting	40

3   SYLLABUS AMENDMENT

As the examination format is being amended to distinguish more clearly between financial management and management accounting, the syllabus will also be amended, although the amendments only represent relabelling of some sections. These amendments will be effective from December 1997.

The syllabus for June 1997 remains unchanged.

The ACCA has released the following explanation of the syllabus amendments.

1   Management Accounting topics and Financial Management topics are currently not clearly identifiable in the paper 8 syllabus.

2   From December 1997, some relabelling will be required to clearly distinguish between Management Accounting and Financial Management, as follows: relabel section 4 as section 6, section 5 as section 4 and section 6 as section 5. New sections 1 - 3 will be designated as Management Accounting and sections 4 - 8 as Financial Management.

7 PRACTICE QUESTIONS

---

1   BORROWS PLC

Borrows plc has decided to embark upon a new investment strategy. Traditionally a mining company operating coal, silver, gold and other mines throughout the world, it has now decided to use its expertise and move into international oil exploration with a view to setting up joint ventures to exploit any oilfields it discovers. The company feels that it requires another £200 million finance to support new operations for the next 8 years and it has identified three possible sources:

(a)   an issue of ordinary shares. The company proposes to make a rights issue at a 10% discount to the current market price.

(b)   an issue of a ten year 7% $300 million Eurodollar bond

(c)   a sale of 8% convertible unsecured loan stock of £100 each. Each of these can be converted by holders at any time into 40 ordinary shares. Any outstanding stocks will be redeemed at par in five years time.

The balance sheet for Borrows at 31 March 1994 is as follows:

	£m	£m
Fixed assets		1,400
Current assets	600	
Less: Current liabilities*	(200)	
Net current assets		400
		1,800
Less: Long term liabilities:		
10% Debentures		(300)
Net assets		1,500
Capital and Reserves		
Issued ordinary shares (50p par)		500
Reserves		1,000
		1,500

* Current liabilities include £80 million overdraft

The current market price per share is 210p, and price per debenture £90 per cent.

The current exchange rate of £1＝$1.50 is expected to be maintained in the medium term.

The profit and loss account (year end 31 March 1994) for the company is:

	£m
Operating profit*	208
- interest	40
Earnings before tax	168
- tax (33%)	55
Earnings attributable to ordinary shareholders	113

* The new finance is expected to increase operating profit by 20% per annum of the amount of the finance, but this may take 4 or 5 years to materialise.

You are required:

(a)   to explain why a rights issue generally results in a fall in the market price of shares. Calculate the theoretical ex-rights price of the share if the issue is undertaken. Under what circumstances would you expect the share price to actually go to this price? Ignore issue costs in this question.

(10 marks)

(b)   to discuss the financial implications of all three options by calculating appropriate accounting ratios.   **(12 marks)**

(c)   to briefly consider the main risks connected with the investment project itself, and how Borrows might attempt to allow for these.   **(8 marks)**

(d)   to advise Borrows on the choice of finance, using the data calculated in the above sections as well as any other information that you perceive to be relevant. What other information would be useful to the company in making this decision?   **(10 marks)**

(Total: 40 marks)

2   TWELLOW PLC

A four year summary of the financial accounts of Twello plc is shown below:

Consolidated profit and loss accounts

	19X0 £m	19X1 £m	19X2 £m	19X3 £m
Sales	742	859	961	1,028
Operating profit	22	25	40	54
Interest (net)	(2)	-	(5)	(6)
Profit on ordinary activities before tax	20	25	35	48
Taxation	(7)	(8)	(12)	(17)
Profit after tax	13	17	23	31
Extraordinary items	(4)	-	(2)	–
Dividends	(4)	(5)	(7)	(9)
Profit retained	5	12	14	22

Consolidated end of year balance sheets

	19X0 £m	19X1 £m	19X2 £m	19X3 £m
Fixed assets				
Tangible assets	142	168	188	225
Long-term investments	4	6	8	8
	146	174	196	233
Current assets				
Stock	43	46	49	52
Debtors	18	24	26	31
Money market investments	11	20	20	12
Cash	4	4	8	6
	76	94	103	101
Current liabilities				
Bank overdraft	8	8	20	18
Trade creditors	66	60	84	89
Taxation	7	7	8	12
Proposed dividend	2	2	3	4
Other short-term creditors	21	26	35	40
	104	103	150	163
Total assets less current liabilities	118	165	149	171

	19X0 £m	19X1 £m	19X2 £m	19X3 £m
Long-term liabilities				
11% convertible debentures 19Y0/19Y4[1]	17	17	17	17
4% deep discount stock[2]	-	-	30	30
	17	17	47	47
Shareholder funds				
Called up share capital (50p)	25	30	30	30
Share premium	30	60	-	-
Profit and loss	46	58	72	94
Capital employed	118	165	149	171

Notes

1   Each £100 debenture is convertible into 12.6 ordinary shares in any year up to 19Y0. The conversion rate has been adjusted for a rights issue in 19X1.

2   Redeemable at a total cost of £60 million in 15 years time in 19Y9 (at face value £100).

	19X0	19X1	19X2	19X3
Average share price	300p	350p	440p	520p
Average earnings yield in the industry	12%	11%	14%	12.5%

Additional notes

(i)   The company's activities (except for import/export) are entirely within the UK.

(ii)   A 1 for 5 rights issue was made in 19X1.

(iii)   The company made an acquisition in 19W7 costing £80 million. The book value of the tangible assets acquired was £20 million.

(iv)   The directors estimate that the current market value of tangible fixed assets is £315 million.

Required:

(a)   Appraise the financial health of Twello plc, commenting upon any possible financial weaknesses.

(13 marks)

(b)   What other information would be useful in your assessment of the company's financial health?

(8 marks)

(c)   What are the advantages of deep discount bonds?

If ordinary debentures have a redemption yield of 12% per year, evaluate whether a second deep discount bond on the same terms as Twello's existing deep discount bond is likely to be attractive to investors. Assume that interest is paid annually. Taxation may be ignored in your evaluation.

(7 marks)

(d)   What factors would the management accountant of Twello take into account in drawing up the budget for 19X4? (NB budgeted figures themselves are not required.)   **(12 marks)**

(Total: 40 marks)

---

3   MANRAY PLC

Manray plc manufactures and distributes automatic security lighting systems, which are purchased primarily by households, but also by business customers. When formed, some dozen years ago, Manray issued four million 25p ordinary shares, and one million £1 nominal 8% cumulative preference shares. Although Manray still relies on a single product, this has been modified numerous times in order to remain abreast of competitors. It is now contemplating investment in computer-controlled manufacturing technology which will further improve the product. It will also significantly alter the cost structure by raising fixed costs by £400,000 but lowering variable cost by £10 per unit, as a result of increased automation.

The improvement in the quality of the product is also expected to raise annual sales by 10,000 units, with no price change. Despite the volume increase, there is expected to be no increase in working capital requirements due to the introduction of a JIT system of stock control. In the trading period ended 31 March 19X3, Manray sold 80,000 units largely to edge-of-town DIY outlets, at a price of £35 per unit.

The new production facility will be financed by borrowing £3m from its present bankers, who currently provide overdraft facilities. The interest rate will be variable, but is initially set at 10% pa. £1m of the loan will be used to repay the existing overdraft. The loan itself will be repaid in three equal instalments, every two years over the anticipated lifetime of the equipment. If the equipment is purchased in the very near future, the company can begin to claim capital allowances against taxation liability. (Tax is paid a year in arrears.) At present, these operate on a **straight-line basis** over four years. The equipment is not expected to have any resale value.

Exhibit 1 shows Manray's profit and loss account for the year ended 31 March 19X3.

Exhibit 1

		£'000
Sales		2,800
Less: Variable expenses	1,600	
Fixed expenses	250	
	———	1,850
Operating profit		950
Less: Interest payable		150
Taxable profit		800
Less: Corporation tax*: at 33%		264
Profit after tax		536
Less: Preference dividend		80
Profit available for ordinary shareholders		456
Less: Dividend		228
Retained profit		228

* Note: a full tax charge was payable, there being no depreciation allowances available for the year in question.

You are required:

(a)   Using a 15% discount rate, to determine whether the project is worthwhile, taking account of corporation tax and the depreciation allowance;   **(12 marks)**

(b)   to calculate the change in earnings per share if Manray introduces the new production facility at once;   **(6 marks)**

(c)   to explain the term 'operating gearing', and illustrate your answer using data relating to Manray;   **(7 marks)**

(d)   to determine the break-even volumes for Manray, both before and after the introduction of the new facility;   **(5 marks)**

(e)   One of Manray's directors argues that the proposed method of finance over-exposes Manray to increases in interest rates.

      What macro-economic factors might be expected to cause increases in interest rates? What difficulties might such an increase cause?   **(10 marks)**
        (Total 40 marks)
        (Pilot Paper)

4   CREDIT PERIODS

(a)   A company is proposing to increase the credit period it gives to its customers from one calendar month to one and a half calendar months in order to raise turnover from the present annual figure of £24 million. The price structure of the company's product is as follows

Variable cost	400p
Fixed cost apportionment	140p
Profit	60p
Selling price	600p

Any increase in sales will give rise to corresponding increase in stock since the company carries finished goods equivalent to one month's turnover. No increase in overhead is envisaged but it is anticipated that whereas bad debts have hitherto been negligible, a figure of 5% of the additional sales should be expected.

You are required to

(a)   calculate the minimum increase in sales which would be necessary to justify the increase in credit on the assumption that all existing customers would take advantage of the new terms and that the company requires a return on investment of 20% per annum.   **(8 marks)**

(b)   summarise the customary methods of establishing the creditworthiness of potential new customers.   **(6 marks)**

(c)   (i)   to specify the factors a company should take into account when considering offering cash discounts to credit customers, and

(ii)   to outline how you would calculate whether or not such a cash discount scheme would increase the company's market value.   **(6 marks)**
(**Total: 20 marks**)

5   CASH SURPLUSES

(a)   The treasurer of B plc has forecast that, over the next year, the company will generate cash flows in excess of its requirements.

List **four** possible reasons for such a surplus, and explain the circumstances under which the board of directors might decide to keep the excess in liquid form.

(8 marks)

(b)   The following table of London money rates shows the relationship between maturity and interest rates for four types of short-term investment, as published in the financial press.

	One month	Three months	Six months	One year
Sterling certificates of deposit	$9\frac{7}{8}$	$10\frac{1}{16}$	$10\frac{3}{16}$	$10\frac{5}{16}$
Local authority bonds	$9\frac{7}{8}$	10	$10\frac{1}{4}$	$10\frac{1}{2}$
Finance house deposits	10	$10\frac{1}{8}$	$10\frac{3}{8}$	$10\frac{9}{16}$
Treasury bills (buy)	$9\frac{11}{16}$	$9\frac{3}{4}$	-	-

You are required:

(i)   to explain the nature of the instruments listed; and

(ii)   to explain the main reasons for the differences in interest rate between the instruments and over time.

(12 marks)

(Total: 20 marks)

6   HEXICON PLC

(a)   Give reasons, with a brief explanation, why the net present value (NPV) method of investment appraisal is thought to be superior to other approaches.

(5 marks)

(b)   Hexicon plc manufactures and markets automatic washing machines. Among the many hundreds of components which it purchases each year from external suppliers for assembling into the finished article are drive belts, of which it uses 40,000 units pa. It is considering converting its purchasing, delivery and stock control of this item to a just-in-time system. This will raise the number of orders placed but lower the administrative and other costs of placing and receiving orders. If successful, this will provide the model for switching most of its inwards supplies on to this system. Details of actual and expected ordering and carrying costs are given in the table below.

			Actual	*Proposed*
O	=	Ordering cost per order	£100	£25
P	=	Purchase cost per item	£2.5	£2.5
I	=	Inventory holding cost (as a percentage of the purchase cost)	20%	20%

To implement the new arrangements will require 'one-off' reorganisation costs estimated at £4,000 which will be treated as a revenue item for tax purposes. The rate of corporation tax is 33% and Hexicon can obtain finance at 12%. The effective life span of the new system can be assumed to be eight years.

You are required:

(i)   to determine the effect of the new system on the economic order quantity (EOQ);

(ii)   to determine whether the new system is worthwhile in financial terms;

Note: EOQ is given by $Q = \sqrt{\dfrac{2 \times D \times O}{I \times P}}$ where D = demand, or usage.   **(10 marks)**

(c)   **You are required:** to briefly explain the nature and objectives of JIT purchasing agreements concluded between components users and suppliers.

(5 marks)

(Total: 20 marks)

(Pilot paper)

7   WHICHFORD PLC

The £25 million annual credit sales of Whichford plc are spread evenly over each of the fifty weeks of the working year. Sales within each week are also equally spread over each of the five working days.

Although Whichford operates from 19 separate locations, all invoicing of credit sales is carried out by the central head office. Sales documentation is sent by post daily from each location to the head office and from these details invoices are prepared. Postal delays affecting the receipt of documentation by the head office, delays and bottlenecks in processing at head office, together with the intervention of the non-working weekend period, all contribute to the considerable range of delays in despatching invoices. As a result of these delays only some of the sales made on Mondays and Tuesdays of each week are invoiced that same week, the remainder of sales made on Mondays and Tuesdays and all sales made between Wednesdays, Thursdays and Fridays are not invoiced until the following week.

An analysis of the delay in invoicing, measured by the delay between the day of sale and the date of despatch of the invoice, indicated the following typical pattern:

No. of days' delay in invoicing	Percentage of week's sales subject to this delay
3	20%
4	6%
5	40%
6	22%
7	12%

A further analysis indicated that debtors take, on average, 35 days' credit before paying. This period is measured from the day of the despatch of the invoice rather than from the date of sale.

It is proposed to hire a number of micro-computers to undertake invoicing at each of the 19 sales locations. The use of computers would ensure that all invoices were despatched either on the day of sale or on the next working day. The revised invoicing would result in 50% of invoices being despatched with no delay, 40% subject to a delay of one day, and 10% subject to a delay of three days.

A computer package, currently in the final stages of development, would assist the follow-up of debtors and, if used, is likely to reduce the number of days' credit taken by customers to 30 - again this is measured from the date of the invoice.

Use of the micro-computers would save head office and postage costs of £48,000 pa spread evenly over the year.

Whichford finances all working capital from a bank overdraft at an interest rate of 15% p.a. applied on a simple daily basis.

You are required:

(a)   by ignoring taxation, to determine the maximum monthly rental that Whichford should consider paying for the hire of the computers if they can be used:

(i)   only to speed the invoicing function;

(ii)   to speed invoicing and reduce the period of credit taken from 35 to 30 days following the despatch of an invoice.   **(12 marks)**

(b)   to describe the main characteristics and features of a factoring agreement.

Clearly distinguish between factoring and invoice discounting. Outline the main issues which should be given consideration before entering into a factoring agreement and illustrate the circumstances in which entering into a factoring agreement may be desirable.   **(8 marks)**
(Total: 20 marks)
(ACCA June 85)

8   MOLLET LTD

(a)   Mollet Ltd prepares a weekly cash budget. Based upon the experience of previous cash inflows and outflows, it has estimated cash flows for the next week, some of which are considered to be definite, and some of which have been assigned probabilities of occurrence:

	£	Probability
Expected cash outflows:		
Wages and salaries:		
Basic	50,000	1
Overtime	0	0.5
	10,000	0.5
Materials	70,000	1
Overheads	10,000	1
Expected cash inflows:		
Cash from debtors	100,000	0.4
	120,000	0.6

Any surplus cash is invested in six month deposits in the money market and shortfalls of cash are funded by withdrawing cash from these money market investments. Mollet currently has £100,000 invested in the money market.

Transactions costs are estimated to be a fixed cost of £10 for each money market deposit and £8 for each money market withdrawal, with a variable cost of 0.05% of the transaction value on both deposits and withdrawals. All money market transactions must be of at least £10,000 in size and in multiples of £10,000.

If withdrawals are made from the six month money market deposits prior to the maturity of the deposits, a penalty equivalent to one week's interest on the amount withdrawn is payable. No deposits are due to mature during the next week.

The interest rate on six month money market deposits is currently 12% per year.

Mollet's directors have decided that the company must maintain a minimum cash balance of £20,000. The cash balance at the start of the next week is expected to be £40,000.

You are required to determine the level of investment in money market deposits at the start of the next week that will maximise the expected net return from the money market for the week.

(12 marks)

(b)   Outline the advantages and disadvantages of using short-term debt, as opposed to long-term debt, in the financing of working capital.

(8 marks)
(Total: 20 marks)
(ACCA June 86)

9   OVERDRAFT REQUIREMENTS

The Finance Director of A & B plc is about to renegotiate the company's overdraft facility. The company currently has annual sales of:

Product A: 50,000 units at £4.50 per unit.
Product B: 60,000 units at £6.50 per unit.
Product C: 75,000 units at £3.50 per unit.

Other information is as follows:

	Product A	Product B	Product C
Cost of sales	50%	60%	30%
Stock conversion period (months)	1.5	2	1
Average debtors credit (months)	2.0	3	1.5
Average suppliers credit (months)	2.5	2.5	1.5
Forecast increase in sales volume	25%	20%	30%

The forecast increase in sales volume is expected to result from aggressive marketing and not as a result of a price reduction. The costs associated with marketing and other administrative activities are included in the average suppliers (creditors) conversion rates.

The Finance Director forecasts three possible scenarios. These are described below. All variations are from the current position.

(1)   The conversion rates of stock, debtors and creditors will remain unchanged.

(2)   The conversion rates for debtors for all three products will deteriorate by 25% because longer credit periods will have to be offered to customers to gain the new business. The conversion rates for stock and creditors will remain unchanged.

(3)   Much of the extra business will be gained by entering a new market of cash-paying customers. As a result, the debtors conversion period for all three products will improve by 25%. The conversion rate for stock will remain unchanged, but the rate for creditors is likely to fall slightly to 2.4 months for Products A and B and to 1.2 months for Product C.

(a)   **You are required**

> (i)   to calculate the net current operating assets (stock, debtors and creditors) and the likely future requirements based on the three scenarios presented above;   **(12 marks)**

> (ii)   to comment on other information which the Finance Director might require before he renegotiates the company's overdraft requirements.   **(5 marks)**

(b)   A detailed forecast based on new marketing data reveals that the overdraft can be substantially reduced in around 6 months' time. In fact, surplus funds will be available for periods of between 1 and 6 months.

> **You are required** to describe **three** possible uses for these surplus funds.   **(3 marks)**
> **(Total: 20 marks)**

10   H N LTD

The directors of HN Ltd, a small manufacturing company, are worried about the company's cash flows during the next three months when sales receipts are at their lowest for the year. Cash budgets have been produced for the next three months under different economic assumptions. The Government's Budget is due in two weeks and there are concerns that there will be changes in corporate tax rates and credit controls. Cash flows in months two and three depend upon previous months' cash flows.

Net cash flow estimates (£000)

Month 1		Month 2		Month 3	
Probable cash flow		Probable cash flow		Probable cash flow	
				.50	25
		.20	20	.50	15
				.50	5
.20	(55)	.50	10	.50	(5)
				.50	(5)
		.30	5	.50	(10)
				.50	5
		.20	10	.50	0
				.50	0
.50	(65)	.50	(5)	.50	(5)
				.50	(10)

		.30	(10)	.50	(15)
				.50	0
		.20	0	.50	(10)
				.50	(10)
.30	(72)	.50	(10)	.50	(20)
				.50	(20)
		.30	(15)	.50	(30)

The company currently has a cash flow of £20,000 which it keeps for 'transactions' and 'precautionary' purposes, and an overdraft facility of £80,000. The current overdraft is £12,000.

Required:

(a)   If the company wishes to maintain a month-end cash float of £20,000 at all times, what is the probability that the overdraft facility will be large enough to maintain this cash balance in each of months one, two and three? Interest on the overdraft can be ignored.   **(11 marks)**

(b)   What is the probability that the company will totally run out of cash (including using the overdraft) in each of months one, two and three?   **(4 marks)**

(c)   If, in better economic times, the company consistently generated a cash surplus and had no plans to increase dividends or to undertake further capital investment, discuss possible alternative uses for this cash flow surplus.   **(5 marks)**

(Total: 20 marks)

(ACCA 3.2 Financial Management June 93)

Tutorial note:

For parts (a) and (b) it is necessary to calculate the effects of each month's possible cash flows on the company's overdraft and cash float. The probabilities and joint probabilities of each cash flow profile will be used in the answer.

Part (c) requires a discussion of the reasons for holding cash and alternative uses for it.

11   COMFYLOT PLC

Comfylot plc produces garden seats which are sold on both domestic and export markets. Sales during the next year are forecast to be £16 million, 70% to the UK domestic market and 30% to the export market, and are expected to occur steadily throughout the year. 80% of UK sales are on credit terms, with payment due in 30 days. On average UK domestic customers take 57 days to make payment. An initial deposit of 15% of the sales price is paid by all export customers.

All export sales are on 60 days credit with an average collection period for credit sales of 75 days. Bad debts are currently 0.75% of UK credit sales, and 1.25% of export sales (net of the deposit).

Comfylot wishes to investigate the effects of each of three possible operational changes:

(1)   Domestic credit management could be undertaken by a non-recourse factoring company. The factor would charge a service fee of 1.5% and would provide finance on 80% of the debts factored at a cost of base rate +2.5%. The finance element must be taken as part of the agreement with the factor. Using a factor would save an initial £85,000 per year in administration costs, but would lead to immediate redundancy payments of £15,000.

(2)   As an alternative to using the factor a cash discount of 1.5% for payment in seven days could be offered on UK domestic sales. It is expected that 40% of domestic credit customers would use the cash discount. The discount would cost an additional £25,000 per year to administer, and would reduce bad debts to 0.50% of UK credit sales.

(3)   Extra advertising could be undertaken to stimulate export sales. Comfylot has been approached by a European satellite TV company which believes that £300,000 of advertising could increase export sales in the coming year by up to 30%. There is a 0.2 chance of a 20% increase in export sales, a 0.5 chance of a 25% increase and a 0.3 chance of a 30% increase. Direct costs of production are 65% of the sales price. Administration costs would increase by £30,000, £40,000 and £50,000 for the 20%, 25% and 30% increases in export sales respectively. Increased export sales are likely to result in the average collection period of the credit element of all exports lengthening by five days, and bad debts will increase to 1.5% of all export credit sales.

Bank base rate is currently 13% per year, and Comfylot can borrow overdraft finance at 15% per year. These rates are not expected to change in the near future.

Taxation may be ignored.

Required:

Discuss whether any of the three suggested changes should be adopted by Comfylot plc. All relevant calculations must be shown.   **(20 marks)**

(ACCA 3.2 Financial Management June 92)

(*Tutorial note:* This question requires an analysis of three possible strategies to improve cash flow. The first two strategies involve working capital management changes. Calculate the extra costs and the extra benefits of each strategy in turn. Remember that holding debtors has an opportunity cost.)

For the third alternative, the company is projecting an increase in sales from extra advertising. Rather than calculate an expected value, the company will find it more useful to know the cost/saving implications of all three possible increases in sales.

12   ENGOT PLC

Three senior managers of Engot plc are discussing the company's financial gearing. Mr R believes that the financial gearing is 55%, Mr Y believes that it is 89% and Mr Z 134%.

Summarised consolidated profit and loss account for
the year ended 31 December 19X1

	£'000
Turnover	56,300
Less: Cost of sales	45,100
Gross profit	11,200
Less: Administrative and other expenses	6,450
Operating profit	4,750
Less: Interest payable	1,154
Profit before taxation	3,596
Less: Taxation	1,259

Profit for the financial year	2,337
Less: Dividends paid and proposed	970
Retained profit for the year	1,367

Summarised consolidated balance sheet as at 31 December 19X1

	£'000
Fixed assets	16,700
Current assets	
Stocks	7,040
Debtors	4,800
Cash at the bank and in hand	2,700
	14,540
Creditors: amounts falling due within one year	
8% loan stock 19X2	1,000
Bank loans and overdrafts	2,800
Trade creditors	7,200
Corporation tax	1,140
Proposed dividends	510
Accruals and deferred income	2,860
	15,510
Net current liabilities	970
Total assets less current liabilities	15,730
Creditors: amounts falling due after more than one year	
Bank loans	(5,600)
12% debentures repayable in 14 years' time	(1,800)
Net assets	8,330
Capital and reserves	£'000
Called-up share capital (10p par value)	2,200
Share premium account	1,940
Profit and loss account	4,190
	8,330

Current market data for Engot plc   Ordinary share price 94p
8% loan stock price £98
12% debentures price £108

You are required:

(a)   to explain how each manager has estimated the financial gearing and suggest how each manager might argue that his is the most appropriate measure of financial gearing. State with reasons which measure of gearing you prefer;   **(7 marks)**

(b)   to explain why financial gearing might be important to a company;   **(3 marks)**

(c)   to discuss what factors might limit the amount of debt finance that a company uses;   **(5 marks)**

(d)   to explain what mezzanine financing is and to describe the situations where it may be used to advantage.   **(5 marks)**

(Total: 20 marks)

13   COMPANY OBJECTIVES

Justify and criticise the usual assumption made in financial management literature that the objective of a company is to maximise the wealth of the shareholders. (Do not consider how this wealth is to be measured).

Outline other goals that companies claim to follow, and explain why these might be adopted in preference to the maximisation of shareholder wealth.

(20 marks)

14   MERCHANT BANKS

When a company seeks a listing for its shares on a stock exchange, it usually recruits the assistance of a merchant bank.

You are required:

(a)   to explain the role of a merchant bank in a listing operation with respect to the various matters on which its advice will be sought by a company;   **(10 marks)**

(b)   to identify the conflicts of interest which might arise if the merchant bank were part of a group providing a wide range of financial services.   **(10 marks)**

(Total: 20 marks)

15   FINANCIAL INTERMEDIARIES

You are required:

(a)   to explain in detail the various functions performed by financial intermediaries in the financial markets;   **(10 marks)**

(b)   to explain briefly, in relation to the London Stock Exchange.

   (i)   the way in which the stock market could be regarded as performing the role of a financial intermediary;

   (ii)   the work done by market makers, agency brokers and broker/dealers respectively.   **(10 marks)**

(Total: 20 marks)

16   EFFICIENT MARKET HYPOTHESIS

You are presented with the following different views of stock market behaviour.

(1)   If a company publishes an earnings figure that is better than the market expects, the shares of that company will usually experience an abnormally high return both on the day of the earnings announcement and over the two or three days following the date of the announcement.

(2)   The return on professionally managed portfolios of equities is likely to be no better than that which could be achieved by a naive investor who holds the market portfolio.

(3)   Share prices usually seem to rise sharply in the first few days of a new fiscal year. However, this can be explained by the fact that many investors sell losing stocks just before the fiscal year end in order to establish a tax loss for Capital Gains Tax purposes. This causes abnormal downward pressure which is released when the new fiscal year begins.

You are required:

(a)   to describe the three forms of the Efficient Market Hypothesis;   **(10 marks)**

(b)   to discuss what each of the above three statements would tell you about the efficiency of the stock market. Where appropriate relate your comments to one or more forms of the Efficient Market Hypothesis.   **(10 marks)**
          (Total 20 marks)

17   FLOW OF FUNDS

(a)   Describe and explain the pattern of the flow of funds that occurs between the major sectors of an economy, and identify the sectors that are normally in surplus and those that are normally in deficit.
          (7 marks)

(b)   Many borrowers wish to borrow large sums of money for long periods of time. Many savers wish to invest small sums of money for short periods of time.

        Explain how financial intermediaries can help to satisfy the needs of both borrowers and lenders and describe the nature and functions of four major types of financial intermediary.   **(13 marks)**
          (Total: 20 marks)
          (ACCA June 86)

18   G PLC

(a)   G plc has a paid-up share capital of 1.2 million ordinary shares of £1 each, the current market price being £1.80 per share. It has no loan capital. Maintainable earnings before tax are forecast at £240,000. The company's effective rate of Corporation Tax is 50%. The company requires to raise a further £768,000 in order to achieve additional earnings of £112,000 per annum and proposes doing this by means of a rights issue. Suggested alternative prices per share for the rights issue are £1.60 and £1.28.

        You are required:

        (i)   to calculate for each alternative the theoretical market price per share of the enlarged capital after the issue (the 'ex-rights' price) and also the market value of a right;

(ii)   to suggest what issue price is most likely to be adopted;

(iii)   to state what factors might, in practice, invalidate the calculations you have made.

(12 marks)

(b)   As a different approach, the company might raise the whole or part of the £768,000 required by means of an issue of 10% loan stock, any balance being covered by a rights issue at £1.60 per share.

You are required to explain and illustrate the likely effect on earnings per share of the use of loan stock in this instance.   **(8 marks)**

(Total: 20 marks)

---

19   LATOST PLC

(a)   What are the main advantages and disadvantages to a company of raising finance by issuing:

(i)   Ordinary shares;
(ii)   Cumulative preference shares;
(iii)   Deferred ordinary shares;
(iv)   Convertible debentures?   **(8 marks)**

(b)   Latost plc wishes to raise £10 million in external finance by issuing ordinary shares, or 14% (nominal rate) preference shares or a 12% unsecured loan stock.

Summarised current financial details of Latost are shown below:

Summarised profit and loss account

	£'000
Turnover	45,320
Operating profit	11,170
Interest	2,280
Profit before tax	8,890
Tax	3,112
Earnings available to ordinary shareholders	5,778
Dividend	3,467
Retained earnings	2,311

Summarised balance sheet

	£'000	£'000
Fixed assets (net)		24,260
Current assets	28,130	
Less: Current liabilities[1]	18,370	9,760
		34,020
13% debentures 19X7–X9		12,000
Net assets		22,020

Shareholders' funds:

Ordinary shares (50 pence par value)	5,000
Share premium	4,960
Other reserves	12,060
	22,020

[1]Including a bank overdraft of £6 million.

The share price is 350 pence.

You are required to prepare a brief report, with supporting evidence, recommending which of these three financing sources the company should use. State clearly any assumptions that you make.

Issue costs may be ignored.

(12 marks)
(Total: 20 marks)

---

20   PROPOSED FLOTATION

(a)   CP plc is a company operating primarily in the distribution industry. It has been trading for 15 years and has shown steady growth in turnover and profits for most of those years, although a failed attempt at diversification into retailing four years ago caused profits to fall by 30% for one year. The figures for the latest year for which audited accounts are available are:

Turnover	£35.2 million
Profit before tax	£13.7 million

The company has been financed to date by ten individual shareholders, three of whom are senior managers in the company, and by bank loans. Shares have changed hands occasionally over the past 15 years but the present shareholders are predominantly those who invested in the company when it was formed.

Some of the shareholders are now keen to realise some of the profits their shareholdings have earned over the years. At the last Annual General Meeting, it was proposed that the company should consider a full listing on the Stock Exchange.

You are required

(i)   to discuss the advantages and disadvantages of a flotation on the stock exchange in the circumstances described above;   **(7 marks)**

(ii)   to explain and compare the following methods by which the company's shares could be brought to the market:

- private placing;
- offer for sale at fixed price;
- offer for sale by tender.   **(6 marks)**

(b)   Describe the services which are likely to be provided by the following institutions in connection with a public offering of shares:

(i)   merchant banks;
(ii)   stockbrokers;
(iii)   institutional investors.   **(7 marks)**
                                                                        (Total: 20 marks)

---

21   ARMADA LEISURE

(a)   Discuss the main factors which a company should consider when determining the appropriate mix of long-term and short-term debt in its capital structure.   **(6 marks)**

(b)   Armada Leisure Industries plc is already highly geared by industry standards, but wishes to raise external capital to finance the development of a new bowling alley in Plymouth. The stock market has recently reached a record level but economic forecasters are expressing doubts about the future prospects for the UK economy.

         You are required to assess the arguments for and against a rights issue by Armada;   **(8 marks)**

(c)   **You are required** to examine the relative merits of leasing versus hire-purchase as means of acquiring capital assets.   **(6 marks)**
                                                                        (Total: 20 marks)
                                                                          (Pilot Paper)

---

22   BRECKALL PLC

Assume that you have been appointed finance director of Breckall plc. The company is considering investing in the production of an electronic security device, with an expected market life of five years.

The previous finance director has undertaken an analysis of the proposed project; the main features of his analysis are shown below.

He has recommended that the project should not be undertaken because the estimated annual accounting rate of return is only 12.3%.

Proposed Electronic Security Device Project

	Year 0 £'000	Year 1 £'000	Year 2 £'000	Year 3 £'000	Year 4 £'000	Year 5 £'000
Investment in depreciable fixed assets	4,500					
Cumulative investment in working capital	300	400	500	600	700	700
Sales		3,500	4,900	5,320	5,740	5,320
Materials		535	750	900	1,050	900
Labour		1,070	1,500	1,800	2,100	1,800
Overhead		50	100	100	100	100
Interest		576	576	576	576	576
Depreciation		900	900	900	900	900
		3,131	3,826	4,276	4,276	4,276

Taxable profit	396	1,074	1,044	1,014	1,044
Taxation	129	376	365	355	365
Profit after tax	240	698	679	659	679

Total initial investment is £4,800,000
Average annual after tax profit is £591,000

All of the above cash flow and profit estimates have been prepared in terms of present day costs and prices as the previous finance director assumed that the sales price could be increased to compensate for any increase in costs.

You have available the following additional information:

(1)   Selling prices, working capital requirements and overhead expenses are expected to increase by 5% per year.

(2)   Material costs and labour costs are expected to increase by 10% per year.

(3)   Capital allowances (tax depreciation) are allowable for taxation purposes against profits at 25% per year on a reducing balance basis.

(4)   Assume that taxation of profits is at a rate of 35% payable one year in arrears.

(5)   The fixed assets have no expected salvage value at the end of five years.

(6)   The company's real after-tax weighted average cost of capital is estimated to be 8% per year, and nominal after-tax weighted average cost of capital 15% per year.

Assume that all receipts and payments arise at the end of the year to which they relate except those in year 0 which occur immediately.

You are required:

(a)   to estimate the net present value of the proposed project. State clearly any assumptions that you make;   **(16 marks)**

(b)   to calculate by how much the discount rate would have to change to result in a net present value of approximately zero.
                                                                        (4 marks)
                                                                (Total: 20 marks)
                                                                    (ACCA June 86)

---

23   ELTERN LTD

Eltern Ltd is an unlisted company with a turnover of £6 million which runs a small fleet of taxis as part of its business. The managers of the company wish to estimate how regularly to replace the taxis. The fleet costs a total of £55,000 and the company has just purchased a new fleet. Operating costs and maintenance costs increase as the taxis get older. Estimates of these costs and the likely resale value of the fleet at the end of various years are presented below.

Year	1	2	3	4	5
	£	£	£	£	£
Operating costs	23,000	24,500	26,000	28,000	44,000
Maintenance costs	6,800	9,200	13,000	17,100	28,000
Resale value	35,000	24,000	12,000	2,000	200

The company's cost of capital is 13% per year.

You are required:

(a)   to evaluate how regularly the company should replace its fleet of taxis;

Assume all cash flows occur at the year end and are after taxation (where relevant). Inflation may be ignored.   **(10 marks)**

(b)   Eltern wishes to finance the replacement of its taxi fleet using part of the proceeds from raising new equity finance.

It has been suggested that it is difficult for a company of Eltern's size to raise new equity finance.

Give reasons why this difficulty might exist and describe the sources of equity finance which might be available to Eltern.   **(10 marks)**
    (Total: 20 marks)
    (ACCA June 88)

24   BANDEN LTD

Banden Ltd is a highly geared company that wishes to expand its operations. Six possible capital investments have been identified, but the company only has access to a total of £620,000. The projects are not divisible and may not be postponed until a future period. After the projects end it is unlikely that similar investment opportunities will occur.

Expected net cash inflows (including salvage value)

Project	Year 1	2	3	4	5	Initial outlay
	£	£	£	£	£	£
A	70,000	70,000	70,000	70,000	70,000	246,000
B	75,000	87,000	64,000			180,000
C	48,000	48,000	63,000	73,000		175,000
D	62,000	62,000	62,000	62,000		180,000
E	40,000	50,000	60,000	70,000	40,000	180,000
F	35,000	82,000	82,000			150,000

Projects A and E are mutually exclusive. All projects are believed to be of similar risk to the company's existing capital investments.

Any surplus funds may be invested in the money market to earn a return of 9% per year. The money market may be assumed to be an efficient market.

Banden's cost of capital is 12% per year.

You are required:

(a)   to calculate:

  (i)   The expected net present value;

  (ii)   The expected profitability index associated with each of the six projects, and rank the projects according to both of these investment appraisal methods.

      Explain briefly why these rankings differ;   **(8 marks)**

(b)   to give reasoned advice to Banden Ltd recommending which projects should be selected;

                                                                                (7 marks)

(c)   A director of the company has suggested that using the company's normal cost of capital might not be appropriate in a capital rationing situation. Explain whether you agree with the director;

                                                                                (5 marks)
                                                                          (Total: 20 marks)
                                                                          (ACCA June 88)

---

25   CEDER LTD

Ceder Ltd has details of two machines which could fulfil the company's future production plans. Only one of these machines will be purchased.

The 'standard' model costs £50,000, and the 'de-luxe' £88,000, payable immediately. Both machines would require the input of £10,000 working capital throughout their working lives, and both machines have no expected scrap value at the end of their expected working lives of four years for the standard machine and six years for the de-luxe machine.

The forecast pre-tax operating net cash flows associated with the two machines are:

	Years hence					
	1	*2*	*3*	*4*	*5*	*6*
	£	£	£	£	£	£
Standard	20,500	22,860	24,210	23,410		
De-luxe	32,030	26,110	25,380	25,940	38,560	35,100

The de-luxe machine has only recently been introduced to the market and has not been fully tested in operating conditions. Because of the higher risk involved, the appropriate discount rate for the de-luxe machine is believed to be 14% per year, 2% higher than the discount rate for the standard machine.

The company is proposing to finance the purchase of either machine with a term loan at a fixed interest rate of 11% per year.

Taxation at 35% is payable on operating cash flows one year in arrears, and capital allowances are available at 25% per year on a reducing balance basis.

You are required:

(a)   to calculate for both the standard and the de-luxe machine:

  (i)   pay-back period;
  (ii)   net present value.

Recommend, with reasons, which of the two machines Ceder Ltd should purchase.

(Relevant calculations must be shown.)   **(14 marks)**

(b)   If Ceder Ltd were offered the opportunity to lease the standard model machine over a four year period at a rental of £15,000 per year, not including maintenance costs, evaluate whether the company should lease or purchase the machine.   **(6 marks)**

(Total: 20 marks)

(ACCA Dec 86)

26   AMBLE PLC

Amble plc is evaluating the manufacture of a new consumer product. The product can be introduced quickly, and has an expected life of four years before it is replaced by a more efficient model. Costs associated with the product are expected to be as follows.

Direct costs (per unit)

Labour

3.5 skilled labour hours at £5 per hour.
4 unskilled labour hours at £3 per hour.

Materials

6 kg of material Z at £1.46 per kg.
Three units of component P at £4.80 per unit
One unit of component Q at £6.40
Other variable costs: £2.10 per unit

Indirect costs

Apportionment of management salaries, £105,000 per year
Tax-allowable depreciation of machinery, £213,000 per year
Selling expenses (not including any salaries), £166,000 per year
Apportionment of head office costs, £50,000 per year
Rental of buildings, £100,000 per year
Interest charges, £104,000 per year
Other overheads, £70,000 per year (including apportionment of building rates £20,000. **Note**: rates are a local tax on property).

If the new product is introduced it will be manufactured in an existing factory, and will have no effect on rates payable. The factory could be rented for £120,000 per year (not including rates) to another company if the product is not introduced.

New machinery costing £864,000 will be required. The machinery is to be depreciated on a straight-line basis over four years, and has an expected salvage value of £12,000 after four years. The machinery will be financed by a four year fixed rate bank loan, at an interest rate of 12% per year. Additional working capital requirements may be ignored.

The product will require two additional managers to be recruited at an annual gross cost of £25,000 each, and one manager currently costing £20,000 will be moved from another factory where he will be replaced by a deputy manager at a cost of £17,000 per year. 70,000 kg of material Z are already in stock and are not required for other production. The realisable value of this material is £99,000.

The price per unit of the product in the first year will be £110, and demand is projected at 12,000, 17,500, 18,000 and 18,500 units in years 1 to 4 respectively. The inflation rate is expected to be approximately 5% per year, and prices will be increased in line with inflation. Wage and salary costs are expected to increase by 7% per year, and all other costs (including rent) by 5% per year. No price or cost increases are expected in the first year of production.

Corporation tax is at the rate of 35% payable in the year the profit occurs. Assume that all sales and costs are on a cash basis and occur at the end of the year, except for the initial purchase of machinery which would take place immediately. No stocks will be held at the end of any year.

Required:

(a)   Calculate the expected internal rate of return (IRR) associated with the manufacture of the new product.

(15 marks)

(b)   Amble is worried that the government might increase corporate tax rates.

Show by how much the tax rate would have to change before the project is not financially viable. A discount rate of 17% per year may be assumed for part (b).

(10 marks)

(Total: 25 marks)

(*ACCA 3.2 Financial Management June 89*)

Tutorial notes:

(1)   In order to calculate a project's IRR, it is necessary to identify the relevant cash flows. You will remember from your studies that the relevant cash flows for investment appraisal are those that are:

-    future not past (sunk)
-    incremental to the project not allocated to it
-    opportunity costs not original costs
-    operating costs to the project not financing costs (these are included in the discount rate).

(2)   This is an example of sensitivity analysis.

27   ZEDLAND

The general manager of the nationalised postal service of a small country, Zedland, wishes to introduce a new service. This service would offer same-day delivery of letters and parcels posted before 10 am within a distance of 150 kilometres. The service would require 100 new vans costing $8,000 each and 20 trucks costing $18,000 each. 180 new workers would be employed at an average annual wage of $13,000 and five managers at average annual salaries of $20,000 would be moved from their existing duties, where they would not be replaced.

Two postal rates are proposed. In the first year of operation letters will cost $0.525 and parcels $5.25. Market research undertaken at a cost of $50,000 forecasts that demand will average 15,000 letters per working day and 500 parcels per working day during the first year, and 20,000 letters per day and 750 parcels per day thereafter. There is a five-day working week. Annual running and maintenance costs on similar new vans and trucks are currently estimated in the first year of operation to be $2,000 per van and $4,000 per truck. These costs will increase by 20% per year (excluding the effects of inflation). Vehicles are depreciated over a five-year period on a straight-line basis. Depreciation is tax allowable and the vehicles will have negligible scrap value at the end of five years. Advertising in year one will cost $500,000 and in year two $250,000. There will be no advertising after year two. Existing premises will be used for the new service but additional costs of $150,000 per year will be incurred.

All the above cost data are current estimates and exclude any inflation effects. Wage and salary costs and all other costs are expected to rise because of inflation by approximately 5% per year during the five-year planning horizon of the postal service. The government of Zedland will not permit annual price increases within nationalised industries to exceed the level of inflation.

Nationalised industries are normally required by the government to earn at least an annual after-tax return of 5% on average investment and to achieve, on average, at least zero net present value on their investments.

The new service would be financed half with internally generated funds and half by borrowing on the capital market at an interest rate of 12% per year. The opportunity cost of capital for the postal service is estimated to be 14% per year. Corporate taxes in Zedland, to which the postal service is subject, are at the rate of 30% for annual profits of up to $500,000 and 40% for the balance in excess of $500,000. Tax is payable one year in arrears. All transactions may be assumed to be on a cash basis and to occur at the end of the year, with the exception of the initial investment which would be required almost immediately.

Required:

Acting as an independent consultant prepare a report advising as to whether the new postal service should be introduced. Include in your report a discussion of other factors that might need to be taken into account before a final decision can be made with respect to the introduction of the new postal service.

State clearly any assumptions that you make.   **(20 marks)**
(ACCA 3.2 Financial Management Dec 89)

Tutorial notes:

(1)   This project must be appraised by the two criteria mentioned in the question, return on investment based upon accounting profit, and NPV based upon cash flows. Assume a 40% tax rate for your answer. Since the required rate is assumed to be a nominal rate (i.e. it includes inflation), then the cash flows to be discounted must include inflation too. Note that the question gives the income expected in year 1, but that all expenses are in current value terms and must therefore have inflation added to find the expected year 1 outflow.

(2)   This is a straightforward question on one method of dealing with uncertainty of cash flows in investment appraisal.

---

28   ULLSWATER

RS Ltd is considering using a machine made by BC Ltd. The machine would cost £60,000 and at the end of a four-year life is expected to have a resale value of £4,000, the money to be received in year 5. It would save £29,000 per year over the method that RS Ltd currently uses. RS Ltd expects to earn a DCF return of 20% before tax on this type of investment.

RS Ltd is currently earning good profits, but does not expect to have £60,000 available to spend on this machine over the next few years. It is subject to corporation tax at 35% and receives capital allowances of 25% on a reducing balance basis.

You are required

(a)   to recommend whether, from an economic viewpoint, RS Ltd should invest in the machine from BC Ltd;   **(5 marks)**

(b)   to calculate which of the following options RS Ltd would be financially better off to adopt:

        Option 1 - Buy the machine and borrow the £60,000 from the bank, repaying at the end of each year a standard annual amount that would comprise principal and interest at 20% per annum; or

        Option 2 - Lease the machine for four years at an annual lease payment equal to the annual amount it would need to pay the bank under *Option 1* above;

        Show your calculations.   **(16 marks)**

(c)   to recommend, with explanations, which of the two options in (b) above RS Ltd should adopt assuming that such a lease was available, but that it would not give RS Ltd the right to acquire the machine at the end of the lease period.   **(4 marks)**

Note: assume that lease payments or loan repayments are made gross at the end of each year and that tax is paid and tax allowances received one year after those profits are earned.

(Total: 25 marks)

---

29   HENSAU LTD

Hensau Ltd has a single production process for which the following costs have been estimated for the period ending 31 December 19X1:

	£
Material receipt and inspection cost	15,600
Power cost	19,500
Material handling cost	13,650

Three products - X, Y and Z are produced by workers who perform a number of operations on material blanks using hand held electrically powered drills. The workers have a wage rate of £4 per hour.

The following budgeted information has been obtained for the period ending 31 December 19X1:

	Product X	Product Y	Product Z
Production quantity (units)	2,000	1,500	800
Batches of material	10	5	16
Data per product unit			
Direct material (sq metres)	4	6	3
Direct material (£)	5	3	6
Direct labour (minutes)	24	40	60
Number of power drill operations	6	3	2

Overhead costs for material receipt and inspection, process power and material handling are presently each absorbed by product units using rates per direct labour hour.

An activity based costing investigation has revealed that the cost drivers for the overhead costs are as follows:

Material receipt and inspection : number of batches of material.

Process power : number of power drill operations.

Material handling : quantity of material (sq metres) handled.

You are required:

to prepare a summary which shows the budgeted product cost per unit for each of the products X, Y and Z for the period ending 31 December 19X1 detailing the unit costs for each cost element:

(a)   using the existing method for the absorption of overhead costs and

(b)   using an approach which recognises the cost drivers revealed in the activity based costing investigation;   **(20 marks)**

```
┌─────────────────────────────────────────────────┐
│ 30      A POLYTECHNIC                             │
└─────────────────────────────────────────────────┘
```

A polytechnic offers a range of degree courses. The polytechnic organisation structure consist of three faculties each with a number of teaching departments. In addition, there is a polytechnic administrative/management function and a central services function.

The following cost information is available for the year ended 30 June 19X7:

(1)   **Occupancy costs**

Total £1,500,000. Such costs are apportioned on the basis of area used which is:

	Square feet
Faculties	7,500
Teaching departments	20,000
Administration/management	7,000
Central services	3,000

(2)   **Administration/management costs**

Direct costs: £1,775,000

Indirect costs: an apportionment of occupancy costs.

Direct and indirect costs are charged to degree courses on a percentage basis.

(3)   **Faculty costs**

Direct costs: £700,000.

Indirect costs: an apportionment of occupancy costs and central service costs.

Direct and indirect costs are charged to teaching departments.

(4)   **Teaching departments**

Direct costs: £5,525,000.

Indirect costs: an apportionment of occupancy costs and central service costs plus all faculty costs.

Direct and indirect costs are charged to degree courses on a percentage basis.

(5)   **Central services**

Direct costs: £1,000,000.

Indirect costs: an apportionment of occupancy costs.

Direct and indirect costs of central services have in previous years been charged to users on a percentage basis. A study has now been completed which has estimated what user areas would have paid external suppliers for the same services on an individual basis. For the year ended 30 June 19X7, the apportionment of the central services cost is to be recalculated in a manner which recognises the cost savings achieved by using the central services facilities instead of using external service companies. This is to be done by apportioning the overall savings to user areas in proportion to their share of the estimated external costs.

The estimated external costs of service provision are as follows:

	£'000
Faculties	240
Teaching departments	800
Degree courses:	
Business studies	32
Mechanical engineering	48
Catering studies	32
All other degrees	448
	1,600

(6)   Additional data relating to the degree courses is as follows:

	Degree course		
	Business Studies	*Mechanical Engineering*	*Catering Studies*
Number of graduates	80	50	120
Apportioned costs (as % of totals)			
Teaching departments	3%	2.5%	7%
Administration/management	2.5%	5%	4%

Central services are to be apportioned as detailed in (v) above.

The total number of graduates from the polytechnic in the year to 30 June 19X7 was 2,500.

You are required:

(a)   to prepare a flow diagram which shows the apportionment of costs to user areas. No values need be shown;   **(3 marks)**

(b)   to calculate the average cost per graduate, for the year ended 30 June 19X7, for the polytechnic and for each of the degrees in business studies, mechanical engineering and catering studies, showing all relevant cost analysis;   **(13 marks)**

(c)   to suggest reasons for any differences in the average cost per graduate from one degree to another, and discuss briefly the relevance of such information to the polytechnic management.   **(4 marks)**
                                                                       (Total: 20 marks)
                                                                       (ACCA June 88)

---

31   PD PLC

Two distinct product ranges are manufactured in one large production department of PD plc. The manufacturing process for one product range, 'Range M', uses equipment operated by skilled labour, paid at £4 per hour. The other product range, 'Range S', is produced on semi-automatic equipment operated by unskilled labour paid at £2 per hour.

The size and specification of the products within each range vary significantly, each product is made to order and stocks of finished goods are not carried.

Individual selling prices are quoted for each order based upon estimated manufacturing costs plus sufficient mark-up to earn 10% profit on selling price.

Shown below is the current year's manufacturing and sales budget for the department.

	Range M £'000	Range S £'000	Total £'000
Sales	1,750.00	1,750.00	3,500.00
Prime cost of sales:			
Materials	450.00	600.00	1,050.00
Labour	450.00	150.00	600.00
Overheads:			
Variable:			
Power	22.50	82.50	105.00
Fixed:			
Plant maintenance	207.50	272.50	480.00
Plant depreciation	140.00	200.00	340.00
Supervision and indirect labour	225.00	150.00	375.00
Building occupancy costs	80.00	120.00	200.00
Total	1,575.00	1,575.00	3,150.00
Profit	175.00	175.00	350.00

The above budget anticipates that sales, production activity and expenses will occur evenly throughout the year. Also the budget anticipates there will be no stocks of work-in-progress at either the beginning or end of the year.

During the first quarter of the year the selling prices for all orders quoted and accepted, for both product ranges, were calculated by:

(1)   estimating the prime cost of each order;
(2)   charging overheads to each order at a rate of 250% of direct wages;
(3)   adding sufficient mark-up to achieve a 10% profit on selling price.

The company operates a full absorption batch costing system, fully integrated with the financial accounts. Overheads are absorbed into production at the above rate of 250% of direct wages.

The actual results for the first quarter of the year were:

	Range M £'000	Range S £'000	Total £'000
Sales	300.00	600.00	900.00
Manufacturing costs:			
Prime cost:			
Materials	63.00	242.50	305.50
Labour	62.00	85.00	147.00
Overheads:			
Variable:			
Power	3.10	46.75	49.85
Fixed:			
Plant maintenance	53.00	70.00	123.00
Plant depreciation	35.00	50.00	85.00
Supervision and indirect labour	60.00	40.00	100.00
Building occupancy costs	20.00	30.00	50.00
Total manufacturing costs	296.10	564.25	860.35

There was no opening stock at the beginning of the year; at the end of the quarter there was one 'Range M' order incomplete on which £3,000 of direct material and £2,000 of direct labour had been incurred.

The first quarter's results have surprised the company's management, the profits are not as they expected, and they cannot understand why quotations for 'Range M' products have not been accepted by their customers and the orders have been taken up by the company's competitors. At the same time the company has taken many more orders than expected for 'Range S' products.

You are required:

(a)   to write up the department's work-in-progress control account and the production overhead control account for the first quarter of the year. Also calculate the actual profit earned by the company during the first quarter;   **(9 marks)**

(b)   to explain to the management of the company possible reasons why the quarter's results are different from that which they expected and suggest any alterations in procedure which may assist the company in future.   **(11 marks)**
(Total: 20 marks)
(ACCA Dec 81)

---

32   A LTD

Product X, one of the products manufactured by A Ltd is sold exclusively to B Ltd. The annual quantity is 250,000 units. A change in the final packing of the product is to be introduced in order to save costs.

Currently the product is packed into boxes, each containing four units of the product. These boxes are then packed in larger boxes (eight small boxes per large box). The new packaging operation will eliminate the packing into small boxes. The product is to be packed into a single box containing twenty units. The new box is available immediately. Savings will result in packaging materials and also in labour and overheads incurred in the packaging operation.

Details of the costs of manufacturing the product currently are as follows:

> Raw materials total £0.452 per unit. Packaging materials (excluding the cost of boxes) total £0.103 per unit. Inner and outer boxes cost £114.00 and £547.20 per thousand boxes respectively. There is 5% wastage on usage of both small and large boxes.

The product is manufactured in batches of 2,000 units, which pass through two stages - fabrication and packaging. 40 units of the product are fabricated per hour of direct labour; units are packaged at a rate of 120 units per direct labour hour. The hourly rates for direct labour in fabrication and packaging are £4.80 and £3.60 respectively.

A direct labour hour rate is established in both the fabrication and packaging departments in order to absorb overheads into the cost of products manufactured. Overheads currently incurred per period are as follows:

	Fabrication £'000	Packaging £'000	General services £'000
Variable	88.0	24.0	-
Fixed	359.4	53.6	253.0

General services overheads are apportioned to fabrication and packaging in the ratio 9:2. Direct labour hours per period in fabrication and packaging are currently 40,000 and 10,000 respectively.

Supplies of the two boxes, currently used for packaging the product, are in stock. These stocks are sufficient to produce 50,000 units. They have no alternative use.

The new box to be used for packaging the product will cost £475.00 per thousand boxes. 5% wastage will occur on usage. Units will be packed at a rate of 400 per direct labour hour. The selling price charged by A Ltd to B Ltd will be reduced from £1.55 to £1.53 per unit when the packaging change is introduced.

You are required:

(a) to calculate the current total manufacturing cost per unit of the product to A Ltd;   **(13 marks)**

(b) to write a letter to the general manager of A Ltd:

    (i) showing the savings that will result from the packaging change;

    (ii) advising him when, from A Ltd's point of view, the packaging change should be introduced. (Explain and demonstrate fully the basis for your advice.)   **(12 marks)**

(Total: 25 marks)
(ACCA Dec 89)

33   LEARNING CURVE

A company has decided to diversify its activities and a new product has been developed which will be included in the master budget preparation for the coming year.

You are required:

(a) to explain ways in which the learning curve effect may create problems in the preparation of the master budget and in its use as a base against which to measure actual results in each four week accounting period;   **(14 marks)**

(b)   to comment on potential problems where short-term profit maximisation is seen as the main objective when setting the budget for the new product.   **(6 marks)**

(Total: 20 marks)

(ACCA Dec 90)

---

34   REDUNDANT MANAGER

A redundant manager who received compensation of £80,000 decides to commence business on 4 January 1988, manufacturing a product for which he knows there is a ready market. He intends to employ some of his former workers who were also made redundant but they will not all commence on 4 January. Suitable premises have been found to rent and second-hand machinery costing £60,000 has been bought out of the £80,000. This machinery has an estimated life of five years from January 1988 and no residual value.

Other data

(1)   Production will begin on 4 January and 25% of the following month's sales will be manufactured in January. Each month thereafter the production will consist of 75% of the current month's sales and 25% of the following month's sales.

(2)   Estimated sales are:

	units	£
January	Nil	Nil
February	3,200	80,000
March	3,600	90,000
April	4,000	100,000
May	4,000	100,000

(3)   Variable production cost per unit:

	£
Direct materials	7
Direct wages	6
Variable overhead	2
	15

(4)   Raw material stocks costing £10,000 have been purchased (out of the manager's £80,000) to enable production to commence and it is intended to buy, each month, 50% of the materials required for the following month's production requirements. The other 50% will be purchased in the month of production. Payment will be made 30 days after purchase.

(5)   Direct workers have agreed to have their wages paid into bank accounts on the seventh working day of each month in respect of the previous month's earnings.

(6)   Variable production overhead: 60% is to be paid in the month following the month it was incurred and 40% is to be paid one month later.

(7)   Fixed overheads are £4,000 per month. One quarter of this is paid in the month incurred, one half in the following month, and the remainder represents depreciation on the second-hand machinery.

(8)   Amounts receivable: a 5% cash discount is allowed on payment in the current month and 20% of each month's sales qualify for this discount. 50% of each month's sales are received in the following month, 20% in the third month and 8% in the fourth month. The balance of 2% represents anticipated bad debts.

You are required:

(a)   to prepare a cash budget for each of the first four months of 19-8, assuming that overdraft facilities will be available;   **(16 marks)**

(b)   to state the amount receivable from customers in May;   **(4 marks)**
                                                                                        (Total: 20 marks)

---

35   JACKSON BROTHERS PLC

In the third week of April the accountant of the SW Division of Jackson Brothers plc is reviewing the division's cash budget up to the end of the company's financial year (31 August). Each of the company's divisions has its own bank account but arrangements are made centrally for transfers among these as a need or opportunity arises. Interest is charged (or allowed) on such inter-company transfers at a market related rate.

The three months of May, June and July are the SW Division's busiest months, providing two-thirds of its annual profit, but there is always a cash flow problem in this period. In anticipation of a cash shortage, arrangements have been made to borrow (internally) £100,000 over the busy period at an annual interest rate of 15% (chargeable monthly). The agreed borrowing and repayment schedule is as follows:

1 May	borrowing of	£30,000
1 June	borrowing of	£70,000
1 July	repayment of	£20,000
1 August	repayment of	£60,000
1 September	repayment of	£20,000

The accountant has in front of him the budgeted divisional profit and loss account figures for the four months to 31 August and the profit and loss accounts for March and April - the latter being an estimated statement. These documents can be summarised as follows:

	Mar £	Apr £	May £	Jun £	Jul £	Aug £
Sales revenue	120,000	120,000	230,000	250,000	300,000	160,000
Factory cost of goods sold	100,000	100,000	182,500	197,500	235,000	130,000
Selling and distribution costs	4,200	4,200	6,400	6,800	7,800	5,000
Administrative costs and						
interest charges	7,000	7,000	7,375	8,250	8,000	7,250
	111,200	111,200	196,275	212,550	250,800	142,250
Divisional profit	8,800	8,800	33,725	37,450	49,200	17,750
	120,000	120,000	230,000	250,000	300,000	160,000

The accountant is using the following assumptions:

(1)   Each factory cost of goods sold figure includes a fixed cost element of £10,000 of which £2,000 is depreciation. The remaining fixed factory cost can reasonably be assumed to be paid as it is charged.

(2)   Direct material cost is approximately 75% of the variable factory cost of the firm's products. The

suppliers of this direct material are paid in the month following its purchase. Other variable factory costs of production are paid in the month in which the production takes place.

(3) Half of the fixed selling and distribution cost is a depreciation charge for motor vehicles. The remaining cost under this heading is paid in the month in which it is charged.

(4) A monthly central administration charge of £1,000 and interest on any borrowings are charged to administrative costs and interest charges and credited to a head office current account. Other administrative costs of approximately £6,000 per month are paid monthly.

(5) The following policies are followed by the division:

   (i) the target month-end stock level for finished goods is £10,000 plus 25% of the variable cost of next month's budgeted sales - finished goods are valued at variable cost for accounting purposes;

   (ii) the target month-end stock level for direct materials is £10,000 plus 25% of the material required for next month's budgeted production.

(6) All sales are on credit terms. 20% of the cash from customers is received in the month following that in which the sales were made, the remainder is received in the next month.

(7) The cash at bank and in hand at the end of April is expected to be approximately £10,000.

You are required:

(a) to prepare the division's cash budget for the months of May and June.

Each cash figure should be rounded to the nearest £1,000. **(10 marks)**

(b) The accountant has been experimenting with the use of the following formula for predicting month-end cash holdings:

$$CB = OB + 0.8S_{i-2} - 0.12S_{i-1} - 0.37S_i - 0.08S_{i+1} - 15$$

where   CB is the predicted closing cash balance in £'000 for month i;
        OB is the (estimated) opening cash balance in £'000 for month i;
and S_i is the sales figure for month i in £'000, actual or budgeted as appropriate.

Assuming that this formula is appropriate, comment on the effect on the division's cash holding at the end of May, of deviations of ±10% in the May sales figure from the budgeted figure.

(*Note:* do not use the formula in part (a) to this question.) **(3 marks)**

(c) The finance director of Jackson Brothers plc is considering a change in the procedures for evaluating divisional performance. Instead of merely charging interest on intra-company cash borrowing, he is considering the charging of interest on the company's total investment in each division.

Comment on this proposal and discuss the difficulties and advantages of such a system.

(7 marks)
(Total: 20 marks)
(ACCA Dec 82)

36   ZBB LTD

ZBB Ltd has two service departments, material handling and maintenance, which are in competition for budget funds which must not exceed £925,000 in the coming year. A zero base budgeting approach will be used whereby each department is to be treated as a decision package and will submit a number of levels of operation showing the minimum level at which its service could be offered and two additional levels which would improve the quality of the service from the minimum level.

The following data have been prepared for each department showing the three possible operating levels for each:

Material handling department

Level 1. A squad of 30 labourers would work 40 hours per week for 48 weeks of the year. Each labourer would be paid a basic rate of £4 per hour for a 35 hour week. Overtime hours would attract a premium of 50% on the basic rate per hour. In addition, the company anticipates payments of 20% of gross wages in respect of employee benefits. Directly attributable variable overheads would be incurred at the rate of 12p per man hour. The squad would move 600,000 kilos per week to a warehouse at the end of the production process.

Level 2. In addition to the level 1 operation, the company would lease 10 fork lift trucks at a cost of £2,000 per truck per annum. This would provide a better service by enabling the same volume of output as for level 1 to be moved to a customer collection point which would be 400 metres closer to the main factory gate. Each truck would be manned by a driver working a 48 week year. Each driver would receive a fixed weekly wage of £155.

Directly attributable overheads of £150 per truck per week would be incurred.

Level 3. A computer could be leased to plan the work of the squad of labourers in order to reduce their total work hours. The main benefit would be improvement in safety through reduction in the time that work in progress would lie unattended. The computer leasing costs would be £20,000 for the first quarter (3 months), reducing by 10% per quarter cumulatively thereafter.

The computer data would result in a 10% reduction in labourer hours, half of this reduction being a saving in overtime hours.

Maintenance department

Level 1. Two engineers would each be paid a salary of £18,000 per annum and would arrange for repairs to be carried out by outside contractors at an annual cost of £250,000.

Level 2. The company would employ a squad of 10 fitters who would carry out breakdown repairs and routine maintenance as required by the engineers. The fitters would each be paid a salary of £11,000 per annum.

Maintenance materials would cost £48,000 per annum and would be used at a constant rate throughout the year. The purchases could be made in batches of £4,000, £8,000, £12,000 or £16,000. Ordering costs would be £100 per order irrespective of order size and stock holding costs would be 15% per annum. The minimum cost order size would be implemented.

Overheads directly related to the maintenance operation would be a fixed amount of £50,000 per annum.

In addition to the maintenance squad it is estimated that £160,000 of outside contractor work would still have to be paid for.

Level 3. The company could increase its maintenance squad to 16 fitters which would enable the service to be extended to include a series of major overhauls of machinery. The additional fitters would be paid at the same salary as the existing squad members.

Maintenance materials would now cost £96,000 per annum and would be used at a constant rate throughout the year. Purchases could be made in batches of £8,000, £12,000 or £16,000. Ordering costs would be £100 per order (irrespective of order size) and stock holding costs would now be 13.33% per annum. In addition, suppliers would now offer discounts of 2% of purchase price for orders of £16,000. The minimum cost order size would be implemented.

Overheads directly related to the maintenance operation would increase by £20,000 from the level 2 figure.

It is estimated that £90,000 of outside contractor work would still have to be paid for.

You are required:

(a) to determine the incremental cost for each of levels 1, 2 and 3 in each department. **(16 marks)**

(b) In order to choose which of the incremental levels of operation should be allocated the limited budgeted funds available, management have estimated a 'desirability factor' which should be applied to each increment. The ranking of the increments is then based on the 'incremental cost × desirability factor' score, whereby a high score is deemed more desirable than a low score. The desirability factors are estimated as:

	Material handling	Maintenance
Level 1	1.00	1.00
Level 2 (incremental)	0.60	0.80
Level 3 (incremental)	0.50	0.20

Use the above ranking process to calculate which of the levels of operation should be implemented in order that the budget of £925,000 is not exceeded; **(4 marks)**

(Total: 20 marks)

(ACCA Dec 88)

---

37   LIMITATION PLC

Limitation plc commenced the manufacture and sale of a new product in the fourth quarter of 19X1. In order to facilitate the budgeting process for Quarters 1 and 2 of l9X2, the following information has been collected:

(1) Forecast product/sales (batches of product):

Quarter 4, 19X1	30 batches
Quarter 1,19X2	45 batches
Quarter 2, 19X2	45 batches

(2) It is estimated that direct labour is subject to a learning curve effect of 90%. The labour cost of batch 1 of Quarter 4, 19X1 was £600 (at £5 per hour). The labour output rates from the commencement of production of the product, after adjusting for learning effects, are as follows:

Total batches produced (batches)	Overall average time per batch (hours)
15	79.51
30	71.56
45	67.28
60	64.40
75	62.25
90	60.55
105	50.15
120	57.96

Labour hours worked and paid for will be adjusted to eliminate spare capacity during each quarter. All time will be paid for at £5 per hour.

(3)   Direct material is used at the rate of 200 units per batch of product for the first 20 batches of Quarter 4, 19X1. Units of material used per batch will fall by 2% of the original level for each 20 batches thereafter as the learning curve effect improves the efficiency with which the material is used. All material will be bought at £1.80 per unit during 19X2. Delivery of the total material requirement for a quarter will be made on day one of the quarter. Stock will be held in storage capacity hired at a cost of 30p per quarter per unit held in stock. Material will be used at an even rate throughout each quarter.

(4)   Variable overhead is estimated at 150% of direct labour cost during 19X2.

(5)   All units produced will be sold in the quarter of production at £1,200 per batch.

Required:

(a)   Calculate the labour hours requirement for the second batch and the sum of the labour hours for the third and fourth batches produced in Quarter 4, 19X1.   **(3 marks)**

(b)   Prepare a budget for each of Quarters 1 and 2, 19X2 showing the contribution earned from the product. Show all relevant workings.   **(14 marks)**

(c)   The supplier of the raw material has offered to deliver on a 'just-in-time' basis in return for a price increase to £1.90 per unit in Quarter 1, 19X2 and £2 per unit thereafter.

    (i)   Use information for Quarters 1 and 2 19X2 to determine whether the offer should be accepted on financial grounds.

    (ii)   Comment on other factors which should be considered before a final decision is reached.
                                                       (8 marks)
                                                       (Total: 25 marks)
(ACCA December 1991 Paper 2.4 Management Accounting Adapted)

---

38   A AND B

A company has two machines - A and B - each of which may be used to produce Products X and Y. The products are fabric, made in a number of widths by passing untreated fabric across one of the machines and then adding a colour dye.

Budget/forecast data for 19X8 are as follows:

(1)   Stocks at 1 January 19X8:

Product X	30,000 metres at 120 cm width
Product Y	5,000 metres at 200 cm width
Untreated fabric:	25,000 sq metres
Fabric dye	25 kilos

(2)   The closing stock of untreated fabric is budgeted at 10% of the required input to production during 19X8. No closing stocks of X or Y are budgeted.

(3)   Fabric yield is budgeted at 90% of input for Machine A and 80% of input for Machine B, due to processing losses.

(4)   Fabric dye is used at the rate of 1 kilo per 500 square metres of **output** for both Products X and Y. The maximum quantity available from suppliers during 19X8 is 520 kilos. If there is insufficient dye to meet production requirements, the output of the narrowest product would be reduced as required.

(5)   The budgeted rates of good output for Machines A and B are the same and vary with the width of products according to the following table:

Product width (cm)	Good output per machine hour (metres)
100	120
120	100
140	90
160	80
180	70
200	50
240	40

(6)   The maximum output width of product from each machine is Machine A: 140 cm, Machine B: 240 cm. It is company policy not to use Machine B for product widths less than 125 cm.

(7)   Each machine is manned for 35 hours per week for 46 weeks in the year. Part of this is budgeted to be lost as idle time as follows, Machine A: 20% of manned hours; Machine B; 30% of manned hours. This idle time does not include any idle time caused by a shortage of fabric dye.

(8)   The sales forecast for 19X8 is as follows:

Product X	90,000 metres at 120 cm width
	70,000 metres at 160 cm width
Product Y	30,000 metres at 200 cm width
	100,000 metres at 100 cm width

(9)   If production capacity is not sufficient to allow the sales forecast to be achieved, the budgets for production on each machine will be set by limiting the quantity of the narrowest product on that machine.

You are required:

(a)   to prepare budgets for 19X8 analysed by product type and width for (i) production quantities and (ii) sales quantities. The budgets should make maximum use of the available resources; **(8 marks)**

(b)   to prepare a purchases budget for untreated fabric. Express the budget in terms of square metres purchased;   **(6 marks)**

(c)   to suggest ways in which the company might attempt to overcome any inability to meet the sales forecast. Comment on any problems likely to arise in the implementation of each of these ways.
    (6 marks)
    (Total: 20 marks)
    (Pilot Paper)

39   RS LTD

RS Ltd makes and sells a single product, J, with the following standard specification for materials:

	Quantity kg	Price per kg £
Direct material R	10	30
Direct material S	6	45

It takes 30 direct labour hours to produce one unit of J with a standard direct labour cost of £5.50 per hour.

The annual sales/production budget is 1,200 units evenly spread throughout the year.

The budgeted production overhead, all fixed, is £252,000 and expenditure is expected to occur evenly over the year, which the company divides into 12 calendar months. Absorption is based on units produced.

For the month of October the following actual information is provided. The budgeted sales quantity for the month was sold at the standard selling price.

	£	£
Sales		120,000
Cost of sales		
Direct materials used	58,136	
Direct wages	17,325	
Fixed production overhead	22,000	
		97,461
Gross profit		22,539
Administration costs	6,000	
Selling and distribution costs	11,000	
		17,000
Net profit		£5,539

Costs of opening stocks, for each material, were at the same price per kilogram as the purchases made during the month but there had been changes in the materials stock levels, viz:

	1 October kg	30 October kg
Material R	300	375
Material S	460	225

Material R purchases were 1,100 kg for £35,000.

Material S purchases were 345 kg for £15,180.

The number of direct labour hours worked was 3,300 and the total wages incurred £17,325.

Work-in-progress stocks and finished goods stocks may be assumed to be the same at the beginning and end of October.

You are required:

(a)   to present a standard product cost for one unit of product J showing the standard selling price and standard gross profit per unit;   **(3 marks)**

(b)   to calculate appropriate variances for the materials, labour and fixed production overhead, noting that it is company policy to calculate material price variances *at time of issue to production*;
(11 marks)

(c)   to present a statement for management reconciling the budgeted gross profit with the actual gross profit;   **(5 marks)**

(d)   to suggest a possible cause for each of the labour variances you show under (b) above, stating whether you believe each variance was controllable or uncontrollable and, if controllable, the job title of the responsible official. Please state the name and amount of each variance about which you write and explain the variance, quantifying it, where possible, in non-financial terms which might be better understood by line management.   **(6 marks)**
(Total: 25 marks)

40   INSPECTION DEPARTMENT

A company has an inspection department in which operatives examine fruit in order to extract blemished input before the fruit is transferred to a processing department.

The input to the inspection department comes from a preparation department where the fruit is washed and trimmed.

Stocks cannot be built up because of the perishable nature of the fruit. This means that the inspection department operations are likely to have some idle time during each working day.

A standard output rate in kilos per hour from the inspection process has been agreed as the target to be aimed for in return for wages paid at a fixed rate per hour irrespective of the actual level of idle time.

The standard data for the inspection department are as follows:

(1)   standard idle time: as a percentage of total hours paid for: 20%;

(2)   standard wage rate per hour: £3.00;

(3)   standard output efficiency is 100% ie, one standard hour of work is expected in each hour excluding idle time hours;

(4)   wages are charged to production at a rate per standard hour sufficient to absorb the standard level of idle time.

The labour variance analysis for November for the inspection department was as follows:

Variances	£	Expressed in % terms
Productivity	525 (F)	2.2 (F)
Excess idle time	150 (A)	2.5 (A)
Wage rate	800 (A)	3.3 (A)

The actual data for the inspection department for the three months December to February are as follows:

	Dec	Jan	Feb
Standard hours of output achieved	6,600	6,700	6,800
Labour hours paid for	8,600	8,400	8,900
Idle time hours incurred	1,700	1,200	1,400
Actual wages earned	£26,660	£27,300	£28,925

The labour variances to be calculated in the operation of a standard cost system are as follows:

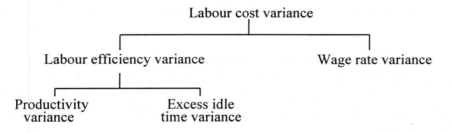

You are required:

(a)   to calculate the labour variances for productivity, excess idle time and rate of pay for each of the three months December to February;   **(8 marks)**

(b)   in order to highlight the trend and materiality of the variances calculated in (a) above, express them as percentages as follows:

Productivity variance: as a percentage of standard cost of production achieved;
Excess idle time variance: as a percentage of expected idle time;
Wage rate variance: as a percentage of hours paid for at standard rates of pay.   **(6 marks)**

(c)   to explain why variance trend and materiality data in percentage terms may provide useful additional control information for management. Comment on the data given for November and calculated for December to February, giving possible explanations for the figures produced.
(6 marks)
(Total: 20 marks)

41   CONSUMER PRODUCTS MANUFACTURER

A company, which manufactures a range of consumer products, is preparing the direct labour budget for one of its factories. Three products are manufactured in the factory. Each product passes through two stages: filling and packing.

Direct labour efficiency standards are set for each stage. The standards are based upon the number of units expected to be manufactured per hour of direct labour. Current standards are:

	Product 1 units/hour	Product 2 units/hour	Product 3 units/hour
Filling	125	300	250
Packing	95	100	95

Budgeted sales of the three products are:

Product 1	850,000 units
Product 2	1,500,000 units
Product 3	510,000 units

Production will be at the same level each month, and will be sufficient to enable finished goods stocks at the end of the budget year to be:

Product 1	200,000 units
Product 2	255,000 units
Product 3	70,000 units

Stocks at the beginning of the budget year are expected to be:

Product 1	100,000 units
Product 2	210,000 units
Product 3	105,000 units

After completion of the filling stage, 5% of the output of Products 1 and 3 expected to be rejected and destroyed. The cost of such rejects is treated as a normal loss.

A single direct labour hour rate is established for the factory as a whole. The total payroll cost of direct labour personnel is included in the direct labour rate.

Hours of direct labour personnel are budgeted to be split as follows:

	% of Total time
Direct work	80
Holidays (other than public holidays)	7
Sickness	3
Idle time	4
Cleaning	3
Training	3
	100%

All direct labour personnel are employed on a full-time basis to work a basic 35 hour, 5 day, week. Overtime is to be budgeted at an average of 3 hours per employee, per week. Overtime is paid at a premium of 25% over the basic hourly rate of £4 per hour. There will be 250 possible working days during the year. You are to assume that employees are paid for exactly 52 weeks in the year.

You are required:

(a)   to calculate the number of full-time direct employees required during the budget year;   **(14 marks)**

(b)   to calculate the direct labour rate (£ per hour, to two decimal places);   **(5 marks)**

(c)   to calculate the direct labour cost for each product (pence per unit to two decimal places).

(6 marks)
(Total: 25 marks)
(ACCA June 88)

42   MATERIAL VARIANCES

A company makes two materials, X and Y, in the production process. A system of standard costing and variance analysis is in operation. The standard material requirement per tonne of mixed output is 60% material X at £30 per tonne and 40% material Y at £45 per tonne, with a standard yield of 90%.

The following information has been gathered for the three months January to March:

	January	*February*	*March*
Output achieved (tonnes)	810	765	900
Actual material input:			
X (tonnes)	540	480	700
Y (tonnes)	360	360	360
Actual material cost (X plus Y) (£)	32,400	31,560	38,600

The actual price per tonne of material Y throughout the January to March period was £45.

You are required:

(a)   to prepare material variance summaries for each of January, February and March which include yield and mix variances in total plus usage and price variances for each material and in total;

(15 marks)

(b)   to prepare comments for management on each variance including variance trend.   **(9 marks)**

(c)   to discuss the relevance of the variances calculated above in the light of the following additional information:

The company has an agreement to purchase 360 tonnes of material Y each month and the perishable nature of the material means that it must be used in the month of purchase and additional supplies in excess of 360 tonnes per month are not available.   **(6 marks)**

(Total: 30 marks)

(ACCA June 91)

43   GENERY PLC

Genery plc makes and sell three types of electronic game for which the following budget/ standard and actual information is available for a four week period:

	Sales	*Budget/Standard*		*Actual sales*
		Unit data		
		Selling price	*Variable cost*	
	Units	*£*	*£*	*Units*
Model A	15,000	50	40	18,000
Model B	25,000	40	25	21,000
Model C	10,000	35	22	9,000

You are required:

(a)   to prepare a summary of sales variances for quantity, mix and volume for each model and in total where individual product standard contribution per unit is used as the variance valuation base;

(6 marks)

(b)   to prepare an alternative summary giving the same range of variances as in (a) above, but using the budgeted weighted average contribution per unit as the variance valuation base;   **(4 marks)**

(c)   Prepare a report to management which specifically comments on each of the following points:

     (i)   similarities and differences between the variances calculated in (a) as compared with those calculated in (b) above;

     (ii)   the arguments which may be put in favour of the individual product quantity and mix variances as calculated in (b) above;

     (iii)   the relevance of the individual product quantity and mix variances to management; and

     (iv)   the use of product units as the base against which quantity and mix effects are measured.
(10 marks)
(Total: 20 marks)
(ACCA June 89)

---

44   FLICK LTD

Flick Ltd make and sell a single product. Demand for the product exceeds the production capacity of Flick Ltd. The production process consists of a single machine operation. All output is sold in the period in which it is produced.

A standard marginal cost system is in operation. Feedback reporting takes planning and operational variances into consideration.

The management accountant has produced the following operating statement for period 3:

Operational statement: period 3

	£	£
Original budget contribution		12,600
Revision variances:		
Material usage		1,440 (A)
Revised budget contribution		11,160
Sales volume variance- due to:		
Capacity utilisation	744 (F)	
Productivity	620 (F)	
Idle time	744 (A)	
		620 (F)
Revised standard contribution from sales achieved		11,780
Other variances:		
Material usage	480 (A)	
Material price	1,075 (A)	
Machine efficiency	300 (F)	
Machine idle time	360 (A)	
Machine expenditure	288 (A)	
		1,903 (A)
Actual contribution		9,877

Other data is available as follows:

(1)   The original standard contribution per unit as determined at period 1 was:

	£	£
Selling price		18
Less: Direct material cost - 2 kg at £4	8	
Less: Machine cost - 0.1 hours at £30	3	11
Contribution		7

(2)   Variable machine costs are charged to product units at a standard rate per productive machine hour. Productive machine hours are budgeted as 80% of gross machine hours. Machine costs are budgeted at £24 per hour for all hours including idle time.

(3)   A permanent change in the product specification was implemented from the beginning of period 3 onwards. It was estimated that this change would require 10% additional material (kg) per product unit.

(4)   Actual direct material used during period 3 was 4,300 kg at £4.25 per kg. Any residual material variances are due to operational problems.

(5)   Budget and actual data for period 3 are:

	Budget	Actual
Production/sales(units)	1,800	1,900
Gross machine hours	225	240
Machine idle time (hours)	45	60

(6)   There have been no permanent changes in the machine standard/budget data.
Actual variable machine costs for period 3 totalled £6,048.

Required:

(a)   Prepare detailed figures showing how each of the materials and machine variances in the period 3 operating statement have been calculated.   **(8 marks)**

(b)   Flick Ltd. wish to prepare an amended forecast in order to check whether a desired total contribution of £40,000 for periods 4 to 6 inclusive will be achieved. The following data should be used in conjunction with period 3 figures and the original budget data in preparing the amended forecast:

   (i)   The direct material price increase is due to short-term market fluctuations and should be eliminated in periods 5 and 6.

   (ii)   The machine variable expenditure variance should be reduced to 60% of the period 3 variance level per hour for each of periods 4 to 6.

   (iii)   Gross machine hours will be 240 hours per period for each of periods 4 to 6. The original budget output was 1,800 units for each of periods 4 to 6.

   (iv)   An increased level of machine maintenance will be implemented from the beginning of period 4 onwards. This should result in:

   -        A reduction of 30% in the rate of the residual material usage variance.

- A reduction in excess idle time to 25% of the period 3 rate of excess.
- Improvement in the productivity ratio to 112% of standard.

Note: The changes in (i) and (iv) should not be incorporated into any revised current standard cost.

Prepare an operating statement in the same format as that for period 3 showing the total forecast contribution for periods 4 to 6 inclusive (individual period figures are not required).   **(12 marks)**

(Total: 20 marks)

(ACCA December 1992 Paper 2.4 Management Accounting)

This question requires you to calculate cost variances, then to assemble these variances into a statement that management can easily understand.

---

45   AB LTD

AB Ltd manufactures a range of products. One of the products, Product M, requires the use of Materials X and Y. Standard material costs for the manufacture of an item of Product M in Period 1 included:

Material X: 9 kilos at £1.20 per kilo.

Total purchases of Material X in Period 1, for use in all products, were 142,000 kilos costing £171,820. 16,270 kilos were used in the period in the manufacture of 1,790 units of Product M.

In Period 2 the standard price of Material X was increased by 6%, whilst the standard usage of the material in Product M was left unchanged. 147,400 kilos of Material X were purchased in Period 2 at a favourable price variance of £1,031.80. A favourable usage variance of 0.5% of standard occurred on Material X in the manufacture of Product M in the period.

Required

(a)   Calculate:

(i)   the total price variance on purchases of Material X in Period 1;   **(2 marks)**

(ii)   the Material X usage variance arising from the manufacture of Product M in Period 1;

(2 marks)

(iii)   the actual cost inflation on Material X from Period 1 to Period 2. Calculate as a percentage increase to one decimal place.   **(4 marks)**

(iv)   the percentage change in actual usage of Material X per unit of Product M from Period 1 to Period 2. Calculate to one decimal place.   **(4 marks)**

(b)   Describe, and contrast, the different types of standards that may be set for raw material usage and labour efficiency.   **(8 marks)**

(Total: 20 marks)

(ACCA June 92)

---

46   MATERIAL A

A company manufacturers two components in one of its factories. Material A is one of several materials used in the manufacture of both components.

The standard direct labour hours per unit of production, and budgeted production quantities, for a 13 week period were:

	Standard direct labour hours	Budgeted production quantities
Component X	0.40 hours	36,000 units
Component Y	0.56 hours	22,000 units

The standard wage rate for all direct workers was £5.00 per hour. Throughout the 13 week period 53 direct workers were employed, working a standard 40 hour week.

The following actual information for the 13 week period is available:

    Production:
      Component X, 35,000 units
      Component Y, 25,000 units
    Direct wages paid, £138,500
    Material A purchases, 47,000 kilos costing £85,110
    Material A price variance, £430 F
    Material A usage (component X), 33,426 kilos
    Material A usage variance (component X), £320.32A

Required

(a)   Calculate the direct labour variances for the period.   **(5 marks)**

(b)   Calculate the standard purchase price for Material A for the period and the standard usage of Material A per unit of production for Component X.   **(8 marks)**

(c)   Describe the steps, and information, required to establish the material purchase quantity budget for Material A for a period.   **(7 marks)**
(Total: 20 marks)
(ACCA Dec 92)

47   GLASS BOTTLES

A manufacturer of glass bottles has been affected by competition from plastic bottles and is currently operating at between 65 and 70 per cent of maximum capacity.

The company at present reports profits on an absorption costing basis but with the high fixed costs associated with the glass container industry and a substantial difference between sales volumes and production in some months, the accountant has been criticised for reporting widely different profits from month to month. To counteract this criticism, he is proposing in future to report profits based on marginal costing and in his proposal to management lists the following reasons for wishing to change:

(1)   Marginal costing provides for the complete segregation of fixed costs, thus facilitating closer control of production costs.

(2)   It eliminates the distortion of interim profit statements which occur when there are seasonal fluctuations in sales volume although production is at a fairly constant level.

(3)   It results in cost information which is more helpful in determining the sales policy necessary to maximise profits.

From the accounting records the following figures were extracted: standard cost per gross (A gross is 144 bottles and is the cost unit used within the business.):

	£
Direct materials	8.00
Direct labour	7.20
Variable production overhead	3.36
	‾‾‾‾
Total variable production cost	18.56
Fixed production overhead	7.52*
	‾‾‾‾
Total production standard cost	26.08
	‾‾‾‾

*The fixed production overhead rate was based on the following computations:

Total annual fixed production overhead was budgeted at £7,584,000 or £632,000 per month.

Production volume was set at 1,008,000 gross bottles or 70 per cent of maximum capacity.

There is a slight difference in budgeted fixed production overhead at different levels of operating:

Activity level Per cent of maximum capacity	Amount per month £'000
50 - 75	632
76 - 90	648
91 - 100	656

You may assume that actual fixed production overhead incurred was as budgeted.

Additional information:

	September	October
Gross sold	87,000	101,000
Gross produced	115,000	78,000
Sales price, per gross	£32	£32
Fixed selling costs	£120,000	£120,000
Fixed administrative costs	£80,000	£80,000

There were no finished goods in stock at 1 September.

You are required:

(a)   to prepare monthly profit statements for September and October using

      (i)   absorption costing; and

      (ii)   marginal costing;   **(16 marks)**

(b)   to comment briefly on the accountant's three reasons which he listed to support his proposal.

                                                 (9 marks)

                                      (Total: 25 marks)

48   MANUFACTURING PRODUCT X

A new subsidiary of a group of companies was established for the manufacture and sale of Product X. During the first year of operations 90,000 units were sold at £20 per unit. At the end of the year, the closing stocks were 8,000 units in finished goods store and 4,000 units in work-in-progress which were complete as regards material content but only half complete in respect of labour and overheads. You are to assume that there were no opening stocks.

The work-in-progress account had been debited during the year with the following costs:

	£
Direct materials	714,000
Direct labour	400,000
Variable overhead	100,000
Fixed overhead	350,000

Selling and administration costs for the year were:

	Variable cost per unit sold £	Fixed cost £
Selling	1.50	200,000
Administration	0.10	50,000

The accountant of the subsidiary company had prepared a profit statement on the absorption costing principle which showed a profit of £11,000.

The financial controller of the group, however, had prepared a profit statement on a marginal costing basis which showed a loss. Faced with these two profit statements, the director responsible for this particular subsidiary company is confused.

You are required:

(a)   to prepare a statement showing the equivalent units produced and the production cost of one unit of Product X by element of cost and in total;   **(5 marks)**

(b)   to prepare a profit statement on the absorption costing principle which agrees with the company accountant's statement;   **(9 marks)**

(c)   to prepare a profit statement on the marginal costing basis;   **(6 marks)**

(d)   to explain the differences between the two statements given for (b) and (c) above to the director in such a way as to eliminate his confusion and state why both statements may be acceptable.
                    (5 marks)
                    (Total: 25 marks)

49   MIOZIP CO

The Miozip Co operates an absorption costing system which incorporates a factory-wide overhead absorption rate per direct labour hour. For 19X0 and 19X1 this rate was £2.10 per hour. The fixed factory overhead for 19X1 was £600,000 and this would have been fully absorbed if the company had operated at full capacity, which is estimated at 400,000 direct labour hours. Unfortunately, only 200,000 hours were worked in that year so that the overhead was seriously under-absorbed. Fixed factory overheads are expected to be unchanged in 19X2 and 19X3.

The outcome for 19X1 was a loss of £70,000 and the management believed that a major cause of this loss was the low overhead absorption rate which had led the company to quote selling prices which were uneconomic.

For 19X2 the overhead absorption rate was increased to £3.60 per direct labour hour and selling prices were raised in line with the established pricing procedures which involve adding a profit mark-up of 50% onto the full factory cost of the company's products. The new selling prices were also charged on the stock of finished goods held at the beginning of 19X2. In December 19X2 the company's accountant prepared an estimated profit and loss account for 19X2 and a budgeted profit and loss account for 19X3. Although sales were considered to be depressed in 19X1, they were even lower in 19X2 but, nevertheless, it seems that the company will make a profit for that year. A worrying feature of the estimated accounts is the high level of finished goods stock held and the 19X3 budget provides for a reduction in the stock level at 31 December 19X3 to the (physical) level which obtained at 1 January 19X1. Budgeted sales for 19X3 are set at the 19X2 sales level.

The summarised profit statements for the three years to 31 December 19X3 are as follows:

Summarised profit and loss accounts

	Actual 19X1		*Estimated 19X2*		*Budgeted 19X3*	
	£	£	£	£	£	£
Sales revenue		1,350,000		1,316,250		1,316,250
Opening stock of finished goods	100,000		200,000		357,500	
Factory cost of production	1,000,000		975,000		650,000	
	1,100,000		1,175,000		1,007,500	
Less: Closing stock of finished goods	200,000		357,500		130,000	
Factory cost of goods sold		900,000		817,500		877,500
		450,000		498,750		438,750
Less: Factory overhead under-absorbed		300,000		150,000		300,000
		150,000		348,750		138,750
Administrative and financial costs		220,000		220,000		220,000
Profit/(loss)		(70,000)		128,750		(81,250)

You are required:

(a)   to write a short report to the board of Miozip explaining why the budgeted income for 19X3 is so different from that of 19X2 when the sales revenue is the same for both years;   **(5 marks)**

(b)   to restate the profit and loss account for 19X1, the estimated profit and loss account for 19X2 and the budgeted profit and loss account for 19X3 using marginal factory cost for stock valuation purposes;   **(7 marks)**

(c)   to comment on the problems which may follow from a decision to increase the overhead absorption rate in conditions when cost plus pricing is used and overhead is currently under-absorbed;

(3 marks)

(d)   to explain why the majority of businesses use full costing systems whilst most management accounting theorists favour marginal costing.   **(5 marks)**

Note: assume in your answers to this question that the value of the £ and the efficiency of the company have been constant over the period under review.

(Total: 20 marks)
(ACCA Dec 82)

---

50   Z LTD, THE RETAILER

Z Ltd is a retailer with a number of shops selling a variety of merchandise. The company is seeking to determine the optimum allocation of selling space in its shops. Space is devoted to ranges of merchandise in modular units, each module occupying seventy square metres of space. Either one or two modules can be devoted to each range. Each shop has seven modular units.

Z Ltd has tested the sale of different ranges of merchandise and has determined the following sales productivities:

Sales per module per week

	1 Module £	2 Modules £
Range A	6,750	6,250
Range B	3,500	3,150
Range C	4,800	4,600
Range D	6,400	5,200
Range E	3,333	3,667

The contribution (selling price - product cost) percentages of sales of the five ranges are as follows:

Range A	20%
Range B	40%
Range C	25%
Range D	25%
Range E	30%

Operating costs are £5,600 per shop per week and are apportioned to ranges based on an average rate per module.

You are required to:

(a)   determine the allocation of shop space that will optimise profit, clearly showing the ranking order for the allocation of modules;   **(13 marks)**

(b)   calculate the profit of each of the merchandise ranges selected in (a) above, and of the total shop;

(5 marks)

(c)   define the term 'limiting factor', and explain the relevance of limiting factors in planning and decision-making.   **(7 marks)**

(Total: 25 marks)

51   SWISH RESTAURANT

(a)   The current average weekly trading results of the Swish Restaurant in Sumtown are shown below:

	£	£
Turnover		2,800
Operating costs:		
Materials	1,540	
Power	280	
Staff	340	
Building occupancy costs	460	
		2,620
Profit		180

The average selling price of each meal is £4; materials and power may be regarded as variable costs varying with the number of meals provided. Staff costs are semi-variable with a fixed cost element of £200 per week; the building occupancy costs are all fixed.

Calculate the number of meals required to be sold in order to earn a profit of £300 per week.

(4 marks)

(b)   The owners of the restaurant are considering expanding their business and using their under-utilised space for diversifying into:

either   (i)   take-away foods;

or   (ii)   high quality meals.

The estimated sales and costs of each proposal are shown below:

	Take-away foods	*High quality meals*
Sales volume, per week	720 meals	200 meals
	£	£
Average selling price, per meal	1.60	6.00
Variable costs, per meal	0.85	4.66
Incremental fixed costs, per week	610.00	282.00

The sales estimate for both of the above proposals is rather uncertain and it is recognised that actual sales volume could be up to 20% either higher or lower than that estimated.

If either of the above proposals were implemented, it has been estimated that the restaurant's existing operations would be affected as follows:

(i)   As a result of bulk purchasing, material costs incurred would be reduced by 10p per meal. This saving would apply to all meals currently produced in the restaurant.

(ii)   Because more people would be aware of the existence of the restaurant it is estimated that turnover would increase. If the take-away food section were opened, then for every ten take-away meals sold the restaurant's current sales would increase by one meal. Alternatively, if the high quality meals section were opened, then for every five such meals sold the restaurant's current sales would increase by one meal.

A special effect of implementing the take-away food proposal would be a change in the terms of employment of the staff in the restaurant, the result of which would be that the staff wages of £340 would have to be regarded as a fixed cost.

Calculate for each of the proposed methods of diversification:

(i)   the additional profit which would be earned by the owners of the restaurant if the estimated sales were achieved;   **(8 marks)**

(ii)   the sales volume at which the owners of the restaurant would earn no additional profit from the proposed diversification.   **(5 marks)**

(c)   Carefully consider the conclusions which may be drawn from your calculations in (b) above.
                                                                                                      (8 marks)
                                                                                          (Total: 25 marks)

52   STOBO PLC

Stobo plc must decide whether to produce and sell either Product X or Product Y in the coming period.

The estimated demand probabilities for the period and the selling prices which have been set are as follows:

	Product X		Product Y	
Selling price per unit	£75		£150	
Sales (units)	5,600	1,400	3,200	1,600
Probability	0.6	0.4	0.3	0.7

The average direct material cost per product unit is expected to vary according to quantity purchased as follows:

Product X		Product Y	
Units purchased up to -	Average material cost per unit £	Units purchased up to -	Average material cost per unit £
1,000	6.50	1,000	33
2,000	6.00	2,000	30
3,000	5.50	3,000	28
4,000	5.00	4,000	26
5,000	4.75		
6,000	4.50		

Each product would pass through two departments - making and finishing - where the maximum available labour hours are sufficient for all possible quantities. It may be assumed that labour hours which are paid for are balanced by natural wastage, so that labour hours which are surplus to actual production requirements do not need to be paid for.

The labour operations are subject to a learning curve effect of 80% for Product X and 90% for Product Y which would apply in both the making and finishing departments.

Initial batch sizes will be 700 units for Product X and 800 units for Product Y. For these sizes, the hours required per product unit are as follows:

	Product X *Hours per unit*	Product Y *Hours per unit*
Making department	4	5
Finishing department	3	4

Wages are paid at £4 per hour in the making department and £3.75 per hour in the finishing department.

Variable overheads would be incurred at 200% on productive wage costs for the making department and 250% on productive wage costs for the finishing department.

Company fixed overheads are normally apportioned to products as a percentage of sales revenue. During the coming period, when total sales revenue of Stobo plc is estimated at £12,000,000, the overheads have been budgeted at 17.5% of sales revenue. The fixed overheads which would be avoidable if Products X or Y were not produced are as follows:

Product X	£36,000
Product Y	£5,000

Production would be adjusted to equate with sales in the period and the purchase of raw material would be matched with production requirements.

You are required:

(a)   showing all relevant calculations, to explain which product Stobo plc should produce and sell;

(14 marks)

(b)   showing all relevant calculations, to explain how the choice of product might be affected if the maximum available labour hours must be retained and paid for in the making and finishing departments but all other conditions are as above. **(6 marks)**

(Total: 20 marks)

(Pilot Paper)

53   A LTD

Budgeted information for A Ltd for the following period, analysed by product, is shown below:

	Product I	Product II	Product III
Sales units (000s)	225	376	190
Selling price (£ per unit)	11.00	10.50	8.00
Variable costs (£ per unit)	5.80	6.00	5.20
Attributable fixed costs (£000s)	275	337	296

General fixed costs, which are apportioned to products as a percentage of sales, are budgeted at £1,668,000.

Required

(a)   Calculate the budgeted profit of A Ltd, and of each of its products. **(5 marks)**

(b)   Recalculate the budgeted profit of A Ltd on the assumption that Product III is discontinued, with no effect on sales of the other two products. State and justify other assumptions made.

(5 marks)

(c)   Additional advertising, to that included in the budget for Product I, is being considered.

Calculate the minimum extra sales required of Product I to cover additional advertising expenditure of £80,000. Assume that all other existing fixed costs would remain unchanged.

(5 marks)

(d)   Calculate the increase in sales volume of Product II that is necessary in order to compensate the effect of profit of a 10% reduction in the selling price of the product. State clearly any assumptions made.
(5 marks)
(Total: 20 marks)
(ACCA June 92)

54   RANGE OF PRODUCTS

C Ltd manufactures a range of products and the data below refer to one product which goes through one process only. The company operates a 13 four-weekly reporting system for process and product costs and the data given below relate to Period 10.

There was no opening work-in-progress stock.

5,000 units of materials input at £2.94 per unit entered the process.

	£
Further direct materials added	13,830
Direct wages incurred	6,555
Production overhead	7,470

Normal loss is 3% of input.

Closing work-in-progress was 800 units but these were incomplete, having reached the following percentages of completion for each of the elements of cost listed:

	%
Direct materials added	75
Direct wages	50
Production overhead	25

270 units were scrapped after a quality control check when the units were at the following degrees of completion:

	%
Direct materials added	$66\frac{2}{3}$
Direct wages	$33\frac{1}{3}$
Production overhead	$16\frac{2}{3}$

Units scrapped, regardless of the degree of completion, are sold for £1 each and it is company policy to credit the process account with the scrap value of normal loss units.

You are required

to prepare the Period 10 accounts for the

(a)   process account; and
(b)   abnormal gain or loss;   **(20 marks)**

55   AMAZON PLC

Amazon plc manufactures two types of industrial sealant by passing materials through two consecutive processes. The results of operating the two processes during the previous month are shown below:

Process 1

Costs incurred (£):

Materials 7,000 kg @ £0.50 per kg	3,500	
Labour and overheads	4,340	

Output (kg):

Transferred to Process 2		6,430
Defective production		570

Process 2

Costs incurred (£):

Labour and overheads	12,129	

Output (kg):

Type E sealant		2,000
Type F sealant		4,000
By-product		430

It is considered normal for 10% of the total output from process 1 to be defective and all defective output is sold as scrap at £0.40 kg. Losses are not expected in process 2.

There was no work in process at the beginning or end of the month and no opening stocks of sealants.

Sales of the month's output from Process 2 were:

Type E sealant	1,100 kg
Type F sealant	3,200 kg
By-product	430 kg

The remainder of the output from Process 2 was in stock at the end of the month.

The selling prices of the products are: Type E sealant £7 per kg and Type F sealant £2.50 per kg. No additional costs are incurred on either of the two main products after the second process. The by-product is sold for £1.80 per kg after being sterilised, at a cost of £0.30 per kg, in a subsequent process. The operating costs of process 2 are reduced by the net income receivable from sales of the by-product.

You are required

(a)   to calculate, for the previous month, the cost of the output transferred from process 1 into process 2 and the net cost or saving arising from any abnormal losses or gains in process 1.   **(6 marks)**

(b)   to calculate the value of the closing stock of each sealant and the profit earned by each sealant during the previous month using the following method of apportioning costs to joint products:

   (i)   according to weight of output,
   (ii)   according to market value of output.   **(10 marks)**

(c)   to consider whether apportioning process costs to joint products is useful. Briefly illustrate with examples from your answer to (b) above.   **(4 marks)**

(Total: 20 marks)

56   JOBBING COMPANY

You have just taken up the position as the first full-time accountant for a jobbing engineering company. Previously the accounting work had been undertaken by the company's auditors who had produced the following summarised profit and loss statement for the financial year which ended on 31 March of this year.

	£	£	£
Sales			2,400,000
Direct material		1,000,000	
Direct labour:			
Grinding department	200,000		
Finishing department	260,000	460,000	
Production overhead:			
Grinding	175,000		
Finishing	208,000	383,000	
Administration costs		118,500	
Selling costs		192,000	2,153,500
Net profit			246,500

The sales manager is currently negotiating a price for an enquiry for a job which has been allocated number 878 and he has been given the following information by his staff:

Preferred price to obtain a return of 16⅔% on selling price	£22,656
Lowest acceptable price	£18,880

These prices have been based on the following estimated costs for proposed Job 878:

	£	£
Direct material		9,000
Direct labour:		
Grinding department 400 hours @ £5	2,000	
Finishing department 300 hours @ £6	1,800	3,800
		12,800
Add: 47.5% to cover all other costs		6,080
Total cost		18,880

The sales manager seeks your advice about the validity of the method he is using to quote for Job 878.

The company is currently busy with a fairly full order book but the Confederation of British Industry has forecast that a recession is imminent for the engineering industry.

You are required, as the accountant:

(a)   to criticise the method adopted for estimating the costs which are used as the basis for quoting prices for jobs;

(8 marks)

(b)   to suggest a better method of estimating job costs and to calculate a revised job cost and price, based on the information available, to give to the sales manager;   **(8 marks)**

(c)   to suggest how you would propose to improve the accounting information to assist with controlling costs and providing information for pricing purposes.   **(9 marks)**

(Total: 25 marks)

ANSWERS TO PRACTICE QUESTIONS

| 1 | **BORROWS PLC** |

(a)   Rights issues tend to reduce the market price of shares because they are sold at a discount to the market price. This is a necessary (but not a sufficient) requirement of a successful rights issue (potential investors still need to be convinced that taking up the rights represents a good investment on their part).

The theoretical ex-rights price is:

New finance required	£200m
Issue price (210p less 10%)	189p
Number of new shares	105.82m
(i.e. £200m ÷ £1.89)	
Existing number of shares	1,000.00m
New number of shares	1,105.82m
Existing market value	
(1,000m × £2.10)	£2,100m
Value of new issue	£200m
New market value	£2,300m
New share price	
(£2,300/1,105.82)	£2.08

The actual market price will be greater than the theoretical ex-rights price if the new money is invested in positive NPV projects, i.e. the money will earn a greater return than the required return for that investment. Thus the market price of the share will only equal the theoretical ex-rights price if the new money earns just the required return for the investment (i.e. the NPV of the investment is zero).

(b)   *Gearing*:

The current market value of debt is:

Long-term debt	£270m
Overdraft	£80m
	———
	£350m
	———

Gearing using market value is currently £350m/£2,100m = 16.7% (use market value in preference to book value to give a more meaningful figure). This is relatively low reflecting the risky nature of current operations.

With a new share issue, gearing will fall to £350m/£2,300m = 15.2%. With more debt, it will rise to £550m/£2,100m = 26.2%

Interest cover and EPS:

The projected P&L account is (£m)

	Ordinary	Eurodollar	CULS
Operating profit	249.6	249.6	249.6
Interest	40.0	54.0*	56.0
EBT	209.6	195.6	193.6
Tax	69.2	64.5	63.9
EAT	140.4	131.1	129.7
Number of shares	1,106	1,000	1,000
EPS	12.7p	13.1p	13.0p

*The existing £40 + ($300m × 7% ÷ 1.50) = £54m

The current EPS is 11.3p.

The higher EPS for debt may compensate for the higher financial risk borne by the ordinary shareholders.

Interest cover is currently 5.2, i.e. 208/40, and changes to:

	Ordinary	Eurodollar	CULS
	6.2	4.6	4.5

All look relatively comfortable.

(c)   The main areas of risk may include:

(i)   Exchange rate risks. Sterling will fluctuate (often significantly) against other currencies. Dealing in 'soft' currencies may also provide problems of convertibility if funds are repatriated. There are various hedging techniques available to insure against these risks, e.g. the forward markets, options etc.

(i)   The risk of finding any oil. This is business risk - the company will rely on survey reports.

(iii)   The risk of fluctuations in the oil price. This is affected by world supply and demand. Fixing long-term contracts, or selling oil forward (thereby confirming the price) may alleviate this problem.

(iv)   The period of time of the investment depends on the success and scale of any oil finds. This will also affect future cash flow profiles.

(d)   This is a risky project. Even though this is a mining company, it is in a different location. Future cash flow requirements are extremely difficult to predict with no guarantee of a return, or when one might occur. This would suggest equity finance so that the company does not commit itself to higher interest charges than necessary. Equity finance is also permanent; the debt will have to be repaid.

Other information that would be useful in this decision includes:

(i)   financial and accounting information relating to other companies in this sector

(ii)   knowledge of the countries where exploration is to take place, with their economic and political profile.

2	**TWELLOW PLC**

(a) Based upon a structured analysis

Liquidity ratios

	19X0	19X3
Current ratio (current assets: current liabilities)	0.73:1	0.62:1
Acid test (current assets less stock: current liabilities)	0.32:1	0.30:1

In both cases, the company's liquidity position has decreased and is at a relatively low level. However, these low levels have occurred throughout the period and so seem to be sustainable; this indicates strong cash inflows for this company.

The company now has 62p of current assets for every £1 of current liabilities and 30p of current assets less stock for every £1 of current liabilities. This reduction in liquidity is more risky (the company has less cover to pay current liabilities) but is more profitable (investment in current assets has an opportunity cost). Looking at the balance sheet, most of the decrease in the ratio is due to the doubling of the overdraft and short-term creditors - this is probably largely due to financing the acquisition with short-term finance. However, it is a risky strategy; short-term finance needs regular renewing and may suddenly be withdrawn. In ratio analysis answers it is only possible to suggest reasons, not reach definite conclusions.

Gearing

	19X0	19X3
$\dfrac{\text{Debt (including bank overdraft)}}{\text{Equity (shares + reserves)}}$	25/101	65/124
	25%	52%

Interest cover cannot be calculated accurately since the interest on the overdraft is not given. Based upon the interest charge on the long-term debt, interest cover looks comfortable (19X0: 22/2 = 11, 19X3: 54/6 = 9).

Gearing has increased (this assumes that the overdraft is being renewed - in effect it operates as long-term finance) and interest cover (the number of times interest can be paid out of profit before interest) has decreased. However, neither figure looks to give cause for concern, especially as there is considerable asset value to act as security. This will increase the company's 'debt capacity'. The increase in gearing probably arose as a result of financing the acquisition. A fall in interest cover is often one of the consequences of increased borrowing and the danger is that however much profit falls, interest still has to be paid (this is the same as the financial risk of gearing).

Although the rise in gearing increases the financial risk of the company, it has an advantage in that debt is cheap to companies due to the tax relief on interest (this assumes that the company pays tax). If a company has high and stable profits, which seems to apply here, high gearing may make good financial sense.

Efficiency (turnover) ratios

	19X0	19X3
Asset turnover (sales/total assets)	3.34	3.08
Debtor collection period (debtors/average daily sales)	9 days	11 days

The sales achieved per £1 of assets has decreased to £3.08, indicating a reduction in the productivity of assets. Investment in tangible assets has taken place throughout this period, and it may take time for them to become fully productive. The debtor collection period is extremely small indicating that this is a business that makes a lot of cash sales.

Profitability

	19X0	19X3
Operating profit margin	3%	5.3%
Return on assets (PBIT/total assets)	10%	16%
Return on shareholder funds (using profit after tax)	13%	25%

There are improvements all around here. Operating profit is used in the first two ratios in order to exclude interest (which is a financing not an operating charge) and tax (which is largely out of the company's control).

Shareholders, on the other hand, will be more interested in the profit attributable to them (after interest and tax). The improvement from a low base in the operating profit margin may be especially significant. Note, however, that the increase in the return on shareholder funds has been helped by effectively writing off the £60 million goodwill on the acquisition against the share premium account.

Market ratios

	19X0	*19X3*
EPS	18p	52p
P/E ratio	11.5	10
Dividend cover	3.25	3.44

$$EPS = \frac{\text{Earnings after tax after extraordinary items}}{\text{Number of shares}}$$

This new definition arises from the requirements of FRS 3. Note the P/E ratio and dividend cover measures above exclude extraordinary items.

Although shareholders now have a significantly higher EPS, shareholders are in a riskier position due to the higher gearing. The P/E ratio indicates that the market has reduced expectations for this company. Dividend cover has remained fairly stable indicating a consistent dividend policy.

(b)   The above analysis is constrained by a lack of important information, for example:

- disaggregated accounting information: cost breakdown, figures for different departments, products, markets
- information about competitors
- information about the markets in which Twello is trading
- company policies and objectives
- other market information such as P/E ratio for the sector
- inflation over this period.

(c)   Deep discount bonds are issued at a discount (at least 15%) to their par value. To achieve this low selling price they must be issued with a low coupon rate. This means that much of the gain to any investor is a capital gain rather than interest income. This will appeal to some investors (probably for tax reasons; although in the UK, some of the capital gain may be taxed as income). Companies also save having to pay lots of interest each year (although, of course, they will not be able to sell them for a very high price in the first place). Some companies will prefer this if they expect to be short of cash in the near future.

The deep discount bonds redeemable at £60 million face value must therefore have originally been sold for £50. This £50 buys £4 p.a. for the next 15 years and a £100 redemption in 15 years' time. This gives a yield to redemption (the same as the IRR) of about 11% (calculate this by linear interpolation). Not only would new investors not like the reduced return compared to the ordinary debentures, they will also require a higher return due to the increased risk of the higher gearing.

(d)   The main points to consider when drawing up the 19X4 budget would be:

- company objectives (new products or markets; growth or consolidation)
- make-up of fixed and variable costs
- state of the market
- projected inflation
- competition.

3   MANRAY PLC

(a)   In order to determine whether or not the project is worthwhile it is necessary to compare the present value of the inflows and outflows of the project after tax adjustments. In this scenario the discount rate (cost of capital) is set at 15%. The actual interest rate of the borrowing being used is therefore irrelevant as this is deemed to be inherent in the discount rate.

The project outflow is £2m (£3m borrowed less £1m used to repay the overdraft).

The project will be eligible for capital allowances of 25% per annum over 4 years. This amounts to £500,000 per annum, assumed to be available from year 1 (when the equipment is brought into use) until year 4 inclusive. After tax this allowance amounts to £500,000 × 33% = £165,000 per annum. The present value of this tax saving is found using the 4-year annuity factor for years 2-5 inclusive (because tax is paid one year in arrears).

15% annuity factor years 1 - 5	=	3.352	
15% annuity factor year 1	=	(0.870)	
15% annuity factor years 2 - 5	=	2.482	

The present value of the capital allowance is thus: £165,000 × 2.482 = £409,530

The change in costs and revenues arising from the project is as follows:

		£
Revenue: Additional 10,000 units @ £35 =		350,000
Variable costs:	New cost = 90,000 × £10 (W1)	
	Old cost = 80,000 × £20 (W1)	
	Saving = (80,000 × £20) - (90,000 × £10) =	700,000
		1,050,000
Fixed costs:	Increase by	(400,000)
Net pre-tax operating inflow		650,000

Since the loan is to be repaid 'in three equal instalments, every two years over the anticipated lifetime of the equipment' the project has a life of 6 years.

The present value of the net pre tax operating inflow is thus found using the 15% annuity factor for years 1–6:

£650,000 × 3.784 = £2,459,600

The tax charge resulting from the increase in pre-tax operating inflow is £650,000 × 33% = £214,500 which will arise in years 2–7 inclusive (because tax is paid 1 year in arrears. The 15% annuity factor for years 2 - 7 inclusive is:

15% annuity factor years 1–7	=	4.160	
15% annuity factor year 1	=	(0.870)	
15% annuity factor years 2–7		3.290	

The present value of the tax charge is thus: £214,500 × 3.290 = £705,705

Present value summary:

	£
Investment outflow	(2,000,000)
Capital allowance inflow	409,530
Operating inflow	2,459,600
Operating tax outflow	(705,705)
Net present value	163,425

Since the project has a positive net present value it is clearly worthwhile.

(b)   Earnings per share $= \dfrac{\text{Profit available for ordinary shareholders}}{\text{Number of ordinary shares}}$

$$= \frac{£456{,}000}{4\text{m}} = 11.4 \text{ pence per share}$$

If the new project is introduced the revised profit and loss account is:

	£'000	£'000
Sales		3,150
Less: Variable expenses	900	
Fixed costs	650	(1,550)
Operating profit		1,600
Less: Interest payable (£3m × 10%) (W2)		(300)
Profit before tax		1,300
Taxation (33% × £800,000 (W3))		(264)
		1,036
Less: Preference dividend		(80)
Profit available for ordinary shareholders		956

The new earnings for share is thus: $\dfrac{£956{,}000}{4\text{m}} = 23.9$ pence per share

This represents an increase of 12.5 pence per share or 110%.

(c)   Operating gearing is the relationship between the level of fixed and variable costs incurred by a business. In relative terms the higher the level of fixed costs the greater is the proportion of revenue required to cover those costs. As a consequence the greater the level of relative fixed costs, the greater the risk of making losses (due to the impact of sales volume changes). In contrast, once the fixed costs have been covered the greater the proportionate fixed costs, the greater is the growth in profits.

Operating gearing can be measured by:

$$\frac{\text{Fixed costs}}{\text{Total costs}} \quad \text{or} \quad \frac{\text{Fixed costs}}{\text{Sales}}$$

In the case of Manray these calculations before and after the introduction of the project are:

Before: $\dfrac{£250{,}000}{£1{,}850{,}000} = 13.5\%$ $\dfrac{£250{,}000}{£2{,}800{,}000} = 8.9\%$

After: $\dfrac{£650{,}000}{£1{,}550{,}000} = 41.9\%$ $\dfrac{£650{,}000}{£3{,}150{,}000} = 20.6\%$

(d)   The breakeven point equals:

$$\frac{\text{Fixed costs}}{\text{Contribution / unit}}$$

In the case of Manray this can be calculated before and after the project is introduced:

Before: $\dfrac{£250{,}000}{(£35 - £20)} = 16{,}667$ units

After: $\dfrac{£650{,}000}{(£35 - £10)} = 26{,}000$ units

Both of these calculations ignore interest, which if included has the following effect:

Before: $\dfrac{(£250,000+£150,000)}{(£35-£20)} = 26,667$ units

After: $\dfrac{(£650,000+£300,000)}{(£35-£10)} = 38,000$ units

(Note: the preference dividend is ignored because although it is fixed rate capital it is an appropriation of profit and not a cost).

(e)   There are a number of economic reasons why interest rates change. Possible reasons for an increase in interest rates include:

(i)   increased borrowing by the government; interest rates rise so as to increase the funds available for gilt purchase by taking funds away from other investments;

(ii)   an increase in the funds demanded by the private sector; again interest rates rise to encourage such investors;

(iii)   a rise in actual price inflation; causing notional interest rates to rise so that real interest rates remain constant;

(iv)   a rise in the expected rate of inflation; so that investors, especially in respect of fixed rate investments, raise their interest rate demands so as to maintain a constant level of real income;

(v)   government legislation to reduce the funds available for lending (eg, by banks); so that interest rates rise to reduce the demand for funds;

(vi)   government action to strengthen the value of currency on the world currency markets.

When measuring difficulties in this way it is necessary to identify how such a difficulty would be measured. In the following it is assumed that the director is concerned about the company's ability to earn profits and make appropriate dividend payments to shareholders. Manray's level of interest cover after the introduction of the new project is:

$$\frac{\text{Operating profit}}{\text{Interest payable}} = \frac{£1,600,000}{£300,000} = 5.33\,\text{times}$$

This means that the interest payable can increase more than five-fold before the operating profit is eliminated, however this would then result in no dividends to either preference or ordinary shareholders. The ordinary shareholders, as the risk-takers, would expect their return to increase in line with interest rate changes in the longer term. Thus it can be stated that any significant increase of the interest cost in isolation has an important implication if it becomes the norm in the longer-term. However, when considering the added effects of reductions in operating income together with increases in interest rates the problem becomes more acute.

WORKINGS

(W1)   Present variable costs are £1,600,000/80,000 = £20/unit

The saving of £10/unit reduces the variable cost to £10/unit.

(W2)   The interest charge assumes that the present overdraft is refinanced - this would appear worthwhile as the present interest rate on the overdraft is 15% (£150,000/£1m) and the new loan rate is only 10%.

(W3)   Taxable profit = £1,300 - £500 (capital allowances).

4	**CREDIT PERIODS**

(a)   Initial workings

Annual sales volume $= \dfrac{£24 \text{ million}}{£6} = 4$ million units.

Stock is equivalent to one month's turnover $= \dfrac{4 \text{ million}}{12} = 333,333$ units.

At a variable cost of £4 per unit, stock value = £1.333 million.

(Tutorial note: in this question we are looking for the 'break-even' increase in sales which will cover the costs of carrying additional stock and of extending the credit period by half a month. Since these costs are dependent on the sales volume, it is necessary to designate the increase in the sales volume as 'q' and solve the problem algebraically.*)*

Let q be the 'break-even' increase in annual sales volume.

Additional contribution from increased sales

For each additional unit sold:

	£
Sales price	6.00
Less bad debts (5%)	0.30
Net sales revenue	5.70
Variable cost	4.00
Contribution per unit (allowing for bad debts)	1.70

Total additional contribution $= 1.7q$

Cost of additional working capital (stock and debtors)

Stock
Stock is equivalent to one month's turnover. Thus, additional stock requirement $= \frac{1}{12}q$.
At a variable cost of £4 per unit this has a value of $£\frac{4}{12}q = £0.333q$.

Debtors

Existing debtors represent one month's sales ie, $\frac{1}{12} \times £24$ million $= £2$ million.

The additional half month's credit will increase existing debtors by $\frac{1}{2} \times £2$ million = £1 million.

(Tutorial note:

New debtors will be $^{1\frac{1}{2}}\!/_{12} \times £6q = £0.75q$.

(£6q is the additional turnover at £6 per unit)

However, it would be unfair to include the profit element of sales in the computation of new debtors. For the purposes of this calculation, the extra financing costs for the additional sales result from having to finance additional variable costs for $1\frac{1}{2}$ months before payment. The additional debtors should therefore be evaluated at variable cost.*)*

New debtors, evaluated at variable cost $= ^{1\frac{1}{2}}\!/_{12} \times £4q = £0.5q$

Thus total increase in working capital requirements (stock plus debtors)

= £0.333q + £1 million + £0.5q
= £1 million + 0.833q.

At 20% per annum, the annual financing cost of this additional working capital is

20% × (£1 million + £0.833q) = (£200,000 + £0.167q)

Break-even sales

Additional contribution must equate to the annual financing cost

$$\therefore 1.7q = 200,000 + 0.167q$$
$$\therefore 1.533q = 200,000$$
$$\therefore q = 130,463$$

The additional sales required to cover the required return of 20% on the increased investment in working capital are 130,463 units with a value of £782,779.

(b)   Customary methods of establishing creditworthiness of potential new customers

Forms of credit evaluation include

(1)   Bank references
(2)   Information from salesmen or other personal visits
(3)   Analysis of company's annual report and accounts
(4)   Extel cards
(5)   DTI and ECGD (for export customers)
(6)   Scrutiny of trade journals/trade association enquiries
(7)   Press comments
(8)   Services of a credit rating agency eg, Dun & Bradstreet
(9)   Information from friendly competitors
(10)   Use of a credit scoring technique
(11)   Supplying goods on a cash basis for a probationary period.

(c)   (i)   Factors to take into account when considering offering cash discounts to credit customers.

The starting point for the analysis is trade practice ie, the level of discounts (if any) currently being offered by competitors.

Beyond this it is a matter of trading off marketing and liquidity benefits against the direct cost of the discount and other hidden costs.

The benefits of offering cash discounts are

(1)   Demand for the company's products may be increased

(2)   Assuming the discounts are offered for prompt payment, liquidity may be immediately improved and a cash crisis avoided

(3)   The consequent reduction in debtors will reduce working capital financing costs

(4)   Sales ledger work will be reduced (fewer reminders)

(5)   Bad debts may be reduced.

The costs are

(1)   The discount itself

(2)   The cost of the debtors who miss the discount date and who consequently take a longer credit period than they otherwise would.

(ii)   Calculation of whether the discount scheme would increase the company's market value.

The factors in (i) above should be quantified. Although subjective, it is relatively easy to make estimates of all the factors listed. These should then be evaluated in a discounted cash flow exercise taking into account the company's cost of capital.

A positive net present value should indicate that the company's market value will increase, provided that the information is communicated to the market. In practice, the company's market value may be influenced by many short-term factors which are likely to obscure the effect of the discount scheme.

5   CASH SURPLUSES

Answer Plan

(a)   The reasons for a cash surplus; the circumstances for keeping the excess in liquid form.

(b)   Nature of the instruments: CD's; local authority bonds; finance house deposits; treasury bills.

Difference in interest rates: between instruments; over time.

(a)   In order to generate a cash surplus a company must be trading profitably. This cash surplus will then partly be used for the payment of dividends and the balance will be retained for investment or expansion.

A company may generate cashflows, in excess of the above requirements for the following reasons.

(i)   There is a lack of worthwhile new investment or the company does not wish to undertake further expansion.

(ii)   Certain sections or divisions of the business have been sold to generate surplus cash.

(iii)   Sales turnover has increased thus enhancing the total profit generated.

(iv)   Improved efficiency and cost control has resulted in cost savings.

The circumstances under which the directors may wish to maintain the surplus in liquid form might include the following.

(i)   To have funds available for the redemption of debenture stock at a future date.

(ii)   To be in a position to repurchase shares from the ordinary shareholders if the company would benefit from such a restructure of its capital.

(iii)   To be able to undertake any large investment projects which become available, such as a takeover of another company where a cash consideration would be required.

(iv)   To take advantage of high bank deposit rates if no preferable alternative investment exists.

(b)   Sterling certificates of deposit (CD's) are a form of investment with a bank. They are issued by a bank to a depositor and state that a certain amount of sterling has been deposited with the bank for a certain period of time during which it will attract interest. Although the CD is issued for a fixed period of time, it represents a flexible investment because CD's are traded on the money market. Therefore if the depositor finds that the cash is required prior to the date of completion, he can sell the CD to obtain immediate cash.

Depositors tend to be either banks or large businesses with surplus cash for investment.

Local authority bonds are securities issued by local authorities in order to raise cash. They have a shorter period to maturity than CD's, but like the latter they are traded on the money market and therefore represent an alternative, flexible investment for excess cash.

Finance houses are usually subsidiaries of banks whose primary function is the lending of money to various parties. In order to do such they need to raise the available funds which is achieved via the issue of finance house deposits. These are non-negotiable and therefore lack the flexibility of the above.

Treasury bills are, on the other hand, negotiable instruments. They are issued by (on behalf of) the government in order to raise the required funds for public spending. They are bought initially on issue by discount houses, which are affiliated to the Bank of England, the body responsible for the issue. The bills are then subsequently traded on the discount market. They carry an effective rate of interest on account of being issued at a discount and redeemed at nominal value.

The reason for interest rate differentials between different types of financial instrument depend on two factors: their marketability and their risk. If we consider initially the marketability of the instruments discussed above, it is the finance house deposits which are not negotiable and which are therefore the least marketable. These will carry the highest rate of interest. There is little to choose between the marketability of the others, but their interest rate differential arises as a result of the varying levels of risk. Treasury bills being associated with the government, bear the least risk. In fact they are often considered to be risk free, since there is no likelihood of the government's defaulting on redemption. As a result, it is the treasury bill interest rate which forms the basis for the interest rates of other financial instruments.

It is usual for interest rates to be higher on longer-term investments. This is commensurate with the level of risk associated with the investment. This can be seen to be true for the data on the four types of instrument in the question. However, if a fall in interest rates is anticipated in the future, it may be possible for a longer-term investment to carry a lower rate of interest. In addition interest rates on particular securities will be affected by specific supply and demand over time.

6   HEXICON PLC

(a) The following reasons may be cited for using the net present value (NPV) method of investment appraisal:

(i) Compared to Accounting Rate of Return (ARR), it discounts real cashflows as opposed to accounting profits which are affected by non-cash items.

(ii) Compared to measuring Internal Rate of Return (IRR), the NPV method only gives one solution. In some circumstances, (when there are a number of outflows occurring at different times), multiple IRR solutions are possible.

(iii) Compared to the payback method, NPV considers all of the cashflows of a project.

(iv) By using a discount rate it measures the opportunity cost of the money invested by a person in a project.

(v) The interest rate used can be increased/decreased depending upon the level of perceived risk in the investment.

(vi) The NPV of a project can be shown to be equal to the increase in the value of shareholder's equity in the company. Thus the method is consistent with the objective of shareholder wealth maximisation.

(b) (i) The present EOQ is $\sqrt{\dfrac{2 \times £100 \times 40,000}{20\% \times £2.50}}$

= 4,000 units/order

The revised EOQ $= \sqrt{\dfrac{2 \times £25 \times 40,000}{20\% \times £2.50}}$

$= 2,000$ units/order

From this it can be seen that the EOQ is halved.

(ii)   The number of orders has increased from (40,000/4,000) 10 orders to (40,000/2,000) 20 orders; however, ordering costs are reduced by:

$(10 \times £100) - (20 \times £25) = £500$ per annum

Average stocks have also reduced from $\dfrac{4,000}{2}$ (2,000 units) to $\dfrac{2,000}{2}$ (1,000 units). Consequently carrying costs have reduced by $20\% \times £2.50 \times 1,000 = £500$ per annum.

Total inventory costs are thereby reduced by £1,000/annum.

Assuming that Hexicon plc pays tax in the same year as it earns profits the present value of the proposal is found by comparing the outflow cost with the discounted after tax savings over the eight-year life of the proposal (using a 12% discount rate).

Discounted savings:

$£1,000 \times 67\%$ (1 - tax rate) $\times$ 12% annuity factor - 8 years

$=$ £670 $\times$ 4.968 $=$ £3,329

Cost of reorganisation (tax deductible)

$= £4,000 \times 67\%$ (1 - tax rate) $=$ (£2,680)

Net benefit   £649

As the present value of the proposal is positive it is worthwhile.

(c)   The main objective of Just In Time (JIT) purchasing is to match the delivery of components from suppliers to their usage in production. If this is achieved there are significant benefits to be gained by both the supplier and the customer.

The customer is likely to use only one supplier for each component and to build up a relationship with the supplier which encourages communication thus enabling the supplier to benefit from advanced production planning and economies of scale. To enhance this relationship the customer makes a long-term commitment to future orders.

The supplier guarantees to deliver goods of an appropriate quality in accordance with an agreed delivery schedule. The benefit to the customer is thereby a reduction(or elimination) of stockholding and significant cost savings. These arise in both holding costs and also in materials handling, because goods are transferred directly from goods inwards to production.

7	**WHICHFORD PLC**

(a)   (i)   Currently the delay in invoicing is:

Percentage of weeks sales subject to delay %	Amount of sales subject to delay £'000	Days delay	£ x days delay
20	100	3	300
6	30	4	120
40	200	5	1,000
22	110	6	660
12	60	7	420
			2,500

This is the equivalent of £2.5 million sales being delayed for one day each week of the 50-week trading year. The cost of this delay in one year amounts to

$$£2,500,000 \times 50 \text{ weeks} \times \frac{0.15}{365} = £51,370 \text{ per year}$$

The revised delay in invoicing will produce:

Percentage of weeks sales subject to delay %	Amount of sales subject to delay £'000	Days delay	£ x days delay
50	250	0	0
40	200	1	200
10	50	3	150
			350

This is the equivalent of £350,000 sales being delayed for one day each week. The cost of this delay in one year amounts to

$$£350,000 \times 50 \text{ weeks} \times \frac{0.15}{365} = £7,192$$

Therefore, the total savings from the introduction of the micro-computers amounts to:

	£	£
Saving of interest:		
Old cost	51,370	
New cost	7,192	
Savings		44,178
Saving of head office costs		48,000
Total saving		92,178

Therefore, the maximum monthly rental is $\dfrac{£92,178}{12}$ £7,681

(ii)   **Average debtors after invoice production**

		£
Old:		
£25 million × $\frac{35}{365}$		2,397,260
New:		
£25 million × $\frac{30}{365}$		2,054,795
Reduction (£25 million × $\frac{5}{365}$)		342,465
Savings £342,465 × 15%		51,370
Savings from increased speed of invoicing		92,178
Total savings		143,548

Therefore, the maximum monthly rental is $\frac{£143,548}{12}$ £11,962

(b)   Factors offer three major services:

(i)   **A sales ledger accounting and credit control service**

The client effectively sells all debts to the factor who administers the debt and collects cash from the debtor. On collection of the cash the factor will usually pass all monies still outstanding, less factoring fees, to the client. The client therefore effectively replaces a great many trade debtors with only one ie, the factor.

(ii)   **Provision of finance**

The factor will normally be prepared to forward immediately to the client a proportion, often between 60% and 80%, of the value of each invoice, thereby assisting the client's cash flow. This service is usually expensive.

(iii)   **Credit insurance**

For a further fee the factor may be willing to provide insurance against bad debts - this is non-recourse factoring as the factor has no recourse to the client in the event of non-payment of the original invoice.

A factoring agreement usually covers all sales by a client.

Invoice discounting is merely the provision of finance against the security of selected invoices. It is the ad hoc use of the 'provision of finance' aspect mentioned above without any other services of factoring.

Issues to be considered include:

(i)   costs of factoring versus costs of keeping one's own sales ledger;

(ii)   expertise which can be provided by the factor;

(iii)   whether factoring will reduce the collection period;

(iv)   whether the contingency nature of the factor's liability to provide finance might be worthwhile;

(v)   whether the intervention of the factor between the client and one's own customers might adversely affect relationships.

Factoring is useful to rapidly growing firms which have previously had little need for a sophisticated sales ledger department but now need the services of experts. Factoring may be suitable for such a firm and may be less expensive than setting up a specialised department within the firm. Factor finance is, however, normally more expensive than overdraft facilities.

---

8   MOLLET LTD

(a)   *Definite cash outflows*

	£
Materials	70,000
Overheads	10,000
Wages and salaries basic	50,000
	130,000

Possible cash outflows

		Probability
Wages and salaries overtime	0	0.5
	10,000	0.5

Overall cash outflows £	Probability	Possible cash inflows £	Probability	Net cash flows £	Probability
		100,000	0.4	(30,000)	0.2
130,000	0.5	120,000	0.6	(10,000)	0.3
140,000	0.5	100,000	0.4	(40,000)	0.2
		120,000	0.6	(20,000)	0.3
					1.0

A maximum net cash outflow of £40,000 is expected during the next week. As the opening balance is expected to be £40,000, and a £20,000 cash balance must be maintained, £20,000 of this requirement can be funded by reducing the money market balance. The minimum level of investment in the money market will, therefore, be £80,000 (£100,000 less £20,000, the maximum that will need to be withdrawn from the money market).

The maximum level of investment in the money market will be £120,000, the existing £100,000 plus £20,000 from the cash balance. However, as expected net cash flows for the week are at best(£10,000), a £120,000 investment in the money market must lead to a withdrawal of cash during the week. As there is a penalty of one week's interest and, in addition, transactions costs, investing £120,000 cannot maximise returns.

The costs and returns of holding cash balances at the start of the week of £80,000 to £120,000 inclusive (in multiples of £10,000) are:

Money market balance at start of week	Expected interest earned at 12%	Amount that might need to be withdrawn during week, and associated probabilities	Expected transactions costs of withdrawals and investments	Expected interest penalty	Expected net earnings
£	£	£	£	£	£
80,000	185	0	18	46	121
90,000	208	10,000 0.2	16	28	164
100,000	231	20,000 0.2	7	14	210
		10,000 0.2			
110,000	254	30,000 0.2	28	30	196
		20,000 0.2			
		10,000 0.3			
120,000	277	40,000 0.2	40	53	184
		30,000 0.2			
		20,000 0.3			
		10,000 0.3			

Note: An example of the full calculations for £110,000 would be:

Expected interest earned $£110,000 \times \dfrac{12\%}{52} = £254$

Expected transactions costs

On amount invested at start of week
  £10 fixed cost + £10,000 × 0.05% variable cost   =   £15

On possible withdrawals during the week:
        If 30,000 withdrawn (8 + 30,000 × 0.05%)0.2   =   5
        If 20,000 withdrawn (8 + 20,000 × 0.05%)0.2   =   4
        If 10,000 withdrawn (8 + 10,000 × 0.05%)0.3   =   4
                            13

Total expected transactions costs are   £28

Expected interest penalty

If £30,000 withdrawn $(£30,000 \times \dfrac{12\%}{52})0.2$ =   14

If £20,000 withdrawn $(£20,000 \times \dfrac{12\%}{52})0.2$ =   9

If £10,000 withdrawn $(£10,000 \times \dfrac{12\%}{52})0.3$ =   7

                            30

The level of money market deposit at the beginning of next week that maximises expected return is £100,000.

(b)   The advantages and disadvantages of short-term and long-term debt relate primarily to:

        Risk
        Cost
        Flexibility

Risk

Short-term debt involves more risk than long-term.

(i)   The risk of overdrafts or loans not being renewed.

(ii)   Risk of more volatile fluctuations in interest rates when compared with a fixed interest long-term loan.

(iii)   Risk of an overdraft being called in at short notice.

Cost

Long-term debt is normally more expensive than short-term debt.

Flexibility

Short-term debt offers greater flexibility.

(i)   If working capital requirements fluctuate because of seasonal or cyclical factors, the company may not want to commit itself to long-term debt.

(ii)   In periods of high interest rates when rates are expected to fall, companies will prefer to borrow on a short-term basis and to refinance (if desired) with long-term debt when interest rates are lower.

Working capital may be divided into two elements: permanent working capital, below which working capital requirements tend not to fall, and fluctuating working capital.

If it is considered desirable to finance long-term assets with long-term funds, it may be argued that permanent working capital should be financed by long-term debts or other long-term sources of funds, and fluctuating working capital by short-term funds.

The choice of how working capital is financed will depend upon the attitudes towards risk and the profitability of the company concerned. Short-term debt is less costly but more risky. A risk-averse company is likely to use a higher proportion of long-term debt even though profitability will be reduced.

---

9   OVERDRAFT REQUIREMENTS

(a)   (i)   The current situation is as follows:

	Product A £	Product B £	Product C £	Total £
Sales (50,000 @ £4.50 etc)	225,000	390,000	262,500	
Cost of sales (50% etc)	112,500	234,000	78,750	
∴ Stock ($^{1.5}/_{12}$ × 112,500 etc)	14,063	39,000	6,562	
Debtors ($^{2}/_{12}$ × 225,000 etc)	37,500	97,500	32,813	
Creditors ($^{2.5}/_{12}$ × 112,500 etc)	(23,438)	(48,750)	(9,844)	
Net current operating assets	28,125	87,750	29,531	145,406

Scenario 1

Under scenario 1 sales of A would increase by 25%, sales of B by 20% and sales of C by 30%, so purchases would have to rise by the same percentages to meet the required volume increases.

	Product A £	Product B £	Product C £	Total £
Net current operating assets (as above)	28,125	87,750	29,531	
Volume increases (25% etc)	7,031	17,550	8,859	
Revised totals	35,156	105,300	38,390	178,846

Scenario 1 requires an increase in net current operating assets of £33,440.

Scenario 2

Debtors will increase by a further 25%.

	Product A £	Product B £	Product C £	Total £
Net current operating assets (per scenario 1)	35,156	105,300	38,390	
Increase in debtors (25% × 37,500 × 1.25 etc)	11,719	29,250	10,664	
Revised totals	46,875	134,550	49,054	230,479

Scenario 2 requires an increase in net current operating assets of £85,073 from the current position.

Scenario 3

Debtors are reduced by 25% while the suppliers credit periods fall slightly.

	Product A £	Product B £	Product C £	Total £
Net current operating assets (per scenario 1)	35,156	105,300	38,390	
Reduction in debtors (same figures as in scenario 2)	(11,719)	(29,250)	(10,664)	
Reduction in creditors ($^{0.1}/_{12}$ × 112,500 × 1.25 etc)	1,172	2,340	2,559	
	24,609	78,390	30,285	133,284

Scenario 3 permits a decrease in net current operating assets of £12,122 from the current position.

(ii)   The finance director might require the following other information before he renegotiates the company's overdraft requirements.

- expected cash flows of a capital nature, eg capital expenditure requirements or receipts from the sale of fixed assets.

- other non-current cash flows eg, payments of tax or dividends.

- other alternative sources of short and medium term funds such as term loans and their relative costs compared with overdrafts.

- what security the bank is looking for when granting the overdraft.

- the seasonality involved in the company's sales. If purchases have to be paid for throughout the year but all the sales are concentrated towards the end of the year, then the maximum overdraft required will be much more than estimated earlier.

- the reliability of the figures in the question. Are the estimated sales figures likely to be achieved? The finance director should look carefully at the basis on which these forecasts were drawn up.

- the relative likelihood of each of the scenarios he has envisaged. There is no point in negotiating a facility for the maximum overdraft under scenario 2, for example, if the probability of its occurring is only remote.

Essentially the finance director must consider the company's cash flow forecasts in the round, rather than just looking at cash from trading activities. The usual practice is to draw up a month-by-month cash flow estimate taking in all anticipated cash receipts and payments, which will reveal the maximum overdraft requirement over the forthcoming year.

(b)   Three possible uses for the surplus funds expected to become available after around six months are as follows:

(i)   Pay creditors more promptly. This would be advantageous if prompt settlement discounts are available which are not currently being taken up. A similar method of profiting by paying creditors is to decide to buy larger quantities than before, in order to qualify for bulk discounts.

(ii)   Place the money in an interest-bearing bank account. Better interest rates may be available if the money is invested in a term deposit, so that a notice period (eg, one month) has to be given before the funds can be withdrawn.

(iii)   Suspend prompt payment settlement discounts offered to debtors. If the money is not needed straight away there is no point in paying discounts to receive it promptly. A tight watch would be needed over this option to ensure that debtors paid up after the agreed period (eg, thirty days) instead and that bad debts did not rise.

(Tutorial note: other possibilities might be investing in other short-term instruments eg, Treasury Bills and commercial paper, increasing the level of dividends or accelerating the capital expenditure programme.)

---

10   H N LTD

(a)   (Note that all the figures refer to £000s)

With an opening overdraft of £(12), if the month 1 cash outflow is £(55), (a 20% probability), then this will increase the overdraft to £(67), keeping the cash balance at the minimum £20. In this case, using joint probabilities, there is a 4% chance that this will be followed by a cash inflow in month 2 of £20 so that the overdraft is reduced to £(47). There is a 2% chance that this will be followed in month 3 by a cash inflow of £25, thereby reducing the overdraft to £(22) and a 2% chance of a cash inflow of £15 which will reduce the overdraft to £(32).

These joint probabilities, cash flows (CFs) and resulting overdrafts (O/Ds) and cash float (Bal) can be summarised in the following table. Note that as soon as the overdraft reaches the maximum permitted £(80), any further deficit must be taken from the cash float (Bal).

| | Month 1 | | | | Month 2 | | | | Month 3 | | |
p	CF	O/D	Bal	jt p	CF	O/D	Bal	jt p	CF	O/D	Bal
.20	(55)	(67)	20	.04	20	(47)	20	.02	25	(22)	20
								.02	15	(32)	20
				.10	10	(57)	20	.05	5	(52)	20
								.05	(5)	(62)	20
				.06	5	(62)	20	.03	(5)	(67)	20
								.03	(10)	(72)	20
.50	(65)	(77)	20	.10	10	(67)	20	.05	5	(62)	20
								.05	0	(67)	20
				.25	(5)	(80)	18	.125	0	(80)	18
								.125	(5)	(80)	13
				.15	(10)	(80)	13	.075	(10)	(80)	3
								.075	(15)	(80)	(2)

	Month 1				Month 2				Month 3		
p	*CF*	*O/D*	*Bal*	*jt p*	*CF*	*O/D*	*Bal*	*jt p*	*CF*	*O/D*	*Bal*
.30	(72)	(80)	16	.06	0	(80)	16	.03	0	(80)	16
								.03	(10)	(80)	6
				.15	(10)	(80)	6	.075	(10)	(80)	(4)
								.075	(20)	(80)	(14)
				.09	(15)	(80)	1	.045	(20)	(80)	(19)
								.045	(30)	(80)	(29)

The probability of keeping the float at £20,000 in month 1 is 50% + 20% = 70%. The same calculation for month 2 is (4% + 10% + 6%) + 10% = 30%. Formonth3itis(2% + 2% + 5% + 5% + 3% + 3%) + 5% + 5% = 30%.

(b)   The probability of running out of cash (including spending even the £20,000 float) is zero for months 1 and 2. The probability of running out of cash in month 3 is (7.5%) + (7.5% + 7.5% + 4.5% + 4.5%) = 31.5%

(c)   Possible alternatives for a cash surplus are:

(i)   repaying loans

(ii)   redeeming shares

(iii)   paying higher wages

(iv)   increasing social or other 'high profile' expenditure such as sponsorships, advertising or donations to charity

(v)   financial investments on the money and capital markets.

11   COMFYLOT PLC

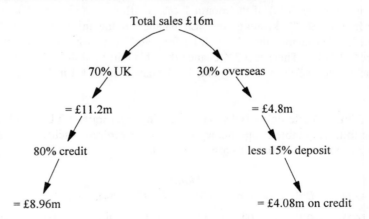

(1)   The costs and savings of domestic factoring can be identified as follows:

Costs of using the factor

	£
Factor charges service fee of 1.5% of all £8.96m credit sales	134,400
Redundancy payments	15,000

80% of the debts are factored at 15.5% The loans only last whilst the debt is outstanding (average 57 days).

The cost of this is therefore:

	£
80% × £8.96m × 15.5% × 57/365	173,505
Investment in the remaining 20% debtors has an opportunity cost (15%) = 20% × £8.96m × 15% × 57/365	41,977
Total cost	364,882

Savings from using the factor

	£
Administration	85,000
Bad debts (0.75% × £8.96m) (the factoring is non-recourse)	67,200
Current opportunity cost of debtors £8.96m × 57/365 × 15%	209,885
	362,085

The net cost of domestic factoring will be £2,797 next year. But redundancy is a non-recurring cost so savings would be expected thereafter.

(2)   The costs and savings associated with the cash discount can be identified as follows:

Costs	£
Administration	25,000
Cost of the discount itself (£8.96m × 0.4 × 0.015)	53,760
	78,760

Savings	£
Reduction in bad debts 0.25% × £8.96m	22,400

The discount results in some earlier payment which will reduce the overall level of debtors from the existing (£8.96m × 57/365 =) £1,399,233 to (£8.96m × 40% × 7/365) + (£8.96m × 60% × 57/365) = £908,274.

The opportunity cost of this reduction in the level of debtors of:

	£
£490,959 is multiplied by 15%	73,644
	96,044

The introduction of this cash discount will save a net £17,284

(3)   The cost/saving implications of all three possible increases in sales will provide the most useful information.

Existing costs are:

	£
The opportunity cost of debtors = £4.08m × 75/365 × 15% =	125,753
Bad debts = £4.08m × 1.25% =	51,000
	176,753

Calculations of the net benefit or loss under each projected possible increase in sales are as follows:

	20%	25%	30%
Sales	£4.896m	£5.1m	£5.304m
Opportunity cost of debtors[1]	160,964	167,671	174,378
Bad debts[2]	73,440	76,500	79,560
	234,1404	244,171	253,938
Less: Current cost (see above)	176,753	176,753	176,753
Net extra costs	57,651	67,418	77,185
Extra administration	30,000	40,000	50,000
Advertising	300,000	300,000	300,000
Total extra cost	387,651	407,418	427,185
Extra contribution			
£960,000 × .35	336,000		
£1.2m × .35		420,000	
£1.44m × .35			504,000
Net benefit (loss)	(51,651)[3]	12,582	76,815

Notes:

(1)   Multiply 80/365 × 15% × £4.896m for 20% sales
× £5.1m for 25% sales
× £5.304m for 30% sales

(2)   Multiply the sales figures by 1.5%.

(3)   But the benefits of this year's advertising expenditure may spill over and increase next year's contribution.

Marking note: Plan your approach before answering this type of question. A little thought would help you to identify and quantify the costs and financial benefits of each option.

12   ENGOT PLC

Answer Plan

(a)   Different measures of financial gearing.

(b)   Importance of financial gearing: risk, interest payments have to be made.

(c)   Limiting factors on the amount of debt finance: existing covenants, available cashflows and interest cover, security to be offered, effect on cost of capital.

(d)   Meaning of mezzanine finance: halfway between senior debt and equity.

(a)   Financial gearing is a measure of the proportionate relationship between a company's borrowings and its equity finance, ie, it is a measure of capital structure. There are a number of ways in which gearing may be calculated: either expressing debt as a proportion of total finance or as a proportion of equity, and either using book values or market values of the capital. In addition, the debt may be calculated to include all borrowings, or simply, those that are deemed to be part of the company's long-term financing.

The three gearing ratios stated in the question have been calculated in the following ways.

Mr R: Ratio based on market values and including all borrowings.

$$\frac{5,600+1,800\times1.08+1,000\times0.98+2,800}{20,680(\text{W1})}=55\%$$

(W1) Market value of equity $=$ Number of shares $\times$ share price

$$=\frac{£2,200,000}{£0.10}\times£0.94$$

$$=£20,680,000.$$

The market value of equity includes all shareholders' funds and therefore the share premium account and retained profit should not be added.

Mr Y: Ratio based on book values and excluding short-term borrowings.

$$\frac{5,600+1,800}{8,330}=89\%$$

Mr Z: Ratio based on book values and including all borrowings.

$$\frac{5,600+1,800+1,000+2,800}{8,330}=134\%$$

Book values are constant over time and therefore give a constant gearing ratio. In the case of debt finance it is probably acceptable to use book values, since generally they do not deviate dramatically from market value. However, the book value of equity often considerably distorts the true value of shareholders' funds and consequently distorts the gearing ratio. For this reason, therefore, it is preferable to use market values.

On the issue of borrowings, the criterion relates to which borrowings actually contribute to the long-term financing of the company. A bank overdraft, although strictly short-term and repayable on demand often is an important source of long-term finance for many companies. Therefore it is reasonable to include the bank loans and overdrafts in the figure for borrowings. The 8% loan stock is classified as a short-term liability since it is due for redemption in a year's time. However, presumably it will need to be replaced by a new issue or some other form of finance, in which case it also should be included as debt, if the gearing ratio is to be meaningful.

Based on the above reasoning the preferred ratio would be 55% based on market values and all borrowings. However, it may be argued the book values are preferable since they do not alter and that current liabilities should be excluded since they fluctuate. Such might be the arguments of Mr Y and Mr Z.

(b) Financial gearing might be important to a company for the following reasons.

(i) High gearing increases the risk perceived by ordinary shareholders, since interest payments are paid first from operating profits and thus cause earnings attributable to ordinary shareholders to fluctuate more significantly. In addition, in the event of liquidation debt holders have priority over the assets of the company.

(ii) A company which has a high level of debt may encounter difficulties in raising further finance.

(iii) At very high levels of gearing the risk of default on interest payments or redemption becomes greater with the associated risk of bankruptcy.

(iv) The company's weighted average cost of capital is likely to increase at very high levels of gearing, due to the factors described above and therefore the company value will fall.

(c)   Factors which might limit the amount of debt finance that a company uses may include the following:

(i)   Existing loan covenants or clauses in the company's articles of association may limit further borrowing.

(ii)   Inadequate cashflows and interest cover may prevent lenders from being willing to subscribe to further debt.

(iii)   The company may have no further assets to offer as security for debt.

(iv)   Higher risk is associated with high gearing and therefore new borrowings may demand a return which is too high for the company to afford.

(d)   Mezzanine finance is a type of funding which may be categorised between debt and equity. It is usually unsecured and has a claim on profits after interest has been paid on 'senior' debt but its return is made by way of interest. To compensate investors for this higher risk it normally has an enhanced coupon rate and may also participate to a certain extent in the equity of the business, perhaps only at a future date by the current issue of a warrant.

Mezzanine finance is used in the following situations:

(i)   In management buyouts or takeovers which are financed by a high proportion of debt, mezzanine finance is a popular option by which to attract investors. In the case of a management buyout where the management team wishes to retain control of the company through their equity stake and yet are unable to raise further debt for their financing requirements, mezzanine finance may represent an intermediate solution.

(ii)   In circumstances of corporate restructuring, mezzanine finance may be a useful tool.

13   COMPANY OBJECTIVES

Financial management is concerned with making decisions about the provisions and use of a firm's finances. A rational approach to decision-making necessitates a fairly clear idea of what the objectives of the decision maker are or, more importantly, of what are the objectives of those on behalf of whom the decisions are being made.

There is little agreement in the literature as to what objectives of firms are or even what they ought to be. However, most financial management textbooks make the assumption that the objective of a limited company is to maximise the wealth of its shareholders. This assumption is normally justified in terms of classical economic theory. In a market economy firms that achieve the highest returns for their investors will be the firms that are providing customers with what they require. In turn these companies, because they provide high returns to investors, will also find it easiest to raise new finance. Hence the so called 'invisible hand' theory will ensure optimal resource allocation and this should automatically maximise the overall economic welfare of the nation.

This argument can be criticised on several grounds. Firstly it ignores market imperfections. For example it might not be in the public interest to allow monopolies to maximise profits. Secondly it ignores social needs like health, police, defence etc.

From a more practical point of view directors have a legal duty to run the company on behalf of their shareholders. This however begs the question as to what do shareholders actually require from firms.

Another justification from the individual firm's point of view is to argue that it is in competition with other firms for further capital and it therefore needs to provide returns at least as good as the competition. If it does not it will lose the support of existing shareholders and will find it difficult to raise funds in the future, as well as being vulnerable to potential take-over bids.

Against the traditional and 'legal' view that the firm is run in order to maximise the wealth of ordinary shareholders, there is an alternative view that the firm is a coalition of different groups: equity shareholders, preference shareholders and lenders, employees, customers and suppliers. Each of these groups must be paid a minimum 'return' to encourage them to participate in the firm. Any excess wealth created by the firm should be and is the subject of bargaining between these groups.

At first sight this seems an easy way out of the 'objectives' problem. The directors of a company could say 'Let's just make the profits first, then we'll argue about who gets them at a later stage'. In other words, maximising profits leads to the largest pool of benefits to be distributed among the participants in the bargaining process. However, it does imply that all such participants must value profits in the same way and that they are all willing to take the same risks.

In fact the real risk position and the attitude to risk of ordinary shareholders, loan creditors and employees are likely to be very different. For instance, a shareholder who has a diversified portfolio is likely not to be so worried by the bankruptcy of one of his companies as will an employee of that company, or a supplier whose main customer is that company. The problem of risk is one major reason why there cannot be a single simple objective which is common to all companies.

Separate from the problem of which goal a company ought to pursue are the questions of which goals companies claim to pursue and which goals they actually pursue.

Many objectives are quoted by large companies. Sometimes these are included in their annual accounts. Examples are:

(a)   to produce an adequate return for shareholders;
(b)   to grow and survive autonomously;
(c)   to improve productivity;
(d)   to give the highest quality service to customers;
(e)   to maintain a contented workforce;
(f)   to be technical leaders in their field;
(g)   to be market leaders;
(h)   to acknowledge their social responsibilities.

Some of these stated objectives are probably a form of public relations exercise. At any rate, it is possible to classify most of them into four categories which are related to profitability:

(a)   Pure profitability goals eg, adequate return for shareholders.
(b)   'Surrogate' goals of profitability eg, improving productivity, happy workforce.
(c)   Constraints on profitability eg, acknowledging social responsibilities, no pollution, etc.
(d)   'Dysfunctional' goals.

The last category are goals which should not be followed because they do not benefit in the long run. Examples here include the pursuit of market leadership at any cost, even profitability. This may arise because management assumes that high sales equal high profits which is not necessarily so.

In practice the goals which a company actually pursues are affected to a large extent by the management. As a last resort, the directors may always be removed by the shareholders or the shareholders could vote for a take-over bid, but in large companies individual shareholders lack voting power and information. These companies can, therefore, be dominated by the management.

There are two levels of argument here. Firstly, if the management do attempt to maximise profits, then they are in a much more powerful position to decide how the profits are 'carved up' than are the shareholders.

Secondly, the management may actually be seeking 'prestige' goals rather than profit maximisation. Such goals might include growth for its own sake, including empire building or maximising turnover for its own sake, or becoming leaders in the technical field for no reason other than general prestige. Such goals are usually 'dysfunctional'.

The dominance of management depends on individual shareholders having no real voting power, and in this respect institutions have usually preferred to sell their shares rather than interfere with the management of companies. There is some evidence, however, that they are now taking a more active role in major company decisions.

From all that has been said above, it appears that each company should have its own unique decision model. For example, it is possible to construct models where the objective is to maximise profit subject to first fulfilling the target levels of other goals. However, it is not possible to develop the general theory of financial management very far without making an initial simplifying assumption about objectives. The objective of maximising the wealth of equity shareholders seems the least objectionable.

---

14   MERCHANT BANKS

Answer Plan

(a)   Role of a merchant bank in a listing: selecting other advisers, compliance with regulations, form of capital, promotion to institutions, underwriting, advice on timing and price.

(b)   Conflicts of interest in conglomerate financial services company: Chinese Walls.

(a)   A company, wishing to raise capital by obtaining a listing on a stock exchange usually employs the services of a merchant bank to augment the skills and knowledge of the management team. The matters to which advice will be sought by the company will include:

      (i)   the need for and selection of other advisers, eg, lawyers, reporting accountants, etc;

      (ii)   compliance with external regulations concerning the issue, eg, statutory provisions in relation to the prospectus and the submission of the detailed information required by the Stock Exchange rules. Specialist legal matters may, however, need to be dealt with by company lawyers;

      (iii)   the form of capital the issue is to take, eg, straight equity or a combination of ordinary and preference shares, voting rights etc and the amount of stock to be issued;

      (iv)   the promotion of the issue. Press advertising is standard but increasingly presentations are made to the larger potential institutional investors;

      (v)   to ensure the success of the venture, the merchant bank will often advise that the issue be underwritten to guard against the possibility of under-subscription. The underwriters, who are usually a syndicate of merchant banks, discount houses and other financial institutions agree to take any shares not subscribed for in return for an underwriting commission;

      (vi)   Perhaps the most important advice sought will be regarding the timing of the flotation and the issue price which must be carefully set in order to ensure as far as possible the success of the issue while at the same time considering the interests of existing stockholders.

(b)   In 1986 the framework regulating the financial services sector was fundamentally changed by the process of deregulation known as 'Big Bang'. Businesses from various different areas of the financial services sector were encouraged to amalgamate within a single organisation. It was claimed that corporate clients would be better served by having the convenience of an all-round service without having to engage several different advisors from different organisations. However, the changes have meant serious problems of conflicts of interest. As an example a financial services company may be advising a client on, say, a new share issue or perhaps an acquisition or even how to handle the sensitive announcement of poor trading results. At the same time another department within the organisation may hold a significant block of the company's shares as a market-maker therein. Yet another department may have been asked to advise an investor whether these particular shares should be bought, sold or held. Such potential conflicts have attempted to be resolved by the introduction of strict rules ensuring departments work independently with little communication between them, ie, the erection of so called 'Chinese Walls' within the organisation so that, for instance, the market-maker would not have access to price sensitive information as in the example above.

However, over the past few years such potential conflicts between various parties involved in major transactions have led to a number of well-publicised problems in the capital market. The Guinness and Blue Arrow affairs have indicated that providing different services in one organisation with only "Chinese Walls" separating departments with extremely sensitive information is sometimes too strong a temptation to resist. The failure of the launch of the Blue Arrow share issue was concealed by companies in the same group as the financial advisor taking up undisclosed positions in the shares. It is quite possible that similar cases to Blue Arrow and Guinness exist but have as yet not come to light.

15   FINANCIAL INTERMEDIARIES

Answer Plan

(a)   Functions performed by intermediaries: definition, examples.

(b)   Why a stock market is an intermediary. Work of market makers, agency brokers and broker/dealers.

(a)   A financial intermediary is an institution which acts as a link between the suppliers of finance and borrowers.

The functions performed are:

(i)   acting as a link between persons wishing to borrow funds and persons wishing to save/invest - an intermediary thus removes the potential marketing problems of borrowers and savers;

(ii)   removing timing problems between borrowers and lenders - for example, a building society is a financial intermediary between long-term borrowers (25 years) and short-term lenders;

(iii)   removing size problems between borrowers and lenders - for example, a bank takes relatively small deposits from savers or temporary surplus funds in current accounts and makes large loans to businesses;

(iv)   reducing risk for an investor - the financial intermediary takes on the risk that the borrower will not pay. Government regulations generally ensure that the financial intermediary will repay investors. The price the investor pays for this protection is a lower rate of return;

(b)   (i)   The London Stock Exchange provides a primary and secondary market in stocks and shares. Companies can raise new funds from investors as there is the knowledge that the shares can be traded on the stock market subsequent to their issue. This is the primary aspect.

Technically the stock market is only a secondary market, ie, it allows the purchase and sale of already issued shares.

The stock market acts as a financial intermediary in its primary market role, ie, it allows borrowers (companies) to be matched with investors (shareholders).

(ii)   **Market makers**

An organisation or part of an organisation which sets prices at which it will buy and sell selected shares. The larger the quoted company, the more market makers are likely to trade in that share.

Agency brokers

These are intermediaries between investors and market makers, ie, the traditional stockbroker.

Broker/dealers

An organisation which is both a broker and a market maker.

16   EFFICIENT MARKET HYPOTHESIS

Answer Plan

Weak form: past price movements only.

Semi-strong form: all current publicly available information.

Strong form: all information, public and non-public.

(a)   The **weak form** of the efficient market hypothesis states that the current share price reflects all information contained in the past price movements of that share. This implies that a study of the trends in share prices over a prior period will not help in predicting the way in which the value or price of those shares will move in the future. In other words there is no place for chartism or technical analysis. Statistical evidence suggests that the efficient market hypothesis does hold in its weak form.

The **semi-strong form** of the efficient market hypothesis encompasses the weak form and adds that share prices also reflect all current publicly available information, for instance information contained in recently published accounts. If the semi-strong form holds, then a detailed analysis of published accounts will not assist in a prediction of future share price movements, since the share price already contains all relevant information shown in those accounts or made public since the issue of those accounts. As such it would only be possible to predict share price movements if unpublished information were known, in other words through insider information. Statistical evidence suggests that the semi-strong form of the efficient market hypothesis is valid.

The **strong form** of the efficient market hypothesis proposes that the current share price reflects all information relevant to the company, whether or not that information has been made public. If this is the case then it will never be possible to predict share price movements. The implication of this statement is that there would be no scope for gains to be made on share trading through the obtaining of inside (unpublished) information. Clearly this appears not to hold in practice, since legislation has been set to prevent insider dealing.

(b)   **Share price rises after announcement of high earnings**

The market will have assessed the likely level of the company's earnings from information which has been available to the public and the share price will be based on that assessment. If subsequent information suggests that the estimate of earnings was inaccurate the share price should adjust immediately under the semi-strong form of the efficient market hypothesis. In the situation described there was an immediate share price movement, but this continued over the following two or three days. This would suggest that the market is not absolutely efficient in the semi-strong form, because if it were the entire adjustment should have occurred immediately on announcement of the earnings figure.

It is also true that the market is not efficient in the strong form, otherwise the high earnings figure would have been known before it was published and as such reflected in the share price. Since the share price moved on announcement of the earnings, the strong form cannot hold.

Return on professionally managed portfolios

The suggestion that the return on professionally managed portfolios is likely to be no better than that which could be achieved by any investor would be supported by the strong form of the efficient market hypothesis. Assuming portfolio managers are not party to inside, unpublished information, this view would also be held by the semi-strong form of the efficient market hypothesis. However, if this proposition were to be unduly accepted there would be no demand for professionally managed portfolios. Since this is not the case, investors must perceive some benefit of placing their funds in the hands of portfolio managers. This would therefore suggest that the market is not efficient in either the semi-strong or strong form.

Share price movements around the fiscal year end

The downward movement on share prices just before the year end followed up a subsequent upward movement is due more to supply and demand effects than the efficient market hypothesis. There is no information specific to a particular security which causes the managers of portfolios or other investors to sell and then re-buy: it is simply the result of tax effects which apply universally to all shares across the market.

17   FLOW OF FUNDS

(a)   For flow of funds purposes the economy may be conveniently divided into four sectors: the personal, business, government and overseas sectors. Direct two-way flows of funds (of differing magnitudes) exist between each of these sectors through wages, payments for goods, taxation and other means. In addition, substantial flows are channelled between and within the four sectors via financial intermediaries which facilitate the flow of funds from those with a surplus of funds to those requiring funds, and also improve the consumption and investment opportunities available to individuals, organisations and the government.

The personal sector is always in surplus whilst the government sector is usually in deficit. In most countries the business sector is normally a net borrower but the overseas sector is more variable and may be either a net provider or a net borrower of funds.

(b)   Most personal sector savers invest relatively small sums of money, wish to maintain a reasonable level of liquidity and do not wish to take substantial risks. Many borrowers, especially in the corporate sector, require large amounts of finance for periods of several years to invest in projects which often involve considerable risk. Financial intermediaries satisfy the requirements of these and other borrowers and lenders by:

     (i)   Collecting together small savings and 'parcelling' them into larger units which may be borrowed by companies and other organisations.

     (ii)   Performing a 'transformational function' by being prepared to borrow funds for a relatively short period of time, and to lend those funds for a longer period of time. Building societies are the extreme example of this transformation, where very short-term deposits are often loaned out for 20 or more years. The financial intermediary relies upon only a proportion of deposits being withdrawn at any time, and keeps sufficient liquid funds to meet such withdrawals.

     (iii)   Spreading risks. The small saver is given the opportunity to obtain a well diversified portfolio with only a small investment eg, via a unit trust or investment trust.

     (iv)   Reducing transactions costs to both borrowers and lenders.

     (v)   Providing financial advice and other services (eg, insurance).

     Four types of financial intermediary (using the United Kingdom as an example) might include:

        (1)   **Deposit institutions**

           (a)   **Clearing banks**

               Clearing banks are the dominant force in retail banking in the United Kingdom, and are also very active in wholesale and international banking. They are responsible for most of the country's cash distribution and money transmission facilities. Clearing banks, especially the 'big four', maintain large branch networks and offer a variety of accounts to the saver, from non-interest earning accounts to accounts yielding money market rates. These banks offer loan facilities, mostly of a short and medium term nature, to industry, commerce and the personal sector.

               In recent years the clearing banks, mainly through subsidiaries, have expanded their operations into merchant banking, hire purchase leasing and other financial activities and are moving towards offering 'universal banking' facilities.

(b)   **Merchant and other banks**

Merchant banks concentrate upon the wholesale market and provide specialist services eg, analysis of investment projects, assistance with mergers and take-overs, underwriting facilities, syndicated credits and portfolio management. They do not maintain large branch networks and rely primarily upon money market funds for their deposit base.

Overseas banks, of which there are approximately four hundred represented in the United Kingdom, are also very active in wholesale banking and provide approximately 30% of bank lending to manufacturing industry. Some of the larger overseas banks are also establishing retail banking branch networks.

(c)   **Savings banks**

The National Savings Bank is operated by the Post Office and collects deposits from small savers which are used to help finance government borrowing requirements.   (Other 'national savings' schemes include National Savings Certificates, Premium Bonds, and Income Bonds.)

(d)   **Finance houses**

Finance houses offer credit facilities (hire purchase especially) and leasing at the point of sale of goods and via branch networks. Their funds are derived partially through deposits, but mainly by borrowing from banks and other sources. Most of the major finance houses are owned by, or controlled by, the clearing banks.

(e)   **Building societies**

Building societies have recently experienced very rapid growth. They rely almost entirely upon personal sector deposits for their funds and exist primarily to provide mortgage finance to the personal sector, although they are now providing some of the retail banking facilities of the clearing banks.

(2)   **Insurance and provident institutions**

(a)   **Insurance companies**

Insurance companies operate both long-term business (life assurance and long-term sickness insurance) and general business (especially motor, property and personal accident insurance). Long-term business generates through the payment of premiums (either on a regular or lump sum basis) funds which are invested often for long periods, mainly in government securities, company securities, land and property. The maturities of investments are approximately matched with the anticipated needs to meet the requirements of policy holders.

(b)   **Pension funds**

Occupational pension funds collect contributions on a regular basis from employees and employers in order to make provision for pensions for employees upon retirement or upon early death. The asset portfolio of pension funds is similar to that of long-term insurance business and some pension funds are managed by insurance companies.

(3)   **Portfolio institutions**

(a)   **Unit trusts.** Unit trusts collect funds from investors and invest these funds primarily in equities. They allow relatively small investors to obtain the benefits of diversified portfolios (although many unit trusts offer portfolios specialising in particular industrial sectors or countries).

      (b)   **Investment trusts**

Investment trusts are not 'trusts' but limited liability companies that can issue both equity and debt (unlike unit trusts). They also offer the benefits of diversification to their investors and invest primarily in corporate shares and government securities.

      (4)   **Other financial intermediaries**

These include 3i plc (including the ICFC division and Ventures division), Equity Capital for Industry and the British Technology Group (incorporating the National Enterprise Board and the National Research Development Corporation).

---

18   G PLC

(a)   (i)   The theoretical ex-rights price is given by

$$\frac{\text{Market value of shares in issue pre-rights} + \text{Proceeds of rights issue}}{\text{Number of shares in issue after rights}}$$

The market value of a right is given by

Theoretical ex-rights price − Price of rights issue share

Rights issue at £1.60 per share

$$\text{Ex-rights price} \quad = \quad \frac{1,200,000 \times £1.80 + £768,000}{1,200,000 + 480,000} \quad = \quad £1.74$$

Market value of a right per rights share = £1.74 − £1.60 = £0.14.

Rights issue at £1.28 per share

$$\text{Number of shares issued} \quad = \quad \frac{£768,000}{£1.28} = 600,000$$

$$\text{Ex-rights price} \quad = \quad \frac{1,200,000 \times £1.80 + £768,000}{1,200,000 + 600,000} \quad = \quad £1.63$$

Market value of a right per rights share = £1.63 − £1.28 = £0.35.

(ii)   The price set for a rights issue is relatively unimportant since the wealth of the shareholders will be unaffected whatever price is determined (since the finance is being raised from the existing body of shareholders and they will automatically participate in any gains).

Therefore the important criterion relates to the success of the issue in terms of its attractiveness to the shareholders. As such it is essential that the issue price is set below the current market price of the shares, otherwise the shareholders will not be willing to subscribe to the new issue.

In addition, it may be noted from the calculations in (i) that the market value of a right is greater the lower the issue price. Although under perfect market conditions this factor is irrelevant, it may nevertheless enhance the attractiveness of the issue in the eyes of the shareholders.

Therefore, in practice, the price set for a rights issue tends to be approximately 20% below the prevailing market price of the shares currently in issue. This would give an issue price of around £1.44 (£1.80 × 80%).

(iii)   The following factors might invalidate the ex-rights price and market values calculated above.

(1)   The ex-rights price has been computed on the assumption that the current market price of the company's existing shares will remain at the same effective level until the rights issue takes place and immediately after. Therefore any factors influencing and changing the share price during that time will render the ex-rights price inaccurate.

(2)   The current share price (assuming the semi-strong form of the efficient market hypothesis is true) should reflect the information available concerning the earnings and net present value to be derived from the investment of the new funds. Any further information which becomes available may alter the share price and invalidate the ex-rights price.

(3)   The increased number of shares resulting from the rights issue may depress the marketability and therefore the price.

(4)   The reaction of shareholders to the issue could influence the share price. For instance, a reluctance to take up the rights could depress the share price.

(b)   The pre-tax return payable on the loan stock is 10%. This compares with a return before tax of 14.6% (£112,000 ÷ £768,000) earned on the new finance. Since the latter is greater, the effect of incorporating 10% loan stock into the capital structure will be to increase the earnings per share of the ordinary shareholders.

The following figures illustrate this effect.

	25% raised by loan stock £	*50% raised by loan stock* £	*75% raised by loan stock* £
Loan stock issued	192,000	384,000	576,000
Rights issue proceeds	576,000	384,000	192,000
	£768,000	£768,000	£768,000
Number of shares issued (@ £1.60)	360,000	240,000	120,000
Existing shares	1,200,000	1,200,000	1,200,000
Shares in issue post rights	1,560,000	1,440,000	1,320,000
	£	£	£
Pre tax maintainable earnings	240,000	240,000	240,000
Additional earnings	112,000	112,000	112,000
	352,000	352,000	352,000
Loan interest @10%	(19,200)	(38,400)	(57,600)
	332,800	313,600	294,400
Tax @50%	166,400	156,800	147,200
Earnings attributable to ordinary shareholders	£166,400	£156,800	£147,200
Shares in issue	1,560,000	1,440,000	1,320,000
Earnings per share	10.67p	10.89p	11.15p

19	**LATOST PLC**

(a) (i) **Ordinary shares**

Advantages

Dividends are an optional payment, unlike interest which is a contractual payment.

Ordinary shares are not normally redeemable, therefore the funds are permanent.

Gearing is reduced, possibly increasing creditworthiness.

Ordinary shares are more easily traded than loan stock or debentures, and are therefore more attractive to investors.

Disadvantages

Issue costs are expensive

Dividends are not allowable for tax purposes.

In a family controlled business, control may be lost.

Low gearing may increase the cost of capital.

(ii) **Cumulative preference shares**

Advantages

Preference shareholders do not normally have full voting rights.

Usually irredeemable.

Dividend is a fixed percentage. If the company does well, more is available for ordinary shareholders.

Disadvantages

Dividends are not a tax allowable expense.

If dividends are not paid in any years, arrears are accumulated, and must be paid before ordinary dividends can be resumed.

(iii) **Deferred ordinary shares**

Advantages and disadvantages

As for ordinary shares. Dividend is usually only paid after the ordinary shareholders have received a certain dividend. Often entitled to a large proportion of the remaining profit. Voting rights may be different.

(iv) **Convertible debentures**

Advantages

Interest paid is a tax deductible expense.

Interest rate may be lower than a 'straight' debenture.

If converted, no funds are necessary for redemption.

Gearing will be reduced when redemption or conversion takes place.

Disadvantages

Fixed interest has to be paid until conversion takes place.

Dilution of earnings per share when conversion is exercised.

Conversion terms may be too generous if the share price rises more than anticipated.

(b)   To................

From................

Date.......

Report on financing sources for Latost plc

The major factors to be considered are the cost and risk of the sources, and the effect of this finance on the capital structure and the existing debenture holders.

The existing gearing (based on book values) is £18m/£22.02m ie, 81.7%. If one excludes the bank overdraft the gearing falls to £12m/£22.02m ie, 54.5%. Alternatively, using market values the gearing is £18m/£35m ie, 51.4% or £12m/£35m ie, 34.3%. This gearing is acceptable.

The current figure for earnings per share is £5,778/10,000 = 57.8p. The choice of financing method will be influenced by its effect on e.p.s., which should not be allowed to fall.

The £10m raised will generate earnings, and for the purposes of the following calculations it is assumed that the new funds will generate the same rate of return as the existing long term funds ie, £11,170/£34,020 = 32.8%, generating profit before interest and tax of £3,280,000.

Ordinary shares:

	£'000
Operating profit (11,170 + 3,280)	14,450
Interest	2,280
Profit before tax	12,170
Tax at 35%	4,260
Earnings available to ordinary shareholders	7,910

Assuming shares were issued as a rights issue at a discount of approximately 15%, a price of £3.00 per share would be reasonable. This would necessitate the issue of a further 3,333,333 shares.

The revised e.p.s. would be £7,910,000 / 13,333,333 = 59.3p.
Gearing would fall to 18m/32,020 = 56.2%

14% Preference shares:

	£'000
Profit after interest and tax (as above)	7,910
Preference dividend	1,400
Earnings available to ordinary shareholders	6,510

The revised e.p.s. would be £6,510 / 10,000 = 65.1p.
The book value gearing increases to 28,000 / 22,020 = 127%

12% unsecured loan stock:

	£'000
Operating profit	4,450
Interest	480
	———
Profit before tax	10,970
Tax	3,840
	———
Earning available to ordinary shareholders	7,130

The revised e.p.s. would be £7,130 / 10,000 = 71.3p.
The book value gearing would be 127%

Summary:	*Present*	*Ordinary shares*	*Preference shares*	*Loan stock*
Gearing	81.7%	56.2%	127%	127%
e.p.s.	57.8p	59.3%	65.1p	71.3p

None of the three methods reduces the e.p.s., but the preference shares and loan stock increase the gearing. There is no obvious case for the preference shares, which give the same gearing as the loan stock, but a lower e.p.s.

The choice is between the ordinary shares and the loan stock.

The loan stock produces a significant increase in e.p.s. but a very high gearing. The ordinary shares raise the e.p.s. a little and lower the gearing to a comfortable level.

It is recommended that the finance be raised by means of a rights issue, as the high level of gearing resulting from the issue of further loan stock may have an adverse effect on the share price.

20   PROPOSED FLOTATION

Answer Plan

(a)   Advantages: realise cash, make takeovers easier, incentive schemes for senior employees.

Disadvantages: costs, may be taken over, have to earn regular profits.

Placing is OK for small issues, shares to institutional clients.

Offer for sale OK for large issues, shares to the public

(b)   Services provided by each.

(a)   (i)   The advantages of a flotation on the stock exchange include:

- Shareholders can realise part of their investments into cash which can then be reinvested or spent however the shareholders wish. Although it would have been legally possible for shareholders to sell shares while the company was unquoted, securing a full listing for the company's shares will enormously add to the liquidity of trading in those shares. So a flotation will make sales of shares much easier.

- Target companies will be much happier receiving a consideration in shares if those shares are listed. So acquisitions will be easier after flotation since a separate cash-raising exercise prior to the takeover will no longer be necessary.

- Employees can be offered tax-efficient share incentive schemes such as share options to motivate them and encourage them to stay with the company.

- Shareholder tax matters will be simplified eg, for capital gains tax and inheritance tax, where there is a clear share price set by the market, rather than having to negotiate with the Inland Revenue on the fair value of a share price.

- The discipline of behaving as a public company under the scrutiny of analysts and journalists should deter the company from being dominated by one headstrong individual who could bring ruin on the company.

The disadvantages of a flotation on the stock exchange include:

- Costs of the flotation itself and of complying with the continuing obligations imposed on listed companies: dealing with the stock exchange, publishing an annual Report and Accounts which is useful to all categories of stakeholder, managing the register of shareholders.

- Shareholders who sell shares on the flotation may be subject to a significant capital gains tax charge.

- A need to consider short-term profitability as well as long-term. While the company was owned by a few individual shareholders, there would be little requirement to publish short-term profits since the shareholders are all committed to the long-term prosperity of the business. However, once public, some investors might have a shorter investment horizon putting pressure on the company to report regular profits and so sustain the short-term share price in order to avoid being taken over on the cheap.

- The failed attempt at diversification four years ago has led to an irregular earnings history over the past five years. This will be noted by the market and the share price marked down accordingly. Perhaps a better price can be achieved by waiting two more years so that the unsuccessful year will fall out of the picture.

- The present ten shareholders will be ceding some control over the company to the new shareholders who arrive after the flotation. In the extreme case they might lose control altogether if they sell more than 50% of the company's shares.

(ii)   **Private placing**

The shares to be sold are first acquired by the issuing house (normally a merchant bank) and those shares are then 'placed' with clients of the issuing house (normally these clients are institutional investors such as pension funds). The stock exchange sets a maximum limit on the size of placings by companies so this method would only be used for small issues. Costs are low since no advertising to the public is required and underwriting is avoided.

Offer for sale at fixed price

The shares to be sold are first acquired by the issuing house (or stockbroker) at an agreed price. These shares are then offered for sale by the issuing house to the public at a marginally higher price, the difference in price covering the cost of underwriting the issue. This method is used by most large issues; it tends to produce a more active after-market than a placing.

If demand for the shares exceeds the number available for sale, the issuing house will decide on the basis by which applicants are scaled down to the number of shares they are allotted with.

Offer for sale by tender

This is similar to the normal offer at fixed price except that the shares are not offered to the public at a fixed price. The prospectus for the share issue will state a minimum price and the public are invited to state the maximum price at which they would be willing to buy shares. The whole issue is then allocated at the highest price which would clear the issue and maintain an orderly after market. Offers by tender are appropriate in periods of market turbulence or where a company is being floated with no directly comparable company already on the market so no one knows what a fair price would be.

(b)   (i)   **Merchant banks**

A merchant bank is likely to control the whole progress of a company's public offering of shares. Specific help will be given with:

- professional advice;
- underwriting the issue;
- marketing the issue.

Advice will be offered as to the other professional advisers to be brought into the team eg, firms of accountants, lawyers and public relations consultants, as well as to the form of capital to be raised (ordinary shares, preference shares etc), the method of issue to be adopted (placing, offer for sale etc) and the price to be set.

Underwriting the issue will guarantee to the company that all the shares will be sold even if demand from the public is low; any shares left after public applications have been satisfied are bought by institutions. Marketing the issue involves promoting it to key institutional shareholders. This aspect is also carried out by stockbrokers (see below).

(ii)   **Stockbrokers**

A firm of stockbrokers is likely to have a relationship with a plc before a merchant bank is appointed to deal with a particular issue, so the stockbrokers have carried out some general work concerning the issue prior to the bank becoming involved. Once the bank has adopted its co-ordinating role, the stockbrokers will concentrate on marketing the issue to the substantial institutional investors with which it has an ongoing relationship.

(iii)   **Institutional investors**

The services provided by institutional investors include:

- agreeing to underwrite the issue;
- conditionally accepting shares subject to clawback;
- communicating their opinions on proposed issue terms.

Clawback is a method of guaranteeing the success of an issue of new shares under a rights issue, for example. All the shares under the rights issue are conditionally allocated to institutional investors, but if existing shareholders wish to take up their rights then the shares are 'clawed back' from the institutions.

---

21   ARMADA LEISURE

Answer Plan

(a)   Cost; risk, flexibility; matching.

(b)   Definition; arguments in favour; arguments against.

(c)   Definitions; merits of leasing; merits of hire-purchase

---

(a)   (i)   The overall cost of long-term and short-term capital borrowing must be considered. The difference in the rates of interest will be affected by the lender's perception of the economy and interest rates, but it is generally accepted that longer-term rates will be higher than shorter term rates for the same level of security. However, shorter term borrowing will require more frequent re-negotiation leading to costs in both management time and arrangement fees.

(ii)   The need to re-negotiate finance is a risk for the company because it may occur at a time when the financial picture of the company is unsuitable for such negotiations. As a consequence there is a greater risk with short-term borrowing, and any failure to re-arrange the finance will merely increase the business' problems.

(iii)   The early repayment of long-term debt usually incurs a penalty, so the use of short-term debt is more flexible in this respect. The use of short-term debt may avoid entering into long-term debt arrangements at unfavourable high interest rates, and give flexibility to switch into longer term debt when interest rates improve. Temporary finance needs can often be serviced by an overdraft facility whereby interest is only charged on finance actually used.

(iv)   A common objective is to match the financing of long-term assets to long-term debt, and to use short-term debt for short-life assets and working capital. This is to avoid the problems of having to repay debt when the asset it was used to acquire is in a non-liquid form. If more funds cannot be found to repay the debt then there is a risk of the company being made insolvent.

(b)   (i)   A rights issue is an offer made to existing shareholders to purchase additional shares in proportion to their existing holding. It is usually underwritten by an issuing house.

(ii)   The following arguments may be made in favour of a rights issue:

(1)   The finance is guaranteed if it is fully underwritten by the issuing house

(2)   There will be no change in the members of the company or their relative voting powers provided the existing members subscribe for the shares.

(3)   As the stock market is rising investors will be seeking to buy shares, therefore the rights issue should be sold with relative ease.

(4)   The rights issue being equity finance will lower the gearing ratio, thereby reducing the debt risk of the company.

(iii)   The following arguments may be used against the making of a rights issue:

(1)   The fees of the underwriters and other issuing costs may be expensive depending upon the underwriter's perception of the success or otherwise of the rights issue.

(2)   A rights issue forces the existing members to either subscribe for the shares or sell the rights; they may resent having to spend money to maintain their existing percentage holding in the company.

(3)   Rights issues have to be made at a discount to encourage their purchase, this usually reduces the share price initially as there is a time-lag between raising the finance and generating the corresponding increase in earnings.

(4)   As future forecasters are expressing doubts about the economy the issue may not be taken up by the members. This would dilute the control and make subsequent attempts to raise equity finance more difficult.

(c)   (i)   Leasing, referred to in financial accounting as operating leases, is the right to use an asset for a defined period of time, by the payment of a rental over the period of that usage.

Hire purchase however, which in financial accounting is a form of finance lease, is the acquisition of an asset by a series of payments, the last of which confers legal title to the asset.

(ii)   The merits of leasing are:

(1)   There is a clear cashflow advantage as payments are made as the asset is being used, instead of a significant part of the cost being paid on acquisition.

(2)   Leasing assets, especially those which are continually being improved by technological development, reduces the risk of obsolescence.

(3) The leases are a means of obtaining off-balance sheet finance, although the notes to the accounts must separately identify their operating lease obligations.

(4) The whole of the rental payment is tax deductible, the lessor retains the right to claim capital allowances. This is more appropriate in companies having relatively low profits and operating in areas where accelerated capital allowances are available.

(iii) The merits of hire-purchase are:

(1) The title to the asset eventually passes to the customer, so a tangible benefit is received in respect of the payments.

(2) The interest element of the hire-purchase payment is tax deductible, and the customer may claim capital allowances on the cost of the asset.

22   BRECKALL PLC

(Tutorial notes:

(1) As different items are inflating at different rates the only realistic approach is to discount money cash flows at the nominal (money) discount rate. This is particularly true as taxation is involved and the amount of tax payable will be based upon a taxable profit figure which in turn is determined by items subject to various rates of inflation.

(2) The general procedure will be:

(a) Determine the corporation tax liability.
(b) Determine other relevant cash flows (in money terms).
(c) Discount these cash flows to present value at the nominal WACC.)

(a) **Calculation of corporation tax liability**

	1	2	3	4	5	
	£	£	£	£	£	
Sales (5% rise pa)	3,675	5,402	6,159	6,977	6,790	
Materials (10% rise pa)	588	907	1,198	1,537	1,449	
Labour (10% rise pa)	1,177	1,815	2,396	3,075	2,899	
Overheads (5% rise pa)	52	110	116	122	128	*Note 2*
Capital allowances	1,125	844	633	475	1,423	*Note 1*
Taxable	733	1,726	1,816	1,768	891	
Tax (35%)	256	604	636	619	312	

Notes:

(1) **Capital allowances**

	Opening balance	Capital allowance
	£	£
Year 1	4,500	1,125
Year 2	3,375	844
Year 3	2,531	633
Year 4	1,898	475
Year 5	1,423	1,423 (balancing allowance)

This assumes that the first capital allowance is available in the first year and that the balancing allowance is taken in year 5. Note that capital allowances are based upon original cost of assets.

(2) Depreciation is replaced by the capital allowance.

Interest is not deducted in calculating the tax liability. The tax deductability of interest will have been allowed for in the calculation of the weighted average cost of capital.

Discount relevant cash flows to present value

Cash flow estimates (£'000)

Year	0	1	2	3	4	5	6
Inflows:							
Sales	-	3,675	5,402	6,159	6,977	6,790	-
Outflows:							
Materials	-	588	907	1,198	1,537	1,449	-
Labour	-	1,177	1,815	2,396	3,075	2,899	-
Overheads *(note 3)*	-	52	110	116	122	128	-
Fixed assets	4,500						
Working capital *(note 4)*	300	120	131	144	156	(851)	-
Taxation *(note 5)*			256	604	636	619	312
Net cash flows	(4,800)	1,738	2,183	1,701	1,451	2,546	(312)
Discount factors at 15%		0.870	0.756	0.658	0.572	0.497	0.432
Present values (£'000)	(4,800)	1,512	1,650	1,119	830	1,265	(135)

NPV = £1,441,000 and on this basis the project should be accepted.

(3)   Once again interest is not included. The cost of interest is taken care of in the discounting process. If we were to charge interest against cash flow and include it in the WACC we would be double counting. This is a very common examination trap and should be avoided.

(4)   We require the incremental investment in working capital each year. Adjusting for inflation this is

Year 0	300		
Year 1	$(400 \times 1.05) - 300$	=	120
Year 2	$(500 \times 1.05^2) - (400 \times 1.05)$	=	131
Year 3	$(500 \times 1.05^3) - (500 \times 1.05^2)$	=	144
Year 4	$(700 \times 1.05^4) - (600 \times 1.05^3)$	=	156
Year 5	$(700 \times 1.05^5) - (700 \times 1.05^4)$	=	42
Year 5	refund of working capital assumed		
	(700×1.05^5)	=	(893)
	Net	=	(851)

(5)   Tax payment lagged by one year.

(b)   *(Tutorial note:* this is roundabout way of asking what is the IRR of the project.)

By normal trial and error procedures this may be determined as follows:

Year	Cashflow	20% discount	PV	27% Discount	PV
0	(4,800		(4,800)		(4,800)
1	1,738	0.833	1,488	0.787	1,368
2	2,183	0.694	1,515	0.620	1,353
3	1,701	0.579	985	0.488	830
4	1,451	0.482	699	0.384	557
5	2,546	0.402	1,023	0.303	771
6	(312)	0.335	(105)	0.238	(74)
			765		5

The discount rate would have to change from 15% to approximately 27% to produce a net present value of zero. This is a change of approximately 80%.

23   ELTERN LTD

(Tutorial note: for replacement decisions the annual equivalent annuity method is used. With common revenues, one is seeking the lowest annual cost. Note it will not effect the decision if replacement is assumed to be at the beginning or at the end of the cycle. The ranking will still be the same.)

(a)

Year		*1* £	*2* £	*3* £	*4* £	*5* £
	Cash flows					
(1)	29,800 × .885	26,373	26,373	26,373	26,373	26,373
	35,000 × .885	(30,975)				
	55,000 × .885	48,675				
(2)	33,700 × .783		26,387	26,387	26,387	26,387
	24,000 × .783		(18,792)			
	55,000 × .783		43,065			
(3)	39,000 × .693			27,027	27,027	27,027
	12,000 × .693			(8,316)		
	55,000 × .693			38,115		
(4)	45,100 × .613				27,646	27,646
	2,000 × .613				(1,226)	
	55,000 × .613				33,715	
(5)	72,000 × .543					39,096
	200 × .543					(109)
	55,000 × .543					29,865
	Present Value	44,073	77,033	109,586	139,922	176,285
	Divide by annuity	0.885	1.668	2.361	2.974	3.517
	Annual Equivalent cost	49,800	46,183	46,415	47,048	50,124

Lowest cost is to replace the fleet every two years.

(b)   Eltern Ltd is only a small company, and as such would incur difficulty in raising equity finance.

The company is not large enough to justify a listing on the full market.

The requirements for a quotation on the USM would make it very expensive for such a small company (see Tutorial note below).

Small companies are perceived as being risky, and institutions tend to favour investment in large companies.

The shares if issued would not be very marketable, and therefore would not command a very high price.

Sources of equity finance which may be available include:

(i)   Issue of new shares by means of a rights issue to existing shareholders.

(ii)   3i group, which has a number of subsidiaries which invest in small companies.

(iii)   The unregulated market is not a part of the stock exchange, but offers opportunities for trading in shares of unlisted companies. Rather risky for investors.

(iv)   Venture Capital. There are now a large number of institutions which have divisions specialising in the provision of debt and equity capital for new and growing businesses.

(v)   Institutions will sometimes provide equity finance for companies which are too small for a full listing, but this facility is usually offered by the venture capital arms as in (v) above.

Tutorial note: since this answer was written, the USM has stopped taking new entrants with a view to its closure by the end of 1996. The Alternative Investment Market (AIM) was opened in June 1995 by the Stock

Exchange to provide a market for the shares of young growing companies not large enough for a full listing. Market capitalisations of companies on the AIM vary from £1 million to £300 million; it is likely that Eltern Ltd could make use of this market for raising capital).

---

24 BANDEN LTD

(Tutorial note: a fairly straightforward question on investment appraisal, including capital rationing and profitability index. An appreciation of linear and integer programming is also required.)

(a) (i) **Calculation of expected Net Present Value**

Project		NPV
A. £70,000 × 3.605 - £246,000	=	£6,350
B. £75,000 × 0.893 + £87,000 × 0.797 + £64,000 × 0.712 – £180,000	=	£1,882
C. £48,000 × 0.893 + £48,000 × 0.797 + £63,000 × 0.712 + £73,000 × 0.636 – £175,000	=	(£2,596)
D. £62,000 × 3.037 – £180,000	=	£8,294
E. £40,000 × 0.893 + £50,000 × 0.797 + £60,000 × 0.712 + £70,000 × 0.636 + £40,000 × 0.567 – £180,000	=	£5,490
F. £35,000 × 0.893 + £82,000 × 0.797 + £82,000 × 0.712 – £150,000	=	£4,993

(ii) **Calculation of Profitability Index**

Present Value of cash inflows/initial outlay:

A. 252,350 / 246,000	=	1.026
B. 181,882 / 180,000	=	1.010
C. 172,404 / 175,000	=	0.985
D. 188,294 / 180,000	=	1.046
E. 185,490 / 180,000	=	1.031
F. 154,993 / 150,000	=	1.033

(Tutorial note: profitability index could be calculated as NPV/initial outlay.)

Ranking	NPV	P.I.
1	D	D
2	A	F
3	E	E
4	F	A
5	B	B
6	C	C

The rankings differ because NPV is an absolute measure of the benefit from a project, while P.I. is a relative measure, and shows the benefit per £ of outlay. Where the initial outlays vary in size the two methods may give different rankings.

(b) In a capital rationing situation, the projects should be selected which give the greatest total NPV from the limited outlay available.

A and E are mutually exclusive.
C is not considered as it has a negative NPV.
Total outlay is limited to £620,000.

Possible selections are:

Projects	Expected NPV (£) £	Total NPV (£) £	Outlay (£) £'000
A.B.D.	6,350 + 1,882 + 8,294	16,526	606
A.B.F.	6,350 + 1,882 + 4,993	13,225	576
A.D.F.	6,350 + 8,294 + 4,993	19,637	576
B.D.E.	1,882 + 8,294 + 5,490	15,666	540
B.D.F.	1,882 + 8,294 + 4,993	15,169	510
D.E.F.	8,294 + 5,490 + 4,993	18,777	510

The recommended selection is projects D, A & F.

(Tutorial note: neither the NPV nor P.I. rankings will necessarily be appropriate because of the 'lumpiness' of the investments. In this particular instance, because of the similarity in size of the projects, only three can be undertaken, and the NPV ranking clearly leads to D,A & F. Profitability index will not work if projects are indivisible or where multiple limiting factors exist. The P.I. might lead to the incorrect solution of D,E & F.)

(c) The director is correct in suggesting that the normal cost of capital might not be appropriate in a capital rationing situation.

In a capital rationing situation, the appropriate discount rate may be the opportunity cost of capital ie, the yield available from the best opportunity foregone.

The appropriate discount rate is therefore the higher of:

(i) the opportunity cost of capital (ie, the IRR of the marginal project rejected due to the capital constraint); and

(ii) the company's normal cost of capital.

25   CEDER LTD

(a)

Calculation of tax liability

	Year 1 £	Year 2 £	Year 3 £	Year 4 £	Year 5 £	Year 6 £
Standard						
Operating cash flows	20,500	22,860	24,210	23,410		
Capital allowance	12,500	9,375	7,031	21,094*		
	8,000	13,485	17,179	2,316		
Taxation (35%)	2,800	4,720	6,013	811		
De-luxe						
Operating cash flows	32,030	26,110	25,380	25,940	38,560	35,100
Capital allowance	22,000	16,500	12,375	9,281	6,961	20,883*
	10,030	9,610	13,005	16,659	31,599	14,217
Taxation (35%)	3,511	3,363	4,552	5,831	11,060	4,976

* Including balancing allowance

Forecast after-tax cash flows

	Year 0 £	Year 1 £	Year 2 £	Year 3 £	Year 4 £	Year 5 £
Standard						
Fixed assets	(50,000)					
Working capital	(10,000)				10,000**	
Operating cash flows		20,500	22,860	24,210	23,410	
Taxation			(2,800)	(4,720)	(6,013)	(811)
	(60,000)	20,500	20,060	19,490	27,397	(811)
Discount factor (12%)		0.893	0.797	0.712	0.636	0.567
Present values	(60,000)	18,307	15,988	13,877	17,424	(460)

Payback period is approximately three years
Net present value is £5,136

	Year 0 £	Year 1 £	Year 2 £	Year 3 £	Year 4 £	Year 5 £	Year 6 £	Year 7 £
Standard								
Fixed assets	(88,000)							
Working capital	(10,000)						10,000**	
Operating cash flows		32,030	26,110	25,380	25,940	38,560	35,100	
Taxation			(3,511)	(3,363)	(4,552)	(5,831)	(11,060)	(4,976)
	(98,000)	32,030	22,599	22,017	21,388	32,729	34,040	(4,976)
Discount factor (14%)		0.877	0.769	0.675	0.592	0.519	0.456	0.400
Present values	(98,000)	28,090	17,379	14,861	12,662	16,986	15,522	(1,990)

Payback period is approximately four years
Net present value is £5,510

** Assumes working capital is released immediately. In reality some time-lag will exist.

Normally the project with the highest NPV would be selected. However, as the projects have unequal lives, it can be argued that although the de-luxe has a higher NPV, this is only achieved by operating for two more years. If the machines are to fulfil a continuing production requirement the time factor needs to be considered.

The annual equivalent cost approach is not appropriate as both machines have different level of risk. In this situation the most useful approach is to assume infinite reinvestment in each machine and calculate their NPVs to infinity.

$$\text{NPV} \infty = \frac{\text{NPV of the investment} \div \text{Present value of an annuity of appropriate years and discount rate}}{\text{Discount rate}}$$

Standard

$$\text{NPV} \infty = \frac{5.136 \div 3.037\#}{.012} = £14,092$$

De luxe

$$\text{NPV} \infty = \frac{5.510 \div 3.889\#}{.014} = £10,120$$

\#   The present values of annuities are taken for four and six years as these are the useful lives of the projects.

As the standard machine has the higher NPV ∞, it is recommended that this machine should be purchased.

An alternative approach to the problem of different lives might be to assume a reinvestment rate for the shorter investment and to use this rate to equalise the lives of the investments.

(b)   Lease payments are usually made at the start of the year.

			Cash flows			
	Year 0	*Year 1*	*Year 2*	*Year 3*	*Year 4*	*Year 5*
	£	£	£	£	£	£
Lease						
Cost of machine saved	50,000					
Capital allowance lost			(4,375)	(3,281)	(2,461)	(7,383)
Lease payments	(15,000)	(15,000)	(15,000)	(15,000)		
Tax relief on lease		5,250	5,250	5,250	5,250	
Net cash flow of lease	35,000	(9,750)	(14,125)	(13,031)	2,789	(7,383)
Discount factor (7.15%) ↑		0.933	0.871	0.813	0.759	0.708
	35,000	(9,097)	(12,303)	(10,594)	2,117	(5,227)

Net present value is (£104).

As the net present value is negative, it appears that the purchase of the machine is the recommended alternative.

↑   The choice of discount rates in lease versus buy analysis is contentious. The approach used here is to regard the lease as an alternative to purchasing the machine using debt finance. The discount rate is, therefore, the amount that the company would have to pay on a secured loan on the machine, the loan being repayable on the terms that are implicit in the lease rental schedule. This discount rate is the after-tax cost of the equivalent loan, 11% (1-0.35) = 7.15%.

This discount rate is only likely to be valid if leases and loans are regarded by investors as being equivalent, and all cash flows are equally risky.

26   AMBLE PLC

(a)   The operating cash flows of Amble

Year	0	1	2	3	4
		£'000	£'000	£'000	£'000
Sales		1,320	2,021	2,183	2,355
Less cash operating costs:					
Direct labour		354	553	608	668
Material Z		102	161	174	188
Component P		173	265	286	308
Component Q		77	118	127	137
Other variables		25	39	42	45
Management salaries		67	72	77	82
Selling expenses		166	174	183	192
Rent		120	126	132	139
Incremental overheads		50	53	55	58
		1,134	1,561	1,684	1,817

Sales less cash operating costs		186	460	499	538
Tax (paid) saved		9	(86)	(100)	(114)
Purchase and sale of machine	(864)				12
Net cash flows	(864)	195	374	399	436

Using linear interpolation to find the IRR of these cash flows:

(i) with a discount rate of 18% NPV = 38
(ii) with a discount rate of 22% NPV = (36).

Therefore the IRR is 18% + [(38/(38 + 36)](22% - 18%) = 20.1%

Notes to the calculation:

Year	1	2	3	4
Sales				
Price (£)	110	115.5	121.3	127.3
Units	12,000	17,500	18,000	18,500
Total (£000)	1,320	2,021	2,183	2,355
Direct labour				
Cost (£)	29.50	31.60	33.80	36.10
Units	12,000	17,500	18,000	18,500
Total (£000)	354	553	608	668

Material Z

Year 1 requires 12,000 units × 6 kg = 72,000 kg. The cost of this is:

the opportunity cost of using the existing 70,000 units	99,000
+ purchase 2,000 units × £1.46	2,920
	£101,920

Year 2 requires 17,500 units × 6 kg = 105,000 kg
× inflating £1.46 by 5%   1.53
£160,650

Year 3 requires 18,000 units × 6 kg = 108,000 kg
£1.53 × 1.05   1.61
£173,880

Year 4 requires 18,500 units × 6 kg = 111,000 kg
£1.61 × 1.05   1.69
£187,590

Management salaries and rent

Both of these require opportunity costs. The best way to find these is to use this formula:

opportunity cost = cost with project less cost without project

Management salaries

Cost with project	=	(2 × £25,000)
		+ £20,000
		+ £17,000
	=	£87,000
Cost without project	=	£20,000
Opportunity cost	=	£67,000

Rent

Cost with project	=	£100,000
Cost without project	=	£100,000 *less* income £120,000
	=	net income £20,000
Opportunity cost	=	£120,000

Tax

Capital allowance based upon straight-line depreciation over 4 years = (£864 - £12)/4 = £213 p.a.

Year	1	2	3	4
Sales less cash operating costs	186	460	499	538
Capital allowances	213	213	213	213
Taxable cash flows	(27)	247	286	325
Tax (paid) (35%)/saved	9	(86)	(100)	(114)

Marking note: The principles of opportunity cost are being tested. Briefly explain these principles for a couple of marks. Always calculate what is required (in this case the IRR), even if you suspect your cash flows are incorrect. You will get a couple of marks for knowing the calculation.

(b)   Discounting the net cash flows identified above at 17% gives a NPV of £58,000. Included in this calculation, the NPV of the tax paid identified above is (£178,000). The overall NPV of the project will disappear if the NPV of the tax payments increases to (£178,000 + £58,000) = £236,000. The tax rate that produces a NPV for tax payments of £236,000 can either be found by trial and error or by solving for x in the following formula using 17% present value factors for the taxable cash flows:

$(-27 \times .855 \times x) + (248 \times .731 \times x) + (286 \times .624 \times x) + (325 \times .534 \times x) = 236$

$x = .46$; this is the break-even tax rate which will produce an overall NPV of zero.

Marking note: Again show the examiner that you know about sensitivity analysis if you find yourself struggling with the calculation.

27   ZEDLAND

(a)   Your report should include the following computations and comments:

There are two investment criteria used by Zedland:

Return on investment

This is defined as: $\dfrac{\text{average after} - \text{tax annual profit}}{\text{average investment}}$

Firstly the calculation of the after-tax annual profit;

	t_1 £'000	t_2 £'000	t_3 £'000	t_4 £'000	t_5 £'000
Sales (letters)[1]	2,048	2,867	3,010	3,160	3,318
(parcels)	682	1,075	1,129	1,185	1,244
Total sales	2,730	3,942	4,139	4,345	4,562
Expenses:[2]					
Wages	2,457	2,580	2,709	2,844	2,986
Premises	158	165	174	182	191
Maintenance:					
vans	210	265	333	420	529
trucks	84	106	133	168	212
advertising	525	276			
depreciation	232	232	232	232	232
Total expenses	3,666	3,624	3,581	3,846	4,150
Taxable profit	(936)	318	558	499	412
Tax (40%)[5]	374*	(127)	(223)	(200)	(165)
Profit after tax	(562)	191	335	299	247

* a loss in this service can be set against profits earned elsewhere in the organisation, in other words, a loss here saves tax elsewhere.

The unit used in this answer is £000. This produces an average annual after-tax profit of £102,000. Average investment is £1,160/2 = £580,000. This gives a return on investment of £102/£580 = 17.6% (this definition has excluded financing costs, such as interest, from the profit calculation).

Notes to the calculation

1   Sales (letters) for year 1   = $0.525 × 15,000 × (52 × 5 working days)
                                   = $2,048

     Sales (letters) for year 2   =   ($0.525 × 1.05) × 20,000 × 260
                                   = $2,867

     There is a 5% p.a. increase after that. Sales (parcels) can be calculated in a similar way.

2   All cost data given are current estimates and so all must be inflated by 5%p.a. to obtain the year 1 expense, for example, year 1 wages = current cost of 180 × $13 = $2,340 × 1.05 to get the t1 figure of $2,457.

3   The five managers would be employed with or without the project, that is the incremental cost to the project is zero.

4   Market research is a committed cost whether the project is carried out or not; it is a sunk cost even if the $50,000 has not actually been paid yet.

5   Since this is an incremental project to the existing business, it is assumed that the existing profits are in excess of $500,000 so that the marginal rate of tax is 40%.

Net present value

Restating the above cash flows for timing, the NPV of this project can be calculated.

	t_0	t_1	t_2	t_3	t_4	t_5	t_6
Initial outlay	(1,160)						
Sales Total		2,730	3,942	4,139	4,345	4,562	
Cash Expense[1]		(3,434)	(3,392)	(3,349)	(3,614)	(3,918)	
Tax[2]			374	(127)	(223)	(200)	(165)
Net cash flow	(1,160)	(704)	924	663	508	444	(165)
14% discount factors[3]	1	.877	.769	.675	.592	.519	.456
Present value	(1,160)	(617)	711	448	301	230	(75)
NPV value	(162)						

Notes:

1   These exclude depreciation.
2   Tax is lagged by one year.
3   The discount rate should reflect the required return relative to the risk of the project.

The reason why this project produced a negative NPV despite a relatively high ROI is:

- t_0 and t_1 had net cash outflows

- the cash inflows didn't start till t_2. With a high discount rate, the present value of these inflows is much reduced

- ROI takes no account of the timing of these cash flows.

Thus the project satisfies only one of the investment criteria. NPV could, of course, be increased by raising prices (this is a monopoly) and/or cutting costs. However, as a nationalised service, social and economic factors must be taken into account as well as financial ones, although they will be difficult to quantify.

Thus, the service may be introduced regardless of its existing negative NPV.

Marking note: Examiners will reward candidates who have inflated the figures appropriately and who know which cash flows to discount. A tidy layout will help prevent confusion, and assist the marker. Remember to discuss the 'other' factors involved.

28   ULLSWATER

(a)   **Investment decision**

(Tutorial note: the question has been made simpler, by the existence of only one cost of finance. In part (a), the investment decision, ignore the later reference to methods of finance and just consider project cash flows. A post-tax analysis is required, therefore a post-tax cost of capital is needed and capital allowances must be found. The diagram shown helps to decide when writing down allowances can be claimed and may avoid having to state some assumptions formally.)

(i)   Timings of capital allowances

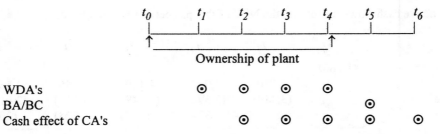

WDA's
BA/BC
Cash effect of CA's

(ii)   Size of capital allowances

	Tax WDV £	Cash saved £	Timing
Purchase price	60,000		
1st WDA	(15,000)	5,250	t_2
	45,000		
2nd WDA	(11,250)	3,937	t_3
	33,750		
3rd WDA	(8,437)	2,953	t_4
	25,313		
4th WDA	(6,328)	2,215	t_5
	18,985		
Proceeds	(4,000)		
BA	£14,985	5,245	t_6
		£19,600	

(iii)   Investment decision

£

$$\text{PV of capital allowances} = \frac{£5,250}{1.13^2} + \frac{£3,937}{1.13^3} + \frac{£2,953}{1.13^4} + \frac{£2,215}{1.13^5} + \frac{£5,245}{1.13^6} = \quad 12,373$$

$$\text{PV of net capital cost} = \frac{£4,000}{1.13^4} - £60,000 \qquad\qquad = \quad (57,547)$$

$$\text{PV of savings} = £29,000 \times 2.97 \qquad\qquad = \quad 86,130$$

$$\text{PV of tax on savings} = -£29,000 \times 2.97 \times 0.35 \times \frac{1}{1.13} \quad = \quad (26,677)$$

£14,279

Note: two-figure factors could be used, although it's a little slower. Tax on savings is 35% of the savings and occurs one year later. Although the scrap proceeds are received in year 5 they are presumed to arrive at t_4; the only significance of the year 5 reference is that 4 WDA's are received rather than 3.

(b)   **Financing decision**

(Tutorial Note:

With option 1 the company receives scrap proceeds, capital allowances and loan interest is allowable against tax. With option 2 there is usually no benefit from scrap proceeds but the whole of the lease payments are allowable against tax. In view of the requirements for (c) it is not clear what the positions are regarding option 2 and scrap proceeds; the answer will show an analysis with and without scrap proceeds being received. The way a payment to a bank in repayment of a loan is split between capital and interest is fairly arbitrary for tax purposes. You could assume that each (presumably equal) repayment contained similar proportions of capital and investment for simplicity's sake. Cash flow is improved, and a more realistic figure obtained, if interest is taken to be calculated on the outstanding capital sum - as shown here. The tax treatment of leasing agreements that allow for acquisition of the asset at the end of the lease has changed recently but have been glossed over here.)

(i)   Annual bank repayment/lease payment

The PV of what the bank gives you (£60,000) must equal the PV of what you repay to the bank. If you repay the bank 4 equal amounts of R, then their PV is 2.59R.

$$\text{Annual (re)payment} = \frac{£60,000}{2.59} = £23,166$$

(ii)   Interest paid on bank loan

You could assume for simplicity's sake that each £23,166 contained £60,000 ÷ 4 = £15,000 repayment of capital and £8,166 of interest.

More appropriately a reducing balance calculation is needed.

Year	Amount at start of year £	Interest @ 20% £	Capital (Balance) £	Amount at end of year £
1	60,000	12,000	11,166	48,834
2	48,834	9,767	13,399	35,435
3	35,435	7,087	16,079	19,356
4	19,356	3,871	19,295	61

Note: the £61 can be ignored, a result of using two figure tables; the annual repayment should be £23,177.35.

(iii) NPV at 13% of cash flows associated with borrowing and buying

	£
Four years repayments £23,166 × 2.97 =	(68,803)
Tax relief on capital allowances (as in (a) (iii)) =	12,373

Tax relief on interest $0.35 \times (\dfrac{£12,000}{1.13^2} + \dfrac{£9,767}{1.13^3} + \dfrac{£7,087}{1.13^4} + \dfrac{£3,871}{1.13^5}) = $ 7,915

Scrap proceeds $\dfrac{£4,000}{1.13^4}$ 2,452

£(46,063)

(iv)   NPV at 13% of cash flows associated with leasing

	£
Four lease payments £23,166 × 2.97	(68,803)
Tax saved on payments £23,166 × 2.97 × 0.35 $\dfrac{1}{1.13}$	21,311

£(47,492)

(v)   Conclusion

The cheapest option in the first, to borrow and buy. It has been assumed that ownership under option

2 rests with the lessor and thus the NPV in (iv) has not been increased by the possibility of having the asset to sell for £4,000 at time 4. If this option was available it would reverse the decision since (iv)'s NPV would improve by $£4,000 \div 1.13^4 = £2,452$.

(c) **Recommendation with no final purchase option**

As mentioned in (b), based on the figures alone, if the lease scheme has the option to acquire the asset at the end of 4 years, the lease is the better policy. If there is no right to acquire the asset at the end of the lease, borrowing and buying is the best policy.

This conclusion has to be viewed in the light of the possibility that the asset has a useful life of more than four years and that the company could earn more than £4,000 from retaining the asset and using it further. However, all this would do would be to reinforce the original decision.

Other factors to take into account are:

- Whether identical machines are available under each option.
- What maintenance arrangements apply to the leased asset.
- Possible changes in tax legislation, interest rates, inflation rates or initial estimates.
- Whether the bank loan carries a fixed or variable interest rate.
- Whether the company wants the responsibility of disposing of the old asset.

29   HENSAU LTD

(a)   The existing overhead absorption rate is:

$$\frac{£15,600+£19,500+£13,650}{(2,000\times {}^{24}\!/_{60})+(1,500\times {}^{4}\!/_{60})+(800\times {}^{6}\!/_{60})} = \frac{£48,750}{2,600} = £18.75 \text{ per hour.}$$

Unit cost

		Product	
	X	*Y*	*Z*
Direct material	5.00	3.00	6.00
Direct labour	1.60	2.67	4.00
Production overhead	7.50	12.50	18.75
	£14.10	£18.17	£28.75

(b)   Cost driver rates

Material receipt and inspection $= \dfrac{£15,600}{10+5+16} = £503.23$ per batch

Process power $= \dfrac{£19,500}{(2,000\times 6)+(1,500\times 3)+(8,000\times 2)}$

$= £1.0773$ per power drill operation

Material handling $= \dfrac{£13,650}{(2,000\times 4)+(1,500\times 6)+(800\times 3)}$

$= £0.70361$ per sq metre handled

	Product		
	X	Y	Z
Direct material	5.00	3.00	6.00
Direct labour	1.60	2.67	4.00
Production overhead			
Material receipt/inspection (W1)	2.52	1.68	10.06
Process power (W2)	6.46	3.23	2.15
Material handling (W3)	2.81	4.22	2.11
Cost per unit	£18.39	£14.80	£24.32

WORKINGS

(W1)   Material receipt/inspection

Cost/unit

Product X   503.23/batch × 10 batches/2,000 units = £2.52/unit

Product Y   503.23/batch × 5 batches/1,500 units = £1.68/unit

Product Z   503.23/batch × 16 batches/800 units = £10.06/unit

(W2)   Process power

Cost/unit

Product X   £1.0773/operation × 6 operations = £6.46

Product Y   £1.0773/operation × 3 operations = £3.23

Product Z   £1.0773/operation × 2 operations = £2.15

(W3)   Material handling

Cost/unit

Product X   £0.70361/m^2 of material × 4m^2 = £2.81

Product Y   £0.70361/m^2 of material × 6m^2 = £4.22

Product Z   £0.70361/m^2 of material × 3m^2 = £2.11

---

30   A POLYTECHNIC

(Tutorial notes: the flow diagram is not difficult, but the time allowance for 3 marks does present problems. However, time spent on ensuring that a correct picture of the cost apportionments is depicted will not only gain these marks but help a great deal in answering part (b).

Part (b) is basically an arithmetic exercise. Good use of the flow diagram will help in breaking this down into a series of apportionments. The model answer uses a 'step' approach. Students should adopt this approach; any attempt to apportion all the costs in a single table is likely to fail.

There is no one answer for part (c). Use your common sense and make brief general statements.)

(a)

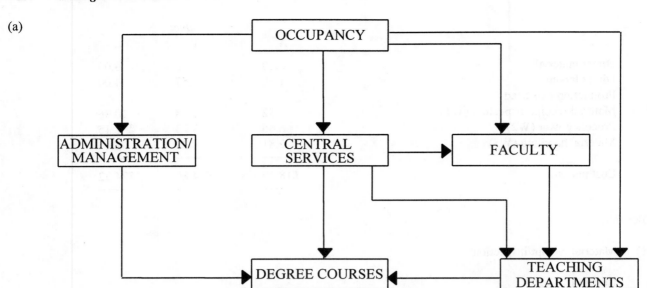

(b)   **Step 1**

Apportion occupancy costs: $\left(\dfrac{£1,500,000}{37,500 \text{ sq ft}} = £40 \text{ per sq ft} \right)$

	£'000
Administration/Management	280
Central Services	120
Faculty	300
Teaching Departments	800
	1,500

Step 2

Apportion central services costs:

$$\left(\frac{£1,000,000 + £120,000}{\text{External Costs } £1,600,000} \right) = 70\text{p per } £ \text{ of external cost}$$

	£'000
Faculty	168
Teaching Departments	560
Degree Courses	392
	1,120

Step 3

Apportion teaching department costs (includes 100% of Faculty costs) and Administration/Management costs, to degree courses.

Teaching department: £800,000 + £560,000 + (£300,000 + £168,000 + £700,000) +
              £5,525,000 = £8,053,000

Administration/management: £280,000 + £1,775,000 = £2,055,000.

Total degree courses costs: £8,053,000 + £2,055,000 + £392,000 = £10,500,000.

Average polytechnic cost per student $= \dfrac{£10,500,000}{2,500 \text{ students}} = £4,200$

Step 4

Analyse £10,500,000 by degree course (in round £'000s).

	Business Studies £'000	Mechanical Engineering £'000	Catering Studies £'000
Teaching department	242	201	564
Administration/management	51	103	82
Central services (based on external costs)	22	34	22
	315	338	668
Average cost per graduate	£3,938	£6,760	£5,567

(c)   The average cost per graduate will differ from one degree course to another for several reasons, the most obvious of which is the very different nature of the courses.

The engineering and catering courses will require much greater use of expensive machinery and equipment, which in turn will need more room. In addition these courses will probably require much greater lecturer input than on the business studies courses. The much lower staff/student ratio will push up the teaching costs per student.

Another factor to be considered is the variability in the student numbers. This variable is unlikely to have an impact on many of the polytechnic costs, which are mainly fixed in nature. For example, if in the following year intake is up to sixty on the mechanical engineering degree, with a similar level of costs, the average cost per student would fall to nearly that being reported for a catering studies student.

These average cost figures must be interpreted with great care by the management. They give a 'rough' guide to the relative cost of degree courses but the arbitrary apportionments render them very nearly useless for decision-making. For decision-making, incremental costs are required.

31   PD PLC

(a)

Work-in-progress control account

	£'000		£'000
Stores ledger account	305.50	Finished goods control (bal fig)	810.00
Wages control account	147.00	Balance c/d	
Production overhead control		(3,000 + 2,000 + (2,000 × 250%))	(10.00)
(250% × 147)	367.50		
	820.00		820.00

Production overhead control account

	£		£
(Incurred)		(Absorbed)	
	49.85	Work-in-progress control	367.50
	123.00	Profit and loss account:	
Cash/Creditors/Accruals	85.00	under-absorption	40.35
	100.00		
	50.00		
	407.85		407.85

Assumption

Even though this quarter is part way through the budget period, it is assumed appropriate to write off the under-absorption to the profit and loss account rather than carry it forward to the next quarter.

Calculation of actual profit earned during the first quarter

	£'000	£'000
Sales		900.00
Cost of sales	810.00	
Under-absorption of overhead	40.35	
		850.35
Actual profit		49.65

(b) (*Tutorial note:* this question demonstrates how overhead absorption based on direct wage cost can result in distorted unit cost of figures. In this case Range M is charged with a disproportionately high charge for overhead, whereas for Range S the charge is correspondingly low.)

Preliminary working

	Range M £'000	*Range S* £'000	*Total* £'000
Per budget:			
Labour cost	450	150	600
Overheads	22.5	82.5	105
	207.5	272.5	480
	140	200	340
	225	150	375
	80	120	200
	675	825	1,500

$$\frac{\text{Overhead}}{\text{Labour cost}} \times 100 \qquad \frac{675}{450} \times 100 \qquad \frac{825}{150} \times 100 \qquad \frac{1,500}{600} \times 100$$

$$= 150\% \qquad = 550\% \qquad = 250\%$$

One possible reason for the results being different from those expected is the blanket overhead rate used. Although in total, overhead is 250% of labour cost, because of the differing wage rates, this is clearly not the case for the individual product lines.

Therefore, Range M is effectively being 'overcharged' with 100% of its labour cost whereas the overhead of Range S is being understated by (550 - 250) = 300% of its labour cost. Hence Range M prices are being overstated and Range S prices understated. This would appear to explain the quarter's results. Adoption of individual absorption rates of 150% and 550% for Range M and Range S respectively should remedy this problem.

A further point to consider is whether there have been any expenditure variances. For example, on fixed overheads the following variances have occurred which will have caused actual profit to be different from budget:

Budget			*Actual*	*expenditure variance (A = Adverse)*
		£'000	£'000	£'000
Plant maintenance	$480 \times \frac{1}{4} =$	120	123	3 (A)
Plant depreciation	$340 \times \frac{1}{4} =$	85	85	Nil
Supervision and indirect labour	$375 \times \frac{1}{4} =$	93.75	100	6.25 (A)
Building occupancy costs	$200 \times \frac{1}{4} =$	50	50	Nil

It would also be necessary to investigate whether any variances have occurred on materials, labour and power costs.

32	A LTD

(Tutorial notes:

(1)   The main advice here is to take one piece of information at a time and gradually build up what is a rather unusual cost per unit figure. It is necessary to use overhead incurred for the absorption rates which would appear to be consistent with budgeted figures.

(2)   It is necessary to identify which costs are affected by changing the packaging method - the obvious changes are in cost of boxes and packaging labour; the less obvious effect is the saving in variance overhead ie, as less hours are worked in packaging, less overhead will be incurred.)

(a)   **Calculation of current total manufacturing cost per unit**

	£
Direct material	0.45200
Packaging materials	0.10300

Packing boxes:

Small boxes 4 units per box $\dfrac{£114}{1,000} \times \frac{1}{4} \times {}^{105}\!/_{100}$ →   0.02990

Larger boxes $4 \times 8 = 32$ units per box $\dfrac{£547.20}{1,000} \times \frac{1}{32} \times {}^{105}\!/_{100}$ →   0.01796

Labour:

Fabrication £4.80 × $\frac{1}{40}$	0.12000
Packaging £3.60 × $\frac{1}{120}$	0.03000

Overhead (see working):

Fabrication £16.36 × $\frac{1}{40}$	0.40900
Packaging £12.36 × $\frac{1}{120}$	0.10300
	1.26486

Working - Overhead recovery rates

	Fabrication £	Packaging £	General £
Variable	88.0	24.0	
Fixed	359.4	53.6	253
General (9:2)	207.0	46.0	
	654.4	123.6	

Recovery rate:

$$\frac{\text{Overhead}}{\text{Direct labour hours}}$$

	Fabrication	Packaging
	$\dfrac{654.4}{40}$	$\dfrac{123.6}{10}$
	= £16.36 per hour	= £12.36 per hour

(b)   Address

Date   XX-X-19XX

General manager, A Ltd

Dear Sir,

                              Change in packaging of Product X

I am writing to advise you on the effect on costs of changing the method of packaging Product X.

(i)   The overall saving possible is shown below, calculated on a per unit basis:

	£	£
Revised cost of boxes: $\frac{475}{1,000} \times \frac{1}{20} \times \frac{105}{100}$		0.02494
Labour for packaging: $£3.60 \times \frac{1}{400}$		0.00900
		0.03394
Existing costs:		
Boxes £(0.02990 + 0.01796)	0.04786	
Labour for packaging	0.03000	
		0.07786
Saving in cost of boxes and labour		0.04392

Add: Saving in labour related variable overhead:

$$\left(\frac{\text{Variable overhead}}{\text{rate for packaging}} = \frac{24}{10} = £2.40 \text{ per hour} \right)$$

$$\therefore \text{ Saving} = £2.40 \times \left(\frac{1}{120} - \frac{1}{400} \right)$$

	£
(saving in labour related variable overhead)	0.01400
Total saving per unit	0.05792

(ii)   This is the saving that can be achieved in the long run. It is in excess of the proposed reduction in selling price of (1.55 - 1.53) = £0.02. The bulk of this saving is not possible until existing stocks of the current boxes have been utilised ie, the figure of £0.05792 assumes the cost per unit of current boxes of £0.04786 can be avoided ie, the saving would initially only be (0.05792 - 0.04786) = £0.01 and therefore not cover the 2p reduction in selling price.

It is assumed:

(1)   that packaging and labour costs can be saved ie, that this labour is a variable cost.
(2)   the costs of packaging materials are not affected;
(3)   fixed overheads are unaffected by the change; and
(4)   that the change will be acceptable to B Ltd.

On the basis of the figures calculated the recommendation is for the packaging change to be introduced once existing box stocks have been exhausted.

Should you require any further information, please contact me again.

Yours faithfully

Cost accountant

33   LEARNING CURVE

(Tutorial notes: the question focuses on the learning curve as it affects budget preparation and calculation of variances for a new product. Answers should focus on these factors and take account of the impact on costs other than labour ie, material usage, variable overheads, fixed overhead recovery.

Part (b) looks at the problems of using short-term profit maximisation as an objective (ie, six to twelve months). The answer is somewhat longer, than the information that could be produced (for six marks) in ten minutes!)

(a)   The learning curve effect refers to the reduction in labour time per unit which may occur as volume of production is increased.

In this case a product has been developed so that any problems will relate to activities carried out after development. During development prototypes would be constructed, probably using various methods. To start volume production it would be necessary to specify the methods which are to be adopted. As production continues and engineers learn more, methods may be changed, making it difficult to calculate a standard cost. Once methods have been chosen the time required must be estimated for each manufacturing operation.

Where the learning curve effect is found to apply, the time for the first unit or batch is vital as it forms the basis for calculating the average time for subsequent batches. It may be difficult to measure this time - there are bound to be 'teething problems' which would cause unusual delays. If part of the production process is carried out on machines, speed of this part of the work is likely to be governed by the machine, though time for loading/setting up may be subject to change.

It is likely that at some stage the time per unit will reach a 'steady' state, after which no further material time savings occur. Before this is reached an average time for, say six months or one year's production could be used as the standard cost. It may not be easy to identify when this steady state will be reached, though once it has been reached the time taken per unit can then be used as a basis for the standard cost. The learning effect makes it more important to budget the level of production - this will be especially difficult with a new product where relatively little is known about demand and therefore sales.

When planning capacity a key element is estimating the number of direct operatives needed - in this case it will be a function of production volume and the learning curve effect and therefore more difficult to predict.

In the early stages, particularly while new methods are being tried out, more highly skilled people may be required. Once the learning curve has improved the performance of the workers, it may be possible/desirable to introduce some lower skilled workers. It may prove difficult to change the mix of the workforce in this way. If the company experiences high labour turnover this would cause the learning effect to fluctuate and make it difficult to predict. As employees learn, the level of material usage (wastage) may decrease, making it difficult to calculate standard material costs.

When comparing budgeted with actual results, it is necessary to 'flex' the budget. With the presence of the learning effect it is necessary to determine the standard hours for the actual output. This will be different for each four week period. If the learning rate remains the same over time, then it would be relatively straightforward but not if the rate of learning fluctuates. In this situation it may also appear unfair to the budget holder to have the time allowed per unit reduced each period. Alternatively, if the more practical alternative of a single standard is used for the whole year, then adverse labour efficiencies would tend to occur early in the year and favourable variances later in the year.

A similar effect may occur on material usage. This would make it difficult to identify any other variance which may occur and which may be controllable. If overheads, particularly fixed, are absorbed on a labour hour basis, recovery is likely to be distorted. If an average standard time is used for the production for the whole year, then the standard hours for actual production early in the year will tend to be low (since production volume will be lower) and result in under-recovery of fixed and variable overheads with a corresponding over-recovery later in the year.

(b)   *Tutorial note:* short-term profit maximisation may be appropriate where the new product is innovative with fairly inelastic demand. This would make it possible to charge high prices for the relatively low volumes in the early stages of the products life. It may also be appropriate if the product has a fairly short life cycle (eg, fashion goods).

If the production is being launched on to an established market, it may be necessary to charge low prices in order to achieve a realistic market share. This would result in low short-term profit or possibly in losses in the early stages but should lead to maximum overall profits in the longer term.

Emphasis on the short term could also result in deliberate 'dysfunctional' decisions to neglect future sales eg,:

(i)   reduce after-sales provision which may not have effect until the subsequent period;
(ii)   reduce advertising in the latter part of the year, causing sales to fall in the subsequent period;
(iii)   reduce research and development expenditure which looks at ways of improving the product;
(iv)   cut stock of replacement parts.

Managers are also likely to be more tempted to build budget slack into the budget if their performance is based on short-term profits (eg, overstate production times, material loss rates).

To maximise profit it would be necessary to set tight standards - this may have a demotivating effect on managers to have high targets which could be near to 'ideal'.

34   REDUNDANT MANAGER

(Tutorial notes:

(1)   This is a fairly difficult question. Careful workings are essential.

(2)   Separate workings should be made for:

> Production in units
> Raw material purchases in £s
> Direct labour costs in £s
> Variable production overheads in £s
> Receipts from customers in £s

(3)   Ensure that depreciation is excluded – inclusion creates a very poor impression of the appreciation of cash flows.

(4)   When practising this type of question, always work within predetermined time limits.

(a)   Cash budget

	Jan £	Feb £	Mar £	Apr £
Receipts:				
From customers	–	15,200	57,100	80,000
Payments:				
Raw material purchases	10,000	11,550	24,500	26,950
Wages	–	4,800	19,800	22,200
Variable production overheads	–	960	4,600	7,080
Fixed overheads	1,000	3,000	3,000	3,000
Total	11,000	20,310	51,900	59,230
Net inflow/(outflow)	(11,000)	(5,110)	5,200	20,770
Balance b/f	20,000	9,000	3,890	9,090
Balance c/f	9,000	3,890	9,090	29,860

(b)   £93,400 (W5)

> *(Tutorial note:* As an alternative, the balance b/f in January could be £80,000 with the £60,000 purchase of machinery shown as a payment in the cash budget.*)*

WORKINGS

(W1)   **Production in units**

Jan	25% of Feb sales	=	800 units
Feb	75% of Feb sales	=	2,400 units
	25% of Mar sales	=	900 units	→ 3,300 units
Mar	75% of Mar sales	=	2,700 units
	25% of Apr sales	=	1,000 units	→ 3,700 units
Apr	75% of Apr sales	=	3,000 units
	25% of May sales	=	1,000 units	→ 4,000 units

(W2)   **Raw material purchases**

Jan	£10,000 (given in question)			Paid Jan.
	3,300 units × 50% × £7	=	£11,550	Paid Feb.
Feb	3,300 units × 50% × £7	=	£11,550	Paid Mar.
	3,700 units × 50% × £7	=	£12,950	Paid Mar.
Mar	3,700 units × 50% × £7	=	£12,950	Paid Apr.
	4,000 units × 50% × £7	=	£14,000	Paid Apr.

(W3)   **Direct labour costs** (assumed strictly variable)

Jan	800 units × £6	=	£4,800	Paid Feb.
Feb	3,300 units × £6	=	£19,800	Paid Mar.
Mar	3,700 units × £6	=	£22,200	Paid Apr.

(W4)   **Variable production overheads**

Jan	Nil			
Feb	800 units × £2 × 60%	=	£960	
Mar	800 units × £2 × 40%	=	£640	
	3,300 units × £2 × 60%	=	£3,960	→ £,4600
Apr	3,300 units × £2 × 40%	=	£2,640	
	3,700 units × £2 × 60%	=	£4,440	→ £7,080

(W5)   **Receipts from customers**

Jan	Nil		
Feb	£80,000 × 20% × 95%	=	£15,200
Mar	£90,000 × 20% × 95%	=	£17,100
	£80,000 × 50%	=	£40,000

£57,100

Apr	£100,000 × 20% × 95%	=	£19,000
	£90,000 × 50%	=	£45,000
	£80,000 × 20%	=	£16,000

£80,000

(Tutorial note: Some forethought would mean the calculations for (a)(ii) would be done here.*)*

May	£100,000 × 20% × 95%	=	£19,000
	£100,000 × 50%	=	£50,000
	£90,000 × 20%	=	£18,000
	£80,000 × 8%	=	£6,400

£93,400

---

35   JACKSON BROTHERS PLC

(Tutorial notes:

(1)   A difficult question on a popular topic. Many students will have chosen to do this question because it relates to cash budgets, but will have subsequently regretted their decision.

(2)   Part (a) is very time consuming - the calculations of purchase, and subsequent payment, of direct materials being particularly difficult.

(3)   Part (b) is easy; just point out in your answer that increased sales levels require extra finance.

(4)   Part (c) is basically a cost/benefit analysis situation.

(5)   Part (d) requires a short discussion on the nature of residual income as a divisional performance measure.

(6)   It may be advisable to attempt parts (b), (c) and (d) first, then move to part (a), spending at most twenty minutes on the preparation of the cash budget.)

(a)   WORKINGS

		£'000
Receipt from sales:		
May: 20% of April sales		24
80% of March sales		96
		120
June: 20% of May sales		46
80% of April sales		96
		142

Payment for direct materials:

	April £'000	May £'000	June £'000	July £'000
Variable cost of sales	90	173	188	225
+ Variable cost of stock c/d (10 + (173 × 25%)) etc	53	57	66	40
- Variable cost of stock b/d	(33)	(53)	(57)	(66)
Variable factory cost incurred	110	177	197	199
Direct material content (× 75%)	83	133	148	149
+ Direct material stock c/d (10 + (133 × 25%))	43	47	47	unknown
- Direct material stock b/d	(31)	(43)	(47)	(47)
Direct material purchases	95	137	148	
	(paid May)	(paid June)		

Payment for other variable factory costs:
May   £177,000 × 25% = £44,250
June   £197,000 × 25% = £49,250

Divisional cash budgets:

	May £'000	June £'000
Receipts:		
Sales	120	142
Internal borrowing	30	70
	150	212
Payments:		
Materials	95	137
Other variable factory costs	44	49
Fixed factory costs	8	8
Selling and distribution costs (see note)	5	6
Administrative costs	6	6
Total	158	206
Net inflow/(outflow)	(8)	6
Balance b/d	10	2
Balance c/d	2	8

Note - **Selling and distribution costs**

The variable element can be estimated as follows:

Increase in selling and distribution costs May to June	£400
Increase in sales May to June	£20,000

which gives a variable selling and distribution cost of 2.0% of sales.

	May £	June £
Variable selling and distribution costs	4,600	5,000
Fixed selling and distribution costs (50% depreciation)	1,800	1,800
	6,400	6,800
∴ Depreciation	900	900

(b)   Employing formula using the budgeted figure:

Cash balance at end of May:

CB = £10,000 + 0.8(£120,000) − 0.12(£120,000) − 0.37(£230,000) − 0.08(£250,000) - £15,000

= £(28,500)

May sales + 10%:

CB = £10,000 + 0.8(£120,000) − 0.12(£120,000) − 0.37(£253,000) − 0.08(£250,000) − £15,000

= £(37,010)

Thus, a 10% increase in budgeted sales would require an additional financing of £8,510.

May sales - 10%:

CB = £10,000 + 0.8(£120,000) − 0.12(£120,000) − 0.37(£207,000) − 0.08(£250,000) − £15,000

= £(19,990)

Thus a 10% decrease in budgeted sales would require less finance.

With internal borrowings of £30,000 in May, the division will require overdraft facilities to finance the expansion.

(c)   The finance director of Jackson Brothers plc is describing a divisional performance measurement commonly referred to as 'residual income'. This income is the residue after deduction of 'imputed' interest on the investments utilised by the division. Thus, residual income is the net operating income which an investment centre is able to earn above some minimum rate of return on operating assets.

The investment centre must have some level of autonomy to make decisions on investment levels, as well as selling price (and sales volume) and expenditure. The finance director should ensure that the divisions of Jackson Brothers plc have such autonomy.

The major advantage claimed for using residual income is that it encourages managers to make profitable investments that will benefit both the division and the company as a whole. Using return on capital employed as a divisional performance measure can result in dysfunctional behaviour, with divisional performance taking precedence over company performance.

The major disadvantages of using the residual income measure relate to the problems of computing divisional profit (eg, include or exclude head office charges), valuing the investment (eg, assets at historical or replacement cost) and calculating the interest percentage.

36   ZBB LTD

(Tutorial notes: a much easier question than it first appears.

Take each department one at a time and consider each level within each department, one at a time. Remember to concentrate on incremental costs for levels 2 and 3. This is especially important for level 3 in the maintenance department.

Note that it is necessary to use the EOQ formula for both levels 2 and 3 of the maintenance department but beware the 2% discount for level 3.

Part (b) is mainly arithmetic, but remember to rank on the basis of the 'score', but use the costs when deciding how to allocate the £925,000.

Part (c) requires use of your general knowledge on qualitative characteristics for decision-making.)

(a) **Material handling department**

Level 1:

	£
Labourers' wages:	
40 hours × £4 × 48 weeks × 30	230,400
5 hours × (£4 × 50%) × 48 weeks × 30	14,400
Employee benefits: (£230,400 + £14,400) × 20%	48,960
Variable overheads: 40 hours × 48 weeks × 30 × 12p	6,912
Incremental costs for level 1 (from zero base)	300,672

Level 2:

Fork lift truck rentals: 10 × £2,000	20,000
Drivers' wages: 48 × 10 × £155	74,400
Truck overheads: 10 × 48 × £150	72,000
Incremental costs of moving from level 1 to level 2	166,400

Level 3:

Computer leasing:	
£20,000 + (£20,000 × 90%) + (£20,000 × 81%) +	
(£20,000 × 72.9%)	68,780
Reduction in labour costs:	
4 hours × £4 × 48 weeks × 30	(23,040)
2 hours × (£4 × 50%) × 48 weeks × 30	(5,760)
Benefits: (£23,040 + £5,760) × 20% (assumed to be variable)	(5,760)
Variable overheads: 4 hours × 48 weeks × 30 × 12p	(691.2)
Incremental cost of moving from level 2 to level 3	33,528.8

Maintenance department

Level 1

	£
Engineers' salaries: £18,000 × 2	36,000
Outside contractor	250,000
Incremental costs for level 1 (from zero base)	286,000

Level 2:

	£
Fitters' salaries: £11,000 × 10	110,000
Maintenance materials	48,000
Ordering costs based on minimum (EOQ) cost orders	

$$\sqrt{\frac{2 \times £100 \times £48,000}{15\%}} = £8,000 \text{ per order}$$

Therefore 6 orders at £100 per order	600

Stock holding costs $\dfrac{£8,000}{2} \times 15\%$	600

Fixed overheads	50,000
Saving on outside contractor	(90,000)
Incremental cost of moving from level 1 to level 2	119,200

Level 3:

Additional fitters' salaries: £11,000 × 6		66,000
Additional maintenance materials		48,000
Ordering costs based on apparent minimum (EOQ) cost orders		

$$\sqrt{\frac{2 \times £100 \times £96,000}{13\frac{1}{3}\%}} = £12,000 \text{ per order}$$

Therefore 8 orders at £100 per order	800	
Stock holding costs $\dfrac{£12,000}{2} \times 13\frac{1}{3}\%$	800	
	1,600	
		114,000
However, with a 2% discount offer –		
Ordering costs at £16,000 per order = 6 × £100	600	
Stockholding costs $\left(\dfrac{£16,000 \times 98\%}{2}\right) \times 13\frac{1}{3}\%$	1,045	
	1,645	
Less: 2% discounts	(1,920)	
Net reduction	(275)	
Incremental benefit – (£275 + £1,200)		(1,475)
Incremental fixed overheads		20,000
Saving on outside contractor		(70,000)
Incremental cost of moving from level 2 to level 3		62,525

(b) **Ranking scores**

Material handling department:

				Score	Ranking
Level 1	£300,672	×	1.00	300,672	1
Level 2	£166,400	×	.60	99,840	3
Level 3	£33,528.8	×	.50	16,764	5

Maintenance department:

				Score	Ranking
Level 1	£286,000	×	1.00	286,000	2
Level 2	£119,200	×	.80	95,360	4
Level 3	£62,525	×	.20	12,505	6

Use of limited budgeted funds:

		Cost £	Cumulative cost £
Ranking item	1	300,672	300,672
Ranking item	2	286,000	586,672
Ranking item	3	166,400	753,072
Ranking item	4	119,200	872,272
Ranking item	5	33,528.8	905,800.8
Ranking item	6	62,525	968,325.8

Therefore material handling department should operate at level 3 and the maintenance department at level 2.

37   LIMITATION PLC

Your answer should look something like that which follows:

(a)   Hours for the first batch of Quarter 4, 19X1 = £600/£5 = 120 hours

Given a 90% learning curve, the average time per batch for all batches is 90% of that for the preceding level each time the number of batches is doubled. We have therefore:

Number of batches	Average time per batch (hours)	Total time (hours)
1	120	120
2	108 (120 × 0.9)	216
4	97.2 (108 × 0.9)	388.8

Hours for batch 2 = 216 - 120 = 96 hours
Hours for batch 3 + batch 4 = 388.8 - 216 = 172.8 hours

(b)   Workings:

Calculation of labour cost:

Time for first 30 batches = 30 × 71.56	=	2,146.8 hrs
Time for first 75 batches = 75 × 62.25	=	4,668.75 hrs
Hence time for Quarter 1 19X2 (45 batches)		2,521.95 hrs
Labour cost for Quarter 1 = 2,521.95 × £5	=	£12,610 approx
Time for first 75 batches = 75 × 62.25	=	4,668.75 hrs
Time for first 120 batches = 120 × 57.96	=	6,955.20 hrs
Hence time for Quarter 2 19X2 (45 batches)	=	2,286.45 hrs
Labour cost for quarter 2 = 2,286.45 × £5	=	£11,432 approx

Calculation of material cost:

Quarter 1 19X2	Units per batch	Total units
First 10 batches 200 × 0.98	196	1,960
Next 20 batches 200 × 0.96	192	3,840
Final 15 batches 200 × 0.94	188	2,820
Total Quarter 1 19X2		8,620

Material cost Quarter 1 19X2 = 8,620 × £1.80 = £15,516

Quarter 2 19X2	Units per batch	Total units
First 5 batches 200 × 0.04	188	940
Next 20 batches 200 × 0.92	184	3,680
Final 20 batches 200 × 0.90	180	3,600
Total Quarter 2 19X2		8,220

Material cost Quarter 2 19X2 = 8,220 × £1.80 = £14,796

Stock holding costs:

Quarter 1, 19X2 (8,620/2) × 30p	=	£1,293
Quarter 2, 19X2 (8,220/2) × 30p	=	£1,233

Limitation plc
Budget Quarters 1 and 2 19X2

	Quarter 1		Quarter 2	
	£	£	£	£
Sales revenue (45 × £1,200)		54,000		54,000
Less: Variable costs:				
Direct material	15,516		14,796	
Holding costs	1,293		1,233	
Direct labour	12,610		11,432	
Variable overhead	18,915	48,334	17,148	44,609
(150% of direct labour)				
Contribution		5,666		9,391

(c) (i)

	Quarter 1		Quarter 2
	£		£
Increased cost (8,620 × £0.1)	862	(8,220 × £0.2)	1,644
Holding costs avoided	1,293		1,233
Net (increase)/decrease in cost	431		(411)

Hence on financial grounds using the information available just-in-time delivery offer would be acceptable in Quarter 1 but should be rejected thereafter.

(ii)   It is unlikely that Limitation plc will accept the offer based on the quarter 1 figures alone, even though they indicate a decrease in cost. Management should consider other factors, however, before rejecting the offer. There may be other costs associated with the present storage method such as transport costs from store due to deterioration and the cost of capital tied up in stock. The just-in-time delivery may cause additional costs if there is no buffer stock to allow for late delivery, changes in demand pattern and changes in level of process losses. Such factors would have an opportunity cost of idle capacity until material was available.

38   A AND B

(a)   There are two constraints:

(i)   the quantity of fabric dye; and
(ii)   the machine time available.

The dye constraint is dealt with first because the question gives a single solution to any shortages; ie, reduce the production of the 100cm width.

Total dye available is 25kgs + 520kgs = 545 kgs.

This can be used to produce:

$$545kgs \times 500m^2/kg = 272,500m^2$$

In order to meet the sales demand production must be:

Product X:	120cm width: (90,000 - 30,000)	60,000m
	160cm width:	70,000m
Product Y:	200cm width: (30,000 - 5,000)	25,000m
	100cm width	100,000m

The area in square metres if this were produced is:

			m^2
Product X:	120cm width		72,000
	160cm width		112,000
Product Y:	200cm width		50,000
	100cm width		100,000
			334,000

As this exceeds the production possible due to the dye constraint, production of the 100cm width must be reduced by (334,000 – 272,500) 61,500m² to 38,500m² (or 38,500m × 100cm).

The machine time available must be considered separately for each machine:

Machine A	Manned hours = 35 × 46 =	1,610
	Lost time @ 20%	322
	Productive hours	1,288

This machine is only used for the 100cm and 120cm widths, therefore time required:

38,500m of 100cm width @ 120m/hour =	320.83 hours
60,000m of 120cm width @ 100m/hour =	600.00 hours
Hours required	920.83

Machine A time is not a binding constraint.

Machine B	Manned hours = 35 × 46 =	1,610
	Idle time @ 30% =	483
	Productive hours	1,127

This machine is only used for the 160cm and 200cm widths, therefore time required:

70,000m of 160cm width @ 80m/hour =	875 hours
25,000m of 200cm width @ 50m/hour =	500 hours
Hours required	1,375

The shortfall of 248 hours means that the 160cm width (being the narrowest on this machine) output must be reduced by:

248 hours × 80m/hour = 19,840m

to (70,000 - 19,840) = 50,160m

Production budget 19X8

Product X:	60,000m @ 120cm width
	50,160m @ 160cm width
Product Y:	25,000m @ 200cm width
	38,500m @ 100cm width

Sales quantity budget 19X8

Product X: 90,000m @ 120cm width
              50,160m @ 160cm width

Product Y: 30,000m @ 200cm width
              38,500m @ 100cm width

(b)   Machine A output:

	m^2
60,000m @ 120cm width =	72,000
38,500m @ 100cm width =	38,500
	110,500
Wastage allowance ($\frac{1}{9}$) (W1)	12,278
	122,778

Machine B output:

	m^2
50,160m @ 160cm width =	80,256
25,000m @ 200cm width =	50,000
	130,256
Wastage allowance ($\frac{2}{8}$) (W1)	32,564
	162,820

Untreated fabric purchases budget

	m^2
Required by production (122,778 + 162,820)	285,598
Required closing stock (10% of 285,598)	28,560
	314,158
Less: Opening stock	(25,000)
Purchase quantity	289,158

(c)   There are two binding constraints, dye and type B machine time; there is a surplus of type A machine time.

The dye constraint may be overcome by using different suppliers or negotiating a greater supply for a higher price. The problems with this approach are:

(i)   that the dye supplied may be of lesser quality than that currently used; and
(ii)   any higher prices will reduce profits on the existing production.

The machine time constraint can be overcome by:

(i)   sub contracting some of the production which uses type B machines - this may be costly and a quality control system is needed for the sub-contract work.

(ii)   installing additional type B machines, this is costly and time consuming - management must be satisfied that there is a long-term need for machine B time,

(iii)   modify type A machines so that they can be used to manufacture the 160cm width and thereby utilise the spare type A machine capacity. The modifications, if possible, may be costly and may reduce the efficiency of the machines which may lead to an overall reduction of profit despite the greater output being achieved.

WORKING

If output is 90% of input, the loss is 10% of input. The adjustment is thus $\frac{10\%}{90\%}$ or $\frac{1}{9}$ of output.

Similarly an 80% yield requires an adjustment of $\frac{2}{8}$ (or $\frac{1}{4}$) of output.

---

39   RS LTD

(a)

Standard product cost

		£
Material R	10 kgs @ £30	300
Material S	6 kgs @ £45	270
Direct labour	30 hrs @ £5.50	165
Production overhead (W1)		210
		945
Standard gross profit (W3)		255
Standard selling price (W2)		1,200

(b)   **Material R**

Price variance

Standard price	=	£30.00
Actual price (£35,000/1,100)	=	£31.82 (rounded)
		1.82 (A)

Price variance = $(300 + 1,100 - 375) \times £1.82$	=	£1,866 (A)

Usage variance

Standard usage = 100 units × 10 kgs	=	1,000 kg
Actual usage	=	1,025 kg
		25 kg (A)

Usage variance = 25 kg × £30	=	£750 (A)

Material S

Price variance

Standard price	=	£45.00
Actual price (£15,180 / 345)	=	£44.00
		1.00 (F)

Price variance = $(460 + 345 - 225) \times £1$	=	£580 (F)

Usage variance

Standard usage = 100 units × 6 kgs	=	600 kg
Actual usage	=	580 kg
		20 kg (F)

Usage variance = 20 kg × £45	=	£900 (F)

Direct labour

Rate variance

Standard rate	=	£5.50
Actual rate (£17,325/3,300)	=	£5.25
		0.25 (F)

Rate variance = 3,300 hrs × £0.25	=	£825 (F)

Efficiency variance

Standard hours = 100 units × 30 hrs	=	3,000
Actual hours	=	3,300
		300 (A)

Efficiency variance = 300 hrs × £5.50	=	£1,650 (A)

Fixed production overhead

Expenditure variance

Budget cost (£252,000/12)	=	£21,000
Actual cost	=	£22,000
Expenditure variance		£1,000 (A)

Capacity variance

Absorption rate per hour:

$$\frac{\text{Unit cost}}{\text{Hrs / unit}} = \frac{£210}{30} = £7/\text{hr}$$

Budget hours = 100 units × 30 hours	=	3,000
Standard hours	=	3,000
Actual hours	=	3,300

Capacity variance = (Budget – Actual hours) × rate/hr

= 300 (F) × £7	=	£2,100 (F)

Efficiency variance

Efficiency variance = (Actual – standard hours) × rate/hr

= 300 (A) × £7	=	£2,100 (A)

(c)

			£
Budgeted gross profit (W4)			25,500

			£ A	£ F	
Cost variances			A	F	
Material R	Price	1,866			
	Usage	750			
Material S	Price		580		
	Usage		900		
Direct labour	Rate		825		
	Efficiency	1,650			
Production overhead	Expenditure	1,000			
	Capacity		2,100		
	Efficiency	2,100			
		7,366	4,405	2,961 A	
Actual gross profit				22,539	

(d) Direct labour rate variance £825 (F)

This variance is controllable by the personnel manager who appears to have settled a wage rate of 25 pence per hour less than that which was anticipated.

The manager may have employed staff of a lower grade than expected.

Direct labour efficiency variance £1,650 (A)

The variance is controllable by the production manager, it means that a total of 300 more hours were used than should have been for the output achieved.

Insufficient training may have been given to the workers.

WORKINGS

(W1) £252,000/1,200 = £210

(W2) $£120,000/\dfrac{1,200}{12} = £1,200$

(W3) Balancing figure

(W4) Budget gross profit = 100 units × £255 = £25,500

40 INSPECTION DEPARTMENT

(Tutorial notes: a question on a topic which most students find difficult. However, this particular question can be answered quickly.

Part (a) is repetitious. The calculations for each of the three months are the same. Therefore concentrate on the computations for December; January and February are the same. There are really 9 marks for being able to compute three variances.

Remember to use the labour cost per standard hour of output, ie, £3 + 80% = £3.75, when calculating the productivity and idle time variances.

Part (b) is a simple arithmetic exercise.

Remember part (c) is worth nearly a third of the marks. Therefore, more than a short paragraph is required. Break the question down into three parts:

(1)   Explain usefulness of percentages
(2)   Comment on data
(3)   Give possible explanations)

(a)

	Actual hours at actual rate £	Actual hours at standard rate £	Wage rate variance £
December	26,660	25,800	860A
January	27,300	25,200	2,100A
February	28,925	26,700	2,225A

Note: labour cost per standard hour of output = £3 + 25% = £3.75

	Actual Idle Time at Standard Rate (£3.75) £	Allowed Idle Time at Standard Rate (£3.75) £	Excess Idle Time Variance £
December	1,700 × £3.75 = £6,375	1,720 × £3.75 = £6,450	75F
January	1,200 × £3.75 = £4,500	1,680 × £3.75 = £6,300	1,800F
February	1,400 × £3.75 = £5,250	1,780 × £3.75 = £6,675	1,425F

	Actual Productive Hours at Standard Rate £	Standard Productive Hours at Standard Rate £	Productivity Variance £
December	6,900 × £3.75 = £25,875	6,600 × £3.75 = £24,750	1,125A
January	7,200 × £3.75 = £27,000	6,700 × £3.75 = £25,125	1,875A
February	7,500 × £3.75 = £28,125	6,800 × £3.75 = £25,500	2,625A

(b)   **Variance %**

	Wage Rate %	Excess Idle Time %	Productivity %
December	$\dfrac{£860}{£25,800} = 3.3\text{A}$	$\dfrac{£75}{£6,450} = 1.2\text{F}$	$\dfrac{£1,125}{£24,750} = 4.5\text{A}$
January	$\dfrac{£2,100}{£25,200} = 8.3\text{A}$	$\dfrac{£1,800}{£6,300} = 28.6\text{F}$	$\dfrac{£1,875}{£25,125} = 7.5\text{A}$
February	$\dfrac{£2,225}{£26,700} = 8.3\text{A}$	$\dfrac{£1,425}{£6,675} = 21.3\text{F}$	$\dfrac{£2,625}{£25,500} = 10.3\text{A}$

(c)   It is possible to assess trends and materiality by looking at variances expressed in absolute terms, but they are much more likely to be meaningful if they are expressed in percentage terms.

The trend of the percentages can be reviewed to see if the variance is nearing unacceptable levels, or, where remedial action had already been taken to reduce an adverse variance, that the expected improvement is materialising. To assess the materiality of a variance, the use of a percentage (together with the absolute values of the variances) is very useful. By establishing control limits expressed in percentage terms an enterprise can concentrate on controlling the costs of those activities which are 'significantly' adrift from their expected position.

The percentages shown in the answer to (b) indicate that the company is now paying labour a wage rate well above the standard, perhaps in an effort to improve productivity and reduce idle time. The figures clearly indicate that the excess idle time has been drastically reduced during the periods of January and February when the higher rates of pay appear to apply. However, there is steady, and probably significant, decline in the productivity achieved in the hours worked. This may be a problem for the inspection department but may also be an indicator of problems in the preparation department. Further investigation is required to find the cause of this trend. The interrelationships of the three variances, and the close working relationship of the preparation and inspection departments, would need to be considered when taking control action. This is essential to ensure that the most advantageous position for the company as a whole is achieved.

41 CONSUMER PRODUCTS MANUFACTURER

(Tutorial notes: a 'number crunching' question. But read it carefully, especially the paragraph giving details of employees' hours and rates of pay.

Part (a) requires careful thought **before** starting the computations. Beware the 5% normal loss and the overtime hours.

Parts (b) and (c) are fairly straightforward, although the question is poorly worded, especially for part (b). It is the standard direct labour rate per hour that is required. For part (c) split your analysis between Filling and Packing. Although not strictly required in the question, this analysis will help ensure a good mark is achieved.)

(a)

	Product 1 Units 000	Product 2 Units 000	Product 3 Units 000
Production sold	850	1,500	510
Closing stock required	200	255	70
	1,050	1,755	580
Less: Opening stock	(100)	(210)	(105)
	950	1,545	475
Filling process	1,000*	1,545	500*
Packing process	950	1,545	475
Labour hours required:			
Filling	8,000	5,150	2,000
Packing	10,000	15,450	5,000
	18,000	20,600	7,000

* (with 5% loss)

Total direct working hours required = 45,600

Direct working hours per employee:

Basic hours	-	250 days × 7 hours × 80%	1,400
Overtime hours	-	3 hours × 50 weeks =	150
			1,550

$$\text{Employees required} = \frac{45,600 \text{ hours}}{1,550 \text{ hours}} = 30$$

Note: it is also possible to assume the 80% direct work applies to overtime. The following figures result from this assumption:

((250 days × 7 hours) + (3 hours × 50 weeks)) × 80% = 1,520 hours

$$\text{Employees required} = \left(\frac{45,600 \text{ hours}}{1,520 \text{ hours}}\right) = 30$$

(b)

	£
Total labour costs = 35 hours × £4 × 52 weeks	7,280
+ overtime = 3 hours × £5 × 52 weeks	780
Per employee	8,060
For 30 employees	£241,800

$$\text{Direct labour rate} = \frac{£241,800}{45,600 \text{ hours}} = £5.30 \text{ (to 2 decimal places)}$$

(c)

Product 1:   *Per Unit*

Filling: for 950,000 units - 8,000 hours × £5.30 = £42,400   4.46p
Packing: for 950,000 units - 10,000 hours × £5.30 = £53,000   5.58p

10.04p

Product 2:

Filling: for 1,545,000 units - 5,150 hours × £5.30 = £27,295   1.77p
Packing: for 1,545,000 units - 15,450 hours × £5.30 = £81,885   5.30p

7.07p

Product 3:

Filling: for 475,000 units - 2,000 hours × £5.30 = £10,600   2.23p
Packing: for 475,000 units - 5,000 hours × £5.30 = £26,500   5.58p

7.81p

42   MATERIAL VARIANCES

(Tutorial note: part (a) is a very basic mix/yield question although it is designed to 'unnerve' students by including variances of zero in January.

In part (b) the zero variances should be mentioned.)

(a)   **Standard cost**

Material X	60% @ £30	18
Material Y	40% @ £45	18
	100%	36
Standard loss	10%	
Standard yield	90%	= $\frac{£36}{90\%}$ = £40 per tonne

Price variance

	January £	*February* £	*March* £
Material Y	Nil	Nil	Nil

Material X:

Total material cost	32,400	31,560	38,600
Less: Cost of Y 360 × £45	16,200	16,200	16,200
	———	———	———
Actual cost of material X	16,200	15,360	22,400
Standard price @ Actual quantity:			
540 × £30	16,200		
480 × £30		14,400	
700 × £30			21,000
	———	———	———
Price variance	Nil	960 A	1,400 A
	———	———	———

Material variance summaries

	January			February			March		
	Product X	Product Y	Total	Product X	Product Y	Total	Product X	Product Y	Total
Mix variance									
Actual quantity @ Actual mix	540	360	900	480	360	840	700	360	1,060
Actual quantity @ Standard mix	540	360	900	504	336	800	636	424	1,060
Mix variance			Nil	24 @ 30 = 720 F	24 @ 45 = 1,080 A	360 A	64 @ 30 = 1,920 A	64 @ 45 = 2,880 F	960 F
Yield variance									
Actual quantity @ Standard mix	540	360	900	504	336	800	636	424	1,060
Standard quantity for actual production @ Standard mix	540	360	$810 \times \dfrac{100}{90}$ = 900	510	340	$765 \times \dfrac{100}{90}$ = 850	600	400	$900 \times \dfrac{100}{90}$ = 1,000
Yield variance			Nil	6 @ 30 = 180 F	4 @ 45 = 180 F	360 F	36 @ 30 = 1,080 A	24 @ 45 = 1,080 A	2,160 A
Usage variance									
Actual quantity @ Actual mix	540	360		480	360		700	360	
Standard quantity for actual production @ Standard mix	540	360		510	340		600	400	
Usage variance			Nil	30 @ 30 = 900 F	20 @ 45 = 900 A	Nil	100 @ 30 = 3,000 A	40 @ 45 = 1,800 F	1,200 A

(b)　　Production in January is exactly according to standard. The price of Y has remained at standard for the whole period. The price of X is £2 $\left(\dfrac{960}{480}\text{ and }\dfrac{1,400}{700}\right)$ in excess of standard in February and March. If this continues the standard price of X will need to be increased. The proportion of X in the mix changed to $\dfrac{4,400}{840}=57\%$ and $\dfrac{700}{1,060}=66\%$ in February and March respectively. The cost increase in February, shown as an adverse mix variance of £360, is caused by dearer Y being used instead of cheaper X. There is an improvement in yield in February. The increased yield could be viewed as an abnormal gain of 9 tons (840 × 90% = (756 - 765) × £40 = £360). There is also a reduction in volume produced in February.

In March the significant increase in the proportion of X (which is cheaper) used has caused a favourable mix variance and may have contributed to the large adverse yield variance. Production in March is considerably higher than for January and February - this may be a reason for the adverse yield variance.

Overall there appears to be a link between mix and yield. If the proportion of Y is increased, causing adverse mix variance as Y is more expensive, the yield is improved - as occurred in February; the opposite took place in March.

There could also be a link between yield and the volume of production - in February production is low and yield is high, whereas in March production is high and yield is low.

(c)　　This information helps to explain the increased proportion of Y used in February - if not used Y would be wasted, which could involve disposal costs. It could therefore be argued that the adverse mix variance on Y of £1,080 in February is a sunk cost ie, using a greater proportion of Y has not increased the purchase quantity. Using more of Y has improved yield.

In March the restriction on Y has resulted in adverse yield arising from the increased proportion of X needed to increase production volume - this has resulted in an overall adverse usage variance of £1,200. This excess cost should be included in the evaluation of decisions to try to obtain more of Y by, for example, paying a premium price.

It would be necessary to ascertain whether and how quality of the final product is affected by changes in mix and whether the quality is then acceptable to customers.

43　　GENERY PLC

(Tutorial notes:

(1)　　A question only for the very well prepared student.

(2)　　The analysis required is specifically mentioned in the syllabus but the need to show individual mix and quantity variances is unusual for the method in part (a). Work using percentage proportions, both budgeted and actual.

(3)　　Part (b) is a straightforward application of the relevant formulae.

(4)　　For part (c) make sure that all the points are covered and answer the specific requirements; do not write a general answer on mix and quantity variances. You are required to discuss comparisons and advantages; very little of the usual critical approach is required.)

(a)

	Proportions		Contribution
	Budgeted	*Actual*	*per unit*
Model A	30%	37.50%	£10
Model B	50%	43.75%	£15
Model C	20%	18.75%	£13

Model A	Sales volume variance	=	$(18{,}000 \text{ units} - 15{,}000 \text{ units}) \times £10$
		=	£30,000 F
	Actual units in budgeted proportion	=	$48{,}000 \times 30\%$
		=	14,400
	Sales mix variance	=	$(18{,}000 \text{ units} - 14{,}400 \text{ units}) \times £10$
		=	£36,000 F
	Sales quantity variance	=	$(14{,}400 \text{ units} - 15{,}000 \text{ units}) \times £10$
		=	£6,000 A
Model B	Sales volume variance	=	$(21{,}000 \text{ units} - 25{,}000 \text{ units}) \times £15$
		=	£60,000 A
	Actual units in budgeted proportion	=	$48{,}000 \times 50\%$
		=	24,000
	Sales mix variance	=	$(21{,}000 \text{ units} - 24{,}000 \text{ units}) \times £15$
		=	£45,000 A
	Sales quantity variance	=	$(24{,}000 \text{ units} - 25{,}000 \text{ units}) \times £15$
		=	£15,000 A
Model C	Sales volume variance	=	$(9{,}000 \text{ units} - 10{,}000 \text{ units}) \times £13$
		=	£13,000 A
	Actual units in budgeted proportion	=	$48{,}000 \times 20\%$
		=	9,600
	Sales mix variance	=	$(9{,}000 \text{ units} - 9{,}600 \text{ units}) \times £13$
		=	£7,800 A
	Sales quantity variance	=	$(9{,}600 \text{ units} - 10{,}000 \text{ units}) \times £13$
		=	£5,200 A
Totals	Sales volume variance	=	£30,000 F - £60,000 A - £13,000 A
		=	£43,000 A
	Sales mix variance	=	£36,000 F - £45,000 A - £7,800 A
		=	£16,800 A
	Sales quantity variance	=	- £6,000 A - £15,000 A - £5,200 A
		=	£26,200 A

(b)

	Budgeted proportion	Contribution per unit	Weighted average contribution per unit
			£
Model A	30%	£10	3.00
Model B	50%	£15	7.50
Model C	20%	£13	2.60
			13.10

Sales volume variances:

	Actual mix		Budgeted mix					£	
Model A	(18,000	-	15,000)	×	£10	=	30,000	F
Model B	(21,000	-	25,000)	×	£15	=	60,000	A
Model C	(9,000	-	10,000)	×	£13	=	13,000	A
Total							43,000A (as for (a))	

Sales quantity variances:

							£	
Model A	(18,000	-	15,000)	×	£13.10 =	39,300	F
Model B	(21,000	-	25,000)	×	£13.10 =	52,400	A
Model C	(9,000	-	10,000)	×	£13.10 =	13,100	A
Total						26,200	A

Sales mix variances:

							£	
Model A	(18,000	-	15,000)	× £(10 - 13.10)	=	9,300	A
Model B	(21,000	-	25,000)	× £(15 - 13.10)	=	7,600	A
Model C	(9,000	-	10,000)	× £(13 - 13.10)	=	100	F
						16,800	A

(c)

To: The management

From: AN Accountant

Date: XX-XX-19XX

Subject: **Summary of sales volume variances**

The sales volume variance in total shows the amount of contribution that has been gained or lost as a result of achieving above or below budgeted sales units, assuming constant unit selling prices and variable costs.

This aggregate variance of £43,000 has been further analysed above and the following points are relevant to an appreciation of the analysis:

(i) The two summaries in the analysis show that, irrespective of the method used, the total sales volume, mix and quantity variances will be the same. However, they highlight the importance of appreciating the calculations involved because the mix and quantity (but not volume) variances attributed to each model are different.

(ii) It would probably benefit the company to show volume variances broken down into mix and quantity variances, because of the additional information which is more readily available when using this approach. If only the volume variance is reported, it would not always be clear what were the underlying reasons for the variances. Where the analysis uses the budgeted average contribution per unit, the sales quantity variances for each model show their proportion of the total sales quantity variance.

The individual sales mix variances reported using the weighted averages emphasise the results achieved by selling more or less of the above or below average contribution models. Reporting in this manner highlights the importance of achieving favourable results with the high contribution products.

(iii)   If management's efforts in planning, controlling and making decisions can be enhanced by reporting individual product quantity and mix variances, then such an analysis is relevant. Management must decide if the analysis is clear enough and accurate enough for them to use. It is likely that they will be most appropriate where there is a real possibility of substituting one product for another.

(iv)   The sales variances have been calculated by standardising the units sold. There may be circumstances where the prices are so different or the physical attributes of the product so different that it would be inappropriate to base the comparison on units. Instead, the variances may be found by standardising in terms of £s value of sales, rather than unit sales.

It is important to understand that this only affects the division between the mix and quantity elements; the sales volume variance is unaffected by the change of approach.

---

44   FLICK LTD

(a)   Period 3 variance calculations:

Revised standard usage per product unit = 2kg × 110% = 2.2kg
Material usage revision variance
(2 – 2.2 kg) × 1,800 units × £4 = £1,440 (A)

Material usage (residual) variance
(revised std. kg per unit × actual units) - (actual kg) × standard price per kilo
= ((2.2 × 1,900) - 4,300) × £4 = £480 (A)

Material price variance
(standard price - actual price) × actual kg = (£4 – £4.25) × 4,300 = £1,075 (A)

Standard productive machine hours per product unit = 1,800/180 = 10 hours

Machine efficiency variance
= (std. productive hours - actual productive hours) × std. rate per productive hour
= ((1,900 × 0.1) – (240 – 60)) × £30
= (190 - 180) × £30 = £300(F)

Machine idle time variance
= (std. idle time - actual idle time) × std. rate per productive hour
= ((240 × 20%) - 60) × £30
= (48 – 60) × £30 = £360(A)

Machine expenditure variance
= (actual gross hours × standard gross rate) – actual cost
= (240 × £24) – £6,048 = £288 (A)

(b)   Forecast operating statement periods 4 to 6 inclusive

	£	£
Original budget contribution (5,400 × £7)		37,800
Revision variances		
material usage (3 × £1,440)		4,320 (A)
Revised budget contribution (5400 × £6.20)		33,480
Sales volume variance - due to:		
Capacity utilisation (note 1)		
360 × £6.20	2,232 (F)	
Productivity (note 1) 680 × £6.20	4,216 (F)	
Idle time (note 1) go × £6.20	558 (A)	5,890 (F)
Revised standard contribution		
for sales forecast		39,370
Other variances:		
Material usage (note 2)	1,123 (A)	
Material price (note 3)	1,188 (A)	
Machine efficiency (note 4)	2,040 (F)	
Machine idle time (note 4)	270 (A)	
Machine expenditure (note 5)	518 (A)	1,059 (A)
Actual contribution forecast		38,311

Workings:

Note 1

	Original budget	*Forecast*
Gross hours	675	720
Standard idle time (20%)	135	144
Expected productive hours	540	576
Forecast productive hours		567 *
Forecast standard hours		635 **

*   Actual idle time in period 3 was 25% of gross hours compared to a budgeted figure of 20% of gross hours. The excess level in periods 4 to 6 is 25% of the period 3 excess i.e. 25% × 5% = 1.25%. The level of idle time for periods 4 to 6 is, therefore 21.25% Hence the forecast productive hours = 720 × (100% - 21.25%) = 567 hours

**   The productivity ratio for periods 4 to 6 is forecast as 112% of standard hence, forecast standard hours = productive hours × productivity ratio = 567 × 112% = 635 hours

Capacity gain = (576 − 540) × 10 = 360 units
Excess idle time = (567 − 576) × 10 = 90 units
Productivity gain = (635 − 567) × 10 = 680 units
Forecast output = 1,800 + (360 − 90 + 680)/3 = 2,117 units per period
The sales volume variance effects are valued at £6.20 per unit. This is the revised standard contribution per unit after allowing for the increased material usage specification.

Note 2

The material usage variance should be reduced to 70% of the period 3 rate and then adjusted to the forecast volume for periods 4 to 6.

We have £480 × 0.7 × 6,350 units/1,900 units = £1,123 (A)

Note 3

The material price variance applies only to period 4. The period 3 price variance will be adjusted to allow for the change in product units and the reduction of 30% in the excess material usage variance.

Using the period 3 figures as the base we have,

Standard material (kg)   = 1,900 × 2.2   =   4 180
Actual material (kg)   =   4 300

Excess usage (100%)   = 120 kg

The reduction in excess usage expected in period 4 = 30% × 120 kg = 36 kg. The revised actual material would be 4,300 − 36 = 4,264 kg. The period 4: period 3 material ratio is therefore 4,264/4,300 = 99.16%

Period 4 material price variance = £1,075 × (2,117 units/1,900 units) × 99.16% = £1,188(A)

Note 4

As per note 1 for the periods 4 to 6 inclusive:
Machine efficiency gain = 635 - 567 = 68 hours × £30 per hour = £2,040(F)
Machine idle time loss = 567 - 576 = 9 hours × £30 per hour = £270(A)

Note 5

The machine variable expenditure variance is reduced to 60% of the period 3 rate per hour. The gross machine hours in each of the periods 4 to 6 are the same as in period 3, viz 240 hours. Machine variable expenditure variance = £288 × 3 × 0.6 = £518(A).

45   AB LTD

(a)   (i)   Actual cost: 142,000 kils at £1.21/kilo = £171,820
Standard cost: 142,000 kilos at £1.20/kilo = £170,400
Price variance = £1,420 A

(ii)   Actual usage (at standard price): 16,270 kilos at £1.20/kilo = £19,524
Standard usage: 1,790 units × £9 × £1.80/unit = £19,332
Usage variance = £192 A

(iii)   Cost inflation:
Standard price = £1.272 (1.20 × 1.06) × 147,400 kilos = £187,492.80
less price variance £1,031.80
= actual cost £186,461 ÷ 147,400 = £1.265 per kil
∴ Cost inflation = $(\frac{1.265}{1.21} - 1) \times 100\% = 4.5\%$

(iv)   Actual usage of Material X:

Period 1: 16,270 kilos ÷ 1,790 units = 9.0894 kilos per unit
Period 2: 9 kilos per unit × 0.995 = 8.955 kilos per unit
∴ Change in usage = $(\frac{9.0894 - 8.955}{9.0894}) \times 100\% = 1.5\%$ improvement.

(b)   There are four types of standards that may be set for raw material usage and labour efficiency:

(i)   *Basic standards*: these are standards which are set out with a view to their remaining unchanged in the longer term, so as to provide a basis for identifying trends over time. They are not frequently used as they do not provide a measure of efficiency, and because actual usage and efficiency can be used instead to establish trends.

(ii) *Current standards*: in stark contrast to basic standards, current standards change frequently (eg, monthly) in order to reflect current operating conditions. If set correctly they can provide motivation to achieve. The danger is that they are frequently reset to what is being achieved rather than what may be reasonably achievable.

(iii) *Normal standards*: these are standards which are expected achievable perfor5mance over a longer period eg, one year. Such standards are most frequently encountered, being an integral part of the normal annual budgeting process. Normal standards shoujld provide a tough but attainable target in order to provide motivation to improve efficiency. Allowances are made for a certain level of wastage, downtime etc, where these are an inevitable aspect of production operations.

(iv) *Ideal standards*: these are standards which can only be achieved under perfect operating conditions. Such standards provide a measure of the additional costs incurred by imperfect operating conditions and thus a target for cost reduction. They can, however, have a negative effect on motivation. They would be changed only when basic operating methods change ie, infrequently.

---

46 MATERIAL A

(a) Standard direct labour cost per unit of production:

Component X, 0.40 hours × £5.00/hour = £2.00/unit
Component Y, 0.56 hours × £5.00/hour = £2.80/unit

Actual hours per period = 53 × 40 × 13 = 27,560 hours

Variances

	£
Actual wages	138,500
− Actual hours at standard rate	137,800
	─────
	700A
	─────

	£	£
Efficiency variance:		
Actual hours at standard rate		137,800
− Standard wages		
(Component X:		
35,000 units × £2.00/unit	70,000	
Component Y:		
25,000 units × £2.80/unit)	70,000	
	─────	
	140,000	
	─────	
		2,200 F
		─────

(b) Standard purchase price of Material A:

	£
Actual cost of purchases	85,110
Plus: favourable price variance	430
	─────
	85,540
	÷ 47,000 kilos
	= £1.82 per kilo

Standard usage of material A per unit of production of Component X:

	£
Actual usage at standard price (33,426 kilos × £1.82/kilo)	60,835.32
Less: unfavourable usage variance	320.32
Standard usage	60,515.00

$$\div £1.82 \text{ per kilo}$$
$$= 33,250 \text{ kilos}$$
$$\div 35,000 \text{ units}$$
$$= 0.95 \text{ kilos per unit of Component X}$$

(c)   The first requirement is to establish the sales budget for components X and Y and to consider whether there is likely to be any factor of production which will prevent demand from being satisfied (limiting factor).

The existence of a limiting factor would influence, in conjunction with expected demand, the determination of the production budget for components X and Y.

In the absence of any limiting factor of production, the production budget will be determined by the sales budget with adjustment as necessary for budgeted changes in the level of finished stock of the components. A planned increase in finished component stock would require a production budget in excess of sales and vice versa.

Once the production budget for the two components has been established, the production quantity of each component multiplied by the expected usage of Material A per unit of component output determines the required quantity of material for production. Expected usage may be different to standard usage depending upon the type of standards that are set.

The budgeted purchase quantity of Material Amust be sufficient to meet budgeted production usage requirements, with an adjustment to take account of any planned change in the level of raw material stock. A required increase in stock will lead to purchases in excess of usage and vice versa.

47   GLASS BOTTLES

(a)   (i)   **Absorption costing**

	September		October	
	£'000	£'000	£'000	£'000
Sales		2,784		3,232
Opening stock	Nil		730.24	
Direct materials	920		624	
Direct labour	828		561.60	
Variable production overhead	386.40		262.08	
Fixed production overhead	864.80		586.56	
	2,999.20		2,764.48	
Closing stock	(730.24)	(2,268.96)	(130.4)	(2,634.08)
Gross profit		515.04		597.92
Over/(under) absorption		208.80		(45.44)
		723.84		552.48
Fixed selling costs	120		120	
Fixed admin costs	80	(200)	80	(200)
Net profit		523.84		352.48

(ii) **Marginal costing**

	September		October	
	£'000	£'000	£'000	£'000
Sales		2,784		3,232
Opening stock	Nil		519.68	
Direct materials	920		624	
Direct labour	828		561.60	
Variable production overhead	386.40		262.08	
	2,134.40		1,967.36	
Closing stock	(519.68)	(1,614.72)	(92.80)	(1,874.56)
Contribution		1,169.28		1,357.44
Fixed costs				
Production	656		632	
Selling	120		120	
Administration	80	(856)	80	(832)
Net profit		313.28		525.44

(b)   Marginal costing separates fixed costs and reports them as a cost of the period in which they are incurred. This causes an immediate effect on the profit of the period and therefore highlights the effect of variable costs on contribution and of the fixed costs on the final profit. This should assist in the control of costs.

Marginal costing will not smooth out the fluctuations in profit which occur when sales fluctuate. If production is constant changes in the level of sales will cause a change in stock levels, so the valuation of stock at variable cost only under a marginal costing system will cause greater fluctuations in profit than absorption costing.

Profits are maximised by the maximisation of contribution in periods of constant fixed costs. The use of marginal costing highlights contribution and management may use this to identify profitable operating levels and thereby improve profitability.

48   MANUFACTURING PRODUCT X

(a)

Input units	Output units		Elements of cost – equivalent units			
			Direct material	Direct labour	Variable overhead	Fixed overhead
102,000	90,000	Sold	90,000	90,000	90,000	90,000
	8,000	Finished goods	8,000	8,000	8,000	8,000
	4,000	Work-in-progress (W1)	4,000	2,000	2,000	2,000
Equivalent units			102,000	100,000	100,000	100,000
Total cost			£714,000	£400,000	£100,000	£350,000
per unit (W2)			£7	£4	£1	£3.5

Total cost per unit of X $= £(7 + 4 + 1 + 3.50) = £15.50$

(b)   **Profit statement based on absorption costing**

				£	£
Sales 90,000 units at £20					1,800,000
Production costs:					
	Direct materials			714,000	
	Direct labour			400,000	
	Variable overhead			100,000	
				1,214,000	
	Fixed overhead			350,000	
				1,564,000	

				£000		
Less:	Closing stock					
	8,000 units	× £15.50	=	124		
	4,000 units	× £7.00	=	28		
	2,000 units	× £4.00	=	8		
	2,000 units	× £1.00	=	2		
	2,000 units	× £3.50	=	7		
				169		

		£	£
		169,000	1,395,000
Gross profit			405,000

					£	£
Less:	Selling costs:	Variable	90,000 × £1.50 =		135,000	
		Fixed			200,000	
	Administration:	Variable	90,000 × £0.10 =		9,000	
		Fixed			50,000	
						394,000
Net profit						11,000

This agrees with the accountant's profit of £11,000.

(c)   **Profit statement based on marginal costing**

	£	£	£

		£	£	£
Sales 90,000 units at £20 each				1,800,000
Production costs:				
Direct materials			714,000	
Direct labour			400,000	
Variable overhead			100,000	
Variable cost			1,214,000	
Less: Closing stock				
8,000 units at £12 each		96,000		
4,000 units at £ 7 each		28,000		
2,000 units at £ 4 each		8,000		
2,000 units at £ 1 each		2,000		
		134,000		
				1,080,000

Gross contribution		720,000
Less: Variable selling costs	135,000	
Variable administration cost	9,000	
		144,000
Net contribution	576,000	
Less: Fixed manufacturing overheads	350,000	
Fixed selling costs	200,000	
Fixed administration costs	50,000	
		600,000
Net loss		(24,000)

(d)

Profit under absorption costing		11,000
Loss under marginal costing		(24,000)
Difference		35,000

The difference arises due to the different treatment of fixed overheads. Using absorption costing, fixed overheads are absorbed into the costs of production during the period. Using marginal costing, all fixed overheads are charged against the profits of the period. When sales and production volumes differ, this will result in different profit figures being stated.

The closing stocks using absorption costing included fixed costs ie:

		£
		£
Finished goods	8,000 at £3.50 =	28,000
Work in progress	2,000 at £3.50 =	7,000
Total difference		35,000

Both statements are acceptable for internal accounting purpose, most accountants preferring marginal costing for decision-making purposes. The absorption costing approach is necessary for external reporting, to comply with the requirements of *SSAP 9.*

WORKINGS

(W1)   4,000 units × degree of completion.
(W2)   Total cost/number of equivalent units.

49   MIOZIP CO

(Tutorial notes:

(1)   An average standard question but, having no 'units' with which to work, does present problems.

(2)   Part (a) is the standard question about absorption costing with changing stock levels resulting in different profits.

(3)   Part (b) is not difficult, but with no variable costs per unit with which to work, it is necessary to use total amounts after deducting the fixed factory overhead.

(4)   Part (c) is reasonably straightforward. Remember the problem of using pre-determined absorption rates in periods of changing activity levels.

(5)   Concentrate on the usefulness of marginal costs in decision-making but full cost systems ensure that no costs are ignored.)

(a)   To: The board of directors, Miozip Co

       From: The company accountant

       Date: XX-XX-19XX

       Subject: **Profitability**

From the summarised profit and loss accounts (estimated 19X2, budgeted 19X3), it is apparent that two periods with equal sales revenue are reporting profits/losses which differ by £210,000. The difference can be entirely attributed to the valuation of opening/closing stock.

The factory cost of goods sold for 19X2 is £60,000 lower than that expected for the level of sales achieved because of the lower overhead absorption rate used in 19X1. Some of the goods produced in this period, being attributed with a lower cost, were sold in 19X2. All units budgeted to be sold in 19X3 carry the full £3.60 overhead.

In addition, the level of activity budgeted in 19X3 (100,000 direct labour hours) is only two-thirds of that achieved in 19X2. This will result in an increased under-absorption of overhead charge of £150,000. This, together with the £60,000 above, accounts for the £210,000 differential.

(b)

WORKINGS

		£	%
19X1:			
	Factory cost of production	1,000,000	100.00
	Fixed factory overhead absorbed		
	(£600,000 - £300,000)	300,000	30.00
	∴ Other variable factory costs	700,000	70.00
19X2 (similar percentage for 19X3):			
	Factory cost of production	975,000	100.00
	Fixed factory overhead absorbed		
	(£600,000 - £150,000)	450,000	46.15
	∴ Other variable factory costs	525,000	53.85

Based on marginal costs:

	Actual 19X1		Estimated 19X2		Budgeted 19X3	
	£	£	£	£	£	£
Sales		1,350,000		1,316,250		1,316,250
Opening stock	70,000		140,000		192,500	
Variable factory cost of production	700,000		525,000		350,000	
	770,000		665,000		542,500	
Closing stock	(140,000)		(192,500)		(70,000)	
Variable cost of goods sold		630,000		472,500		472,500
Contribution		720,000		843,750		843,750

Fixed costs:

Factory overheads	(600,000)	(600,000)	(600,000)
Administrative and financial costs	(220,000)	(220,000)	(220,000)
Net profit/(loss)	(100,000)	23,750	23,750

(c) The decision to increase the selling price by using the cost-plus formula without considering the effect upon demand from customers, could result in an increase in the under-absorbed overhead. The higher price might result in a fall in demand and a fall in the number of direct labour hours worked. Thus, the absorption of overheads would fall with the reduction in direct labour hours and a larger proportion of the overheads incurred would not be absorbed.

(d) Management accounting theorists favour marginal costing because it will tend to give the most relevant costs to assist a decision-maker. Marginal costs are usually differential, incremental costs and are important in most decisions, including pricing special orders, production scheduling with limiting factors, and make or buy decisions. By contrast, full costing systems, by including fixed costs in product costs, can often lead to sub-optimal decisions being taken if the effect of 'fixed costs per unit' is not fully understood.

However, full costing systems appear to be used extensively in practice. This could be for the following reasons:

(i) automatically ensures compliance with SSAP 9;

(ii) provides more realistic matching of total costs with revenues;

(iii) a large part of the costs of most companies are now fixed; using marginal costing may result in these substantial costs being overlooked eg, under-pricing using a marginal cost-plus formula resulting in losses;

(iv) analysis of under/over-absorbed overhead is useful to identify inefficient utilisation of production resources.

50   Z LTD, THE RETAILER

(a)

	Total sales from 1 module £	Total sales from 2 modules £	Incremental sales from 2nd module £
Range A	6,750	2 × 6,250 = 12,500	5,750
Range B	3,500	2 × 3,150 = 6,300	2,800
Range C	4,800	2 × 4,600 = 9,200	4,400
Range D	6,400	2 × 5,200 = 10,400	4,000
Range E	3,333	2 × 3,667 = 7,334	4,001

Note that the sales figures in the question are per module. For instance for Range A if there is only 1 module the sales are £6,750. If there are 2 modules the sales are £6,250 per module, ie, £12,500 in total, of which £6,750 comes from the 1st module, therefore £5,750 (the remainder) must come from the 2nd module.

Modules	Sales £	C/S Ratio	Contribution per module £	Priority
Range A - No 1	6,750	20%	1,350	3rd
No 2	5,750	20%	1,150	5th
Range B - No 1	3,500	40%	1,400	2nd
No 2	2,800	40%	1,120	6th
Range C - No 1	4,800	25%	1,200	4th
No 2	4,400	25%	1,100	7th
Range D - No 1	6,400	25%	1,600	1st
No 2	4,000	25%	1,000	
Range E - No 1	3,333	30%	999.9	
No 2	4,001	30%	1,200.3	

Note that although the 2nd module for range E provides a contribution of £1,200.3, in order to open the 2nd module, the first must also be opened. The net result is an increase in contribution of £2,200.2, in effect an average increase of £1,100.1 per module. This increase is not as good as Range B module 2 and Range C module 2.

(b)   Operating costs are £5,600 per week for 7 modules = £800 per week per module.

Range	Contribution £	Operating costs £	Profit £
A	2,500	1,600	900
B	2,520	1,600	920
C	2,300	1,600	700
D	1,600	800	800
			3,320

(c)   A limiting factor is that factor which prevents a company from achieving the level of activity that it would wish. Examples of possible limiting factors include sales demand, machine capacity, availability of skilled labour, etc.

When preparing a budget or any other plan, the starting point is usually the limiting factor as this sets the overall level of activity for the business. For instance, for most companies the limiting factor is sales demand and the sales budget would therefore be the starting point for the budgeting process. Once the sales budget has been completed the company will then be able to determine the required production and thus the required material usage, etc.

With limiting factor decisions, the 'rule' is to maximise the contribution per unit of scarce resource. If a resource is in short supply, it makes sense to ensure the greatest return from each unit of that resource.

51   SWISH RESTAURANT

(a)   **Calculation of number of meals required to be sold to earn a profit of £300 per week**

$$\text{Sales volume required} = \frac{\text{Fixed costs} + \text{Required profit}}{\text{Contribution per meal}}$$

		£	£
Fixed costs - Staff			200
Building occupancy			460
			660

Contribution per meal:

Selling price (average volume = $\frac{2,800}{4}$ = 700)   4.00

Variable costs:

Materials $\frac{1,540}{700}$ 2.20

Power $\frac{280}{700}$ 0.40

Staff $\frac{340-200}{700}$ 0.20
                                                      ———
                                                      2.80
                                                      ———
Contribution per meal   1.20
                                                      ———

Sales volume required $= \frac{660+300}{1.20} = $ 800 meals
                                                  ————

*(**Tutorial note:** an alternative approach is to calculate the contribution sales ratio ie:*

	£	£
Sales		2,800
Variable costs:		
Materials	1,540	
Power	280	
Staff £(340 - 200)	140	
	———	1,960
Contribution		840

Contribution sales ratio $= \frac{\text{Contribution}}{\text{Sales}} \times 100$

$= \frac{840}{2,800} \times 100$

$= 30\%$

Sales value required $= \left(\frac{\text{Fixed}}{\text{costs}} + \frac{\text{Required}}{\text{profit}}\right) \times \frac{100}{\text{Contribution sales ratio}}$

$= (660 + 300) \times \frac{100}{30} = £3,200$

Sales volume $= \frac{£3,200}{£4}$

$=$ 800 meals
    ————

If unit data is provided it is best to show the answer in revenue and units.)

(b)   *(**Tutorial note:** the question is asking for:*

(i)   the additional profit from each of the two options; and
(ii)   the break-even sales volume for each of the two options.

It is necessary to identify the net effect on profit of selling take-away or high quality meals. This is complicated by the fact that the present meals in the restaurant are 'complementary' to the new proposals. Hence, one meal sold under, for example, the take-away option increases contribution in two ways, ie.

(i)   contribution earned on the take-away meal itself; and
(ii)   contribution earned from additional sales in the restaurant.

To derive the figures required by the examiner it is advisable to show contribution per meal as the total of these two effects.

A second problem is that the cost structure is different for each alternative (staff costs). Hence, contribution per meal must be calculated for each proposal.)

The bulk discount is going to take effect in two stages:

(i)   a 'lump sum' reduction of 700 meals @ 10p on meals;
(ii)   a 10p per meal reduction on all additional meals.

This may be demonstrated graphically:

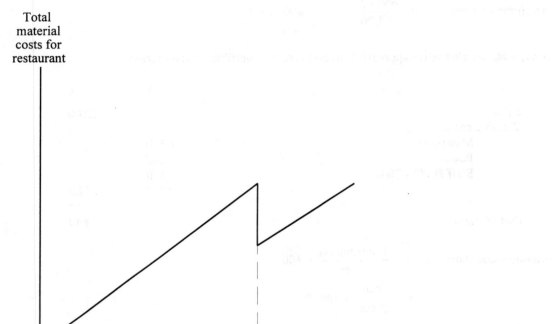

(i)   **Take-away meals**

	Contribution from take-away meals £		Contribution from present restaurant meals £	£
Selling price	1.60			4.00
Variable costs	0.85			
Materials			2.20	
			(0.10)	
Power			0.40	
				2.50
Contribution per meal	0.75			1.50

Ten take-away meals sold will increase present sales by one.

One take-away meal sold will increase sales by $\frac{1}{10}$ of a meal.
Effective increase in contribution from selling one take-away meal = £0.75 + $\left(\frac{1}{10} \times £1.50 \right)$ = £0.90.

		£	£
(A)	Contribution from selling 720 take-away meals 720 × £0.90		648
	Bulk material discount 700 × £0.10	70	
	Incremental fixed costs	(610)	
			(540)
	Net increase in profit		108

(B) Break-even sales volume $= \dfrac{\text{Fixed costs}}{\text{Contribution per meal}}$

$= \dfrac{610-70}{0.90}$

$= 600$ meals

(ii)   **High quality meals**

	Contribution from take-away meals	Contribution from present restaurant meals	
	£	£	£
Selling price	6.00		4.00
Variable costs	4.66		
Materials		2.20	
		(0.10)	
Power		0.40	
Staff		0.20	
			2.70
Contribution per meal	1.34		1.30

Incremental/extra contribution from selling one high quality meal $= £1.34 + \left(\tfrac{1}{5} \times £1.30\right) = £1.60$

		£	£
(A)	Contribution from selling 200 high quality meals 200 × £1.60		320
	Less: Fixed costs	(282)	
	Bulk material discount	70	
			(212)
	Net increase in profit		108

(B) Break-even sales volume $= \dfrac{282-70}{£1.60}$

$= 133$ meals

(c)   *(Tutorial note:* when asked to comment on these proposed courses of action the two primary pieces of information to consider are:

(i)   estimated profits; and
(ii)   break-even point and margin of safety.

In this particular question it is also necessary to consider the effect of the possible 20% change (higher or lower) in estimated sales volume.)

Conclusions which may be drawn from the calculations in (b)

(i)   Profits will be the same under both proposals if the estimated volume is achieved.

(ii)		*Take-away meals*	*High quality meals*
Margin of safety:			
Estimated sales			
Less: Break-even sales		720 - 600 = 120 meals	200 - 133 = 67 meals
Margin of safety ratio:			

$$\frac{\text{Margin of safety}}{\text{Estimated sales}} \times 100 \qquad \frac{120}{720} \times 100 = 17\% \qquad \frac{67}{200} \times 100 = 33\%$$

These figures illustrate that the take-away option comes with a higher risk of losses being incurred.

On the basis of the estimate of 20% given in the question, if sales were 20% below the estimated level, the restaurant would be worse off by [£108 - (720 × 20% × 0.90)] ie, £22 than it would be without selling take-away meals. If sales were 20% less than estimated for the high quality option, profits would still be increased above existing levels.

(iii)   If sales were 20% higher, estimated incremental profits would be increased to:

	Take-away meals £	*High quality meals* £
Original estimate	108.00	108.00
20% contribution increase:		
720 × 20% × 0.90	129.60	
200 × 20% × 1.60		64.00
	237.60	172.00

Hence, the take-away option offers the chance of earning higher overall profits but involves the risk of profits being reduced below existing levels.

52   STOBO PLC

(a)   Product costs/unit:

	Product X		*Product Y*	
Volume	5,600	1,400	3,200	1,600
	£	£	£	£
Material cost	4.50	6.00	26.00	30.00
Wages cost (W3):				
Making	8.19	12.80	16.20	18.00
Finishing	5.76	9.00	12.15	13.50
Variable overheads:				
Making (200%)	16.38	25.60	32.40	36.00
Finishing (250%)	14.40	22.50	30.38	33.75
Variable costs/unit	49.23	75.90	117.13	131.25
Selling price	75.00	75.00	150.00	150.00
Contribution/unit	25.77	(0.90)	32.87	18.75

Total gross contribution (W4)	£144,312	(£1,260)	£105,184	£30,000
Demand probability	0.6	0.4	0.3	0.7
Expected gross contribution	£86,587	(£504)	£31,555	£21,000
Expected product gross contribution		£86,083		£52,555
Relevant avoidable fixed costs		£36,000		£5,000
Expected relevant profit		£50,083		£47,555

Product X is preferred because it has the higher expected relevant profit.

(b)   If the maximum labour hours must be paid for then it is a fixed cost and the contribution/unit must be adjusted:

	Product X		Product Y	
Volume	5,600	1,400	3,200	1,600
	£	£	£	£
Contribution/unit (a)	25.77	(0.90)	32.87	18.75
Add:				
Wages cost:				
Making	8.19	12.80	16.20	18.00
Finishing	5.76	9.00	12.15	13.50
Revised contribution/unit	39.72	20.90	61.22	50.25
Total gross contribution (W4)	£222,432	£29,260	£195,904	£80,400
Demand probability	0.6	0.4	0.3	0.7
Expected gross contribution	£133,459	£11,704	£58,771	£56,280
Expected product gross contribution		£145,163		£115,051
Relevant avoidable fixed costs		£36,000		£5,000
Expected relevant profit		£109,163		£110,051

Product Y now has the higher expected profit value and may be preferred.

WORKINGS

(W1)   Average unit times - Product X:

700 units	=	7 hours	
1,400 units	=	80% of 7 hours	= 5.6 hours
2,800 units	=	80% of 5.6 hours	= 4.48 hours
5,600 units	=	80% of 4.48 hours	= 3.584 hours

(W2)   Average unit times - Product Y:

800 units	=	9 hours	
1,600 units	=	90% of 9 hours	= 8.1 hours
3,200 units	=	90% of 8.1 hours	= 7.29 hours

(W3)   Making: X 5,600 = $\frac{4}{7}$ × £4 ×   3.584 hours   =   £8.19
                 X 1,400 = $\frac{4}{7}$ × £4 ×   5.6 hours   =   £12.80
                 Y 3,200 = $\frac{5}{9}$ × £4 ×   7.29 hours   =   £16.20
                 Y 1,600 = $\frac{5}{9}$ × £4 ×   8.1 hours   =   £18.00

        Finishing: X 5,600 = $\frac{3}{7}$ × £3.75 × 3.584 hours =   £5.76
                   X 1,400 = $\frac{3}{7}$ × £3.75 × 5.6 hours   =   £9.00
                   Y 3,200 = $\frac{4}{9}$ × £3.75 × 7.29 hours   =   £12.15
                   Y 1,600 = $\frac{4}{9}$ × £3.75 × 8.1 hours   =   £13.50

(W4)   Contribution/unit × volume

53   A LTD

(a)

	Product I £'000	Product II £'000	Product III £'000	Total £'000
Sales	2,475	3,948	1,520	7,943
Contribution	1,170	1,692	532	3,394
Attributable fixed costs	(275)	(337)	(296)	(908)
General fixed costs	(520)	(829)	(319)	(1,668)
	(795)	(1,166)	(615)	(2,576)
Profit	375	526	(83)	(818)
	= £1.6/unit	= £1.40/unit	= (£0.04/unit)	

(b)   If Product III is discontinued it may be assumed that, as well as variable costs, the fixed costs attributable to the product would be saved. The term 'attributable' fixed costs refers to costs which, although not variable with activity in the short-term, are directly incurred by a particular product and thus should be avoidable in the event of the activity ceasing altogether. However, an important question is whether the cost quoted is the true opportunity cost.

It is reasonable to assume that the level of general fixed costs would be unaffected by Product III's discontinuation as they are not specific to the product. Over time, however, it could be expected that they would be affected to some extent by large changes in activity.

The analysis would be as follows:

	£'000
Contribution of Products I and II	2,862
Attributable fixed costs of Products I and II	(612)
General fixed costs	(1,668)
	(2,280)
Profit	582

Thus profit would be reduced by £236,000, the net contribution (variable contribution minus attributable fixed costs) budgeted for Product III (ie, £532,000 – £296,000).

(c)   On the assumption that all existing fixed costs would be unaffected by any change in activity the extra sales units required would be:

$$\frac{£80,000 \text{ expenditure}}{£5.20 \text{ contribution per unit}} = 15,385$$

(d)   As with (iii) above it is reasonable to assume that fixed costs would be unaffected by the change in activity. Product contribution would become:

Selling price	£9.45/unit
Variable cost	6.00
Contribution	3.45

Required sales would be:

$$\frac{£1,692,000}{£3.45} \quad \frac{\text{existing total contribution}}{\text{new contribution per unit}}$$

= 490,435 units, an increase of 30.4%
over the budgeted sales of 376,000 units

---

54   RANGE OF PRODUCTS

(a)

Process

	Units	£		Units	£
Direct materials	5,000	14,700	Normal loss	150	150
Direct materials		13,830	Closing WIP (W1)	800	5,160
Direct wages		6,555	Abnormal loss (W1)	120	696
Production overhead		7,470	Output (W1)	3,930	36,549
	5,000	42,555		5,000	42,555

(b)

Abnormal loss

	£		£
Process	696	Normal loss (W2)	120
		P&L a/c	576
	696		696

WORKINGS

(W1)   **Equivalent units table**

	Total	Input %	Input eu	Material added %	Material added eu	Wages %	Wages eu	Ohd %	Ohd eu
Normal loss	150	0	-	0	-	0	-	0	-
Closing WIP	800	100	800	75	600	50	400	25	200
Abnormal loss	120	100	120	$66\frac{2}{3}$	80	$33\frac{1}{3}$	40	$16\frac{2}{3}$	20
Output	3,930	100	3,930	100	3,930	100	3,930	100	3,930
			4,850		4,610		4,370		4,150

	£	£	£	£
Costs	14,700	13,830	6,555	7,470
Normal loss scrap val	(150)			
	£14,550	£13,830	£6,555	£7,470
£/eu		£3	£3	£1.50	£1.80

Valuations

Closing WIP	£5,160	2,400	1,800	600	360
Abnormal loss	£696	360	240	60	36
Output	£36,549	11,790	11,790	5,895	7,074

The output quantity is a balancing figure from the process account.

(W2)

Normal loss

	£		£
Process	150	Bank (W3)	270
Abnormal loss	120		
	270		270

(W3)   Actual loss of 270 units @ £1 each

---

55   AMAZON PLC

(a) $\text{Cost per kg} = \dfrac{\text{Total cost} - \text{Scrap value of normal loss}}{\text{Expected output}}$

$= \dfrac{3,500 + 4,340 - (700 \times 0.40)}{7,000 - (10\% \times 7,000)}$

$= £1.20/\text{kg}$

Transfer to process 2 = 6,430 kg × 1.20 = £7,716

Expected output	= 7,000 − (10% × 7,000) =	6,300 kg
Actual output		6,430 kg
Abnormal gain		130 kg

Net gain = 130 kg × (1.20 − 0.40) = £104

(b)   *Costs of process 2*

		£
Transfer from process 1	6,430 × 1.20	7,716
Labour and overhead		12,129
		19,845
Less net income of by-product (1.80 − 0.30) × 430		645
		19,200

(i)

	Weight of output kg		Share of joint costs £
E	2,000	$\dfrac{2,000}{6,000} \times 19,200$	6,400
F	4,000	$\dfrac{4,000}{6,000} \times 19,200$	12,800
	6,000		19,200

Cost/kg

Type E	£6,400/2,000kg = £3.20/kg
Type F	£12,800/4,000kg = £3.20/kg

Profits/(losses)

Type E	1,100kg × (7 − 3.20) = £4,180
Type F	3,200kg × (2.50 − 3.20) = (£2,240)

Stock values

Type E	(2,000 kg − 1,100kg) × 3.20 = £2,880
Type F	(4,000kg − 3,200kg) × 3.20 = £2,560

(ii)

	Market value of output £		Share of joint costs £
Type E	2,000kg × £7 = 14,000	14/24 × 19,200	11,200
Type F	4,000kg × £2.50 = 10,000	10/24 × 19,200	8,000
	24,000		19,200

Cost/kg

Type E	£11,200/2,000kg =	£5.60/kg
Type F	£8,000/4,000kg =	£2/kg

Profits

Type E	(7 − 5.60) × 1,100kg =	£1,540
Type F	(2.50 − 2) × 3,200kg =	£1,600

Stock values

Type E	(2,000kg − 1,100kg) × 5.60 =	£5,040
Type F	(4,000kg − 3,200kg) × 2 =	£1,600

(c)   The main purpose of apportioning joint costs is for financial reporting. We apportion the joint costs in order to calculate the stock value and the cost of sales. The main problem is that the choice of apportionment method is subjective and can have a profound effect on stock values and profits. For instance in part (b) above:

(1)   Type E was valued at £3.20/kg or £5.60/kg and gave a profit of £4,180 or £1,540.
(2)   Type F was valued at £3.20/kg or £2/kg and gave a loss of £2,240 or a profit of £1,600.

56   JOBBING COMPANY

Tutorial note: this question involves identifying what is wrong with the method used for calculating the cost of jobs. The main things to note are that

(1)   a single 'blanket' recovery rate (47.5%) is used for all overheads;
(2)   the fact the company uses total cost as the lowest acceptable selling price; and
(3)   a recession is imminent making (2) a dangerous approach to use.

(a)   **Criticism of method for estimating costs**

The essential feature of job costing is that all jobs are potentially different. The cost is therefore likely to differ. The method used for charging costs to jobs should aim at reflecting the incidence of the costs ie the costs caused by the job. In this case all overheads are charged to products on the basis of a single blanket recovery rate of 47.5% of direct materials and direct labour. It is extremely unlikely that such a direct method will provide an accurate basis for charging overheads eg if higher priced higher quality material is used the amount of variable overhead may be less if, for example, less labour time is needed to work on the better quality material. The above absorption rate would result in a higher overhead charge.

Similarly it may be that direct labour rates vary in which case higher wage rates would **not** necessarily result in higher overheads being incurred whereas with this method more overhead is charged to the job.

Another weakness of the existing system is that no attempt is made to split cost between fixed and variable. With the imminent recession it will be extremely important for managers to know the variable cost of jobs so that, with increased competition, it is possible to quote lower prices which will still generate contribution. If the existing total cost plus pricing system is continued the company is likely to start losing jobs to competitors.

As shown for job no. 878 the current system is to use total cost ie fixed cost and variable costs, as the lowest acceptable price. This is misleading since the lowest price should be as mentioned above the variable cost. This is because a price above variable cost will generate contribution which will increase profit/reduce losses. In a time of recession the firm may be forced to accept very low prices in order to win orders from customers.

A further criticism is the method for calculating the mark up of 47.5%. This is based on the actual costs for the year just ended.

$$\left(\text{ie, } \frac{383,000 + 118,500 + 192,000}{1,000,000 + 460,000} \times 100 = 47.5\% \right)$$

There are several factors which will result in costs being different in the current period from the previous period:

(i)   The level of activity may be lower – this will cause average fixed overheads to increase as a proportion of direct costs.

(ii)   Inefficiency may have arisen in the previous year which is not expected to recur.

(iii)   Inflation would cause the level of costs to alter.

(iv)   Changes in production method may have occurred.

(b)   In this circumstance it would be more accurate to calculate separate production overhead recovery rates for each of the production departments ideally based on budgeted figures. Direct labour hours or machine hours would be suitable bases for recovery but the information given means direct labour hours must be used below:

Based on last year's actual figures	*Grinding*	*Finishing*
Direct labour hours	$\dfrac{200,000}{5} = 40,000$	$\dfrac{260,000}{6} = 43,333$

Overhead recovery rates $= \dfrac{\text{Overhead}}{\text{Direct labour cost}} \times 100$ $\dfrac{175,000}{40,000} = £4.375 \text{ per hour}$ $\dfrac{208,000}{43,333} = £4.80 \text{ per hour}$

Administration and selling costs, as a percentage of production costs

$$\frac{118,500 + 192,000}{1,000,000 + 460,000 + 383,000} \times 100 = 16.85\%$$

$$\text{Mark up} = \frac{\text{net profit}}{\text{sales}} \times 100 = \frac{246,500}{2,400,000} \times 100 = 10.27\%$$

Revised estimate for job 878

		£	£
Direct material			9,000
Direct labour			3,800
Production overhead:			
Grinding:	400 × 4.375 =	1,750	
Finishing:	300 × 4.80 =	1,440	3,190
			15,990
Admin. and selling costs			
16.85% × 15,990 =			2,694
Revised total cost			18,684
Mark up 10.27% × 18,684 =			1,919
Revised selling price			20,603

or if based on 'preferred return'

Cost	$83\tfrac{1}{3}$
Mark up	$16\tfrac{2}{3}$
Selling price	100

Selling price $= 18,684 \times \dfrac{100}{83\tfrac{1}{3}} = £22,421$

(c)   The following changes should be made to improve the accounting information:

(i)   Preparation of budgets. This would include calculation of predetermined overhead recovery rates and a separation of fixed and variable costs. The latter will be needed to identify the minimum acceptable selling price for each job. This will enable adoption of a more flexible attitude to pricing (ie, not just use a margin of $16\tfrac{2}{3}\%$) which will be particularly important in the recession when prices may need to be determined by demand.

(ii)   When actual costs are available for each job these should be compared with budget to identify variances. These variances may indicate that current activities must be amended or that it is necessary to vary future estimates.

(iii)   It could be beneficial to obtain information about competitors eg costs, profits, quality of product and selling prices charged.

(iv)   It may be possible to establish more accurate job costs by using activity based costing.

9 NEW SYLLABUS EXAMINATIONS

JUNE 1994 QUESTIONS

Section A – This question is compulsory and MUST be attempted

57 (Question 1 of examination)

1   Netherby plc manufactures a range of camping and leisure equipment, including tents. It is currently experiencing severe quality control problems at its existing fully-depreciated factory in the south of England. These difficulties threaten to undermine its reputation for producing high quality products. It has recently been approached by the European Bank for Reconstruction and Development, on behalf of a tent manufacturer in Hungary, which is seeking a UK-based trading partner which will import and distribute its tents. Such a switch would involve shutting down the existing manufacturing operation in the UK and converting it into a distribution depot. The estimated exceptional restructuring costs of £5m would be tax-allowable, but would exert serious strains on cash flow.

Importing, rather than manufacturing tents appears inherently profitable as the buying-in price, when converted into sterling, is less than the present production cost. In addition, Netherby considers that the Hungarian product would result in increased sales, as the existing retail distributors seem impressed with the quality of the samples which they have been shown. It is estimated that for a five-year contract, the annual cash flow benefit would be around £2m pa before tax.

However, the financing of the closure and restructuring costs would involve careful consideration of the financing options. Some directors argue that dividends could be reduced as several competing companies have already done a similar thing, while other directors argue for a rights issue. Alternatively, the project could be financed by an issue of long-term loan stock at a fixed rate of 12%.

The most recent balance sheet shows £5m of issued share capital (par value 50p), while the market price per share is currently £3. A leading security analyst has recently described Netherby's gearing ratio as 'adventurous'. Profit-after-tax in the year just ended was £15m and dividends of £10m were paid.

The rate of corporation tax is 33%, payable with a one-year delay. Netherby's reporting year coincides with the calendar year and the factory will be closed at the year end. Closure costs would be incurred shortly before deliveries of the imported product began, and sufficient stocks will be on hand to overcome any initial supply problems. Netherby considers that it should earn a return on new investment projects of 15% pa net of all taxes.

Required

(a)   Is the closure of the existing factory financially worthwhile for Netherby?   (5 marks)

(b)   Explain what is meant when the capital market is said to be information-efficient in a semi-strong form.

       If the stock market is semi-strong efficient and without considering the method of finance, calculate the likely impact of acceptance and announcement of the details of this project to the market on Netherby's share price.   (6 marks)

(c)   Advise the Netherby board as to the relative merits of a rights issue rather than a cut in dividends to finance this project.   (6 marks)

(d)   Explain why a rights issue generally results in a fall in the market price of shares.

   If a rights issue is undertaken, calculate the resulting impact on the existing share price of issue prices of £1 per share and £2 per share, respectively. (You may ignore issue costs.)   (6 marks)

(e)   Assuming the restructuring proposal meets expectations, assess the impact of the project on earnings per share if it is financed by a rights issue at an offer price of £2 per share, and loan stock, respectively.

   (Again, you may ignore issue costs.)   (4 marks)

(f)   Briefly consider the main operating risks connected with the investment project, and how Netherby might attempt to allow for these.   (8 marks)
   (Total 35 marks)

Section B – This question is compulsory and MUST be attempted

Answer five of the six parts of this question

---
58   (Question 2 of examination)
---

2   (a)   Briefly explain, with examples, the nature and purpose of 'supply-side economic policies'.   (5 marks)

(b)   'The financial manager needs to identify and realise surplus assets.' Explain briefly the benefits to an organisation of adopting this policy.   (5 marks)

(c)   Name and comment on the factors which should be considered in the establishment of a normal loss in a process costing environment.   (5 marks)

(d)   Explain ways in which the management accountant can monitor the effects of the external environment in which their firm operates.   (5 marks)

(e)   'We have a budget of £196,000 for the service which we are providing this year. I propose we put in for that plus the rate of inflation for our next year's budget allocation.' Critically evaluate the above comment and explain briefly how zero-based-budgeting (ZBB) could help to avoid such a situation.(5 marks)

(f)   Explain briefly how time series analysis can assist the management accountant.   (5 marks)
   (Total 25 marks)

Section C – ONE question ONLY to be attempted

---
59   (Question 3 of examination)
---

3   The Perseus Co Ltd a medium sized company, produces a single product in its one overseas factory. For control purposes, a standard costing system was recently introduced and is now in operation.

The standards set for the month of May were as follows:

Production and sales	16,000 units
Selling price (per unit)	£140

Materials

- Material 007   6 kilos per unit at £12.25 per kilo
- Material XL90   3 kilos per unit at £3.20 per kilo

Labour

4.5 hours per unit at £8.40 per hour

— marginal costing.

Overheads (all fixed) £86,400 per month, they are not absorbed into the product costs.

The actual data for the month of May, is as follows:

Produced 15,400 units which were sold at £138.25 each.

Materials

Used 98,560 kilos of material 007 at a total cost of £1,256,640 and used 42,350 kilos of material XL90 at a total cost of £132,979.

Labour

Paid an actual rate of £8.65 per hour to the labour force. The total amount paid out, amounted to £612,766.

Overheads (all fixed)

£96,840

Required

(a)   Prepare a standard costing profit statement, and a profit statement based on actual figures for the month of May.   (6 marks)

(b)   Prepare a statement of the variances which reconciles the actual with the standard profit or loss figure.   (9 marks)

(c)   Explain briefly the possible reasons for inter-relationships between material variances and labour variances.   (5 marks)
                                                                                                                                (Total 20 marks)

60 (Question 4 of examination)

4   Cepheus Transport Co Ltd currently does around 60% of its work for its holding company and the remainder for a small number of local manufacturers. It operates from a garage and warehouse complex located close to an airport and within two hours drive of the nearest seaport.

Their management accounting information is very limited and what they do have is shown below for the quarter which has just ended:

Type of vehicle	Type F	Type P	Type U	
Number of vehicles owned	8	4	7	
Mileage	*Miles*	*Miles*	*Miles*	
Holding company work	26,000	8,120	12,080	
Work for other companies	14,600	7,400	12,400	

Revenue	£	£	£	£
From holding company	47,450	13,601	14,798	75,849
From other companies	46,720	19,573	23,560	89,853
	94,170	33,174	38,358	165,702

Operating costs	£	£	£	£
Fuel (diesel at £2 per gallon)	4,368	1,404	1,752	7,524
Drivers' wages				
Fixed	12,800	6,000	10,500	29,300
Variable	7,200	1,625	3,750	12,575
Overtime premium	1,200	250	500	1,950
Other operating costs and maintenance costs	4,415	2,371	2,604	9,390
Fixed costs of vehicles (including insurance etc.)	3,850	2,142	2,881	8,873
*Depreciation	9,000	3,000	4,000	16,000
	42,833	16,792	25,987	85,612

* Depreciation is charged at 20% of cost per annum, taking a full year's depreciation in the year of purchase and none in the year of sale.

The company's administrative costs, garage and warehouse rent and other fixed overheads amounted to £58,220.

Edith Cepheus, the chief executive, has assured you that this data is quite typical and that to date the company has not experienced any violent fluctuations in trading conditions.

Required

Prepare a report for submission to Mrs Cepheus in which, from the limited supply of data available, you evaluate and comment on current performance and explain how the company can improve its recording system to assist them with planning, control and decision-making.

(20 marks)

Section D – ONE question ONLY to be attempted

---

61   (Question 5 of examination)

---

5   Ewden plc is a medium-sized company producing a range of engineering products which it sells to wholesale distributors. Recently, its sales have begun to rise rapidly following a general recovery in the economy as a whole. However, it is concerned about its liquidity position and is contemplating ways of improving its cash flow. Ewden's accounts for the past two years are summarised below.

Profit and loss account for the year ended 31 December

	1992 £'000	1993 £'000
Sales	12,000	16,000
Cost of sales	7,000	9,150
Operating profit	5,000	6,850
Interest	200	250
Profit before tax	4,800	6,600
Taxation*	1,000	1,600
Profit after tax	3,800	5,000
Dividends	1,500	2,000
Retained profit	2,300	3,000

* After capital allowances

Balance sheet as at 31 December

	1992 £'000	1992 £'000	1993 £'000	1993 £'000
Fixed assets (net)		9,000		12,000
Current assets				
Stock	1,400		2,200	
Debtors	1,600		2,600	
Cash	1,500		100	
		4,500		4,900
Current liabilities				
Overdraft	–		200	
Trade creditors	1,500		2,000	
Other creditors	500		200	
		(2,000)		(2,400)
10% Loan stock		(2,000)		(2,000)
Net assets		9,500		12,500
Ordinary shares (50p)		3,000		3,000
Profit and loss account		6,500		9,500
Shareholders' funds		9,500		12,500

In order to speed up collection from debtors, Ewden is considering two alternative policies. One option is to offer a 2% discount to customers who settle within 10 days of despatch of invoices rather than the normal 30 days offered. It is estimated that 50% of customers would take advantage of this offer. Alternatively, Ewden can utilise the services of a factor. The factor will operate on a service-only basis, administering and collecting payment from Ewden's customers. This is expected to generate administrative savings of £100,000 pa and, it is hoped, will also shorten the debtor days to an average of 45. The factor will make a service charge of 1.5% of Ewden's turnover. Ewden can borrow from its bankers at an interest rate of 18% pa.

Required

(a)   Identify the reasons for the sharp decline in Ewden's liquidity and assess the extent to which the company can be said to be exhibiting the problem of 'overtrading'.

Illustrate your answer by reference to key performance and liquidity ratios computed from Ewden's accounts.   (13 marks)

(Note: it is not necessary to compile a FRS 1 statement.)

(b)   Determine the relative costs and benefits of the two methods of reducing debtors, and recommend an appropriate policy.   (7 marks)
                                                                                         (Total 20 marks)

62   (Question 6 of examination)

6   (a)   Explain how inflation affects the rate of return required on an investment project, and the distinction between a real and a nominal (or 'money terms') approach to the evaluation of an investment project under inflation.   (4 marks)

(b)   Howden plc is contemplating investment in an additional production line to produce its range of compact discs. A market research study, undertaken by a well-known firm of consultants, has revealed scope to sell an additional output of 400,000 units pa. The study cost £0.1 m but the account has not yet been settled.

The price and cost structure of a typical disc (net of royalties), is as follows:

	£	£
Price per unit		12.00
Costs per unit of output		
Material cost per unit	1.50	
Direct labour cost per unit	0.50	
Variable overhead cost per unit	0.50	
Fixed overhead cost per unit	1.50	
		(4.00)
Profit		8.00

The fixed overhead represents an apportionment of central administrative and marketing costs. These are expected to rise in total by £500,000 pa as a result of undertaking this project. The production line is expected to operate for five years and require a total cash outlay of £11m, including £0.5m of materials stocks. The equipment will have a residual value of £2m. Because the company is moving towards a JIT stock management policy, it is expected that this project will involve steadily reducing working capital needs, expected to decline at about 3% pa by volume. The production line will be accommodated in a presently empty building for which an offer of £2m has recently been received from another company. If the building is retained, it is expected that property price inflation will increase its value to £3m after five years.

While the precise rates of price and cost inflation are uncertain, economists in Howden's corporate planning department make the following forecasts for the average annual rates of inflation relevant to the project:

Retail Price Index	6% pa
Disc prices	5% pa
Material prices	3% pa
Direct labour wage rates	7% pa
Variable overhead costs	7% pa
Other overhead costs	5% pa

Note: you may ignore taxes and capital allowances in this question.

Required

Given that Howden's shareholders require a real return of 8.5% for projects of this degree of risk, assess the financial viability of this proposal. (10 marks)

(c)   Briefly discuss how inflation may complicate the analysis of business financial decisions.

(6 marks)

(Total 20 marks)

EXAMINER'S COMMENTS

General comments

There were two common reasons why candidates performed badly on this paper: insufficient preparation for the examination; and inability to read and answer the question set. In particular, many candidates were ill-equipped to answer the case study question.

In a large number of cases, candidates were particularly badly prepared for Financial Management topics, even for such a basic building block as investment appraisal.

Question 1: examined various areas connected with the effect of project financing on a company's share price.

In part (a), although there were a relatively easy five marks to be obtained here, many candidates seemed to overlook the word 'financially' in the question, and provided instead a lengthy discussion of the logistic aspects. There was ample indication in the question that an investment appraisal was required. For the majority who did conduct a NPV analysis (some offered payback or ARR), common errors were failure to allow for tax and failure to discount at 15% as instructed, using 12% instead, having apparently assumed debt financing. Where tax was allowed for, many candidates introduced 25% capital allowances. No mention of this was made in the question, and in many answers, the year 6 tax outflow mysteriously disappeared. Many answers attempted to incorporate interest outflows in the cash flow profile, betraying a fundamental misunderstanding of the distinction between an investment, a financial decision and the rationale for DCF analysis.

In part (b), many candidates wasted time by providing lengthy descriptions of all types of market efficiency. There was widespread misunderstanding of the meaning of information-efficient; it means that all publicly available information relevant to a company's future prospects is impounded in today's share price. Many candidates declared that it means that all information is available or that the market uses all available information, suggesting strong-form market efficiency. Candidates who understood the subject went on to explain that, in a semi-strong efficient market, it is impossible to make excess returns by trading on recently released information, and that the announcement of Netherby's new project would tend to raise share price as long as the market agrees with the company's assessment of the project (although this depends on how much information is released).

Too many candidates ignored the instruction in the question to abstract from the method of finance. Very few candidates went on to quantify the likely impact on share price. This would be done by spreading the NPV of the project across the existing number of shares or by applying the existing P/E ratio to the increase in EPS.

In part (c), the question implies an assessment of the case for a rights issue rather than a dividend cut, and hence a discussion of the pros and cons of the former. Many candidates did not understand the definition of a rights issue, confusing it with a scrip issue. Most answers gave only two or three good points, limiting their discussion to the respective implications for control, gearing and share price. Many compared a rights issue to other methods of raising equity, and many said that a rights issue does not affect gearing.

In part (d), the key word in the question is 'generally'. It is true that a rights issue can lead to a higher price if the market views the intended use of the funds with favour. More frequently, the share price falls initially, due to uncertainty over the proposed investment or other use of the funds. The second, and more technical, reason for a share price fall is earnings dilution due to issuing more shares and at a discount to the pre-issue market price which is necessary to make the issue look attractive and ensure its success.

There was widespread failure to identify the correct number of shares, the amount which the company would have to raise (it is clear from the question that any such rights issue would be undertaken to finance the restructuring project) and hence the terms of the issue. Most candidates assumed issue terms (eg,) 1-for-4, and then applied it to both cases. Even candidates who could identify the respective numbers of newly-issued shares were unable to compute the resulting theoretical ex-rights price.

In part (e), many candidates assumed that the project would replace all of Netherby's existing activities and that tent distribution would be the only source of income, an incorrect interpretation of the question. Any resulting calculation would show a dramatic reduction in EPS, although the answer would be consistent with the change in EPS due to the project and its financing, ie, equity financing of the project lowers the EPS by 19p from £1.50 to £1.31, and loan financing raises it by 9p to £1.59. Many answers ignored the impact of the project entirely. Although some credit was given to all these approaches, the highest marks were awarded to those who considered both impacts.

A common failing was to ignore taxation in the computation of the EPS. Another error was to work in terms of dividend per share.

Part (f), in many cases, was a lifeline for weaker candidates, but all too often candidates seemed unable to appreciate the distinction between operating or business risk and financial risk. This is fundamental in Managerial Finance. The former relates to factors which impact on operating profit such as security of supply, exchange rate variations, etc, and the latter to the impact of gearing in the financial structure. Marks were not awarded for discussing financial risk.

It was also important that candidates should offer a brief explanation/discussion of the factors they identified rather than a listing, and also suggest how the various risks may be allowed for, as clearly stated in the question.

Question 2: required 5 short written answers.

Part (a) was not well done. This type of question was clearly flagged in the Examiner's article in the *Students' Newsletter*, March 1994. The clear implication was that candidates have not prepared for the economics element of the syllabus. Of those who did attempt an answer, the vast majority confused supply-side policies with control of the money supply, or wrote vague generalities about supply and demand. Attention to the supply side was a keynote of US and UK economic policies in the 1980s, and has been adopted by many other nations. Candidates must develop a greater awareness of the prevailing economic environment and of government economic policy options and priorities.

In part (b), the majority of candidates performed well. However, some candidates failed to appreciate that there can be surplus fixed assets, current assets and investments and also failed to identify the benefits.

Part (c) was one of the questions where candidates did not answer the question set. The definition of a normal loss and its accounting treatment is covered in Paper 3. This question was an attempt to build on that knowledge and asked about the factors needed to be taken into account when establishing a normal loss in process costing.

In part (d), simply listing the definition of 'the environment' was not enough; the question asked how the management accountant monitors the external environment. For those who included the use of budgets and standards in their answer, it was important also to explain how they could assist in monitoring and possibly provide an example. The same is true of financial ratios, market research etc.

Part (e) required consideration of the two questions; one required a critical view of the existing budgeting system and the other an explanation as to how ZBB could overcome its deficiencies. Many candidates did not do justice to the first part and did not really explain how ZBB could overcome its deficiencies. Again, many candidates did not answer the question set but the one that they hoped would be set.

In part (f), most candidates were awarded approximately two or three marks. Although candidates only had to attempt five out of the six sections, many wasted valuable exam time by attempting all six parts. Another cohort of candidates did less than five parts, perhaps because of not revising the areas covered or a shortage of time.

Question 3: required candidates to calculate and comment on the inter-relations of variances in a manufacturing situation.

Overall this question was very well done and candidates did gain high marks.

There were a number of alternative answers which were acceptable eg, using a volume variance in the reconciliation where a flexed budget had not been used in part (a).

However, workings for this type of computational question are important, but it was evident that many candidates lost a lot of valuable exam time by the method they used to compute the variances. Workings for this type of question need to be clear and concise. In part (c), on inter-relationships, many candidates failed to gain marks because they did not look at the inter-relationships between the variances.

Question 4: dealt with interpreting management information.

This was not a very popular question and there were not many answers. Some candidates did not provide their answer in report form. Other failings included: few computations with the figures provided and no attempt to express costs as, for example, a cost per mile; no attempt to discuss the problems being caused by the holding company; and ignoring the request in the question to advise the company as to how it could improve its recording system.

Question 5: concentrated on ratio analysis and the management of working capital.

This question was poorly done, given that ratio analysis is also covered in Paper 1. In part (a), most answers offered a sprinkling of ratios, but often included largely irrelevant ones such as EPS, with little or no attempt to incorporate the figures into the answer. This required an analysis of the company's liquidity problems and an assessment of the extent to which it is overtrading. It was debatable whether many candidates actually understood the meaning of overtrading; relatively few defined, explained or illustrated it, using the figures provided.

Few answers spotted that the increase in fixed assets appeared to have been largely financed out of working capital and that the company now needed to raise long-term finance. The better candidates queried the wisdom of the dividend increase in these circumstances.

In part (b), the main errors were: failure to include the interest savings due to lower debtor levels under one or both options; confining the discount cost to the debtors figure rather than to 50% of the total sales. Few answers offered much in the way of a concluding assessment, although several went to the opposite (and unrewarding) extreme of giving no calculation at all, but providing a lengthy discussion of the pros and cons of each option. Many candidates omitted this section altogether.

Question 6: was concerned with investment appraisal and the impact of inflation upon decision making.

This was considerably less popular than question 5, but for candidates with good knowledge of DCF methods, offered relatively easy marks. In part (a), candidates seemed generally aware of the corrosive impact of inflation, and the need to achieve a higher nominal return, and were often able to reproduce the Fisher equation. However, very few were able to give a coherent distinction between the two approaches to project evaluation under inflation.

In part (b), candidates had some idea how to inflate cash flows. Common errors were: inclusion of the sunk cost; neglect of the opportunity cost of the building; neglect of the residual values of the equipment and/or building; failure to allow for working capital release, either with or without any adjustment; and over-inclusion of fixed overheads. However, the main and most culpable error was incorrect specification of the discount rate, even among those who had specified the Fisher equation correctly in section (a).

In part (c), candidates failed to read the wording of this section. Most answers were applied to investment decisions although this was not specified in the question, the intention being to elicit a broader appreciation of the problems which inflation inflicts on business financial decision-makers in general.

Those who discussed the problems of forecasting general inflation and also rates specific to investment projects were given credit but it was disappointing that so few answers went beyond this and drew to any extent upon knowledge of economics.

ANSWERS TO JUNE 1994 EXAMINATION

57   **(Answer 1 of examination)**

1   (a)   Assuming that the restructuring cost is a revenue item, and that all costs are incurred in year 0, the estimated cash flow profile is:

Cash flow profile (£m)

Item	0	1	2	3	4	5	6
			Year				
Closure costs	(5)						
Tax saving		1.65					
Cash flow increase		2.00	2.00	2.00	2.00	2.00	
Tax payment			(0.66)	(0.66)	(0.66)	(0.66)	(0.66)
	(5)	3.65	1.34	1.34	1.34	1.34	(0.66)

$$\text{NPV (£m)} = -5 + 1.65(\text{PVIF}_{15,1}) + 2(\text{PVIFA}_{15,5}) - 0.66(\text{PVIFA}_{15,6} - \text{PVIFA}_{15,1})$$

$$= -5 + 1.65(0.870) + 2(3.352) - 0.66(3.784 - 0.870)$$

$$= -5 + 1.44 + 6.70 - 1.92 = +1.22 \ (\text{ie}, +£1.22\text{m})$$

Hence, the restructuring appears worthwhile.

(b)   A semi-strong efficient capital market is one where security prices reflect all publicly-available information, including both the record of the past pattern of share price movements and all information released to the market about company earnings prospects. In such a market, security prices will rapidly adjust to the advent of new information relevant to the future income-earning capacity of the enterprise concerned, such as a change in its chief executive, or the signing of a new export order. As a result of the speed of the market's reaction to this type of news, it is not possible to make excess gains by trading in the wake of its release. Only market participants lucky enough already to be holding the share in question will achieve super-normal returns.

In the case of Netherby, when it releases information about its change in market-servicing policy, the value of the company should rise by the value of the project, assuming that the market as a whole agrees with the assessment of its net benefits, and is unconcerned by financing implications.

Net present value of the project = £1.22m

Number of 50p ordinary shares in issue = £5m × 2 = 10m shares

Increase in market price = £1.22m/10m = 12.2p per share.

(Alternatively, the answer could be expressed in terms of Netherby's price-earnings ratio. This would necessitate an assumption about Netherby's sustainable future earnings per share after tax).

(c)   Arguments for and against making a rights issue include the following:

For

(i)   A rights issue enables the company to at least maintain its dividends, thus avoiding both upsetting the clientele of shareholders, and also giving negative signals to the market.

(ii)   It may be easy to accomplish on a bull market.

(iii)   A rights issue automatically lowers the company's gearing ratio.

(iv)   The finance is guaranteed if the issue is fully underwritten.

(v)   It has a neutral impact on voting control, unless the underwriters are obliged to purchase significant blocks of shares, and unless existing shareholders sell their rights to other investors.

(vi)   It might give the impression that the company is expanding vigorously, although this appears not to be the case with Netherby.

Against

(i)   Rights issues normally are made at a discount, which usually involves diluting the historic earnings per share of existing shareholders. However, when the possible uses of the proceeds of the issue are considered, the *prospective* EPS could rise by virtue of investment in a worthwhile project, or in the case of a company earning low or no profits, the interest earnings on un-invested capital alone might serve to raise the EPS.

(ii)   Underwriters' fees and other administrative expenses of the issue may be costly, although the latter may be avoided by applying a sufficiently deep discount.

(iii)   The market is often sceptical about the reason for a rights issue, tending to assume that the company is desperate for cash. The deeper the discount involved, the greater the degree of scepticism.

(iv)   It is difficult to make a rights issue on a bear market, without leaving some of the shares with the underwriters. A rights issue which 'fails' in this respect is both bad for the company's image and may also result in higher underwriters' fees for any subsequent rights issue.

(v)   A rights issue usually forces shareholders to act, either by subscribing direct or by selling the rights, although the company may undertake to reimburse shareholders not subscribing to the issue for the loss in value of their shares. (This is done by selling the rights on behalf of shareholders and paying over the sum realised, net of dealing costs.)

(d)   (*Note:* candidates are not expected to display a knowledge of SSAP 3 which is the province of Paper 10).

A rights issue normally has to be issued at a discount in order, firstly, to make the shares appear attractive, but more importantly, to safeguard against a fall in the market price below the issue price prior to closure of the offer. If this should happen, the issue would fail as investors wishing to increase their stakes in the company could do so more cheaply by buying on the open market. Because of the discount, a rights issue has the effect of diluting the existing earnings per share across a larger number of shares, although the depressing effect on share price is partly countered by the increased cash holdings of the company.

The two possible issue prices are now evaluated:

(i)   *A price of £1*

It is assumed that to raise £5m, the company must issue £5m/£1 = 5m new shares at the issue price of £1.

In practice, it is possible that the number of new shares required might be lower than this, as the post-tax cost of the project is less than £5m due to the (delayed) tax savings generated. The company might elect to use short-term borrowing to bridge the delay in receiving these tax savings, thus obviating the need for the full £5m.

Ignoring this argument, the terms of the issue would be '1-for-2' ie, for every two shares currently held, owners are offered the right to purchase one new share at the deeply-discounted price of £1.

The ex-rights price will be:

[Market value of 2 shares before the issue + cash consideration]/3

$$= [(2 \times £3) + £1]/3 = £7/3 = £2.33$$

(ii) *Similarly, if the issue price is £2*, the required number of new shares = £5m/£2 = 2.5m, and the terms will have to be '1 -for-4'

The ex-rights price will be [(4 × £3) + £2]/5 = £14/5 = £2.80.

Clearly, the smaller the discount to the market price, the higher the ex-rights price.

(e) Ignoring the impact of the benefits of the new project:

The rights issue at £2 involves 2.5m new shares.

The EPS was £15m/10m = £1.50p per share.

Hence, EPS becomes $\dfrac{£15m}{10m + 2.5m} = £1.20$

With the debt financing, the interest charge net of tax = [12% × £5m] [1 − 33%] = £0.40m

Hence, EPS becomes $\dfrac{£15m − £0.40m}{10m} = £1.46$

Allowing for the benefits of the new project

The annual profit yielded by the proposal, after tax at 33% = (£2m × 0.67) = £1.34m, although the cash flow benefit in the first year is £2m due to the tax delay.

After the rights issue, the prospective EPS will become:

[£15m + £1.34m]/12.5m = £1.31 per share

With debt finance, the financing cost, net of tax relief, of £0.40m pa reduces the net return from the project to (£1.34m − £0.40m) = £0.94m pa.

(In the first year, the cash flow cost will be the full pre-tax interest payment. Thereafter, Netherby will receive annual cash flow benefits from the series of tax savings.)

The EPS will be: £15.94m/10m = £1.59 per share.

Therefore, in terms of the effect on EPS, the debt-financing alternative is preferable, although it may increase financial risk.

(f) A range of factors could be listed here. Among the major sources of risk are the following:

(i) *Reliability of supply.* This can be secured by inclusion of penalty clauses in the contract, although these will have to be enforceable. The intermediation of the European Bank for Reconstruction and Development may enhance this.

(ii) *The quality of the product.* Again, a penalty clause may assist, although a more constructive approach might be to assign a UK-trained total quality management (TQM) expert to the Hungarian operation to oversee quality control.

(iii)   *Market resistance to an imported product.* This seems less of a risk, if retailers are genuinely impressed with the product, and especially as there are doubts over the quality of the existing product.

(iv)   *Exchange rate variations.* Netherby is exposed to the risk of sterling depreciating against the Hungarian currency, thus increasing the sterling cost of the product. There are various ways of hedging against foreign exchange risk, of which use of the forward market is probably the simplest. Alternatively, Netherby could try to match the risk by finding a Hungarian customer for its other goods.

(v)   *Renewal of the contract.* What is likely to happen after five years? To obtain a two-way protection, Netherby might write into the contract an option to renew after five years. If the product requires re-design, Netherby could offer to finance part of the costs in exchange for this option.

58   (Answer 2 of examination)

2   (a)   As the difficulties of aggregate demand management (eg, crowding out of the private sector by the public sector, and the inflationary dangers of financing a state deficit) have become more apparent, governments have increasingly turned to 'Monetarist' policy nostrums, which, *inter alia,* urge the removal of barriers to the free flow of resources between alternative uses. So-called supply-side policies are designed to allow the supply of goods and services to adjust rapidly and smoothly to alterations in the pattern of demand, as expressed by the signals emitted by freely-functioning markets ie, prices.

Monetarists argue that a dynamic economy can only operate efficiently if market prices offer clear signals to resource owners regarding their most profitable uses. Rather than using budgetary policies to manage demand, they argue that the authorities should create a stable, non-inflationary economic framework to allow the economy to reach its own natural equilibrium. In their view, the role of the state should be merely to ensure that impediments to the free flow of resources, including labour, should be minimised.

Examples of measures to improve the efficiency of the market system are re-training schemes and mobility allowances to enable workers to switch between alternative occupations and locations, and abolition of minimum wage legislation, which, by artificially inflating wages above the market level, may have prevented some firms from offering more employment.

(b)   A vast amount of finance can be tied up in surplus assets. Surplus assets can be unwanted fixed assets such as plant, machinery, fixtures, equipment etc, or unwanted current assets eg, stocks of finished goods, components, fuels and raw materials.

If such assets can be identified and disposed of the cash which is generated can be used to purchase fixed assets or to finance working capital or to buy stocks and shares.

However, the disposal of surplus assets does provide other benefits. The space used for the fixed assets or inventory can be used for other purposes or even sub-let or sold. Thus the company could expand its operations without having to find more premises. Also, if inventory levels are reduced certain holding costs eg, insurance will tend to decrease.

The down side to this strategy is, firstly, it is difficult to identify surplus assets and secondly, it is not always easy to find a buyer.

(c)   The computation of a 'normal loss' is not an easy task. It is quite difficult to define in quantitative terms what is normal and acceptable.

The 'normal loss' is the loss which is expected to occur under normal operating conditions.

The computation of the normal loss will involve a certain degree of subjective judgement and take account of past performance and future expectations regarding:

- the expected level of activity
- the efficiency of the equipment used
- the competence of the labour force
- the quality of the materials etc.

The normal loss, because it is expected, is regarded as part of the cost of the process to which it relates. It is therefore valued at nil and the cost of the normal loss units absorbed by the good units. The effect being to increase the cost per unit.

(d)   The management accountant has to make assumptions about the external environment in which the firm operates eg, for the purpose of setting budgets and standards. The management accountant can monitor the following areas of the external environment:

- political factors eg, proposed legislation
- social influences eg, 'green issues'
- economic considerations eg, fiscal policy
- technological developments eg, new equipment,

using a variety of sources of data eg, TV, quality newspapers, professional and trade journals, government statistics and information from Chambers of Commerce etc.

In addition, there is also the need to monitor factor markets, product markets and competitors eg, changes in the availability of certain sources of finance and/or changes in the pricing policies of competitors.

A change in the external environment can dramatically affect the budgets, standards and other information generated by the management accounting function. Such monitoring may also help to highlight threats and opportunities and thus contribute towards the firm's long-term survival.

(e)   The statement made indicates that the organisation concerned is currently using an incremental budgeting approach. This approach can in addition to taking into account the previous year's figures plus inflation, also take account of anticipated changes.

This cannot be regarded as a satisfactory way of setting targets. One of the aims of budgetary control is to set targets against which actual performance can be measured. Thus, the targets set should be realistic, fair and achievable.

Zero-based-budgeting (ZBB) attempts to change the attitudes of managers, from the expectation of receiving an incremental increase each year to one of justifying why they need the budget. In ZBB, managers have to assign priorities and justify each activity/programme. The overall aim is to increase efficiency by obtaining better value for money eg,. by getting rid of obsolete activities, thus making better use of scarce resources between competing factions. However, it should be noted that the introduction of ZBB could prove to be quite costly.

(f)   The management accountant can use time series analysis to help make assumptions about the future. It can be particularly helpful during the budget preparation period eg, sales forecasting, predicting future product demand. However, the use of time series data rests on the assumption that the historical relationships between past and future sales will continue.

It can enable the management accountant to detect/identify trends eg, by using graphical representations and/or moving averages. These can be classified into:

- seasonal trends ie, those fluctuations which change each year, and
- cyclical trends ie, changes which take place every so many years eg, every five years.
- abnormal, irregular or erratic fluctuations ie, 'one off happenings.'

59	**(Answer 3 of examination)**

3 **(a)** **Profit statements**

(15,400 units)*

	Standard		Actual	
	£	£	£	£
Sales (at £140)		2,156,000	(at £138.25)	2,129,050
Less: Costs				
Materials				
Mat. 007				
(6 kilos × 15,400)				
= 92,400 × £12.25	1,131,900		1,256,640	
			(given)	
Mat. XL90				
(3 kilos × 15,400)				
= 46,200 × £3.20	147,840		132,979	
			(given)	
Labour				
(4.5 hours × 15,400)				
= 69,300 × £8.40	582,120		612,766	
			(given)	
Fixed overheads	86,400		96,840	
	(given)		(given)	
		1,948,260		2,099,225
Profit		207,740		29,825

* A standard based on the original budget of 16,000 units could have been used in part (a) and then adjusted by means of a sales volume variance in part (b).

(b) **Reconciliation**

				£
Standard profit on 15,400 units (as above)				207,740

		(+)	(−)
Variance		Favourable	Adverse
	£	£	£
Sales price			
Standard − Actual			
(£2,156,000 − £2,129,050)			26,950
Materials			
Mat. 007 usage			
(Standard − Actual) × Standard price			
(92,400 − 98,560) × £12.25**			75,460
Mat. XL90 usage			
(Standard − Actual) × Standard price			
(46,200 − 42,350) × £3.20		12,320	
Mat. 007 Price			
(Actual quantity × Actual price)	1,256,640		
(Actual quantity × Standard price)	1,207,360		
			49,280

Mat. XL90 Price

(Actual quantity × Actual price)	132,979	
(Actual quantity × Standard price)	135,520	

2,541

Labour

Efficiency
  Standard hours – Actual hours*
   (69,300 – 70,840) = 1,540 × Standard rate £8.40   12,936
Rate
  Standard – Actual
   (£8.40 – 8.65) = £0.25 × Actual hours 70,840   17,710

Overheads

Fixed overheads
  Standard – Actual
   (£86,400 – £96,840)   10,440

                        (adverse)
               14,861   192,776   (177,915)

Actual profit   29,825

$$* \ \frac{£612,766}{£8.65} = 70,840 \ \text{hours}$$

** Note that it was not really necessary to do a material mix and material yield variance, but provided they added back to the material usage variances they were acceptable.

(c)   Variances may be inter-related eg, the reason why one variance is favourable could also help explain why another variance is adverse.

Using poor quality materials could result in a favourable price variance because of paying a lower price. The poor quality material could be the cause of an adverse material usage variance and an adverse labour efficiency variance eg, materials more difficult to work with, more rejects/spoilt work, more waste.

If a higher grade of labour was used, compared with that which was planned, there would most certainly be an adverse labour rate variance. The higher skill level employed could well be the reason for a favourable labour efficiency variance and a favourable material usage variance eg, a lower number of rejects and less waste of materials.

---

60   (Answer 4 of examination)

---

4   **REPORT**

To: Mrs Cepheus   15 January 19X5
    Chief Executive
    Cepheus Transport Co Ltd

An evaluation of current performance and the management accounting information

I have now completed my evaluation of the data which you supplied on 5 January 19X5. From the limited amount of data which you provided, it can be observed that currently, your company is making an overall profit of £21,870 which is computed as follows:

	£
Revenue received	165,702
Less: Operating costs (including depreciation)	85,612
Gross profit	80,090
Less: Administration costs and other fixed overheads (including rent)	58,220
Net profit	21,870

The revenue generated *per mile* is:

Type of vehicle	Type F	Type P	Type U
From holding company	£1.825	£1.675	£1.225
From other companies	£3.200	£2.645	£1.900
Operating cost (per mile) (including depreciation)	£1.055	£1.082	£1.062

The revenue per mile for each type of vehicle is in excess of the operating cost per mile. However, the revenue per mile from the holding company is well below that which is generated from dealing with other companies. This will have the effect of increasing the holding company's own profits, because they are apparently paying below market rates for the service which you provide, and reducing your own profits. If you are to be judged on your performance, it is important that you take up this matter with the holding company. If the holding company can pay rates which are nearer to the market rates this will raise your profits and provide you with funds for the expansion of your business and for the replacement of motor vehicles and other fixed assets.

Depreciation policy

In my opinion, in view of the high cost of motor vehicles, it would be fairer to compute your depreciation using the 'time apportionment' basis ie, you charge depreciation on say a month-by-month basis, from the date of purchase to the date of disposal.

Information needed

Should you wish me to do a more in depth appraisal of your performance I would need copies of your published accounts and access to your financial accounting recording system.

Pricing policy

There was also insufficient data relating to your pricing policy. However, I must stress the need for you to monitor:

– your costs;

– your competitors eg, their prices and services;

– the economic environment eg, social factors, legislation etc. which may have a direct impact on your business.

Improvements to the management accounting information system

I suggest that you consider giving a higher priority to management accounting, so that you may receive information which is up-to-date, and relevant, information which will help you with planning, control and decision-making. I propose that you consider making the following improvements:

More detailed records for each individual motor vehicle of:

– the revenue, analysed between the holding company and others;
– their operating costs in terms of fuel, wages, insurance, etc;

–   the amount spent on repairs and maintenance;
–   the depreciation charged to date, using the time apportionment basis;
–   the mileage;
–   an analysis of waiting time;
–   the revenue per mile, cost per mile, fuel consumption per mile etc.

At the moment, the fuel consumption can only be calculated for each group of vehicles, as follows:

Vehicle	Type F	Type P	Type U
Diesel (gallons) (Fuel cost ÷ 2)	2,184	702	876
Miles	40,600	15,520	24,480
Miles per gallon	18.59	22.11	27.95

The information above provides the average miles per gallon for each class of motor vehicle. Hidden in the average, could be one or more vehicles which for various reasons are performing badly. The information needed to produce this analysis can be extracted from the log sheets/records which are kept by the drivers.

Using budgetary control

Budgets will provide the company with targets for revenues and costs and provide a means of control via the frequent comparison of budgeted and actual figures. This should help the company to take appropriate corrective action to put right that which is not going according to plan. All the aspects of the business would be taken into account in producing the 'master budget' ie, a budgeted trading and profit and loss account, balance sheet and cash budget.

To illustrate the need for budgeting, consider its application to the repairs and maintenance of vehicles expenditure. The budgeting process will require planning of what maintenance is to be done and when it is to be done for each vehicle. Spending targets will be compared with actuals on say, a monthly basis, and significant adverse variances highlighted on reports and investigated so that management can decide upon what action needs to be taken.

Devoting more time/resources to the management accounting activities

You need information for planning, control and decision-making purposes. You need information which can help you:

–   make vehicle-by-vehicle internal comparisons;

–   to decide whether or not to use a sub-contractor;

–   to compare buying vehicles with leasing vehicles;

–   to review the possibility of using other forms of transport eg, rail, air, sea;

–   to evaluate the cost of carrying out your own maintenance of vehicles with the cost of using a garage;

–   to formulate your pricing policy;

–   to assess the performance of vehicles loaned to you for testing purposes.

Improving efficiency

Other areas which you will need to look at are:

–   route planning, to avoid hold-ups that could cost you time and money;
–   scheduling, to make the best possible use of vehicles in terms of capacity, loading etc;
–   monitoring the efficiency of keeping to delivery times;
–   making use of idle capacity, especially on return journeys.

Fixed costs

One final observation which needs to be drawn to your attention is the high level of fixed costs which you have to recover. The fixed costs make up around 63% of the operating costs, excluding the overtime premium and the fixed element, if any, included in the operating and maintenance costs. The company's current break-even point, based on the above assumptions, may be computed as follows:

	£'000
Revenue	166
Less: Variable costs	31
Contribution	135 (81 % of the revenue)

Fixed costs £54,000 $\times \dfrac{100}{81}$ = £67,000 break-even point (40% of revenue)

To break even, the company needs to operate at around 40% of current capacity. In the event of a downturn in the economy causing the company's operations to fall below its break-even point, a loss-making situation would arise.

Conclusions and recommendations

One of the principal findings to the lower earnings made was in connection with the work performed for the holding company. If you are to stand on your own feet and be responsible for your own performance, you need to be able to charge the holding company a fair price. This should enable you to generate more funds for re-investment and make you better able to assess your profitability.

More resources need to be devoted to the provision/ supply of management accounting information which will assist you to plan and control the company more effectively and help you with your decision-making. This includes introducing a system of budgetary control which provides targets for both costs and revenues, and by continuous comparison with actuals, provides an 'early warning' of where things are going wrong.

In view of the limited amount of data which was provided, and the wide scope of this report, I will be pleased to discuss any of the above matters with you personally in greater detail.

Philip Loch Ness FCCA

61   (Answer 5 of examination)

5   (a)   Comparison of the two balance sheets reveals that Ewden has suffered a significant fall in liquidity – cash balances have fallen sharply from £1.5m (probably an unnecessarily high level) in 1992 to just £0.1m in 1993 while an overdraft of £0.2m has appeared, reflecting a reduction in net cash resources of £1.6m. However, company profitability remains satisfactory, indicating that the run-down in liquidity has been required to finance the acquisition of assets.

Analysis of the financial statements reveals that Ewden has been able to reinvest £3.0m of retained earnings (plus an unspecified amount of depreciation provisions) in order to fund a substantial net increase in fixed assets of £3.0m, presumably to support an output expansion. It is possible that this significant capacity increase might have been obtained via acquisition of another company. Such a large increase implies that during the past recession, Ewden had cut back its capacity in order to reduce costs.

But as well as an increase in fixed assets, Ewden has invested £0.8m in stocks and £1.0m in debtors. This substantial investment in working capital is partially offset by an increase in trade and other creditors of £0.2m making a total increase in working capital of £1.6m.

No additional external long-term finance has been raised, so the increased investment in fixed assets and working capital has had to be financed by a significant reduction in cash balances and the opening-up of a bank overdraft, resulting in a heavy net outflow of liquid resources of £1.6m.

Overtrading is the term applied to a company which rapidly increases its turnover without having sufficient capital backing, hence the alternative term 'under-capitalisation'. Output increases are often obtained by more intensive utilisation of existing fixed assets, and growth tends to be financed by more intensive use of working capital. Overtrading companies are often unable or unwilling to raise long-term capital and thus tend to rely more heavily on short-term sources such as creditors and bank overdrafts. Debtors usually increase sharply as the company follows a more generous trade credit policy in order to win sales, while stocks tend to increase as the company attempts to produce at a faster rate ahead of increases in demand. Overtrading is thus characterised by rising borrowings and a declining liquidity position in terms of the quick ratio, if not always according to the current ratio.

The accounts indicate some of the signs of overtrading, although the case is not proven.

Checking Ewden's ratios against the common symptoms of overtrading:

(i)   Fall in the liquidity ratios. For Ewden, the current ratio falls from 2.25 to 2.04, which does not seem to indicate a serious decline in liquidity, although the extent of the decline in the quick ratio, (ie, excluding stocks), from 1.55 to 1.13, might give more cause for concern, especially as the bulk of its quick assets (96%) are in the form of debtors.

(ii)   Rapid increase in turnover – 33% for Ewden.

(iii)   Sharp increase in the sales-to-fixed assets ratio. For Ewden, this has remained steady at 1.33 because the increase in sales has been supported by an increase in fixed assets, suggesting that the output increase was well-planned.

(iv)   Increase in stocks in relation to turnover. For Ewden, the increase is from 11.7% (43 days) to 13.8% (50 days), which is marked but hardly dramatic.

Measured against cost of sales, the equivalent figures are 20% (73 days) for 1992 and 24% (88 days) for 1993, a more pronounced increase in stockholding.

(v)   Increase in debtors. Ewden's accounts receivable rise as a percentage of sales from 13.3% (49 days) to 16.3% (59 days). This does seem to represent a significant loosening of control over debtors.

(vi)   Increase in the trade credit period. The ratio of trade creditors to cost of goods sold rises slightly from 21.4% (78 days) to 21.8% (80 days). The trade credit period is considerably longer (80 days versus 59 days) than the debtor collection period, suggesting that the company is exploiting the generosity of suppliers in order to enhance sales.

(vii)   Increase in short-term borrowing and a decline in cash balances. Clearly, this has happened to Ewden.

(viii)   Increase in gearing. Taking the ratio of long and short-term debt-to-equity as the appropriate measure, gearing has actually fallen (from a relatively low level of 21% to 18%) despite the opening of the overdraft, primarily due to the increase in equity via retentions.

(ix)   Fall in the profit margin. In terms of its gross profit margin (operating profit-to-sales), Ewden actually achieves an increase from 42% to 43%, although there is a marginal fall in the ratio of profit after tax-to-sales from 31.7% to 31.3%. This does not suggest that Ewden is using aggressive price discounting in an attempt to increase sales.

It seems that Ewden's liquidity is under pressure but the company displays by no means all the classic signs of overtrading. Ewden might consider issuing further long-term securities if it wishes to support a further sales surge. If sales are expected to stabilise, the recent increase in capacity should be sufficient to produce the desired output, enabling the liquidity position to be repaired via cash flow, which was substantial in 1993, before allowing for the financing of the capital investment.

(b)   **The discount**

At December 1993, debtors were £2.6m. The debtor collection period was: £2.6m/£16m × 365 = 59 days.

The 2% discount would lower this to 10 days for 50% of customers reducing average debtor days to:

$$(50\% \times 59) + (50\% \times 10) = 34.5 \text{ days}$$

The cost of the discount (ignoring any beneficial impact on sales volume) would be:

$$(2\% \times 50\% \times £16m) = £160,000$$

The revised sales value estimate would be (£16m – £160,000) = £15.84m

Average debtors would become $\dfrac{34.5}{365} \times £15.84m = £1,497,206$

The interest saving would be 18% × (£2.6m – £1.497m) = £198,540

Set against the cost of the discount, the net benefit would be:

$$(£198,540 – £160,000) = £38,540$$

Factoring

Reduction in debtor days = (59 – 45)	=	14 days
Reduction in debtors = $\dfrac{14}{365} \times £16m$	=	£613,699
Interest saving = (18% × £613,698)	=	£110,466
Administrative savings	=	£100,000
Service charge = (1.5% × £16m)	=	£240,000
Net cost = (£240,000) + £100,000 + £110,466	=	(£29,534)

The figures imply that the discount policy is preferable but this relies on the appropriate percentage of customers actually taking up the discount and paying on time. Given that debtor days are currently 59, it seems rather optimistic to expect that half of Ewden's customers will be sufficiently impressed by the discount as to advance their settlement by 49 days. Conversely, the assessment of the value of using the factor depends on the factor successfully lowering Ewden's debtor days. Any tendency for the factor to retain these cash flow benefits for himself, rather than passing them on to Ewden, will further increase the net cost of the factoring option. In this respect, the two parties should clearly specify their expectations and requirements from the factoring arrangement.

62   (Answer 6 of examination)

6   (a)   Investors advance capital to companies expecting a reward for both the delay in waiting for their returns (time value of money) and also for the risks to which they expose their capital (risk premium). In addition, if prices in general are rising, shareholders require compensation for the erosion in the real value of their capital.

If, for example, in the absence of inflation, shareholders require a company to offer a return of 10%, the need to cover 5% price inflation will raise the overall required return to about 15%. If people in general expect a particular rate of inflation, the structure of interest rates in the capital market will adjust to incorporate these inflationary expectations. This is known as the 'Fisher effect'.

More precisely, the relationship between the real required return (r) and the nominal rate, (m), the rate which includes an allowance for inflation, is given by: $(1 + r) \times (1 + p) = (1 + m)$ where p is the expected rate of inflation.

It is essential when evaluating an investment project under inflation that future expected price level changes are treated in a consistent way. Companies may correctly allow for inflation in two ways each of which computes the real value of an investment project:

(i)   Inflate the future expected cash flows at the expected rate of inflation (allowing for inflation rates specific to the project) and discount at m, the fully-inflated rate – the 'money terms' approach.

(ii)   Strip out the inflation element from the market-determined rate and apply the resulting real rate of return, r, to the stream of cash flows expressed in today's or constant prices – the 'real terms' approach.

(b)   First, the relevant set-up cost needs identification. The offer of £2m for the building, if rejected, represents an opportunity cost, although this appears to be compensated by its predicted eventual resale value of £3m. The cost of the market research study has to be met irrespective of the decision to proceed with the project or not and is thus not relevant.

Secondly, incremental costs and revenues are identified. All other items are avoidable except the element of apportioned overhead, leaving the incremental overhead alone to include in the evaluation.

Thirdly, all items of incremental cash flow, including this additional overhead, must be adjusted for their respective rates of inflation. Because (with the exception of labour and variable overhead) the inflation rates differ, a disaggregated approach is required.

The appropriate discount rate is given by:

$$(1 + p) \times (1 + r) - 1 = m = (1.06) \times (1.085) - 1 = 15\%$$

Assuming that the inflated costs and prices apply from and including the first year of operation, the cash-flow profile is:

Cash flow profile	(£m)			Year		
Item	0	1	2	3	4	5
Equipment	(10.50)					2.00
Foregone sale of buildings	(2.00)					
Residual value of building						3.00
Working capital*	(0.50)					0.50
Revenue		5.04	5.29	5.56	5.83	6.13
Materials		(0.62)	(0.64)	(0.66)	(0.68)	(0.70)
Labour and variable overhead		(0.43)	(0.46)	(0.49)	(0.52)	(0.56)
Fixed overhead		(0.53)	(0.55)	(0.58)	(0.61)	(0.64)
Net cash flows	(13.00)	3.46	3.64	3.83	4.02	9.73
Present value at 15%	(13.00)	3.01	2.75	2.52	2.30	4.84

NPV = +£2.42m, therefore, the project appears to be acceptable.

However, the financial viability of the project depends quite heavily on the estimate of the residual value of the building and equipment.

Note: the working capital cash recovery towards the end of the project is approximately equal to the initial investment in stocks because the rate of material cost inflation tends to cancel out the JIT-induced reduction in volume, leading to roughly constant stock-holding in value terms throughout most of the project life-span.

(c)   In addition to the problems offered for investment appraisal such as forecasting the various rates of inflation relevant to the project, inflation poses a wider range of difficulties in a variety of business decision areas.

Inflation may pose a problem for businesses if it distorts the signals transmitted by the market. In the absence of inflation, the price system should translate the shifting patterns of consumer demand into price signals to which producers respond in order to plan current and future output levels. If demand for a product rises, the higher price indicates the desirability of switching existing production capacity to producing the good or of laying down new capacity.

Under inflation, however, the producer may lose confidence that the correct signals are being transmitted, especially if the prices of goods and services inflate at different rates. He may thus be inclined to delay undertaking new investment. This applies particularly if price rises are unexpected and erratic.

Equally, it becomes more difficult to evaluate the performance of whole businesses and individual segments when prices are inflating. A poor operating performance may be masked by price inflation, especially if the price of the product sold is increasing at a rate faster than prices in general or if operating costs are inflating more slowly. The rate of return on capital achieved by a business is most usefully expressed in real terms by removing the effect on profits of generally rising prices (or better still, the effect of company-specific inflation). The capital base of the company should also be expressed in meaningful terms. A poor profit result may translate into a high ROI if the capital base is measured in historic terms. Unless these sorts of adjustment are made, inflation hinders the attempt to measure company performance on a consistent basis and thus can cloud the judgement of providers of capital in seeking out the most profitable areas for investment.

DECEMBER 1994 QUESTIONS

Section A – This question is compulsory and MUST be attempted

63 (Question 1 of examination)

1 The budgeted balance sheet data of Kwan Tong Umbago Ltd is as follows:

1 March 19X5

	Cost £	Depreciation to date £	Net £
Fixed assets			
Land and buildings	500,000	–	500,000
Machinery and equipment	124,000	84,500	39,500
Motor vehicles	42,000	16,400	25,600
	666,000	100,900	565,100

Working capital

Current assets			
Stock of raw materials (100 units)		4,320	
Stock of finished goods (110 units)*		10,450	
Debtors (January £7,680, February £10,400)		18,080	
Cash and bank		6,790	
		39,640	
Less: Current liabilities			
Creditors (raw materials)		3,900	
			35,740
			600,840

Represented by		
Ordinary share capital (fully paid) £1 shares		500,000
Share premium		60,000
Profit and loss account		40,840
		600,840

* *The stock of finished goods was valued at marginal cost*

The estimates for the next four month period are as follows:

	March	April	May	June
Sales (units)	80	84	96	94
Production (units)	70	75	90	90
Purchases of raw materials (units)	80	80	85	85
Wages and variable overheads at £65 per unit	£4,550	£4,875	£5,850	£5,850
Fixed overheads	£1,200	£1,200	£1,200	£1,200

The company intends to sell each unit for £219 and has estimated that it will have to pay £45 per unit for raw materials. One unit of raw material is needed for each unit of finished product.

All sales and purchases of raw materials are on credit. Debtors are allowed two months' credit and suppliers of raw materials are paid after one month's credit. The wages, variable overheads and fixed overheads are paid in the month in which they are incurred.

Cash from a loan secured on the land and buildings of £120,000 at an interest rate of 7.5% is due to be received on 1 May. Machinery costing £112,000 will be received in May and paid for in June.

The loan interest is payable half yearly from September onwards. An interim dividend to 31 March 19X5 of £12,500 will be paid in June.

Depreciation for the four months, including that on the new machinery is:

–   Machinery and equipment £15,733
–   Motor vehicles £3,500

The company uses the FIFO method of stock valuation. Ignore taxation.

Required

(a)   Calculate and present the raw materials budget and finished goods budget in terms of units, for each month from March to June inclusive.   (5 marks)

(b)   Calculate the corresponding sales budgets, the production cost budgets and the budgeted closing debtors, creditors and stocks in terms of value.   (5 marks)

(c)   Prepare and present a cash budget for each of the four months.   (6 marks)

(d)   Prepare a master budget ie, a budgeted trading and profit and loss account for the four months to 30 June 19X5, and budgeted balance sheet as at 30 June 19X5.   (10 marks)

(e)   Advise the company about possible ways in which it can improve its cash management.
                                                                            (9 marks)
                                                                    (Total 35 marks)

Section B – This question is compulsory and MUST be attempted

64   (Question 2 of examination)

2   Answer FIVE of the six parts of this question

Each part carries five marks

(a)   The following two debenture stocks are both traded on the London Stock Exchange:

      (i)   9% debentures issued by Hammer plc, redeemable in early 1996 at their £100 par value. Each debenture is convertible at any time from now onwards into 20 ordinary shares. The current market price per ordinary share is £3.50 (ex dividend).

      (ii)   7% debentures issued by Nail plc, redeemable in five years time at their £100 par value. Each debenture is convertible into 25 ordinary shares in three years time. The current ordinary share price is £4.10 (ex dividend).

Explain what factors will influence the respective *current* market values of these two convertible stocks.

(Note: you are not required to perform precise valuations.)   (5 marks)

(b)   Briefly explain the methods whereby a company can obtain a quotation for its shares on the London Stock Exchange.

(5 marks)

(c)   It is becoming increasingly common for companies to offer their shareholders a choice between a cash dividend or an equivalent scrip issue of shares.

Briefly consider the advantages of scrip dividends from the viewpoint of:

(i)   the company; and
(ii)   the shareholders.

(5 marks)

(d)   Distinguish between factoring and invoice discounting, explaining the benefits which companies obtain from each.

(5 marks)

(e)   Explain the main *economic* objectives underlying the widespread practice of privatising state-owned companies.

(5 marks)

(f)   Explain briefly the relevance of the concepts of 'price elasticity' and the 'cross elasticity' of demand to the product pricing decision.

(5 marks)

(Total 25 marks)

Section C – ONE question ONLY to be attempted

65   (Question 3 of examination)

3   The following budget and actual data relates to Cassiop plc for the past three periods:

Budget	Period 1	Period 2	Period 3
Sales (units)	10,000	14,000	12,200
Production (units)	8,000	14,200	12,400
Fixed overheads	£10,400	£19,170	£17,360
Actual			
Sales (units)	9,600	12,400	10,200
Production (units)	8,400	13,600	9,200
Fixed overheads	£11,200	£18,320	£16,740

The value of the opening and closing stock of the units produced is arrived at by using FIFO. The budgeted and actual opening stock for period 1 was 2,600 units and its valuation included £3,315 of fixed overheads. The company absorbs its fixed overheads via a predetermined fixed overhead rate per unit which is the same for each period. It is assumed that variable costs per unit and selling prices per unit remained the same for each of the periods.

Required

(a)   Calculate the under- or over-recovery of fixed overhead for each period and indicate how it will affect the profit or loss.

(6 marks)

(b)   'Absorption costing will produce a higher profit than marginal costing.' Explain why you agree or disagree with this statement, making reference to the data provided above as appropriate.   (6 marks)

(c)   Explain briefly why absorption costing is usually considered to be unsuitable as an aid for decision-making. Justify your answer.

(8 marks)

(Total 20 marks)

66   (Question 4 of examination)

4   Your company will shortly be completing its acquisition of a small manufacturing company which is engaged in producing a range of products via a number of processes. The production side of that company is well established. However, its cost and management accounting function is not so well developed. This type of multi-process production system is new to your company.

You are required to:

Prepare a report for management which clearly explains the problems associated with process costing, and which looks particularly at:

–   the treatment of overheads;
–   valuation problems;
–   normal and abnormal gains and losses.   **(20 marks)**

Section D – ONE question ONLY to be attempted

67   (Question 5 of examination)

5   Newsam plc is a quoted company which produces a range of branded products all of which are well-established in their respective markets, although overall sales have grown by an average of only 2% per annum over the past decade. The board of directors is currently concerned about the company's level of financial gearing, which although not high by industry standards, is near to breaching the covenants attaching to its 15% debenture issue, made in 1982 at a time of high market interest rates. Issued in order to finance the acquisition of the premises on which it is secured, the debenture is repayable at par value of £100 per unit of stock at any time during the period 1994 –1997.

There are two covenants attaching to the debenture, which state:

> 'At no time shall the ratio of debt capital to shareholders' funds exceed 50%. The company shall also maintain a prudent level of liquidity, defined as a current ratio at no time outside the range of the industry average (as published by the corporate credit analysts, Creditex), plus or minus 20%.'

Newsam's most recent set of accounts is shown in summarised form below. The buildings have been depreciated since 1982 at 4% per annum, and most of the machinery is only two or three years old, having been purchased mainly via a bank overdraft. The interest rate payable on the bank overdraft is currently 9%. The finance director argues that Newsam should take advantage of historically low interest rates on the European money markets by issuing a medium-term Eurodollar bond at 5%. The dollar is currently selling at a premium of about 1% on the three-month forward market.

Newsam's ordinary shares currently sell at a P/E ratio of 14, and look unattractive compared to comparable companies in the sector which exhibit an average P/E ratio of 18. According to the latest published credit assessment by Creditex, the average current ratio for the industry is 1.35.

The debentures currently sell in the market at £15 above par.

The summarised financial accounts for Newsam plc for the year ending 30 June 1994 are as follows:

Balance sheet as at 30 June 1994

Assets employed	£m	£m	£m
Fixed (net)			
Land			5.0
Premises			4.0
Machinery and vehicles			11.0
			20.0
Current			
Stocks	2.5		
Debtors	4.0		
Cash	0.5		
		7.0	
Current liabilities			
Creditors	(4.0)		
Bank overdraft	(3.0)		
		(7.0)	
Net current assets			0.0
Total assets less current liabilities			20.0
Long-term creditors			
15% Debentures 1994 – 1997			(5.0)
Net assets			15.0
Financed by			
Ordinary shares (25p par value)			5.0
Reserves			10.0
Shareholders' funds			15.0

Profit and loss account extracts for the year ended 30 June 1994

	£m
Sales	28.00
Operating profit	3.00
Interest payable	(1.00)
Profit before tax	2.00
Taxation	(0.66)
Profit after tax	1.34
Dividend	(0.70)
Retained profit	0.64

Required

(a)   Calculate appropriate gearing ratios for Newsam plc using:

      (i)   book values; and

      (ii)   market values.

(3 marks)

(b)   Assess how close Newsam plc is to breaching the debenture covenants.

(3 marks)

(c)   Discuss whether Newsam plc's gearing is in any sense 'dangerous'.

(4 marks)

(d)   Discuss what financial policies Newsam plc might adopt:

(i)   in order to lower its capital gearing; and
(ii)   to improve its interest cover.

(10 marks)

(Total 20 marks)

---

68   (Question 6 of examination)

6   (a)   Distinguish between 'hard' and 'soft' capital rationing, explaining why a company may deliberately choose to restrict its capital expenditure.

(5 marks)

(b)   Filtrex plc is a medium-sized, all equity-financed, unquoted company which specialises in the development and production of water- and air-filtering devices to reduce the emission of effluents. Its small but ingenious R & D team has recently made a technological breakthrough which has revealed a number of attractive investment opportunities. It has applied for patents to protect its rights in all these areas. However, it lacks the financial resources required to exploit all of these projects, whose required outlays and post-tax NPVs are listed in the table below. Filtrex's managers consider that delaying any of these projects would seriously undermine their profitability, as competitors bring forward their own new developments. All projects are thought to have a similar degree of risk.

Project	Required outlay £	NPV £
A	150,000	65,000
B	120,000	50,000
C	200,000	80,000
D	80,000	30,000
E	400,000	120,000

The NPVs have been calculated using as a discount rate the 18% post-tax rate of return which Filtrex requires for risky R & D ventures. The maximum amount available for this type of investment is £400,000, corresponding to Filtrex's present cash balances, built up over several years' profitable trading. Projects A and C are mutually exclusive and no project can be sub-divided. Any unused capital will either remain invested in short-term deposits or used to purchase marketable securities, both of which offer a return well below 18% post-tax.

Required

(i)   Advise Filtrex plc, using suitable supporting calculations, which combination of projects should be undertaken in the best interests of shareholders.

(ii)   Suggest what further information might be obtained to assist a fuller analysis.

(9 marks)

(c)   Explain how, apart from delaying projects, Filtrex plc could manage to exploit more of these opportunities.

(6 marks)

(Total 20 marks)

EXAMINER'S COMMENTS

General comments

There were two striking features about the pattern of marks in this diet. First was the importance of the case-study question, which few students failed, and which often contributed well over half of their overall marks. As with the June 1994 paper, marks on the MA questions were higher than on the FM areas. Once again, it seems that candidates are seeing paper 8 as an exam in MA with a little FM tacked on, and/or are relying on knowledge gained in earlier MA studies to carry them through.

Question 1 part (a): required the calculation of the raw materials budget and finished goods budget in units for each month for a four month period.

Candidates lost marks through not calculating the closing stock of raw materials and finished goods. It was unusual to find some students calculating to closing stocks of raw materials correctly and then calculate the stocks of finished goods incorrectly.

Part (b): required the calculation of sales and production budgets and budgeted closing debtors, creditors and stocks.

Most candidates had no difficulty computing the sales budget. A large number of candidates failed to use FIFO in computing the value of the raw materials used when trying to arrive at the production budget and did not appreciate that stocks were being valued at marginal cost.

Part (c): required the preparation of a cash budget.

Overall, this part of the question was done very well. Those who lost marks, made errors through dealing incorrectly with the periods of credit on debtors and creditors and failed to account for the loan correctly.

Part (d) some candidates re-computed figures, in particular the production costs, which had already been calculated, so wasting valuable examination time. Candidates who did include the production cost, also included the purchase figure, when it was already included in the production cost. Another common error was to exclude the loan interest and to deal incorrectly with the profit and loss appropriations.

In the balance sheet the loan was treated at a current liability falling due within one year by a significant number of candidates and the loan interest outstanding was not included at all.

Part (e): required advice about ways of improving the company's cash management.

In this wide 'open ended' question it was pleasing to see knowledge from other studies being applied, eg, auditing in particular. A lot of the points made needed to be expanded, eg, by explaining why and how such advice would be of benefit and where appropriate giving brief examples.

Question 2 part (a): required assessment of the factors influencing the current market values of two specified convertible debenture stocks.

This question was poorly done, mainly due to neglecting to use the copious information given in the question for answering the question set. The wording of the question clearly referred to 'those two convertible stocks'. Failure to answer the question, however good a survey was provided of the influences on the valuation of convertibles, necessarily restricted maximum marks obtainable.

Part (b): required knowledge of how companies can obtain a listing on the London Stock Exchange.

A straightforward question which was generally well done. Those who did not perform well, wrote about the process of obtaining a listing and/or the listing requirements. The other recurrent error was the inclusion of a rights issue as a method of obtaining a listing.

Part (c): required explanation of the advantages of scrip dividends for both companies and their share-holders.

The wording of this question was carefully phrased to make the distinction between a scrip dividend (which is optional) and a scrip issue (received by all shareholders). Unfortunately, the majority of candidates ignored this distinction, it being clear from their answers that they were writing about the latter. However, many points relating to scrip dividends also apply to scrip issues such as cash flow savings, avoidance of issue costs, reduction in gearing (below what it would otherwise have been). The basic point about scrip dividends is that they offer shareholders a choice and this makes the shares more appealing to a wider clientele of investors.

Part (d): required distinction between factoring and invoice discounting, specifying the advantages of each.

This was quite well done, except for the misconception that invoice discounting is the offer of discounts to customers for prompt payment. Apart from this, the only significant errors were those of omission, eg, failing to explain that factoring normally involves all of a company's sales whereas invoice discounting involves selected invoices (sometimes only one), and failure to explain that factoring will save book-keeping and administration costs, whereas with invoice discounting, the task of collection from customers remains with the company.

Part (e): required explanation of the main economic aims underlying privatisation of state-owned companies.

The key word in the question was 'economic'. Many candidates instead discussed the political aims of promoting wider share ownership. This only scored marks if it was explained that wider share ownership, by encouraging greater interest in share-holding, may augment the flow of new funds onto the capital markets. The core of the answer should have been the impact of privatisation on industrial efficiency, prompted by exposure to new competitive pressures and the opportunity to diversify into areas previously forbidden by statute. The efficiency improvements would thus enhance the technical and allocative efficiency of the nation's industrial structure.

The majority of answers tended to emphasise aims such as; reducing the Public Sector Borrowing Requirement raising revenue and enabling tax cuts, all of which do have economic spin-offs (eg, lower interest rates), but all too often these economic benefits were glossed over. This part of question 2 provided a good example of the need to look beyond the obvious answer.

Part (f): required a brief explanation of the concepts of 'price elasticity' and 'cross elasticity' in relation to the product pricing decision.

A lot of attempts were of a good standard. Weaker answers, either failed to make an mention of 'cross elasticity' or focused on supply and demand.

Question 3 part (a): required the calculation of the under or over recovery of overheads.

Candidates who applied the rules correctly and who demonstrated that they understood the concept of under or over absorption received full marks, provided that they knew the correct treatment in the profit and loss account. On the whole this section was very well done.

Part (b): required an explanation of the statement, 'absorption costing will produce a higher profit than marginal costing'.

Those who agreed and provided some satisfactory reasons as to why, did get some marks. However, a number of candidates did make the point very clearly about fixed production overheads being carried forward in closing stocks and then failed to take account of the fixed production overheads brought into the period via the opening stocks. Many candidates did not make any attempt to relate their answer to or illustrate their answer by reference to the data in part (a) which was asked for in the question. On the whole this part was not answered well.

Part (c): required an explanation as to why absorption costing is usually considered to be unsuitable for decision making.

It was encouraging to find candidates applying terms such as sunk costs, relevant costs and Activity Based Costing in their answers to this question.

Question 4: required a report about process costing with particular emphasis on the treatment of overheads valuation problems and normal/abnormal gains and losses.

Some answers were not in the required report format. Others did not make any recommendations or try to draw any conclusions. Not many candidates attempted this question and from those who did there were not many answers that could be described as being of a high quality.

Question 5: required knowledge of the measurement of gearing, implications of 'excessive' gearing levels, and of policies to reduce both capital and income gearing.

This question was poorly done. It offered a substantial amount of accounting information to enable candidates to illustrate their answers numerically but more importantly, to allow an opportunity to express their expertise in interpreting accounting statements. However, apart from the calculation of gearing ratios, candidates tended to ignore much of the information given. Candidates also seemed unable to work out market values of equity, and even where this was done, a common error was to add on the reserves. The dangers of 'high' gearing and the implications of breaking a debt covenant were not highlighted by many candidates.

Part (d) was generally poorly done, with too many answers consisting of a set of odd jottings without any attempt to explain or justify the suggestions made, or to illustrate them numerically. The opportunity to issue the Eurobond was generally ignored, and those who did recommend it over-looked the exchange rate risk. Finally, whereas it is true that increasing sales/profits and/or reducing costs will likely raise interest cover, the question does specify 'financial policies'.

Question 6: required knowledge of types of capital rationing, of how to evaluate capital expenditure under rationing and of how to exploit the benefits of projects under these conditions.

Most candidates could make the distinction between external and internal rationing, but often could offer no reasons for the latter.

In part (b), a number of candidates seemed to think that mutual exclusivity meant that both projects A and C could be done together or even had to be done together. Others also ignored the information that projects were indivisible. Most students omitted to specify the NPV-preferred project (E), the usual starting point in a rationing exercise, but did calculate the Profitability Indices. Several appeared to think the PI was outlay divided by NPV, and many referred to it as the return on capital, or even more explicitly, as the ROCE. Few candidates seemed to be aware of the role of the IRR in a rationing situation.

Part (c) required a certain amount of creativity – the wording used was 'exploit more of these opportunities', ie, it was intended to point towards avenues other than finding more capital, such as selling the patent, forming a Joint Venture, licensing, etc. Many students simply wrote down a 'shopping list' of points with little or no accompanying explanation. Candidates should remember that the Examiner uses words such as 'discuss' and 'explain' rather than 'list' to encourage analysis and discussion.

ANSWERS TO DECEMBER 1994 EXAMINATION

It should be noted that some of the following answers are perhaps fuller than would be expected from most students under exam conditions. The answers are provided in this degree of detail to offer guidance on the approach required and on the range and depth of knowledge that would be expected from an excellent student.

63   (Answer 1 of examination)

1   (a)

	(Units)			
	March	*April*	*May*	*June*
Raw materials				
Opening stock	100	110	115	110
Add: Purchases	80	80	85	85
	180	190	200	195
Less: Used in production	70	75	90	90
Closing stock	110	115	110	105
Finished production				
Opening stock	110	100	91	85
Add: Production	70	75	90	90
	180	175	181	175
Less: Sales	80	84	96	94
Closing stock	100	91	85	81

(b)

	(Units)				
	March	*April*	*May*	*June*	*Total*
Sales					
(at £219 per unit)	£17,520	£18,396	£21,024	£20,586	£77,526
Production cost					
Raw materials (using FIFO)	3,024*	3,321**	4,050	4,050	14,445
Wages and variable costs	4,550	4,875	5,850	5,850	21,125
	£7,574	£8,196	£9,900	£9,900	£35,570

Debtors

Closing debtors = May + June sales = £41,610

Creditors

June, raw materials = 85 units × £45 = £3,825

$$* \left(£4,320 \times \frac{70}{100} \right) = £3,024$$

$$** \left(£4,320 \times \frac{30}{100} \right) = £1,296 + 45 \text{ units at } £45 = £3,321$$

Closing stocks

Raw materials 105 units × £45 = £4,725
Finished goods 81 units × £110 = £8,910
(Material £45 per unit + Lab overhead £65 per unit)

(c) **Cash budget**

	March £	April £	May £	June £
Balance b/f	6,790	4,820	5,545	132,415
Add: Receipts				
Debtors (two months credit)	7,680	10,400	17,520	18,396
Loan	–	–	120,000	–
(A)	14,470	15,220	143,065	150,811
Payments				
Creditors (one month's credit)	3,900	3,600	3,600	3,825
Wages and variable overheads	4,550	4,875	5,850	5,850
Fixed overheads	1,200	1,200	1,200	1,200
Machinery	–	–	–	112,000
Interim dividend	–	–	–	12,500
(B)	9,650	9,675	10,650	135,375
Balance c/f (A) – (B)	4,820	5,545	132,415	£15,436

(d) **Master budget**

**Budgeted trading and profit and loss account
for the four months to 30 June 19X5**

	£	£
Sales		77,526
Less: Cost of sales		
Opening stock finished goods	10,450	
Add: Production cost	35,570	
	46,020	
Less: Closing stock finished goods	8,910	
		37,110
		40,416
Less: Expenses		
Fixed overheads (4 × £1,200)	4,800	
Depreciation		
Machinery and equipment	15,733	
Motor vehicles	3,500	
Loan interest (two months)	1,500	
		25,533
		14,883
Less: Interim dividends		12,500
		2,383
Add: Profit and loss account balance b/f		40,840
		43,223

Budgeted balance sheet as at 30 June 19X5

Employment of capital	Cost £	Depreciation to date £	Net £
Fixed assets			
Land and buildings	500,000	–	500,000
Machinery and equipment	236,000	100,233	135,767
Motor vehicles	42,000	19,900	22,100
	778,000	120,133	657,867
Working capital			
Current assets			
Stock of raw materials		4,725	
Stock of finished goods		8,910	
Debtors		41,610	
Cash and bank balances		15,436	
		70,681	
Less: Current liabilities			
Creditors	3,825		
Loan interest owing	1,500		
		5,325	
			65,356
			723,223

Capital employed	£
Ordinary share capital £1 shares (fully paid)	500,000
Share premium	60,000
Profit and loss account	43,223
	603,223
Secured loan (7$\frac{1}{2}$%)	120,000
	723,223

(e)   Possible ways in which the company can improve its cash management are as follows:

–   Employing a *treasury function* to invest surplus cash and thereby improving the productivity of the capital employed. Even a small company such as Kwan Tong Umbago Ltd could switch funds from its bank current account to an account on which it can earn some interest. Many businesses fail to make full use of their cash budget, in that it provides them with an indication of when they will have surplus cash in addition to highlighting when they have a shortage.

–   Its cash budget can only be as accurate as the data which it uses to estimate the figures. To arrive at more relevant and realistic estimates it may be possible to use computer packages eg, which take account of the numerous variables involved, and statistical techniques such as time series analysis for forecasting sales.

–   It may be possible to improve its *credit control*. It currently takes around two months to collect the amounts owing from its debtors whilst paying off its creditors within one month.

It needs to make an effort to collect what is owing more quickly without offering cash discounts which could prove to be expensive eg, by more prompt invoicing and chasing slow payers etc. It could take a little longer to pay creditors provided that it does not lose cash discounts. A small percentage cash discount does have a high implicit annual interest cost!

– It could generate more cash by identifying and disposing of surplus assets eg, unwanted stocks of raw materials and/or finished goods, production and/or office equipment which is no longer required, provided that it can find a buyer. Finding a buyer of the surplus assets may not be easy. Another benefit of disposing of surplus assets which can have a significant impact on cash, is that the disposal may free valuable production, office or storage space. It may also be possible to secure a reduction in insurance premiums at the next renewal date relating to the assets disposed of.

– The company's cash position may also be improved via using more debt financing. The company is low geared and a large proportion of its fixed assets have not already been pledged as security. This should enable it to benefit from low cost financing eg, secured loans or debentures, but would expose it to a higher degree of risk caused by the obligation to make regular payments of capital and interest.

– The management could also consider other ways of financing assets eg, renting or leasing plant and machinery. This should enable them to generate the payments out of the earnings of the plant and machinery concerned.

– Finally, the company could opt to make greater use of sub-contractors which frees it from having to find additional sums for financing the expansion involved. The sub-contractor would have to finance the purchase of the necessary fixed assets, the remuneration of its labour force and the purchase and holding of stocks of raw materials, work in progress and finished goods. The downside from the company's point of view would be the problem of exercising quality control over the supplier.

64   (Answer 2 of examination)

2   (a)   (i)   The market price of Hammer's debentures will be largely determined by their essential debenture characteristics because conversion does not appear to be an attractive proposition. At present, the value of 20 shares is only £70, considerably less than the redemption value of £100. Although there is over a year to go until redemption, the share price would have to rise more than £1.50 (over 40%) over this period to make conversion the better alternative. Consequently, Hammer's stock will be valued as debentures, based on the future interest payments plus the redemption consideration. There will still, however, be some (probably small) option premium to add to this.

(ii)   In the case of Nail's stock, the share conversion value (25 × £4.10 = £102.50) already exceeds the stock redemption value of £100. Conversion is not due for another three years, and although share prices could fall, there is the prospect of further capital gains at conversion. These convertibles will be valued based on the remaining interest payments and the expected ordinary share price at conversion. The critical factors in valuation are thus the actual and expected share price and the length of time to conversion, especially if the share price is volatile.

(b)   There are three main ways in which a company can 'come to the market'.

(i)   *Offer for sale by prospectus.* Shares are offered at a fixed price to the public at large, including both investing institutions and private individuals. Application forms and a prospectus, setting out all relevant details of the company's past performance and future prospects, as stipulated by Stock Exchange regulations laid down in 'The Yellow Book', must be published in the national press. An offer for sale is obligatory for issues involving £30m or more.

A variant on this method is the offer for sale by tender, where no prior issue price is announced, but prospective investors are invited to bid for shares at a price of their choosing. The eventual 'striking price' at which shares are sold is determined by the weight of applications at various prices. Essentially, the final price is set by supply and demand.

(ii)   *A placing* occurs when shares (up to £15m value) are 'placed' or sold to institutional investors, such as pension funds and insurance companies, selected by the merchant bank advising the company, and the company's stockbroker. In a placing, the general public have to wait until official dealing in the shares begins before they, too, can buy the shares.

An intermediaries' offer is a placing with financial intermediaries, which allows brokers other than the one advising the issuing company to apply for shares. These brokers are allocated shares which they can subsequently distribute to their clients.

(iii)   *Introduction.* In some cases, the proportion of shares held by the public *(25% for a full listing)* may already meet Stock Exchange requirements, and the company is seeking a listing merely to open up a wider market for its shares rather than seeking new capital. No new shares are issued, and new investors can only participate if some of the existing shareholders decide to liquidate their holdings after the listing.

(c)   (i)   From the company's point of view, the scrip alternative preserves liquidity, which may be important at a time of cash shortage and/or high borrowing costs, although it may become committed to a higher level of cash outflows in the future if shareholders revert to a preference for cash. However, having issued more shares, the company's reported financial gearing may be lowered, possibly enhancing borrowing capacity. In this respect, the scrip dividend resembles a rights issue.

In addition, the company is not required to make an advance corporation tax (ACT) payment to the Inland Revenue. This may be of particular value to companies facing difficulties in 'relieving' ACT ie, offsetting it against mainstream corporation tax (MCT).

For example, a company which declares cash dividends of £10m (net of tax), and half of whose shareholders choose the scrip alternatives would make the following cash flow savings:

[dividend payment saved (£5m) plus ACT saved (20/80 × £5m)] = £6.25m

The latter element would be only a temporary saving for a company with a MCT liability. In reality, a considerably lower proportion of shareholders elect for the scrip alternative. This is largely due to the inability of tax-exempt shareholders to reclaim a tax credit, no ACT having been paid by the company in respect of the scrip issue.

(ii)   For shareholders wishing to increase their holdings, the scrip is a cheap way into the company as it avoids dealing fees. The conversion price used to calculate the number of shares receivable is based on the average share price for several trading days after the 'ex dividend day'. Should the market price rise above the conversion price before the date at which shareholders have to declare their choice, there is the prospect of a capital gain, although if the share price appreciation exceeds 15%, any such gain is taxable.

A scrip dividend has no tax advantages for shareholders as it is treated as income for tax purposes. Nor can a tax credit be reclaimed as no ACT was originally payable.

If the capital market is efficient, there is no depressing effect on the share price by the scrip dividend through earnings dilution. This is because the scrip simply replaces a cash dividend which would have caused share price to fall anyway due to the 'ex dividend' effect. In other words, shareholder wealth is unchanged.

However, if the additional capital retained is invested wisely, then share price may be maintained or even rise, although this would depend on the proportion of shareholders who opt for the scrip.

(d)   Factoring and invoice discounting are two ways in which a company can obtain speedier payment in respect of credit sales made to customers. The shorter working capital cycle will quicken the rate of cash flow and in turn enable the company to reduce its reliance on other, perhaps less dependable, sources of short-term finance, such as bank overdrafts.

Factoring is the service provided by a financial institution which will lend the firm up to around 80% of the value of its debtors. The factor will then administer the sales accounts and undertake the collection of the debts. The remaining 20% or so of the value of debtors will be paid over to the client company either when all of the invoices have been settled or after some agreed time period, net of administration fees and interest charges. The service charge will vary between 0.5%–2.5% of turnover, and the interest charge will typically be in the range of 1–3% above base rate.

There is a distinction between 'non-recourse' factoring, whereby bad debts are the responsibility of the factor, and 'with recourse' factoring under which bad debts remain the liability of the client company. An additional fee, typically, 0.5% of turnover, will be required for the factor to provide protection against bad debts.

Sometimes, for reasons of goodwill, a company with a need to quicken its cash flow may not wish to reveal that it has enlisted the aid of a factor, preferring to retain the role as debt collector. In this case, it may utilise *invoice discounting,* a less comprehensive service which involves the financial institution purchasing selected invoices from the client at a discount. The interest cost of this provision of finance is reflected in the discount. For example, if a bundle of invoices with an average maturity of two months were sold at a discount of 2%, the effective interest cost would be $(1.02)^6 =$ 12.6% (approximately). The administration of the customer accounts remains with the company which settles the debt to the invoice discounter out of the payments duly collected from its customers.

Thus, the main additional benefit provided by full service-and-finance factoring are the administrative costs avoided by not having to operate the credit management function. The factor, perhaps by utilising information about customers obtained from operating the sales accounts of other firms, may also be a more efficient collector of debt than the client company, although there may be adverse goodwill implications.

(e)   The following reasons are often cited to support the *economic* case for privatisation:

To increase competition

Many formerly state-owned firms enjoyed statutory monopoly positions in their respective industries, often for sound reasons, such as to avoid the wasteful duplication of facilities which, say, competing water utilities would entail. Unless closely regulated, monopolies may exploit the consumer by charging high prices. In the UK, several of the statutory monopolies, such as gas, electricity and telephonic communications have now been broken, allowing new firms like Mercury in telecommunications, to compete for a share of the market. Competition of this nature is likely to lead to lower end prices and greater allocative efficiency.

To increase operating efficiency

Monopoly power is said to promote complacency and inertia, allowing excessively bureaucratic management structures to emerge. Exposure to market forces may force managerial economies, as the enterprise is forced to pare its costs in order to compete effectively. This has been seen most dramatically in the case of British Airways, in 1993, the most profitable airline in the world. Even an enterprise which preserves its monopoly is forced to improve its performance relative to other comparable private companies in order to build a stock market rating which ensures access to fresh supplies of capital.

Another way in which efficiency can be improved is by freeing enterprises from government interference in pricing and investment policies and thus allowing managers greater independence to plan effectively for the future. Moreover, enterprises are freer to diversify into other activities eg, some UK water companies have acquired or developed waste management subsidiaries. Some privatised industries are still regulated by the oversight of an industry 'watchdog' such as Oftel, in telecommunications, which by imposing tight pricing formulae, has forced BT to become considerably more cost-conscious.

To reduce the public sector borrowing requirement

The first UK asset sale, in 1977, that of BP shares under pressure from the IMF, was explicitly designed to raise funds for the public purse. The revenue raised from the subsequent and more significant privatisations, such as BT, British Gas and the water companies, made major inroads into the government's borrowing needs, and for a short spell, helped to convert the deficit into a surplus. The rationale behind reducing or eliminating the state's need to borrow is twofold. First, lower state borrowing moderates upward pressure on interest rates, thus reducing the tendency for state expenditure to 'crowd out' private investment expenditure. Secondly, higher state income increases the scope for reduction of taxes in order to raise incentives to work. In these respects, privatisation is part of the monetarist 'supply-side' philosophy.

(f)   The 'elasticity of demand' concept measures the extent to which the demand for a product will respond to a given change in some economic variable eg, price.

If there is a more than proportionate change in demand which results from a price change, ie, the price change has a significant effect on the number of units sold, demand is described as elastic. If the price change has little or no effect on demand ie, a less than proportionate change in the quantity demanded, demand is then described as inelastic. Price elasticity can be calculated as follows:

$$\frac{\% \text{ change in quantity of product demanded}}{\% \text{ change in product's own price}}$$

The concept of 'cross elasticity' describes the situation which exists, where the demand for one product is affected by a change in the price of a related product.

Management would need to monitor very frequently and very carefully, all of their products for which demand is elastic or subject to cross elasticity. This would involve keeping an eye on competitors' pricing and the development of a pricing policy which ensures that a satisfactory contribution is generated and is flexible enough to respond to the activities of competitors. For example, if a substitute made by a competitor is reduced in price, the company will have to decide reasonably quickly as to how it is going to react. Pricing cannot simply be done using cost-plus methods, it has to take account of, the effect it could have on demand and the prices of competitors.

65   (Answer 3 of examination)

3   (a)   **Cassiop plc**

Calculation of fixed overhead absorption rates

	Period 1 £	Period 2 £	Period 3 £
Budgeted FOH	10,400	19,170	17,360
Budgeted production (units)	8,000	14,200	12,400
FOH absorption rate (per unit)	1.30	1.35	1.40
Actual production (units)	8,400	13,600	9,200
FOH absorbed (actual units × rate)	10,920	18,360	12,880
Less: Actual FOH	11,200	18,320	16,740
	Under 280	Over 40	Under 3,860
Effect on the profit or loss	Deducted in P&L	Added back in P&L	Deducted in P&L

(Tutorial note: the wording of the question could imply a constant absorption rate across the three periods. This would be £(10,400 + 19,170 + 17,360)/(8,000 + 14,200 + 12,400) = £1.36 per unit. Resulting over/(under) absorptions would then be: Period 1 £224, Period 2 £176, Period 3 (£4,228).*)*

(b)   **The calculation of the closing stock figures (actual)**

	Period 1 (Units)	Period 2 (Units)	Period 3 (Units)
Opening stock	2,600	1,400	2,600
Add: Production	8,400	13,600	9,200
	11,000	15,000	11,800
Less: Sales	9,600	12,400	10,200
Closing stock	1,400	2,600	1,600

Whether or not a profit is higher (or a loss lower) under an absorption costing system compared with a marginal costing system depends on the value of the fixed overheads included in both the opening and closing stocks.

If the closing stock value of FOH is greater than the opening stock value of FOH, the profit will be greater (or loss lower) computed according to absorption costing principles compared with marginal costing, and vice versa.

The differences between the absorption costing profit and the marginal costing profit or loss can be computed as follows:

	Period 1 £	Period 2 £	Period 3 £
Closing stock	1,820	3,510	2,240
	(1,400 × £1.30)	(2,600 × £1.35)	(1,600 × £1.40)
Opening stock (given)	3,315	(Period 1) 1,820	(Period 2) 3,510
	(1,495)	1,690	(1,270)

Absorption profit lower than marginal profit in periods 1 and 3, higher in period 2.

(c)   Absorption costing cannot produce costs which are accurate, its principal aim is simply to ensure that all costs are covered. It depends upon a high degree of subjective judgement and thus should not be used for decision-making purposes.

The following areas of absorption costing involve subjective judgement.

–   The predetermination of costs and revenues. These take account of perceived assumptions about the environment in which the firm operates.

–   Those costs which can be allocated ie, charged direct to cost centres are still only estimates and their division depends upon assumptions eg, the estimated time which factory cleaners spend in each cost centre in which they clean.

–   The selection of methods of apportioning overheads to cost centres is at the discretion of the person doing the selecting such as the management accountant. Some overheads could be shared according to floor area, or cubic capacity eg, rent of premises, but yet only one or the other can be used.

–   The selection of the method by which the service cost centres are apportioned. Some of the methods favoured have their drawbacks eg, stores cost apportioned according to the number of requisitions take no account of weight, value, handling/storage problems etc.

–   The choice of the absorption (recovery) rate eg, direct labour hours, machine hours, percentage of prime cost etc.

–   The estimation of the denominator in the absorption rate eg, machine hours, direct labour hours etc.

–   The way in which administration, selling and distribution, research and development expenditure will be dealt with ie, will it be absorbed into the product cost or written off to the profit and loss account?

–   The treatment of any under- or over-recovery of overheads.

Thus, because of the high degree of subjectivity involved in producing an absorption rate and costs which cannot be classed as accurate, absorption costing is not recommended for decision-making purposes.

66   (Answer 4 of examination)

4   To the Board of Directors   Date: 18 December 19X4

Report on the problems associated with process costing

I have now completed my review of the problems associated with using process costing and describe my findings below.

My findings have been divided between five principal areas which are:

–   The treatment of overheads

–   Valuation at the point of separation of by-products and joint products

–   Normal and abnormal gains and losses

–   The valuation of work-in-progress and finished good (equivalent units) including the valuation of materials used

–   Others (sub-contractors etc)

The treatment of overheads

Overheads, the indirect expenditure such as non-manufacturing labour and maintenance materials, light and heat etc. has to be included in process costs using marginal costing or absorption costing.

Marginal costing only includes the variable overheads in the process costs ie, those overheads which vary directly with production.

Absorption costing includes all the manufacturing overheads in the process costs. Those overheads which cannot be identified and traced to a specific process are apportioned between the processes according to some arbitrary basis such as floor area, number of employees, etc.

The overheads are then charged to production via a direct labour or machine hour rate. For example, for every direct labour hour worked an amount will be added to the cost of the process to recover the overheads. Costs can only be described as accurate up to the point of their marginal cost. Costs attributed to products via absorption costing can in no way be described as accurate and should not therefore be used for decision-making purposes.

The main problem here is whether to use marginal costing or absorption costing. It must be stressed that if absorption costing is used, the data which it provides should not be used for decision-making purposes.

The valuation at the point of separation

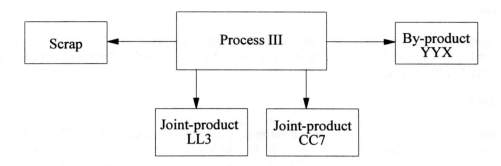

Figure 1: A valuation problem

The above diagram illustrates the problem which has to be faced. How much of process III should be charged, if any, to scrap, the by-product and the two joint products respectively? All three products and the scrap were produced in the same process. There are a number of treatments which can be used. Some examples are:

–   Scrap – of low saleable value, value at nil.

–   The by-product – value it at its selling price. This reduces the process cost.

–   The joint products – share the remaining process cost out in proportion to their weighted selling prices or weighted market values. Sharing the process cost between them using weight alone eg, the process cost per kilo, fails to recognise the fact that the two products are different.

The problem here is that a selection has to be made of the method for valuing the products at the point of separation. It must also be emphasised that the methods used simply share the process costs between the products, and cannot be regarded as accurate.

Normal and abnormal gains and losses

The principle of not charging abnormal losses or including abnormal gains in the process cost is well-established. The key problem to be solved is arriving at what is abnormal. This would involve consultation with the appropriate production personnel and would to a large extent depend upon past experience and future expectations.

The valuation of work-in-progress and finished goods

The valuation depends upon:

–   The estimation of the degree of completion. This should be done by those production personnel who are competent to make such an assessment. The estimation will need to take account of opening stocks, inputs from an earlier process, materials, labour and overheads.

–   The recording of labour for each process and the treatment of idle time, bonus payments and overtime.

–   A selection will also have to be made of the method of valuation of materials which are issued to each process eg, FIFO (first in, first out), LIFO (last in, first out), AVE CO (average cost), STD CO (standard cost) etc. The method adopted could have a significant impact on the process costs eg, FIFO in times of rising prices could in effect be understating the process costs in terms of the material content. The above-mentioned valuation methods also have an impact where stocks are brought forward in cases where there have also been movements in labour rates and overhead rates.

Others

Sub-contractors

The work undertaken by sub-contractors can be included as a direct cost of the next process or the finished product in cases where there is no further processing. The concern here is the maintenance of quality and the keeping of delivery pledges.

Activity-based costing (ABC)

An alternative to the marginal costing and absorption costing approaches is ABC. This method shares out the overheads via 'cost drivers' ie, the reason why the cost has been incurred eg, the number of purchase orders. However, this would need careful consideration and could be the focus of a future report.

Please do not hesitate to consult me should you want more information about the contents of this report.

Margaret Redwick, FCCA

---

67 (Answer 5 of examination)

5   (a)   The covenant does not give a precise measure of gearing in so far as it fails to stipulate whether short-term debt should be included in the calculation. It seems prudent to consider gearing measures with and without the bank overdraft.

        (i)   **Using book values**

$$\frac{\text{Long-term debt}}{\text{Shareholders' funds}} = £5m/£15m = 33\%$$

$$\frac{\text{Total debt}}{\text{Shareholders' funds}} = £8m/£15m = 53\%$$

        (ii)   **Using market values**

The market value of the debentures	=	$1.15 \times £5m = £5.75m$
The price of the ordinary shares	=	P/E ratio × Earnings per share
	=	$14 \times \dfrac{\text{Profit after tax}}{\text{Number of shares}}$
	=	$14 \times \dfrac{£1.34m}{20m} = 14 \times 6.7p = 94p$
Market value of equity	=	$20m \times 94p = £18.8m$

The gearing ratios are:

$$\frac{\text{Long-term debt}}{\text{Shareholders' funds}} = \frac{£5.75m}{£18.8m} = 31\%$$

$$\frac{\text{Total debt}}{\text{Shareholders' funds}} = \frac{£8.75m}{£18.8m} = 47\%$$

    (b)   It would seem that, in terms of its borrowing, Newsam has already breached the covenant if a combination of book values and total debt is used, while it is very near to doing so if the market value base is used in conjunction with total indebtedness. It could be argued that short-term creditors also constitute part of Newsam's indebtedness, inclusion of which would increase the gearing measures, but as they are covered by cash and debtors, they have been excluded.

Regarding the liquidity stipulation, at present, Newsam's current ratio is precisely one, compared to a permissible range of (1.35×0.8) to (1.35×1.2) ie, 1.08 to 1.62. It seems, therefore, that Newsam is also breaching the liquidity requirement in the covenant and will have to take steps to improve its liquidity, especially as the quick ratio is only £4.5m/£7m = 0.64 (although no industry standard is given).

(c)   Financial gearing exposes the company to the risk of inability to meet required interest payments, should the company's profitability falter. If the creditors decide to demand repayment of their capital, the company faces the problem of liquidating assets, and possibly, the whole enterprise, in order to meet these claims. Hence, the first consideration is the degree of safety implied by the firm's interest cover, the ratio of profit before tax and interest to interest payable, in the light of the stability of the firm's sales and profits.

Interest cover is £3m/£1m = 3 times, which might appear low to some analysts, but if the firm's operations are stable, this may be tolerable. In the case of Newsam, although sales growth has been sluggish, its products are branded and well-established, and probably not subject to wide fluctuations. This seems a safe cover.

The second consideration is the value of the firm's assets in relation to the debt capital. In the first instance, the ability to repay the debentures is critical, but if debenture holders demanded repayment, it is inconceivable that Newsam's bankers would not call in the overdraft. Hence, Newsam's ability to repay *all* its debt needs to be assessed.

At book values, fixed assets appear in the accounts at £20m. Whether Newsam could actually achieve this figure in a forced sale is questionable, although it is possible that the value of the land and premises on the open market might exceed their historic cost values. The current state of the property market is important in this respect.

The final consideration is the action which Newsam's debenture holders are empowered to take in the event of breach of covenant, and, more pertinently, what they are *expected* to do in the circumstances. Newsam is likely to have some idea of their probable reaction as precautionary discussions are likely to have taken place already.

(d)   (i)   To lower its gearing ratio, Newsam could adopt a number of policies:

Revalue its fixed assets

Despite the depression in the UK property market in the early 1990s, it is still likely that a revaluation could reveal a surplus. However, this is likely to be a purely cosmetic adjustment – unless the revaluation conveys information which is genuinely new to the market, the share price is unlikely to respond, despite an increase in the book value of assets.

Place a value on its brands

Again, this may be a purely cosmetic exercise, as the market will already have taken into account the value of these brands in setting the share price. Nevertheless, this ploy has been adopted by a number of UK firms.

Tighten working capital management

The bank overdraft could be lowered by a more aggressive working capital management policy. For example, the debtor collection period could be shortened and/or the trade credit period lengthened. There does appear to be some scope regarding debtor days which currently stand at: $4/28 \times 365 = 52$ days which appears quite lengthy, although the trade credit period, currently: $4/20 \times 365 = 73$ days, already is excessively long and would give rise to fears over suppliers' reaction if any further delay was attempted.

The stock turnover at 20/2.5 = 8 times (or 46 days) may look fairly long and capable of reduction, but overall, the working capital cycle at (52 + 46) − 73 = 25 days is quite rapid already.

It may be possible to achieve economies in this area but the scope appears limited.

(Tutorial note: In order to calculate the credit period, you have to assume a reasonable figure for purchases. The examiner has assumed £20 million*).*

Issue more shares

In theory, it should not matter when a rights issue is made, because the share price in an efficient market would always indicate the correct value of the shares, and the only market reaction would be the technical adjustment caused by earnings dilution when shares are sold at a discount. In reality, it is often difficult to convince a flat stock market of the positive reasons for a rights issue. In the present case, the announcement that a moderately performing and poorly-rated company like Newsam was planning to make a rights issue on a weak stock market merely in order to reduce indebtedness would be likely to induce a negative reaction.

This problem could possibly be eased if the company were able to make a placing of new shares with supportive financial institutions after persuading shareholders to forgo pre-emptive rights of purchase.

(ii)   To raise the interest cover, Newsam could do the following:

Refinance the debenture with a bank overdraft

The interest saving, assuming no change in the total debt, would be: (15% − 9%) × £5m = £0.3m. This would raise the interest cover to £3.0m/£0.7m = 4.3 times.

Refinance the debenture with a Eurodollar issue

On the face of it, this alternative appears to offer bigger interest savings − ie, (15% − 5%) × £5m = £0.5m, which would raise the interest cover to £3.0m/£0.5m = 6 times. However, aside from the issue costs likely to be involved, there are dangers here. The forward market quotation for the dollar suggests that the dollar will appreciate against sterling by 1% over three months, or about 4% over one year. Although it is possible that the dollar could actually depreciate, thus lowering the sterling value of the debt, the foreign exchange market consensus is for a dollar appreciation of sufficient magnitude to eliminate the interest differential between Eurobonds and an overdraft from a domestic bank.

In addition, there are dangers in replacing long-term debt with short-term debt. For example, a bank overdraft is, in principle (if not always in practice), repayable on demand, nor is the bank obliged to extend overdraft facilities indefinitely, while the company is exposed to the risk of adverse interest rate movements over the duration of its short-term financing. Newsam must balance these risks and their consequences against the interest cost differential.

68   (Answer 6 of examination)

6   (a)   *Hard capital rationing* applies when a firm is restricted from undertaking all apparently worthwhile investment opportunities by factors external to the company, and over which it has no control. These factors may include government monetary restrictions and the general economic and financial climate, for example, a depressed stock market, precluding a rights issue of ordinary shares.

Soft capital rationing applies when a company decides to limit the amount of capital expenditure which it is prepared to authorise. The capital budget becomes a control variable, which the company may relax if it chooses. Segments of divisionalised companies often have their capital budgets imposed by the main board of directors.

A company may purposely curtail its capital expenditure for a number of reasons:

(i)   It may consider that it has insufficient depth of management expertise to exploit all available opportunities without jeopardising the success of both new and ongoing operations.

(ii) It may be deliberate board policy to restrict the capital budget to concentrate managerial attention on generating the very best and most carefully thought out and analysed proposals. In this regard, self-imposed capital rationing may be an exercise in quality control.

(iii) Many companies adopt the policy of restraining capital expenditure to the amounts which can be generated by internal resources ie, retained earnings and depreciation provisions (or in reality, cash flow). This reluctance to use the external capital markets may be due to a risk-averse attitude to financial gearing, possibly because of the operating characteristics of the industry eg, high operating gearing in a cyclical industry. Alternatively, it may be due to reluctance to issue equity in the form of a rights issue, for fear of diluting earnings, or in the case of an unlisted company, reluctance to seek a quotation owing to the time and expense involved and the dilution of ownership.

(b) (i) Assuming Filtrex wishes to maximise the wealth of its shareholders, it will seek the set of investment projects with the highest combined NPVs.

As a first approximation, it may examine the projects ranked according to their estimated NPVs, and select the projects with the highest NPVs, consistent with the budget limitation. However, this approach would confine the programme to project E alone, which apart from losing any benefits of diversification, is a solution which can be improved upon. This is because it overlooks the relationship between the NPV itself and the amount of capital required to yield the estimated NPV. Under capital rationing, it is often considered desirable to examine the productivity of each pound of scarce capital invested in the various projects. This information is given by the profitability index (PI). The ranking of the five projects according to their PIs is:

A	65/150	=	0.43
B	50/120	=	0.42
C	80/200	=	0.40
D	30/80	=	0.37
E	120/400	=	0.30

Moving down the ranking, Filtrex would select projects A and B. but then, due to the indivisibility problem, and also the fact that projects A and C are mutually exclusive, it would have to depart from the rankings and move down as far as D, whereafter the remaining project E is too demanding of capital. The selected programme of ABD would require an outlay of £350,000 and generate an NPV of £145,000. £50,000 of scarce capital would remain unspent and according to the stated policy, would be invested in short-term assets. Although of low risk, these offer a return less than the 18% required by shareholders. Consequently it might be preferable to return this unspent capital to shareholders in the form of a dividend or share repurchase, if shareholders are able to invest for higher returns in alternative activities. Perhaps, closer liaison with major shareholders is required to determine their preferences.

It is possible to improve on both of the previous selections by trial and error, in an attempt to utilise the whole of the capital budget. The optimal selection is BCD which offers a joint NPV of £160,000. However, even this result is suspect as it relies on evaluating the projects at the rate of return required in the absence of rationing, in this case, 18% post-tax. This neglects the impact of capital rationing on the cost of capital − if apparently worthwhile projects are rejected, there is an opportunity cost in the form of the returns otherwise obtainable on the rejected projects. Projects should be evaluated at the discount rate reflecting the rate of return on the best of the rejected projects. Unfortunately, until the evaluation and selection is made, this remains an unknown! Unless project indivisibility is a problem, ranking and selection using the internal rate of return (IRR) will yield the same solution – it would therefore be helpful to find the IRR for each project.

(ii)   In addition to IRRs, other information which may aid the decision-maker might include:

    (1)   Whether the rationing is likely to apply over the long-term, in which case,

    (2)   The degree of postponability of projects should be more closely assessed ie, whether a project can be postponed and the impact of postponement on its profitability. If projects can be postponed, it may be desirable for Filtrex to select projects in the base period offering a rapid return flow of cash in order to provide funds to enable investment in postponed projects in the next time period. In other words, it would be helpful to examine the cash flow profiles of these projects and hence their rates of payback.

    (3)   The respective degrees of risk of these projects. It is implied that all projects have a similar degree of risk which is unlikely in practice, especially for the types of new product development planned by Filtrex. A capital-constrained company may use its limited access to finance to justify rejecting a high risk activity, especially if it is reliant on subsequent cash flows to finance postponed projects.

    (4)   The likelihood of obtaining marginal supplies of finance and on what terms.

(c)   There are two basic ways in which a company in Filtrex's position might still manage to exploit more projects. On one hand, it can involve other parties in the project, and on the other, it can resolve to seek outside capital.

Sharing the projects

(i)   To the extent that some part of the project(s) still require further development eg, design and market research, some of this work can be sub-contracted to specialist agencies, who may be able to perform the work at lower cost, or even to take payment out of the project cash flows.

(ii)   The production and/or sale of the products can be licensed or franchised to another party, with Filtrex arranging to receive a royalty or a percentage of sales. This is particularly appropriate for overseas activities.

(iii)   A joint venture could be mounted with a competitor, although for commercial reasons, it is often safer to arrange such alliances with companies outside the industry, or with overseas companies wishing to penetrate the UK market. Clearly, such an agreement would have to be carefully negotiated.

(iv)   The patent rights to one or more products could be sold and the purchaser allowed to develop the projects.

Raising external finance

(i)   A certain amount of marginal finance could be squeezed out of more intensive use of working capital, although this could be counter-productive eg, reducing credit periods for customers may lose sales.

(ii)   Some equipment could be leased.

(iii)   If Filtrex has assets of sufficient quality, it may be possible to raise a mortgage or issue debentures secured on these assets.

(iv)   Alternatively, good quality property assets could be sold to a financial institution and their continued use secured via a leaseback arrangement.

(v)   Filtrex might approach official sources of aid such as a regional development agency, if relevant, or perhaps the European Investment Bank.

(vi)   Filtrex might approach a venture capitalist such as 3i, which specialises in extending development capital to small-to-medium-sized firms. However, they may require an equity stake, and possibly insist on placing an appointee on the Board to monitor their interests.

(vii)   Filtrex may decide to seek a Stock Exchange quotation, either on the main market or the USM. However, this would be time-consuming and costly, and involve releasing at least 25% of the equity (10% for the USM) to a wider body of shareholders.

*(**Tutorial note:** it is now no longer possible to enter the USM, which is due to be closed by the end of 1996. The Alternative Investment Market (AIM) was launched in June 1995 to provide a market for the shares of young fast growing companies not yet ready for a full listing; its entry requirements are less onerous than those for the USM.)*

Section A – This question is compulsory and MUST be attempted

┌───┐
│ **69**   **(Question 1 of examination)**   │
└───┘

1   (a)   For what *economic* reasons do central governments periodically impose limits on the capital expenditure of regional authorities?   (5 marks)

(b)   How does the required return for public sector investment decisions differ from that in the private sector?   (5 marks)

(c)   The regional authority of Arctica, the most northerly province of Northland, (a member of the European Union which uses sterling as its currency) received many complaints from the general public during the past winter for its poor performance in clearing the local roads in snowy weather conditions. The roads department operates a fleet of five vehicles all beyond their optimum operating lifetimes and consequently having a high rate of breakdowns. Their second-hand value is estimated at £2,000 each. Modern replacements cost £50,000 each. After a life span of six years, it is expected that each vehicle could be resold for £5,000 after overhaul, or for £2,000 as scrap. The vehicles will require overhauls every two years costing £14,000 per vehicle.

A consultant, hired to assess the size of fleet required to provide an acceptable level of service to avoid future complaints, estimates that 10 vehicles would suffice in all but exceptional weather conditions. However, Arctica is concerned about the recent tightening by central government, (on whom regional authorities rely for most of their capital funding), of controls over capital spending. The vehicles would only be needed for the six months from October to March, although they could be hired during the summer months for a maximum of five years to a nearby quarry for a fixed annual contract fee for *all* 10 vehicles of initially £200,000, but declining by £40,000 each year to reflect ageing of the fleet. However, Arctica is concerned that the quarry workings are approaching exhaustion and may be closed in the near future. Indeed, the quarry company will not sign a firm contract for a period exceeding two years out of a similar concern.

During the winter, the 10 vehicles would be kept on stand-by, to be driven, when needed, by refuse disposal truck drivers, assigned from normal duties and paid overtime wage rates if necessary. Incremental operating costs, including salt to treat the roads, will depend on winter weather conditions according to the following probability distribution:

Cost of drivers' wages, fuel, maintenance and salt

Winter weather	*Probability*	*Annual cost (£m)*
Severe	0.2	1.5
Average	0.5	0.8
Good	0.3	0.3

Instead of buying 10 vehicles, Arctica is considering contracting-out the whole operation. It has received an unofficial tender from a waste management company, Dumpex plc, which might be willing to perform the required services at an all-in fee of £1m pa, payable at the end of each year.

Central government guidelines require regional authorities to evaluate capital expenditures at a discount rate of 5% expressed in real terms. The real rate of return in the private sector for transport and related activities is currently 8% net of all taxes.

All estimates of costs and benefits have been made in constant price terms. As a public sector organisation, Arctica is not liable to pay taxes.

Required

(i)   Is it financially more worthwhile for Arctica to purchase the new vehicles or to accept the tender from Dumpex?

Explain your answer.

(11 marks)

(ii)   What is the maximum annual tender figure at which Arctica would contract out the operation?

Explain your answer.

(2 marks)

(d)   Find the break-even value of the annual contract fee payable to Dumpex plc on the assumption that Arctica is unable to conclude any form of contract with the quarry company.

Comment on your results.

(6 marks)

(e)   Discuss *three* alternative ways in which Arctica could finance this project.

(6 marks)
(Total 35 marks)

Section B – This question is compulsory and MUST be attempted

70	(Question 2 of examination)

2   Answer *five* of the six parts of this question. Each part carries five marks.

(a)   Explain the process whereby commercial banks can create the short-term credit required by business and other borrowers, and the constraints on this process.

(5 marks)

(b)   'If an organisation applies zero-base budgeting, (ZBB), it is essential that all levels of management understand the 'decision package' concept.'

Explain briefly what the 'decision package concept' is and how it is used in ZBB.

(5 marks)

(c)   The following cost information relates to product ZIM 3A, which is produced in one continuous process by Chemacca Ltd:

	£
Actual quantity of materials at standard price	103,500
Actual quantity of materials at actual price	103,250
Actual yield at standard materials cost	102,500
Standard yield from actual input of materials at standard cost	100,000

Required

Calculate and present the following material cost variances:

(i)   price;
(ii)   usage;
(iii)   mix and yield, and

comment briefly on your findings.

(5 marks)

(d)   Explain why statistical information is important to the operation of the management accounting function of an organisation.

(5 marks)

(e)   Sellmoor plc is considering a proposal to change its credit policy from allowing its debtors a credit period of 50 days, to either 40 days or 60 days, and supplied you with the following data:

Period of credit allowed to debtors Days	Annual turnover (all on credit) £'000
50 (current)	420
40	350 (estimated)
60	520 (estimated)

The average profit/volume ratio for the company is 22% and the cost of financing debtors is 12%.

Required

Compute and explain briefly what the effect on profit of each proposal would be, if adopted. (5 marks)

(f)   Explain briefly the principal steps which management would have to take in order to draw up their capital expenditure budget.   (5 marks)

(Total 25 marks)

Section C – ONE question ONLY to be attempted

71   (Question 3 of examination)

3   You have been provided with the following operating statement which represents an attempt to compare the actual performance for the quarter which has just ended with the budget:

	Budget	Actual	Variance
Number of units sold ('000)	640	720	80
	£'000	£'000	£'000
Sales	1,024	1,071	47
Cost of sales (all variable)			
Materials	168	144	
Labour	240	288	
Overheads	32	36	
	440	468	(28)
Fixed labour cost	100	94	6
Selling and distribution costs			
Fixed	72	83	(11)
Variable	144	153	(9)
Administration costs			
Fixed	184	176	8
Variable	48	54	(6)
	548	560	(12)
Net profit	36	43	7

Required

(a)   Using a flexible budgeting approach, re-draft the operating statement so as to provide a more realistic indication of the variances, and comment briefly on the possible reasons (other than inflation) why they have occurred.   (12 marks)

(b)   Explain why the original operating statement was of little use to management.   (2 marks)

(c)   Discuss the problems associated with the forecasting of figures which are to be used in flexible budgeting.

(6 marks)

(Total 20 marks)

72	**(Question 4 of examination)**

4   The following budgeted information relates to Brunti plc for the forthcoming period:

	Products		
	XYI	*YZT*	*ABW*
	('000)	*('000)*	*('000)*
Sales and production (units)	50	40	30
	£	£	£
Selling price(per unit)	45	95	73
Prime cost (per unit)	32	84	65
	Hours	*Hours*	*Hours*
Machine department (machine hours per unit)	2	5	4
Assembly department (direct labour hours per unit)	7	3	2

Overheads allocated and apportioned to production departments (including service cost centre costs) were to be recovered in product costs as follows:

Machine department at £1.20 per machine hour
Assembly department at £0.825 per direct labour hour

You ascertain that the above overheads could be re-analysed into 'cost pools' as follows:

Cost pool	*£'000*	*Cost driver*	*Quantity for the period*
Machining services	357	Machined hours	420,000
Assembly services	318	Direct labour hours	530,000
Set up costs	26	Set ups	520
Order processing	156	Customer orders	32,000
Purchasing	84	Suppliers' orders	11,200
	941		

You have also been provided with the following estimates for the period:

	Products		
	XYI	*YZT*	*ABW*
	('000)	*('000)*	*('000)*
Number of set-ups	120	200	200
Customer orders	8	8	16
Suppliers' orders	3	4	4.2

Required

(a)   Prepare and present profit statements using:

(i)   conventional absorption costing; and   (5 marks)
(ii)   activity-based costing.   (10 marks)

(b)   Comment on why activity-based costing is considered to present a fairer valuation of the product cost per unit.

(5 marks)

(Total 20 marks)

Section D – ONE question ONLY to be attempted

---
73   (Question 5 of examination)
---

5   Armcliff Ltd is a division of Shevin plc which requires each of its divisions to achieve a rate of return on capital employed of at least 10% pa. For this purpose, capital employed is defined as fixed capital and investment in stocks. This rate of return is also applied as a hurdle rate for new investment projects. Divisions have limited borrowing powers and all capital projects are centrally funded.

The following is an extract from Armcliff's divisional accounts:

Profit and loss account for the year ended 31 December 1994

	£m
Turnover	120
Cost of sales	(100)
Operating profit	20

Assets employed as at 31 December 1994

	£m	£m
Fixed (net)		75
Current assets (including stocks £25m)	45	
Current liabilities	(32)	
		13
Net capital employed		88

Armcliff's production engineers wish to invest in a new computer-controlled press. The equipment cost is £14m. The residual value is expected to be £2m after four years operation, when the equipment will be shipped to a customer in South America.

The new machine is capable of improving the quality of the existing product and also of producing a higher volume. The firm's marketing team is confident of selling the increased volume by extending the credit period. The expected additional sales are:

Year 1	2,000,000 units
Year 2	1,800,000 units
Year 3	1,600,000 units
Year 4	1,600,000 units

Sales volume is expected to fall over time due to emerging competitive pressures. Competition will also necessitate a reduction in price by £0.5 each year from the £5 per unit proposed in the first year. Operating costs are expected to be steady at £1 per unit, and allocation of overheads (none of which are affected by the new project) by the central finance department is set at £0.75 per unit.

Higher production levels will require additional investment in stocks of £0.5m, which would be held at this level until the final stages of operation of the project. Customers at present settle accounts after 90 days on average.

Required

(a)   Determine whether the proposed capital investment is attractive to Armcliff, using the average rate of return on capital method, as defined as average profit-to-average capital employed, ignoring debtors and creditors.

[*Note:* Ignore taxes]

(7 marks)

(b)   (i)   Suggest *three* problems which arise with the use of the average return method for appraising new investment.

(3 marks)

       (ii)   In view of the problems associated with the ARR method, why do companies continue to use it in project appraisal?

(3 marks)

(c)   Briefly discuss the dangers of offering more generous credit, and suggest ways of assessing customers' creditworthiness.

(7 marks)

(Total 20 marks)

---

74   (Question 6 of examination)

6   Collingham plc produces electronic measuring instruments for medical research. It has recorded strong and consistent growth during the past 10 years since its present team of managers bought it out from a large multinational corporation. They are now contemplating obtaining a stock market listing.

Collingham's accounting statements for the last financial year are summarised below. Fixed assets, including freehold land and premises, are shown at historic cost net of depreciation. The debenture is redeemable in two years although early redemption without penalty is permissible.

Profit and loss account for the year ended 31 December 1994

	£m
Turnover	80.0
Cost of sales	(70.0)
Operating profit	10.0
Interest charges	(3.0)
Pre-tax profit	7.0
Corporation tax (after capital allowances)	(1.0)
Profits attributable to ordinary shareholders	6.0
Dividends	(0.5)
Retained earnings	5.5

Balance sheet as at 31 December 1994

	£m	£m	£m
Assets employed			
Fixed:			
Land and premises	10.0		
Machinery	20.0		
			30.0
Current:			
Stocks	10.0		
Debtors	10.0		
Cash	3.0		
		23.0	
Current liabilities:			
Trade creditors	(15.0)		
Bank overdraft	(5.0)		
		(20.0)	
Net current assets			3.0
Total assets less current liabilities			33.0
14% Debenture			(5.0)
Net assets			28.0
Financed by:			
Issued share capital (par value 50p)			
Voting shares			2.0
Non-voting 'A' shares			2.0
Profit and loss account			24.0
Shareholders' funds			28.0

The following information is also available regarding key financial indicators for Collingham's industry.

Return on (long-term) capital employed	22% (pre-tax)
Return on equity	14% (post-tax)
Operating profit margin	10%
Current ratio	1.8:1
Acid-test	1.1:1
Gearing (total debt equity)	18%
Interest cover	5.2
Dividend cover	2.6
P/E ratio	13:1

Required

(a) Briefly explain why companies like Collingham seek stock market listings. (4 marks)

(b) Discuss the performance and financial health of Collingham in relation to that of the industry as a whole. (8 marks)

(c)   In what ways would you advise Collingham:

(i)   to restructure its balance sheet *prior* to floatation,   (5 marks)
(ii)   to change its financial policy *following* floatation?   (3 marks)
                                                                    (Total 20 marks)

EXAMINER'S COMMENTS

General comments

Paper 8 has now been examined under the new syllabus on three occasions. As with the earlier papers, marks on the MA questions were higher than on the FM areas. Again, it seems that candiates (particularly those from overseas) are seeing Paper 8 as an exam in MA with a little FM tacked on, and/or are relying on knowledge gained in earlier MA studies to carry them through. This is exacerbated by the number of candidates who fail to read the questions properly. Also of concern is the 'bullet point syndrome' – the tendency to confine answers to a list of points without offering any supporting discussion or explanation.

It continues to be disappointing to see such a poor level of knowledge and ability to apply that knowledge in both the FM area and also in Economics. It is certain that those who were poorly prepared for FM but knew enough MA to scrape through will struggle on Paper 14, and probably Paper 9, both of which require a sound grasp of project appraisal in particular.

Another area of concern is poor layout and presentation in numerical answers.

Question 1: the case study question, centred on a regional authority facing capital spending restrictions imposed by central government, but wishing to invest in new snow-clearing equipment. Essentially a question on project appraisal, but requiring knowledge of the economic context and of sources of finance available to the public sector.

Part (a): many candidates appeared to be unaware of economic principles, and of the role of the state in managing the economy. Most answers were a list of possible reasons for intervention which may or may not have been relevant. These were expressed in vague terms such as 'to control inflation', 'to restrain interest rates', 'to reduce borrowing', etc with little or no attempt to place these points in the context of an economic stabilisation policy. A particular difficulty was a lack of understanding of the interrelationships between the various factors cited. For example, candidates should ask themselves why is it government borrowing may affect interest rates, the exchange rate and perhaps the balance of payments? (There was great confusion between the PSBR and the balance of payments.)

Part (b): the intention of this section was to elicit discussion from candidates of the required rates of return, ie, discount rates, for investment projects, in the public and private sectors respectively. Candidates could also earn some marks (as most did), by talking generally about the nature of the returns in the two sectors, and about respective objectives, ie, profit motive in the private sector and social benefits in the public sector. Few candidates focused on the differential in time horizon risk as between the two sectors, or on the possible risk disparity, although some did focus on the tax aspect.

There was some confusion in the distinction between public and private sector – some candidates read public as 'publicly quoted' and private as 'unquoted'. The correct interpretation should have been clear from the context of the whole question.

Part (c)(i): many different approaches were possible here. For example, the decision problem could be treated in terms of the respective NPVs of the two options, in incremental terms or in terms of Equivalent Annual Costs (EAC). All such approaches would produce the same answer. It was however, essential to use DCF analysis (which was why discount rates were provided) over six years, incorporating Arctica's cut-off rate of 5%. Many candidates attempted to find a one-year cost which included all the initial outlay, for which only limited credit could be offered. Many candidates seemed unsure of how to approach a cost minimisation problem.

Part (c)(ii): this section revealed candidates' lack of knowledge of the EAC concept – a common error was to divide the NPV figure from the previous section by the number of years rather than by the relevant annuity factor.

Part (d) was frequently totally ignored, but for candidates who understood the question, this offered some very easy marks. All that was required was removal of the PV of the hire income and conversion of the resulting higher cost figure into a higher EAC. Many candidates could only associate 'break-even' with cost-volume-profit analysis. Commentary was generally very sparse.

(Candidates can be assured that incorrect answers to earlier sections were not penalised twice – markers applied the 'own answer principle' to give appropriate credit for method even where answers were numerically incorrect.)

In part (e), answers were generally weak. Although the requirement said 'discuss', most responses were little more than lists, often with no acknowledgement of the context of the question. Some answers were completely irrelevant, talking about companies and rights issues, debentures and convertibles, etc. To gain marks, answers had to be relevant to the public sector, and where appropriate, eg, in the case of aspects like government grants or borrowing, to reflect the more stringent regime being applied, ie, the regional authority might have to make a special case to the central authorities to overcome the new restrictions.

Question 2: part (a) required a knowledge of how commercial banks create credit via the operation of the bank multiplier, and the constraints on the process.

This was very badly done, partly as a result of poor knowledge of Economics and partly due to misinterpretation. The question required explanation of the credit creation process and associated constraints, such as central bank restrictions on reserve ratios. The trigger words should have been 'credit creation' and 'process'. Actual answers ranged from the trivial (such as 'banks receive deposits and lend them out as loans'), through general explanations of the nature of financial intermediation to broad explanations of lending procedures (ie, interviews, credit checks, etc), and/or of the range of bank lending facilities (ie, overdrafts, loans, etc). For properly prepared candidates, interpretation should not have been a problem – the bank multiplier process is commonplace. Responses were especially poor on knowledge of central bank measures to restrict lending.

Part (b) was about 'the decision package concept' in zero-base budgeting.

This part was not answered very well. Many candidates did not answer the question set, instead writing down all they knew about ZBB.

Part (c) required candidates to calculate material variances, including the mix and yield variances from the information supplied and then to comment briefly on their findings.

The majority of candidates made a poor attempt at answering this part. The calculation of the material price variance did not present too much difficulty. However, a large number of candidates scored few or no marks for their calculations of the other material variances. Quite a number of answers described one of the variances as 'the mix and yield variance'. Many of the attempts made no comment at all about their findings.

Part (d). This 'open ended' question asked for an explanation as to why statistical information is important to the management accountant. The majority of candidates did reasonably well here. It was pleasing to find satisfactory explanations of why it is important in areas such as budgeting and decision making and also to find examples of the uses to which the management accountant can put certain statistical techniques/government statistics.

Part (e) concerned the effects on profit of changing the period of credit which is offered to debtors.

Overall this was very well down but quite a number of candidates lost marks by not providing the brief explanation that was required.

Part (f) concerned the steps needed to draw up a 'capital expenditure budget'.

The performance on this part was very mixed. Candidates tending to produce either very good or very poor answers. Quite a number of candidates just wrote about capital investment appraisal eg, NPV, pay-back etc which was just one small component part of the answer. Those who produced better answers looked at inter-relationships with other budgets, financing considerations, alternatives to outright purchase etc.

Question 3: involved the calculation of variances using a flexible budgeting approach and commenting briefly on the possible reasons for the variances.

(a)   Many candidates scored well on this question. Those who did not tended either not to flex the budget at all, or flex both variable and fixed costs.

(b)   The majority of candidates had no problem with this part.

(c)   This section was about the problems associated with forecasting the figures which are used in flexible budgeting.

This was not very well answered and represents the area in this question where candidates did not pick up many marks. This was yet another prime example of a question where candidates did not answer the question set. Quite a number of answers were all about the advantages and disadvantages of flexible budgeting or just looked at the problem of distinguishing between fixed and variable costs.

Question 4: this question looked at activity based costing (ABC).

Most candidates were very well prepared for this question and scored very good marks on both the computational and the written parts.

Question 5: required calculation of the average rate of return for a new investment project, and discussion of the reasons for and against using this method, then testing knowledge of the dangers of extending additional credit to customers and of ways of screening them for credit-worthiness.

Part (a) seemed to highlight candidates' unease with the whole topic of project appraisal. For example, many candidates elected to conduct an NPV calculation, totally ignoring the thrust of the question. Overheads were often ignored, as is correct for a DCF exercise but not in an ARR calculation, although there were many errors of inconsistency here. Depreciaton was frequently ignored, as was the investment in stock required by the new project. Many return on investment calculations were based on initial investment. Although the average could be calculated in several ways, it was important to allow for the residual value, which was deducted by the majority of candidates rather than added.

(The correct calculation of average investment in its simplest form was:

[£14m + £0.5m + £2m]2 = £16.5m/2 =£8.25m or £16m/2 + £0.5m = £8.5m, ignoring the stock rundown, either being acceptable).

Many answers neglected to indicate whether the project met the 10% required standard, and the vast majority neglected to compare the project's ARR with the divisions's current ROI of 20%, which also has a bearing on project acceptability.

In part (b) too many answers were in bullet point form with little or no explanation. There was considerable repetition eg, candidates saying that the ARR ignored the time value of money and then saying it ignored the timing of cash flows. Few candidates seemed aware of coherent reasons for using ARR beyond its 'simplicity' and 'ease of calculation' and the fact that managers appear to understand it. It is difficult to award marks for such vague answers unsupported by discussion. Candidates should ask themselves questions like 'What is it about the ARR which makes it 'understandable'?'

It was clear that many candidates were referring to the IRR in their answers rather than the ARR.

Part (c) was answered quite well by most candidates, with typical answers displaying good knowledge of the problems involved in extending additional credit. As is common across the board, too many responses to the second part failed to offer any supporting discussion/explanation of credit assessment methods, relying solely on bullet points.

Question 6: required knowledge of the reasons why companies seek a stock market quotation, and use of ratio analysis to underpin evaluation of company performance (to judge the attractiveness of the issue), and then how obtaining a quotation might affect company financial policy.

(a)   Few candidates could cite reasons beyond raising new finance and easier access to capital (oddly, borrowed capital was mainly cited) in the future. Some insisted on explaining the drawbacks with obtaining a listing.

(b)   This section, as in previous papers, highlighted candidates' lack of knowledge of basic accounting and ratio analysis. Many curious ratios were given, especially in the areas of ROCE, ROE and dividend and interest cover. Unaccountably, quite a sizeable proportion of candidates chose to ignore Collingham's accounts (and hence the wording of the question) and discussed the industry ratios. Perhaps the main failing was the superficiality of the analysis of the company's 'financial health' in the light of the given and calculated figures.

(c)   The distinction between pre- and post-flotation is somewhat artificial so credit was given for valid points wherever they appeared. Answers were generally disappointing, again showing up lack of basic accounting understanding. A common error was to focus on presentation of the accounts rather than on the underlying financial indicators. Few candidates explained the need to enfranchise the 'A' shares and the desirability of a scrip issue.

ANSWERS TO JUNE 1995 EXAMINATION

It should be noted that the following answers are fuller than would be expected from the average student under exam conditions. Answers are provided in some degree of detail to offer guidance on the approach required, and on the range and depth of knowledge that would be expected from an excellent student.

69   (Answer 1 of examination)

1   (a)   Central governments apply periodic restrictions on public expenditure, both current and capital, as part of their discretionary fiscal policy. Such intervention in the economy seeks to smooth the oscillations of the business cycle by adjusting the balance between public expenditure and revenue from taxes. Specifically, when an economic downturn is expected, the government will plan to operate a budget deficit ie, spend more than its tax revenue, in order to inject demand into the economy when economic activity is flagging, and conversely, when an economic expansion, with consequent inflationary pressures, is expected.

This contra-cyclical budgetary policy can dampen fluctuations in the economy, thus increasing business confidence and readiness to invest. However, successful operation of this policy requires considerable skill in forecasting future economic trends, perception in recognising the need to act and speed in putting appropriate measures into effect so that they have an impact when required.

When a government wishes to restrict its expenditure it is often easier to cut capital expenditure. Although once approved and begun, capital projects acquire a momentum which is difficult to reverse, design specifications can be changed for subsequent phases of a lengthy project, later phases postponed or cancelled, or projects yet to be undertaken can be delayed indefinitely.

(b)   Private sector companies are obliged to earn a return at least as great as the opportunity cost incurred by the owners who subscribe capital to them, that is, to at least match the returns offered by comparable investments in which they might otherwise have invested. This reflects the required compensation to reward the individual for waiting for his money, (his rate of 'time preference'), plus some compensation for risk.

In the public sector, many investments such as civil engineering works, have far longer lives than private sector projects, and may also involve costs and benefits which are not priced by the market – so-called externalities such as pollution or congestion costs. For these reasons, it is often argued that a different discount rate should be applied to public sector projects.

One approach is to adopt the social rate of time preference argument. Society has a longer time horizon than private individuals and to reflect this, a lower rate of discount is warranted, so as not to over-discount the distant benefits which would be valued by future generations.

However, this approach may overlook the opportunity cost incurred by society in undertaking the project in question. Since capital can be invested in a number of ways, it is appropriate to examine what projects and hence what returns are foregone by allocating capital to particular uses. Consequently, the correct discount rate would reflect the rate of return on the best alternative use of public funds, including all externalities – the so-called social opportunity cost return.

(In the Arctica example, the government requires a return of 5% in real terms, below the yield on comparable private sector investments. In the UK in recent years, the Treasury has tended to overlook the externalities argument and focus on the post-tax returns which would otherwise have been achieved in the private sector. In this case, it is more likely that the lower percentage reflects the differential advantage enjoyed by the government in raising capital compared to private sector companies.)

(c)   (i)   **Evaluation of alternatives**

The optimal course of action from a financial viewpoint is that which minimises the present value of the net costs of meeting the service targets.

The offer

The present value of the annual contract payments sought by Dumpex is found by applying the six-year annuity factor at 5% to the annual payments:

Present value = £1m × PVIFA$_{5,6}$ = £1m × 5.076 = £5.08.

Purchase of new fleet

Expected value of operating costs (£m)

= (0.2 × 1.5) + (0.5 × 0.8) + (0.3 × 0.3) = 0.3 + 0.4 + 0.09 = 0.79

				Cash flow profile (£m)			
				Year			
Item	*0*	*1*	*2*	*3*	*4*	*5*	*6*
Outlay	(0.50)						
Residual values	0.01						0.02
Overhaul*			(0.14)		(0.14)		
Operating costs		(0.79)	(0.79)	(0.79)	(0.79)	(0.79)	(0.79)
Contract income		0.20	0.16	0.12	0.08	0.04	
Net outflows	(0.49)	(0.59)	(0.77)	(0.67)	(0.85)	(0.75)	(0.77)
Discount factor	1.000	0.952	0.907	0.864	0.823	0.784	0.746
Present value	(0.49)	(0.56)	(0.70)	(0.58)	(0.70)	(0.59)	(0.57)

Present value of net outflows = (4.19) (ie, £4.19m).

**Note:* the overhaul profile recognises that the expenditure in year 6 of £0.14m required to make the vehicles saleable for £5,000 each is uneconomic. The best alternative is to sell for scrap.

Based upon this information, the in-house option is less costly ie, the net present value of in-house costs is less than the present value of the contracted-out costs. This may be because Dumpex seeks a higher return for an activity of this degree of risk, and/or it must provide for tax liabilities. However, there remains the uncertainty surrounding the period over which Arctica can expect to receive income from the quarry company. In addition, the operating costs are based on expected values – a run of bad winters could result in costs higher than the contracted-out figure.

(Tutorial note: the above evaluation ignores the possibility of Arctica still having the benefit of the scrap values of its current fleet if it contracts out the operation. If this was included, it would reduce the PV of the costs of this option by £10,000 to £5.07m. This does not change the conclusion.)

(ii) To encourage Arctica to contract out the operation, an annual fee which generates the same or lower present value would have to be offered. The equivalent contract fee is found by dividing the present value of outflows by the appropriate annuity factor ie:

£4.19m/5.076 = £0.83m

which is considerably below the unofficial offer of £1m.

(d) There is a distinct danger that the in-house cost is understated as the income from the quarry contract is highly unreliable. As a form of sensitivity analysis, the impact of losing all income from that source can be assessed. The break-even value of the contract fee can be found by removing the given contract income figures from the cash flows, finding the present value of the resulting cost stream and converting it into an equivalent annuity ie, the annual figure which yields the same present value as the series of costs which Arctica expects to incur.

Cash flow profile from part (c) (£m)
Year

	0	1	2	3	4	5	6
Net outflows	(0.49)	(0.59)	(0.77)	(0.67)	(0.85)	(0.75)	(0.77)
Contract income		(0.20)	(0.16)	(0.12)	(0.08)	(0.04)	
Revised net outflows	(0.49)	(0.79)	(0.93)	(0.79)	(0.93)	(0.79)	(0.77)
Discount factor	1.000	0.952	0.907	0.864	0.823	0.784	0.746
Present value	(0.49)	(0.75)	(0.84)	(0.68)	(0.77)	(0.62)	(0.57)

Total present value = (4.72) (ie, £4.72m).

Hence to break even, the fee for the contract with Dumpex would have to be:

[Present value of costs]/$PVIFA_{5,6}$ = £4.72/5.076 = £0.93m.

This means that to cover the risk attaching to the contract with the quarry company, Arctica would have to pay an annual fee to Dumpex of £0.93m, a little below the unofficial tender of £1m. However, it is likely that the latter figure is above the minimum valuation which Dumpex attaches to the contract, being merely an 'opener' in the negotiation process. There seems to be scope for negotiation.

(e)   Possible alternative sources of finance including the following:

(i)   *Private finance input.* In some countries, (eg, in the UK under the Private Finance Initiative), efforts are being made to involve the private sector in partially or wholly financing public sector investment. This reflects the government's conviction that some services may be more efficiently provided by the private sector. In the case of Arctica, there may be scope for operating a joint venture, sharing control with a private sector company willing to assume a portion of the financial outlay and associated risk in return for a guaranteed service contract.

(ii)   *Official aid sources.* If the central government is unwilling to fund the project, Arctica may look to external funding agencies such as the range of loan facilities offered by the European Investment Bank, or grants from the European Union Regional Fund which aims to promote economic development in less-developed areas of the EU.

(iii)   *Leasing.* Leasing is a means of transferring expenditure from capital account to revenue account. Instead of incurring a 'lumpy' investment outlay at the outset of the project, the authority may arrange to pay a series of rentals to a leasing company for the use of the asset(s) concerned. With a finance lease, the length of the agreement approximates to the lifetime of the asset(s), and the contract cannot easily be cancelled without prohibitive penalty clauses. Hence, the lessee (user) assumes the risk of equipment obsolescence and idle time. An operating lease is similar to a plant-hire contract whereby the equipment is rented for a limited period corresponding to the requirements of a particular task. Operating leases are usually more expensive than finance leases per period of use, but, as in the case of Arctica, where there are long periods of idle time, they may represent the soundest option.

70   (Answer 2 of examination)

2   (a)   The working capital cycle of most companies is financed to some degree by bank loans and overdrafts (advances). To fulfil their function of providers of short-term finance, banks rely on their ability to create money via the bank multiplier process.

The banks are able to create money in the form of credit because they are confident, on the basis of experience, that when a deposit is made, the customer is unlikely to wish to withdraw the whole balance at any one time. However much she/he does withdraw, there is a high probability that she/he will make payments to people who will, in turn, deposit their receipts at the bank. Consequently, bankers know that only a relatively small cash reserve is required to support a given level of deposits so that the remainder can be safely lent to other customers in order to earn interest income.

For instance, if a new customer makes a cash deposit of £1,000 and the bank deems it prudent to retain only 10% of this ie, £100, it can be shown that the deposit can be used to support loans of £9,000. In this case, there is a 'bank deposit multiplier' of 10 at work, given by the reciprocal of the prudential reserve ratio [1/0.1 = 10]. The initial deposit has been multiplied 10 times and new money in the form of credit of £9,000 has been created. There is thus also a *credit* multiplier of nine at work.

Clearly, this process is limited by the banker's own notions of prudence and also by the demand for loans. The reserve ratio may also be controlled by the nation's monetary authorities, who may also impose other restrictions on the structure of banks' balance sheets to limit their ability to lend. The full multiplier also relies on there being no cash leakages from the banking system. If the general public and businesses also require to hold liquid cash reserves, this will dampen the operation of the multiplier- each time an expenditure is made, the recipient will hold back some proportion in cash form before banking the remainder. Such cash leakages may be mitigated by the prevalence of cheque and credit card usage. Finally, if the recipients of loan-financed expenditures deposit their receipts at other banks, the ability of the original lender to create further credit ceases. However, the credit-creating capacity of the banking system as a whole is unimpaired, unless other banks apply stricter reserve requirements to back their own lending.

(b)   In ZBB (zero-base budgeting), past budget allocations are irrelevant and managers are called upon to justify their requests. This means that managers have to produce 'decision packages' and to rank them in their order of importance.

Decision packages represent units of intended activity, such as a proposed new internal transport system or a research and development project.

A typical 'decision package' is a document which will indicate and try to justify, why the proposal is necessary and indicate:

–   the capital and revenue expenditure required
–   details of other resource needs
–   the assumptions which have had to be made eg, the operating level of activity
–   details of alternative courses of action
–   forecasts of income etc
–   the expected benefits

It has been found that ZBB, using its 'decision package concept' has been of particular value in service and support areas. The fact that it calls upon management to justify and explain their claims on the organisation's scarce resources makes it into quite a powerful tool. The ranking process forces managers to state their priorities and enables top management to allocate resources accordingly.

The formulation of 'decision packages' requires the active participation of lower levels of management and subordinates, which should result in more accurate/ realistic information and better co-ordination/communications within the organisation.

(c)   **Product ZIM 3A**

Calculation of variances

		£
(A)	Actual quantity at actual price	103,250
(B)	Actual quantity at standard price	103,500
(C)	Standard yield at standard cost	100,000
(D)	Actual yield at standard cost	102,500

		£
Material: price variance	(A – B)	250 (F)
Usage variance	(B – D)	1,000 (A)
Cost variance	(A – D)	750 (A)

The usage variance is made up of the mix and yield variances as follows:

Mix variance	(B – C)	3,500 (A)
Yield variance	(C – D)	2,500 (F)
		1,000 (A)

The mix and yield variance are the component parts of the adverse material usage variance, which has cost the company more than it planned. The cause needs to be investigated and could be caused by using poor quality materials or the input of a greater than planned proportion of the more expensive materials.

(d)   The role of the management accountant has been described as being that of an 'information manager'. In order to fulfil this role the management accountant must use and provide statistical information. Statistical information is needed to help to:

–   set targets eg, information on trends, market research data, inflation rates, etc

–   set objectives eg, quantitative information via statistical techniques such as probability and regression analysis

–   monitor performance eg, what is happening to stocks, order, prices, etc, and quality measures

–   control eg, comparative data, statistical data needed in the setting of standards

–   assist with decision making eg, the assessment of risk

–   define what the problem is, using statistical data eg, number of customers in restaurant, their average expenditure, consumer spending etc

–   understand their environment eg, economic factors such as supply and demand etc

–   present reports which are supported by facts and appropriate figures/tabulation/graphs etc

(e)   **Proposed credit policies**

	40 days £	60 days £
40 days debtors = £350,000 × $^{40}/_{365}$	38,356	
60 days debtors = £520,000 × $^{60}/_{365}$		85,479
Less: Existing debtors £420,000 × $^{50}/_{365}$	57,534	57,534
Effect on debtors	(19,178)	27,945
Cost of debtors (12%)	2,301	(3,353)
Effect on contribution (£70,000)/100,000 × 22%	(15,400)	22,000
Profit/(loss)	(13,099)	18,647

As indicated above, the 40 day policy will result in a reduction of profit and the 60 day policy will result in an increase. However, it should also be noted that the 40 day policy could reduce the level of bad debts and the 60 day policy increase the level of bad debts. It would be advisable also to look at the policy re the payment of creditors at the same time.

(f)   The principal steps which management would have to take in order to produce their capital expenditure budget, could include:

–   The assessment of needs in terms of fixed assets such as buildings, machinery, equipment and fixtures for the short, medium and long terms.

–   The production of a timetable so as to ensure the proper consultation takes place and that the budget is ready for implementation by the due date. The meetings involved should provide the opportunity for participation by the various managerial levels and shop floor representatives.

–   Matching the requirements to the other budgets, as budgets are inter-related eg, the expansion of the production could well involve the acquisition of new fixed assets.

–   Taking the 'principal budget factor' (also called the limiting factor) into account as it places a constraint on the activities of the organisation. If the availability of finance is the 'principal budget factor', the capital expenditure budget will be affected.

–   Appointing someone to co-ordinate the capital expenditure budget eg, the accountant/budget controller. Their role would include communicating with all those involved, providing information/data to assist preparation, chairing meetings, etc.

71   (Answer 3 of examination)

3   (a)   **Revised operating statement based on sales of 720,000 units**

	Budget £'000	Actual £'000	Variance £'000	Possible reasons *for the variance*
Sales	1,152	1,071	(81)	Sales made to certain segments at lower prices. Bulk discounts given to customers.
Cost of sales				
Materials	189	144	45	Buying in bulk and attracting discount. Buying lower quality materials.

Labour (variable)	270	288	(18)	More time taken to work, lower quality material. More overtime worked to cope with increased volume.
Labour (fixed)	100	94	6	Fixed lower than budget could be caused by employees leaving and not being replaced.
Overheads	36	36	Nil	
	595	562	33	
Gross profit	557	509	(48)	(As above)

Other overheads
Selling and distribution

Fixed	72	83	(11)	Additional fixed advertising cost.
Variable	162	153	9	Better vehicle utilisation.
Administration				
Fixed	184	176	8	Staff leave but not replaced
Variable	54	54	Nil	immediately
	472	466	6	
Net profit	85	43	(42)	(As above)

The principal reasons for the variation between budgeted and actual net profits are the sales revenue being lower than planned and the £45,000 less than planned expenditure on materials plus the increased variable labour costs.

Note: The above statement could have used a marginal costing format, and other reasons for variances are possible.

(b)   When budget and actual figures are compared, and variances extracted, it is most important that 'like is compared with like' ie, that the budgeted 'level of activity' is the same as the actual 'level of activity'. The statement provided is not a fair and valid comparison, as it is comparing sales and costs for 640,000 units with an actual of 720,000.

(c)   The problems associated with forecasting figures which are to be used in flexible budgeting are:

–   Using past information to forecast the future does not always provide reliable forecasts. What happened in the past does not always hold true for the future eg, records showing how much material was used are just a starting point in the assessment of what quantities should be used.

–   Flexible budgeting relies on being able to separate costs into their fixed and variable elements. This is not always an easy task eg, direct labour can be fixed or variable or a combination of the two such as a fixed salary plus a bonus based on output.

–   The computation of step-fixed costs also needs to be considered. Fixed costs can go up or down as output increases/decreases eg, shedding labour, hiring/renting more machinery and equipment.

–   Another problem is concerned with sorting out the underlying assumptions upon which the budget is to be based eg, the rate of inflation, the level of sales, constraints imposed by limiting factors, judgements re probability etc.

72	(Answer 4 of examination)

4 (a) (i) **Absorption costing profit statement**

		Products			
	XYI '000		YZT '000		ABW '000
Sales/production (units)	50		40		30

	£'000	£'000	£'000	£'000	£'000	£'000
Sales		2,250		3,800		2,190
Less: Prime cost	1,600		3,360		1,950	
Overheads						
Machine dept	120		240		144	
Assembly dept	288.75	2,008.75	99	3,699	49.5	2,143.5
Profit (loss)		241.25		101		46.5

Total <u>£388.75</u>

			Cost pools		
	Machining services	Assembly services	Set-ups	Order processing	Purchasing
(£'000)	357	318	26	156	84
Cost drivers	420,000 machine hours	530,000 direct labour hours	520 set-ups	32,000 customer orders	11,200 suppliers' orders
	£0.85 per machine hour	£0.60 per direct labour hour	£50 per set-up	£4.875 per customer order	£7.50 per suppliers' order

(ii)   **Activity-based costing profit statement**

	XYI '000		YZT '000		ABW '000	
Sales/production (units)	50		40		30	
	£'000	£'000	£'000	£'000	£'000	£'000
Sales		2,250		3,800		2,190
Less: Prime cost	1,600		3,360		1,950	
Cost pools						
Machine dept at 0.85	85		170		102	
Assembly dept at 0.60	210		72		36	
Set-up costs at £50	6		10		10	
Order processing at £4.875	39		39		78	
Purchasing at £7.50	22.5		30		31	
		1,962.5		3,681		2,207.5
Profit/(loss)		287.5		119		(17.5)

Total <u>£389</u>

(b)   Activity-based costing (ABC) is considered to present a fairer valuation of the product cost per unit for the following reasons:

–   It overcomes some of the problems which are associated with conventional absorption costing. In part (a) (i) all of the production overheads and some other overheads had to be allocated or apportioned to the two cost centres, machine department, assembly department and to service cost centres. Those overheads which could not be identified with a particular cost centre would have had to be shared between cost centres using some arbitrary basis such as floor area or the number of employees. In addition, the service department costs would have been apportioned to production cost centres using some arbitrary basis or technical estimates. The total overheads for each production cost centre would then be divided by the estimated number of machine hours or direct labour hours, as appropriate. This meant, that costs which could have been more accurately related to the product were not eg, set up costs vary more with the number of set-ups than with the number of machine hours or direct labour hours.

–   In (a) (ii) it can be observed that by having a number of 'cost pools' and dividing them by their 'cost driver' ie, the activity which causes the cost, a more accurate and realistic assessment can be produced. The information so produced using ABC, can be significantly different to that which is generated by traditional absorption costing. The differing levels of activity incurred on behalf of each product in terms of the 'cost drivers' eg, the number of set-ups, customer orders etc, can, and do, have quite a significant impact on the product cost per unit.

---

73   (Answer 5 of examination)

5   (a)   **Current return on capital employed**

= Operating profit/capital employed = £20m/(£75m + £25m) = £20m/£100m = 20%

Analysis of the project

Project capital requirements are £14m fixed capital plus £0.5m stocks. The annual depreciation charge (straight line) is:

(£14m − expected residual value of £2m)/4 = £3m pa

Profit profile (£m)

Year	1	2	3	4
Sales	(5.00 × 2m) = 10.00	(4.50 × 1.8m) = 8.10	(4.00 × 1.6m) = 6.40	(3.50 × 1.6m) = 5.60
Op. costs	(2.00)	(1.80)	(1.60)	(1.60)
Fixed costs	(1.50)	(1.35)	(1.20)	(1.20)
Depreciation	(3.00)	(3.00)	(3.00)	(3.00)
Profit	3.50	1.95	0.60	(0.20)

Capital employed (start-of-year):

Fixed	14.00	11.00	8.00	5.00
Stocks	0.50	0.50	0.50	0.50
Total	14.50	11.50	8.50	5.50

$$\text{Average rate of return} = \frac{\text{Average profit}}{\text{Average capital employed}} = \frac{£5.85/4}{£40.0/4} = \frac{£1.46}{£10.0} = 14.6\%$$

Note that if debtors were to be included in the definition of capital employed, this would reduce the calculated rate of return, while the inclusion of creditors would have an offsetting effect. However, using the ARR criterion as defined, the proposal has an expected return above the minimum stipulated by Shevin plc. It is unlikely that the managers of Armcliff will propose projects which offer a rate of return below the present 20% even where the expected return exceeds the minimum of 10%. To undertake projects with returns in this range will depress the overall divisional return and cast managerial performance in a weaker light.

However, it is unlikely that the senior managers of the Armcliff subsidiary would want to undertake the project.

(b)　(i)　The ARR can be expressed in a variety of ways, and is therefore susceptible to manipulation. Although the question specifies average profit to average capital employed, many other variants are possible eg, average profit to initial capital, which would raise the computed rate of return. It is also susceptible to variation in accounting policy by the same firm over time, or as between different firms at a point in time. For example, different methods of depreciation produce different profit figures and hence different rates of return.

Perhaps, most fundamentally, it is based on accounting profits expressed net of deduction for depreciation provisions, rather than cash flows. This effectively results in double-counting for the initial outlay ie, the capital cost is allowed for twice over, both in the numerator of the ARR calculation and also in the denominator. This is likely to depress the measured profitability of a project and result in rejection of some worthwhile investment. Finally, because it simply averages the profits, it makes no allowance for the timing of the returns from the project.

(ii)　The continuing use of the ARR method can by explained largely by its utilisation of balance sheet and profit-and-loss-account magnitudes familiar to managers, namely 'profit' and 'capital employed'. In addition, the impact of the project on a company's financial statements can also be specified. Return on capital employed is still the commonest way in which business unit performance is measured and evaluated, and is certainly the most visible to shareholders. It is thus not surprising that some managers may be happiest in expressing project attractiveness in the same terms in which their performance will be reported to shareholders, and according to which they will be evaluated and rewarded.

(c) Armcliff intends to achieve a sales increase by extending its debtor collection period. This policy carries several dangers. It implies that credit will be extended to customers for whom credit is an important determinant of supplier selection, hinting at financial instability on their part. Consequently, the risk of later than expected, or even no payment, is likely to increase. Although losses due to default are limited to the incremental costs of making these sales rather than the invoiced value, Armcliff should recognise that there is an opportunity cost involved in tying up capital for lengthy periods. In addition, companies which are slow payers often attempt to claim discounts to which they are not entitled. Armcliff may then face the difficult choice between acquiescence in such demands versus rejection, in which case, it may lose repeat sales.

The creditworthiness of customers can be assessed in several ways:

Analysis of accounting statements

In the case of companies which publish their annual accounts, or file them at Companies House, key financial ratios can be examined to assess their financial stability. However, these almost certainly will be provided in arrears and may not give a true indication of the companies' current situation. Some customers may be prepared to supply more up-to-date accounts directly to the seller, although these are unlikely to have been audited.

Analysis of credit reports

It may be possible to obtain detailed assessment of the creditworthiness of customers from other sources, such as their bankers, specialist credit assessment agencies such as Dun & Bradstreet, and from trade sources such as other companies who supply them. These assessments are likely to be more up-to-date than company accounts, but will inevitably be more subjective.

Previous experience

If the firm has supplied the customer in the past, its previous payment record will be available.

Cash-only trial period

If accounting and other data is sparse, and there is no previous trading record with the customer, the seller may offer a trial period over which cash is required, but if the payment record is acceptable (eg, if the customer's cheques always clear quickly), further transactions may be conducted on credit.

Background information

General background information on the industry in which the customer operates will generate insights into the financial health of companies in that sector, and by implication, that of the customer. Many agencies supply such information, although it should only be used as a back-up to other assessments.

---

74 (Answer 6 of examination)

6 (a) Seeking a quotation places many strains on a company, in particular, the need to provide more extensive information about its activities. However, the costs involved in doing this may seem worthwhile in order to pursue the following aims:

(i) *To obtain more capital to finance growth.* Companies which apply for a market listing are often fast-growing firms which have exhausted their usual supplies of capital. Typically, they rely on retained earnings and borrowing, often on a short-term basis. A quotation opens up access to a wider pool of investors. For example, large financial institutions are more willing to invest in quoted companies whose shares are considerably more marketable than those of unlisted enterprises.

Companies with a listing are often perceived to be financially stronger and hence may enjoy better credit ratings, enabling them to borrow at more favourable interest rates.

(ii) *To allow owners to realise their assets.* After several years of successful operation, many company founders own considerable wealth on paper. They may wish to liquidify some of their holdings to fund other business ventures or simply for personal reasons, even at the cost of relinquishing some measure of voting power. Most flotations allow existing shareholders to release some of their equity as well as raising new capital.

(iii) *To make the shares more marketable.* Existing owners may not wish to sell out at present, or to the degree that a floatation may require. A quotation, effected by means of a Stock Exchange introduction, is a device for establishing a market in the equity of a company, allowing owners to realise their wealth as and when they wish.

(iv) *To enable payment of managers by stock options.* The offer to senior managers of payment partially in the form of stock options may provide powerful incentives to improve performance.

(v) *To facilitate growth by acquisition.* Companies whose ordinary shares are traded on the stock market are more easily able to offer their own shares (or other traded securities, such as convertibles) in exchange for those of target companies whom they wish to acquire.

(vi) *To enhance the company's image.* A quotation gives an aura of financial respectability, which may encourage new business contracts. In addition, so long as the company performs well, it will receive free publicity when the financial press reports and discusses its results in future years.

(b) The table below compares Collingham's ratios against the industry averages:

	Industry	*Collingham*		
Return on (long term) capital employed	22%	10/33	=	30.3%
Return on equity	14%	6/28	=	21.4%
Operating profit margin	10%	10/80	=	12.5%
Current ratio	1.8:1	23/20	=	1.15:1
Acid-test	1.1:1	13/20	=	0.65:1
Gearing (total debt/equity)	18%	10/28	=	35.7%
Interest cover	5.2	10/3	=	3.33 times
Dividend cover	2.6	6/0.5	=	12 times

Collingham's profitability, expressed both in terms of ROCE and ROE, compares favourably with the industry average. This may be inflated by the use of a historic cost base, in so far as assets have never been revalued. Although a revaluation might depress these ratios, the company appears attractive compared to its peers. The net profit margin of 12.5% is above that of the overall industry, suggesting a cost advantage, either in production or in operating a flat administrative structure. Alternatively, it may operate in a market niche where it is still exploiting first-comer advantages. In essence, it is this aspect which is likely to appeal to investors.

Set against the apparently strong profitability is the poor level of liquidity. Both the current and the acid-test ratios are well below the industry average, and suggest that the company should be demonstrating tighter working capital management. However, the stock turnover of $(10/70 \times 365) =$ 52 days and the debtor days of $(10/80 \times 365) = 46$ days do not appear excessive, although industry averages are not given. It is possible that Collingham has recently been utilising liquid resources to finance fixed investment or to repay past borrowings.

Present borrowings are split equally between short-term and long-term, although the level of gearing is well above the market average. The debenture is due for repayment shortly which will exert further strains on liquidity, unless it can be re-financed. Should interest rates increase in the near future,

Collingham is exposed to the risk of having to lock-in higher interest rates on a subsequent long-term loan or pay (perhaps temporarily) a higher interest rate on overdraft. The high gearing is reflected also in low interest cover, markedly below the industry average. In view of high gearing and poor liquidity, it is not surprising that the pay-out ratio is below 10%, although Collingham's managers would presumably prefer to link high retentions to the need to finance ongoing investment and growth rather than to protect liquidity.

(c)　It is common for companies in Collingham's position to attempt to 'strengthen' or to 'tidy up' their balance sheets in order to make the company appear more attractive to investors. Very often, this amounts to 'window dressing', and if the company were already listed, it would have little effect in an information-efficient market. However, for unlisted companies, about whom little is generally known, such devices can improve the financial profile of the company and enhance the prospects of a successful floatation.

(i)　Some changes in the balance sheet that Collingham might consider prior to floatation are:

Revalue those fixed assets which now appear in the accounts at historic cost. The freehold land and premises are likely to be worth more at market values, although the effect of time on second-hand machinery values is more uncertain. If a surplus emerges, a revaluation reserve would be created, thus increasing the book value of shareholders' funds, and hence the net asset value per share. The disadvantage of this would be to lower the ROCE and the return on equity, although these are already well above the industry averages. Asset revaluation would also reduce the gearing ratio.

Dispose of any surplus assets in order to reduce gearing and/or to increase liquidity which is presently low, both absolutely, and also in relation to the industry.

Examine other ways to improve the liquidity position, by reducing stocks, speeding up debtor collection or slowing payment to suppliers, although it already appears to be a slow payer with a trade credit period of $(15/70 \times 365) = 78$ days.

Conduct a share split, because at the existing level of earnings per share, the shares promise to have a 'heavyweight' rating. Applying the industry P/E multiple of 13 to the current EPS of $(£6m/£4m \times 2) = 75p$, yields a share price of $(13 \times 75p) = £9.75$. While there is little evidence that a heavyweight rating is a deterrent to trading in already listed shares, it is likely that potential investors, certainly small-scale ones, will be deterred from subscribing to a highly-priced new issue. A one-for-one share split whereby the par value is reduced to 25p per share and the number of shares issued correspondingly doubles, would halve the share price, although other configurations are possible.

It will have to enfranchise the non-voting 'A' shares, because, under present Stock Exchange regulations, these are not permitted for companies newly entering the market.

(ii)　Following the floatation, Collingham would probably have to accept that a higher dividend pay-out is required to attract and retain the support of institutional investors. If it wishes to persist with a high level of internal financing, a compromise may be to make scrip issues of shares, especially if the share price remains on the 'heavy' side. Scrip issues are valued by the market because they usually portend higher earnings and dividends in the future.

Finally, if the company has not already done so, it might consider progressively lowering the gearing ratio. It might begin this by using part of the proceeds of the floatation to redeem the debenture early. However, it must avoid the impression that it requires a floatation primarily to repay past borrowings as that might cast doubts on the company's financial stability.

DECEMBER 1995 QUESTIONS

Section A – This question is compulsory and MUST be attempted

75   (Question 1 of examination)

1   The YZPK Packing Co Ltd, a family-owned company, has now been trading for six years and has provided you with the following data relating to its last four trading years:

Extracts from its balance sheets

	19X3 £'000	19X4 £'000	19X5 £'000	19X6 £'000
Issued ordinary shares	26	75	75	255
Retained earnings	49	109	396	819
Bank overdraft (secured)	Nil	90	187	94

Extracts from its profit and loss accounts

	19X3 £'000	19X4 £'000	19X5 £'000	19X6 £'000
Turnover	725	1,335	2,496	4,608
Net profit (after tax)	18	48	212	334
Dividends proposed	Nil	Nil	Nil	51

All sales and purchases are made on credit.

Financial analysis

	*Industry	19X3	19X4	19X5	19X6
Current ratio	1.47	1.11	1.02	1.19	1.24
Acid test	0.85	1.03	0.90	0.94	0.95
Debtors, average collection period (days)	51	63	72	76	64
Creditors, period of credit taken (days)	72	103	146	121	118
Stockholding (days)	62	14	22	45	52
Net profit after tax to capital employed	21%	24%	26%	45%	31%

* The industry averages have been around this level for the whole of the four year period.

Required

(a)   Comment on the company's growth in turnover and profits over the four years, and suggest possible problems which such rapid growth may cause.   (4 marks)

(b)   Suggest reasons why the company's stockholding in days has been less than the industry average. (6 marks)

(c)   The board of directors is concerned about the cash flow position of the company. As chief accountant, write a memo to the board setting out various ways in which credit control could be improved and point out the potential threat posed by creditors.   (9 marks)

(d)   From the additional information supplied below:

         (i)   prepare and present a cash budget and comment briefly on your findings;   (7 marks)
         (ii)   prepare a budgeted profit and loss account,   (5 marks)

for the four months from 1 January 19X7 to 30 April 19X7.

On 1 January 19X7, the bank overdraft amounted to £94,000 and the stock of raw materials amounted to £288,000. All sales and purchases are on credit.

| | 19X6 | | | | 19X7 | | | | Period of |
	Sept £'000	*Oct* £'000	*Nov* £'000	*Dec* £'000	*Jan* £'000	*Feb* £'000	*Mar* £'000	*Apr* £'000	credit
Debtors	420	560	640	250	480	520	500	440	2 months
Creditors	200	220	101	200	210	210	180	190	4 months
Operating expenses	30	30	50	50	30	30	40	40	Nil
Other expenses	36	36	44	40	42	43	41	37	2 months
New equipment					560				2 months
Sale of old equipment					40				3 months
Bank charges				4				2	Nil

An ordinary dividend of £51,000 (ignore ACT), for the year to 31 December 19X6 is due to be paid in April 19X7, and tax for that year amounting to £184,000 is due to be paid in March 19X7.

The closing stock of raw materials amounted to £254,000 as at 30 April 19X7.

The net book value of plant, machinery and motor vehicles etc, at 31 December 19X6 was £426,000. The net book value of the equipment sold was £56,000. Depreciation on these assets is charged at 20% per annum of net book value.

(e)   The company is now considering acquiring more long-term financing and has asked you to comment on the matters which would have to be taken into account by the directors if they converted the company into a plc.

(4 marks)

(Total 35 marks)

Section B – This question is compulsory and MUST be attempted

Answer *five* of the six parts of this question.

Each part carries five marks.

---

76   (Question 2 of examination)

---

2   (a)   What is the significance of the forward market for foreign exchange in the management of overseas debtors?

(5 marks)

(b)   Explain the functions of financial intermediaries in bringing together individual savers and borrowers.

(5 marks)

(c)   Identify the major limitations of the payback method of project appraisal and suggest reasons why it is widely used by companies.

(5 marks)

(d)   Briefly explain the purpose and expected benefits of JIT purchasing agreements concluded between the users and suppliers of components and materials.

(5 marks)

(e)   Identify, and briefly explain, the nature of *two* problems associated with the use of fiscal policy to control cyclical variations in the macro-economy.

(5 marks)

(f)   (i)   Explain briefly why forecasting is a very important part of the planning and control process.(2 marks)

(ii)   What information should be considered when producing a sales forecast?

(3 marks)

(Total 25 marks)

Section C – ONE question ONLY to be attempted

```
┌─────────────────────────────────────────────────────────┐
│  77      (Question 3 of examination)                      │
└─────────────────────────────────────────────────────────┘
```

3   Acca-chem Co plc manufacture a single product, product W, and have provided you with the following information which relates to the period which has just ended:

Standard cost per batch of product W

Materials	Kilos	Price per kilo £	Total £
F	15	4	60
G	12	3	36
H	8	6	48
	35		144
Less: Standard loss	(3)		
Standard yield	32		

Labour	Hours	Rate per hour £	
Department P	4	10	40
Department Q	2	6	12
			196

Budgeted sales for the period are 4,096 kilos at £16 per kilo. There were no budgeted opening or closing stocks of product W.

The actual materials and labour used for 120 batches were:

Materials	Kilos	Price per kilo £	Total £
F	1,680	4.25	7,140
G	1,650	2.80	4,620
H	870	6.40	5,568
	4,200		17,328
Less: Actual loss	(552)		
Actual yield	3,648		

Labour	Hours	Rate per hour £	
Department P	600	10.60	6,360
Department Q	270	5.60	1,512
			25,200

All of the production of W was sold during the period for £16.75 per kilo.

Required

(a) Calculate the following material variances:

(i) price;
(ii) usage;
(iii) mix;
(iv) yield.

(5 marks)

(b) Prepare an analysis of the material mix and price variances for each of the materials used.

(3 marks)

(c) Calculate the following labour variances:

(i) cost;
(ii) efficiency;
(iii) rate,

for each of the production departments.

(4 marks)

(d) Calculate the sales variances.

(3 marks)

(e) Comment on your findings to help explain what has happened to the yield variance.

(5 marks)
(Total 20 marks)

78 (Question 4 of examination)

4 (a) In an attempt to win over key customers in the motor industry and to increase its market share, BIL Motor Components plc have decided to charge a price lower than their normal price for component TD463 when selling to the key customers who are being targeted. Details of component TD463's standard costs are as follows:

Standard cost data

Component TD463
Batch size 200 units

	Machine Group 1 £	Machine Group 7 £	Machine Group 29 £	Assembly £
Materials (per unit)	26.00	17.00	–	3.00
Labour (per unit)	2.00	1.60	0.75	1.20
Variable overheads (per unit)	0.65	0.72	0.80	0.36
Fixed overheads (per unit)	3.00	2.50	1.50	0.84
	31.65	21.82	3.05	5.40
Setting-up costs per batch of 200 units	£10	£6	£4	–

Required

Compute the lowest selling price at which one batch of 200 units could be offered, and critically evaluate the adoption of such a pricing policy.

(8 marks)

(b)   The company is also considering the launch of a new product, component TDX489, and have provided you with the following information.

Product TDX489   *Standard cost*
                                             per box
                                               £

Variable cost   6.20
Fixed cost   1.60
                                              ────
                                              7.80
                                              ────

Market research – forecast of demand

Selling price (£)	13	12	11	10	9
Demand (boxes)	5,000	6,000	7,200	11,200	13,400

The company only has enough production capacity to make 7,000 boxes. However, it would be possible to purchase product TDX489 from a sub-contractor at £7.75 per box for orders up to 5,000 boxes, and £7 per box if the orders exceed 5,000 boxes.

Required

Prepare and present a computation which illustrates which price should be selected in order to maximise profits.   (8 marks)

(c)   Where production capacity is the limiting factor explain briefly the ways in which management can increase it without having to acquire more plant and machinery.   (4 marks)
                                                                          (Total 20 marks)

Section D – ONE question ONLY to be attempted

79   (Question 5 of examination)

5   Burnsall plc is a listed company which manufactures and distributes leisurewear under the brand name Paraffin. It made sales of 10 million units world-wide at an average wholesale price of £10 per unit during its last financial year ending at 30 June 1995. In 1995/96, it is planning to introduce a new brand, Meths, which will be sold at a lower unit price to more price-sensitive market segments. Allowing for negative effects on existing sales of Paraffin, the introduction of the new brand is expected to raise total sales value by 20%

To support greater sales activity, it is expected that additional financing, both capital and working, will be required. Burnsall expects to make capital expenditures of £20m in 1995/96, partly to replace worn-out equipment but largely to support sales expansion. You may assume that, except for taxation, all current assets and current liabilities will vary directly in line with sales.

Burnsall's summarised balance sheet for the financial year ending 30 June 1995 shows the following:

Assets employed	£m	£m	£m
Fixed (net)			120
Current			
Stocks	16		
Debtors	23		
Cash	6		
		45	
Current liabilities			
Corporation tax payable	(5)		
Trade creditors	(18)		
		(23)	
Net current assets			22
Long-term debt at 12%			(20)
Net assets			122
Financed by			
Ordinary shares (50p par value)			60
Reserves			62
Shareholders' funds			122

Burnsall's profit before interest and tax in 1994/95 was 16% of sales, after deducting depreciation of £5m. The depreciation charge for 1995/96 is expected to rise to £9m. Corporation tax is levied at 33%, paid with a one-year delay. Burnsall has an established distribution policy of raising dividends by 10% pa. In 1994/95, it paid dividends of £5m net.

You have been approached to advise on the extra financing required to support the sales expansion. Company policy is to avoid cash balances falling below 6% of sales.

Required

(a)   By projecting its financial statements, calculate how much additional *external* finance Burnsall must raise.

       Notes

       (1)   It is not necessary to present your projection in FRS 1 format.
       (2)   You may ignore advance corporation tax in your answer.
       (3)   You may assume that all depreciation provisions qualify for tax relief.

                    (8 marks)

(b)   Evaluate the respective merits *of four* possible external long-term financing options open to Burnsall.(12 marks)
                    (Total 20 marks)

---

80   (Question 6 of examination)

---

6   (a)   The Cleevemoor Water Authority was privatised in 1988, to become Northern Water plc (NW). Apart from political considerations, a major motive for the privatisation was to allow access for NW to private sector supplies of finance. During the 1980s, central government controls on capital expenditure had resulted in relatively low levels of investment, so that considerable investment was required to enable the company to meet more stringent water quality regulations. When privatised, it was valued by the merchant bankers advising on the issue at £100 million and was floated in the

form of 100 million ordinary shares (par value 50p), sold fully-paid for £1 each. The shares reached a premium of 60% on the first day of stock market trading.

Required

In what ways might you expect the objectives of an organisation like Cleevemoor/NW to alter following transfer from public to private ownership?   (5 marks)

(b)   Selected *bi-annual* data from NW's accounts are provided below relating to its first six years of operation as a private sector concern. Also shown, for comparison, are the *pro forma* data as included in the privatisation documents. The *pro forma* accounts are notional accounts prepared to show the operating and financial performance of the company in its last year under public ownership as if it had applied private sector accounting conventions. They also incorporate a dividend payment based on the dividend policy declared in the prospectus.

The activities of privatised utilities are scrutinised by a regulatory body which restricts the extent to which prices can be increased. The demand for water in the area served by NW has risen over time at a steady 2% per annum, largely reflecting demographic trends.

Key financial and operating data for year ending 31 December (£m)

	1988 (pro forma)	1990 (actual)	1992 (actual)	1994 (actual)
Turnover	450	480	540	620
Operating profit	26	35	55	75
Taxation	5	6	8	10
Profit after tax	21	29	47	65
Dividends	7	10	15	20
Total assets	100	119	151	191
Capital expenditure	20	30	60	75
Wage bill	100	98	90	86
Directors' emoluments	0.8	2.0	2.3	3.0
Employees (number)	12,000	11,800	10,500	10,000
P/E ratio (average)	–	7.0	8.0	7.5
Retail Price Index	100	102	105	109

Required

Using the data provided, assess the extent to which NW has met the interests of the following groups of stakeholders in its first six years as a privatised enterprise.

If relevant, suggest what other data would be helpful in forming a more balanced view.

(i)   shareholders;   (5 marks)

(ii)   consumers;   (2 marks)

(iii)   the workforce;   (4 marks)

(iv)   the government, through NW's contribution to the achievement of macro-economic policies of price stability and economic growth.   (4 marks)

(Total 20 marks)

EXAMINER'S COMMENTS

General comments

There is a lot of evidence that many of the candidates are not reading the questions properly and not answering the questions set. In many cases, this practice leads to the loss of valuable examination time eg, including irrelevant material in answers. It would also appear to be the case that there is a tendency for candidates to produce marginally relevant answers in the latest paper which would have been more appropriate to the previous paper. In addition, there was also a failure on the part of quite a number of candidates to make good use of the information provided in the questions.

Recurring problems with which candidates tended to struggle were: their understanding of financial ratios, project appraisal methods eg, the difference between profit and cash flow, and economics. There were also a significant number of candidates who attempted all six parts of Section B question 2, when only FIVE were required, and a small number who did both questions in Section C, when only ONE was required. The structure of this examination should now be well known and such unfortunate errors should no longer be occurring.

There are still many candidates who do not appear to have had an adequate preparation for the financial management part of the paper. Candidates are reminded that the financial management element occupies 60% of the paper 8 syllabus.

SECTION A

Question 1: this five part mini case study type question provided candidates with a mix of financial management and management accounting material which required them to demonstrate their analytical and comprehensive skills.

(a) **Required the candidate to comment on the growth in turnover and profits and to suggest possible problems which could be caused by rapid growth.**

Quite a large number of candidates commented on the growth in turnover and profits without making any use of the data which was provided. Some candidates dealt with the growth in turnover and ignored the growth in profits, and others failed to tie up the growth in turnover with the decline in the profit margin. At the other extreme, some candidates went over-board on the growth aspects and did not attempt to answer the second part of this question concerning the problems of rapid growth.

Although 'over-trading' was indeed part of the answer, quite a large number of students focused on this one aspect and ignored the numerous other problems which could have been mentioned.

(b) **This part asked for reasons why the company's stockholding in days was below the average for the industry.**

JIT (just-in-time) featured in many of the answers which were submitted. A lot of the answers tended to concentrate on the reasons for why the rapid growth in sales had taken place rather than answering the question set which was about the reasons for the low level of stock holding days. The rapid growth in turnover was just one of many possible reasons.

However, it was very pleasing to find answers in which candidates could integrate and display their knowledge of economics and statistical techniques in response to the open-ended question which was set.

(c) **The question focused on credit control and the threat posed by the creditors.**

This part was answered very well by the majority of candidates. However, some answers failed to focus on the two parts of the question, deviating in all directions, covering inventory control and sources of finance etc.

Although quite a number of candidates answered the credit control part well, many then did not attempt to provide an answer to the other part of the question which concerned the threat posed by the creditors. It was surprising to find a significant number of candidates confusing debtors and creditors. At this level, such confusion should not exist.

(d)   **Required the preparation of a Cash Budget and a Budgeted Profit and Loss Account.**

Overall the candidates did very well on this part and scored high marks. Errors which were made in attempting the cash budget tended to be related to the period of credit, leaving out the opening overdraft (or treating it as a credit balance), calculation errors and failing to include the tax payment.

In the profit and loss account, the calculation of the depreciation and the loss and the disposal, proved to be difficult for a number of candidates.

A number of candidates lost valuable examination time by preparing a cash budget which covered each month from September to April, and others also lost time by preparing a budgeted profit and loss account for each month on an individual basis, rather than for the four month period in total, which is all that was required. Other candidates lost even more time by attempting to prepare a budgeted balance sheet which was also not called for.

(e)   **A considerable number of candidates did not focus on the question set, which asked for comments on matters which the directors of the family owned company would have to take into account if they converted their company into a plc.**

A significant number of candidates looked at the various types of long term financing and others described the advantages of becoming a plc which did not match up with the question set. The 'control' aspect, one of the key matters was however, one of the few areas which was picked up and well answered by a pleasing number of candidates.

The overall performance by candidates on question 1 was quite pleasing, particularly in part (d). Certain candidates lost valuable examination time by not answering the question set and/or providing material which was not necessary eg, the budgeted balance sheet mentioned above.

SECTION B

Question 2: (a) this question required explanation of the use of forward markets in managing overseas debtors.

There was considerable confusion in this area, due in large measure to candidates' inability to understand the difference between debtors and creditors, but mainly due to lack of knowledge about currency markets and methods of payment. Many answers declared that the issue concerned fixing prices before the sale, and/or was a way of ensuring payment from customers, suggesting some form of international factoring. Of those who did understand the use of forward contracts (including forward options but not currency options!), most talked of buying currency forward as would be done by an importer wishing to hedge payments to creditors - the question clearly stated debtors.

(b)   **This question required a discussion of the general functions of financial intermediaries.**

Some good answers were given by candidates but many superficial ones. Candidates seemed to grasp the pooling function of intermediaries and how they solve the problem of the double coincidence of wants, but not the more complex functions such as risk spreading. Many answers simply concentrated on a specific institution and described their functions. Banks were a particular favourite, no doubt because credit creation appeared on the previous paper. There was considerable confusion between financial intermediaries and independent financial advisers.

(c)   **This section required a discussion of the problems with the payback method and the reasons for its continued use.**

This was probably the best answered section of question 2. Candidates were generally aware that payback overlooks the time value of money and ignores cash flows beyond the payback point, and that it is simple to use. However, there was some confusion between cash flows and profits revealed in the answers, and relatively few candidates identified the advantages of payback in risky and cash-constrained situations (many said it totally ignored risk).

(d)   **This section required explanation of the purpose of JIT agreements and the benefits to both parties.**

Again, quite well-answered with good awareness of the purpose of JIT and the benefits to the recipient of supplies. However, answers generally neglected the benefits conferred to the sender of supplies. There were widespread assertions that JIT helped the cash flow of the sender by speeding up debtor collection. Although this may be a product of closer relationships between the two parties, it does not follow that it will necessarily happen.

(e)   **This section required an explanation of two problems in the conduct of fiscal policy.**

This part was very poorly-done, reflecting candidates' apparent weakness in the economics area. There was little attempt to answer the question, beyond saying that counter-cyclical policy may create unemployment and sometimes lead to inflation, although discussion in terms of policy conflicts obtained credit. Few candidates really understood what fiscal policy tries to achieve over the business cycle, and many confused it with monetary policy, discussing interest rate changes and monetary contractions/expansions. While it is true that fiscal policy may have monetary implications, it is important to clearly distinguish the two types of policy.

(f)   **This short scenario question was about the importance of forecasting and the information requirements relating to sales forecasts.**

The majority of candidates performed well on both parts to this question. It was again pleasing to see candidates demonstrating their knowledge of economics, statistical techniques and marketing etc in a constructive way to produce numerous and quite different acceptable answers.

SECTION C

Question 3: candidates were required to calculate and comment on a number of variances.

(a) and (b) The answers submitted were generally very disappointing as a very large proportion of candidates could not calculate the material mix variance and the material yield variance. A significant number of candidates computed the usage variance and the mix variance as the same figure.

(c)   The majority of those who attempted this question performed very well on this part and their answers tended to accord with the published suggested answers. There were other alternative acceptable answers to this part for which marks were awarded.

(d)   The sales variances were reasonably well done. Here also, there were some quite acceptable alternative answers, in addition to those published in the suggested answers for which marks were awarded.

(e)   This tended to be neglected in terms of the time and thought required to produce a sensible answer. Many of the answers submitted failed to explain what had happened to the yield variance and to link it up with the other variances.

Question 4: the first two parts of this question called for the application of marginal costing techniques to help resolve some pricing problems plus some comments relating to the pricing strategy. Part (c) required brief explanations of possible management action which could be taken to increase production capacity.

(a) and (b) Many candidates did not take a marginal costing approach. However, marks were still awarded to those candidates who took and justified taking an absorption costing approach.

It was observed that in part (b), a considerable number of candidates were unable to deal with the 'buying-in' aspect of the question.

This question was not as popular as question three, and parts (a) and (b) were not very well answered. However, part (c) presented few problems to all those who attempted it, and was generally well done.

SECTION D

Question 5: **(a) This section required candidates to use a projection of a company's current financial statements to identify the extent to which a proposed capital programme could be funded internally, and hence, how much external finance was required.**

This part was done extremely badly by candidates. Candidates failed to recognise the need to predict the operating cash flow to be generated by the company, and the amount of external funding required, despite the strong hint in note 1 to the requirement and the very context of the question. Most candidates tried to project the balance sheet which had some merit if they could then identify an aspect of long-term finance as a balancing item, but such answers came adrift in attempting to measure profits and hence tax liability, which was irrelevant to the question. Once again, it seems that candidates do not appreciate the difference between profits and cash flow. Hence, credit was given to those who did work in cash flow terms, but most answers failed to treat depreciation correctly, or time the tax and dividend payments correctly. Interest payments were generally ignored, and many neglected the need to provide more working capital. A remarkably high proportion failed even to calculate the new level of sales correctly.

(b)   **This section required an evaluation of four long-term financing options relevant to the company in this question.**

This should have been a straightforward elaboration of the respective merits of different financing options applicable to the company. Instead, very few answers gave the remotest acknowledgement to the company, (eg,) recommending debt finance without considering the company (eg,) present capital or income gearing, and advising public issues of shares, oblivious of the fact that the company is already quoted and existing shareholders will have pre-emption rights. Some recommended that it should obtain a stock market quotation and then went through the various methods. Many candidates gave highly repetitive answers eg, debentures/deep discount bonds/zero coupon bonds/convertibles are effectively all variations on the long-term debt theme, similarly, long-term loans from banks. There was little attempt to qualify answers eg, venture capital could have a role to play although it could be argued that the company is too large to qualify.

Many candidates gave methods of short-term finance eg, bank overdrafts, factoring and invoice discounting. Some recommended devices like bonus issues and warrants which do not raise cash, although the former may conserve cash to allow internal financing, which is not relevant to the question, and the latter can only be of relevance for future financing. Inevitably, there were many recommendations to use reserves.

Question 6: a very topical question which might have led the unwary into quasi political discussion. Fortunately, the vast majority avoided this temptation. However, there was widespread inability to utilise the information contained in the question, even to the extent of calling for information actually given, or easily calculable from that data.

(a)   **This section required discussion of how the aims of a water utility would alter following privatisation.** This section was answered reasonably well in the main, but answers should have gone beyond merely stating the service/profit dichotomy. Issues relevant to objectives which deserved a mention were the dimensions of shareholder aims (profit, EPS, dividends, share price) and removal of much government interference, and the need to serve a new master in the form of the stock exchange, but which opened up new avenues of finance. Nor does it follow that the utility would abandon quality objectives - indeed, the regulators might even tighten up on these. A major deficiency was the weak or lack of emphasis on aims prior to privatisation and hence, discussion of how they had changed.

(b)   **This section sought discussion of the extent to which the utility's performance over time had met the interests of different stakeholders.**

Candidates seemed unaware that most shareholders look for some combination of dividends and capital gain. There was great misunderstanding about the meaning of PE ratios. Movements in these do not tell us much, unless coupled with EPS data, with which we can then derive share prices. All the required information to do this was given in the question. Very little use was made of the information provided to calculate growth rates, either in nominal or real terms.

Candidates seemed unable to appreciate that if volume of output rose by 2% per annum, then the additional turnover growth is probably due to price increases, in this case, well above the movement in the RPI. Candidates seemed incapable of using index numbers to measure this discrepancy. Many said that if volume increased, consumers must have been happy, ignoring the monopoly position of the supplier. There were very few mentions of the role of the regulator. Credit was given for mentions of capital expenditure and presumed improvements in quality.

Candidates seemed happier with discussing labour issues, although few could use the data provided to calculate changes in real pay per head. Most recognised the higher rewards for directors. The contribution of the company to general economic aims was not well understood. Many said that since the RPI went up by some 2% pa, the price stability aim was not satisfied, appearing to blame the company for the movement in the RPI! There was little evidence of understanding that higher capital expenditure and greater efficiency was likely to assist economic growth, although most recognised the unemployment created by the firm, which might detract from growth, especially if it required higher public expenditure. Against this, the utility was generating more and more tax revenue, recognition of which obtained credit.

ANSWERS TO DECEMBER 1995 EXAMINATION

It should be noted that the following answers are probably fuller than would be expected from the average student under exam conditions. Answers are provided in this degree of detail on the principle of offering guidance on the approach required, and on the range and depth of knowledge that would be expected from an excellent student.

75   (Answer 1 of examination)

1   (a)   YZPK Packing Co Ltd has experienced quite remarkable growth over the past four years in both turnover and profits. Turnover has gone up by over 635% and the net profit after tax has increased by over 1,855%.

A rapid growth company such as this may suffer from the following problems:

–   As a company grows, all business functions do not always keep pace with the growth eg, the management accounting function and the monitoring and control processes.

–   Going for market share and growth in turnover may be at the expense of the productivity of the capital employed eg, using low mark-ups to attract sales volume.

–   Cash flow is a problem. Cash is needed to finance the expansion of both fixed and current assets eg, more machinery, higher stockholdings of raw materials and more debtors. Thus, such companies, high in terms of growth, tend to be faced with cash flow problems.

(b)   **Inventory management**

	Industry average	19X3	19X4	19X5	19X6
Stockholding (days)	62	14	22	45	52

The stocks of raw materials will have grown over the years to support the increased turnover. However, the company's stockholding period is still less than the industry average. The possible reasons for this are:

–   The company being a 'rapid growth company' and in need of all the cash which it generates to help finance its continued expansion, has been keeping stocks low out of necessity.

–   To ensure that a minimum amount of capital is tied up and so avoid expensive holding costs such as interest on loans used to finance the holding of stocks, storage, lighting, heating, insurance, etc.

–   They may be using MRP (material requirements planning) or JIT (Just-in-time) both of which try to ensure that stocks are kept to an acceptable minimum and are used in production very soon after they arrive and that finished goods eg, packing cases, are despatched soon after completion.

The current 52 days may be improved via more use of MRP or JIT and also by searching out and disposing of stock which is obsolete or surplus to requirements.

However, 'trade-offs' and compromises may have to be reviewed/made eg, having lower stock levels but losing discounts for buying in bulk.

(c)   **Memo to the directors**

Credit control – The management of debtors

	Industry average	19X3	19X4	19X5	19X6
Average collection period (days)	51	63	72	76	64

The performance here is not what one would expect from a 'rapid growth' company ie, being in need of cash flow tends to dictate a better than average performance regarding the average collection period.

It could well be that the credit control function of this company has not been able to keep pace with the growth and is not being seen as a high priority.

The company is currently taking 13 days longer than the industry average. Even though it has improved its performance, it would appear that there is still room for further improvement. They could attempt to improve their credit control by:

–   Making a full review of their credit control system and credit policy and giving the function a higher priority.

–   Chasing slow payers and sending out invoices and statements more promptly eg, telephoning debtors to find out why they haven't paid, or sending invoices along with the goods when they are delivered.

–   Consider a COD (cash on delivery) system for certain types of customer.

–   Investigate prompt settlement discounts. However, this could be expensive. A small discount can have a high APR (annual percentage rate) of interest.

Although the liquidity ratios ie, the current ratio and acid test appear to be satisfactory, when compared with the industry average, this area is a cause for concern. The company is in a dangerous position. It is taking far too long to pay its creditors, currently 118 days compared with an industry average of 72 days. A combination of cash flow problems together with pressure from creditors could bring about the downfall and liquidation of the company.

Once again, 'trade-offs' may be necessary. One of the reasons for the increased turnover could be generous credit terms. If credit terms are reduced, sales could be lost. Improving credit control could release much needed cash which could be used for other purposes eg, paying off creditors and/or reducing the bank overdraft.

(d)   (i)   **Cash budget 19X7**

	Jan £'000	Feb £'000	Mar £'000	Apr £'000
Balance b/f	(94)	272	232	(215)
Inflows				
Debtors	640	250	480	520
Sale of machine	–	–	–	40
(A)	546	522	712	345
Outflows				
Creditors	200	220	101	200
Operating expenses	30	30	40	40
Other expenses	44	40	42	43
Dividends	–	–	–	51
New equipment	–	–	560	–
Taxation	–	–	184	–
Bank charges	–	–	–	2
(B)	274	290	927	336
Balance (A) – (B) c/f	272	232	(215)	9

The cash budget indicates that the overdraft limit will be exceeded in March. The company can, armed with the figures, arrange an increase in the limit with their bankers or take internal action. The internal action could include delaying paying the tax or for the new equipment, or by improving their credit control and collecting their debts more quickly.

(ii)   **Budgeted profit and loss account**

		£'000	£'000
Sales			1,940
Less:	Cost of sales		
	Opening stock	288	
	Add: Purchases	790	
		1,078	
	Less: Closing stock	254	
			824
Gross profit (57.53%)			1,116
Operating and other expenses		303	
Bank charges		2	
Depreciation*		62	
Loss on sale of old plant		16	
			383
Net profit (37.78%)			733

*(£426,000 − £56,000 + £560,000) × 20% ÷ 3 = £62,000

(e)   **The ordinary shares**

YZPK Ltd is a family company with the initial share capital subscribed by family friends and relatives. This could also be true of the further injections received in 19X4 and 19X6.

In the future, if more finance is to be raised in this way, the company will most likely have to become a plc so that it can issue shares to the public. However, to be successful in attracting prospective investors, the company will need to have a satisfactory performance record and reasonable future expectations. One of the key issues as to whether or not the company would select this route is the control factor. The existing directors, most probably own a major stake in the shares. To issue lots of shares to the public, could bring about a loss of a controlling interest. To retain control, the directors would have to find funds so that they could buy sufficient shares.

76   (Answer 2 of examination)

2   (a)   The forward exchange market sets a price for delivery of currency at some future specified date, thus providing a mechanism whereby exporters can achieve protection against fluctuations in foreign exchange rates, and hence forecast their future cash inflows more accurately.

A major problem for exporters is uncertainty over future exchange rates and hence over the domestic currency value of goods sold on credit. Even in currency blocks like the Exchange Rate Mechanism, quite sizeable variations are permitted in the relative values of different currencies. One way of avoiding exposure to foreign exchange variability is to insist on payment in one's own currency, thus shifting the exchange risk to the customer. However, this ploy risks loss of competitive advantage to rivals who are willing to shoulder the exchange risk. An alternative policy is to utilise the forward market as explained in the following example.

A UK firm sells goods with a sterling value of £1m on three months credit to a customer in the Netherlands which will pay in Guilders. If the exchange rate at the date of signing the export deal is 2.40 Guilders per pound sterling, the value of the deal is £1m × 2.40 = 2.4m Guilders. The exporter is concerned that sterling will appreciate over the period before settlement thus reducing the sterling value of the Guilders receivable. If after three months, the spot rate moves to 2.80 Guilders per pound. the amount of sterling receivable will have dropped over 14% to 2.4m/2.80 = £857,143 possibly wiping out the profit on the export sale.

Protection can be obtained by hedging on the forward exchange market. Assume that when the export contract is signed, the three-month forward rate for Guilders is 2.45. This is above the spot rate, reflecting the market's expectation that sterling will strengthen. The exporter can lock in this rate by arranging with a bank to deliver Guilders to be exchanged for sterling at 2.45 in three months time, thus yielding sterling proceeds of 2.4m/2.45 = £979,592. This is some 2% lower than the sterling value as at the date of the export order, but it is guaranteed (unless the bank fails) and hence offers protection against more pronounced sterling appreciation. Conversely, if sterling weakens, the exporter is precluded from enjoying the windfall gains accruing to recipients of payments in overseas currency.

(b)   A financial intermediary is an institution which brings together units seeking funds with others wishing to invest surplus funds. Using their size and expertise, they offer important services to the financial system.

Maturity transformation

It would be difficult for individuals wishing to lend capital to find potential borrowers wishing to borrow for the same length of time. By pooling the funds of many individuals, the intermediary can extend loans of varying terms while using its liquidity to safeguard individuals' rights to withdraw their capital.

Risk spreading

Individuals would find it difficult to assess the riskiness of potential borrowers, lacking both the time and resources to undertake a detailed credit evaluation. They would also be wary about over-exposing themselves to risk by lending to small numbers of borrowers. Pooling of funds allows the intermediary not only to specialise in credit risk assessment but also to spread the risk over a large number of clients.

Scale economies

Finding people wanting to borrow can be expensive and time-consuming, so-called 'shoeleather costs'. An institution can utilise its size to exploit economies of scale in marketing its services to a broad range of potential customers.

Access to managed investment portfolios

Some financial institutions, such as unit trusts and investment trusts in the UK, allow investors access to well-diversified portfolios of securities. By pooling the funds of a large number of people, they enable smaller investors to achieve a degree of diversification which they could not otherwise attain due to the transactions costs and the time necessary for active portfolio management. Investors receive returns in the form of regular dividends and capital value appreciation.

(c)   The payback method relies on comparing the period over which the initial outlay of a project is expected to be recovered with some arbitrarily-defined required payback period. If the former period is less than the stipulated time-span, the project is acceptable.

The major limitations of this method are that it does not consider expected cash flows in all future periods, and ignores the timing of cash flows, by failing to discount cash flows to present values. As a result it gives an indication neither of the project's profitability nor the contribution which it is expected to make to shareholders' wealth.

However, it does serve some useful purposes, explaining why so many companies continue to use it:

(i)   It is simple to operate and to understand, and is thus appealing to firms which may lack the resources to conduct more sophisticated analysis.

(ii)   For the same reason, it may be a useful device for communicating information about the minimum requirements for an acceptable project. For example, a minimum required return of 25% approximates to a four-year payback period.

(iii)   It is useful as a screening device to sift out the obviously inappropriate projects from those which merit more detailed scrutiny.

(iv)   Under conditions of capital rationing, it may be desirable to bias project selection in favour of projects which offer a rapid rate of return cash flow in order to provide capital for further investment.

(v)   It is an important safeguard against two forms of risk. First, by minimising the period over which capital is exposed to risk of non-recovery, the firm is better protected against the risks of market failure or entry into its markets by new competitors. Secondly, by favouring projects with a quick and early return and thus enhancing short-term liquidity, it lowers the risk of inability to meet financial obligations as they fall due.

(d)   The main purpose of JIT purchasing is to compress the time period elapsing between delivery and use of materials and components as far as is physically possible. In extreme cases, this can involve new deliveries being transferred direct to the production line from the receiving bay. The concept is not new, having been operated, for example in the delivery of building materials such as ready-mixed concrete for many years. However, JIT has increasingly been applied in recent years to a wider range of manufacturing, assembly and even retail activities. The essence of a JIT arrangement is close cooperation between user and supplier. The supplier is required to guarantee product quality and reliability of delivery while the user offers the assurance of firmer long-term contracts. Users will tend to concentrate their purchasing on fewer (and perhaps only single) suppliers, thus enabling the latter to achieve greater scale economies and efficiency in production planning. The user would expect to achieve savings in materials handling, inventory investment and store-keeping costs since (ideally) supplies will now move directly from unloading bay to the production line. If a JIT system operates efficiently, it effectively precludes the need for stock control although the receiving company must ensure efficiency in the receipt and handling of supplies.

(e)   Economies tend to grow in cyclical fashion, with periods of recession following periods of recovery and prosperity. However, excessive economic instability is considered undesirable. First, slack activity imposes costs in terms of unemployed resources and lost output, and second, overheating at times of rapid expansion imposes costs in terms of inflation and lost international competitiveness. Governments periodically intervene in the economy in order to moderate cyclical fluctuations, raising expenditure and/or cutting taxes at times of recession, and restricting expenditure and/or raising taxes in boom times.

Some problems arising from the use of fiscal policy are:

Forecasting problems

The conduct of fiscal policy requires knowledge of where the economy is now and how it is likely to develop in the future. Forecasting economic trends usually involves the construction of complex economic models which embody assumptions about the relationships between economic magnitudes, based on past behaviour. The validity of the forecast depends on the extent to which such relationships are likely to apply in the future, and also on the volume and reliability of data about the present state of the economy which provides the forecasting base.

Time-lags

Policy-makers are often hampered by inability to recognise the need for action and to assess the scale of the required intervention. Consequently, it is often argued that discretionary fiscal policy can be counter-productive because of the time-lags involved – by the time the policy measures are introduced and begin to impact on people's behaviour, the nature of the problem may have changed.

Crowding-out

Some economists argue that an increase in government expenditure, far from supplementing aggregate demand, will only displace or 'crowd out' private sector expenditure. Increased command over resources by the state may simply lower the ability of firms and individuals to obtain resources. For example, if the state wishes to computerise more of its activities, the increased demand for skilled systems analysts may drive up the salary levels which all organisations will have to pay to recruit and retain such specialists.

Financing problems

A public sector deficit has to be financed in some way. If the state borrows on the financial markets, the resulting increase in demand for funds may raise interest rates, thus dampening the incentive of firms to invest. Alternatively, the government may borrow from the central bank ('printing money'). Because this usually involves an increase in the monetary aggregates, it poses the risk of raising the rate of inflation, although this effect is likely to depend on the current level of unemployed resources.

(f)   (i)   Forecasting is a very important part of the planning and control process. Management in all sectors of the economy need to forecast trends to assist them to plan for the future. They have to make decisions based on the best available information now, on what they expect may happen in the future eg, sales forecasts and cash flow forecasts may affect the labour budget and investment plans.

(ii)   In arriving at its sales forecast, a company could review economic trends such as employment levels, interest rates, inflation and those concerned with international trade. For example, high interest rates could affect the company's ability to invest in new projects and also affect demand for its products because of a reduction in disposable income.

Industry forecasts could also prove to be very useful. The company could, by taking into account its market share and the expected market conditions, produce useful data which would help to forecast sales.

The sales forecast could also benefit from surveys of buyers' intentions information/feedback from sales personnel and advice from experts.

Use can also be made of statistical techniques such as index numbers and time-series analysis.

---

77   (Answer 3 of examination)

3   (a)   **Material variances**

(i)   Actual quantity at actual price (given)   £17,328

(ii)   Actual quantity at standard price:

	£	
F $1,680 \times £4$	6,720	
G $1,650 \times £3$	4,950	
H $870 \times £6$	5,220	
		£16,890

(iii)   Standard yield × Standard cost
$(32 \times 120) \times £4.50$ (W1)   £17,280

(iv)   Actual yield × Standard cost
$3,648 \times £4.50$ £16,416

Variances		£
Price	(i) – (ii)	438 A
Usage	(ii) – (iv)	474 A
Cost	(i) – (iv)	912 A
Mix	(ii) – (iii)	390 F
Yield	(iii) – (iv)	864 A
Usage (as above)		474 A

WORKINGS

(W1)   Standard cost per kilo = $\dfrac{£144}{32 \text{ kilos}}$ = £4.50

Variances

A = Adverse   F = Favourable

(b)   **Further analysis of material variances**

Mix		F	G	H
Standard (kilos)		1,800	1,440	960
Actual (kilos)		1,680	1,650	870
		120 F	210 A	90 F
× Standard price (£)		4	3	6
	£390 F	£480 F	£630 A	£540 F

Price		F	G	H
		£	£	£
Standard		4.00	3.00	6.00
Actual		4.25	2.80	6.40
		0.25 A	0.20 F	0.40 A
× Actual kilos used		1,680	1,650	870
	£438 A	£420 A	£330 F	£348 A

(c)   **Labour variances**

Cost variances	*Total* £	*Dept P* £	*Dept Q* £
Standard cost	6,240	4,800	1,440
Actual cost	7,872	6,360	1,512
(i)	£1,632 A	£1,560 A	£72 A

	Total £	Dept P £	Dept Q £
Efficiency variances			
Standard hours		480	240
Actual hours		600	270
		120 A	30 A
× Standard rate per hour (£)		10	6
(ii)	£1,380 A	£1,200 A	£180 A

	£	£	£
Rate variances			
Standard rate		10.00	6.00
Actual rate		10.60	5.60
		0.60 A	0.40 F
× Actual hours worked		600	270
(iii)	£252A	£360A	£108 F

Proof: (i) = (ii) + (iii)

(d)   **Sales variances**

	£
Budgeted sales for actual level of activity (120 × 32 × £16)	61,440
Actual sales (3,648 × £16.75)	61,104
	£336 A

Made up of:

Volume variance(3,840 − 3,648 kilos) × £16	3,072 A
Price variance (£0.75 × 3,648)	2,736 F
	£336 A

(Tutorial note: these are other equally acceptable ways of calculating the volume variance.*)*

(e)   The actual mix used had the same weight as the standard mix ie, 4,200 kilos but used a different combination to the standard mix [as indicated in (b)]. It used less than planned of materials F and H, and more than planned of material G, a lower cost material. In addition to substituting the lower cost material for F and H which could affect the yield, the adverse yield variance could have also been caused by using materials of a lower quality than that which was planned eg, the lower price per kilo of G gives a favourable price variance, but this could be due to buying a lower quality material.

The labour efficiency variance could have been caused by poor quality materials taking longer to process. It could also be caused by a lack of motivation on the part of employees eg, the employees in department Q getting a pay rise lower than expected, could have caused them to work more slowly and to waste more material because of not taking as much care as they should. This could also help to explain the actual yield, 30.4 kilos per batch being lower than the standard yield of 32 kilos per batch.

78   (Answer 4 of examination)

4   (a)

Per unit	←		Machine group	→	
	1	*7*	*29*	*Assembly*	*Total*
	£	£	£	£	£
Total cost	31.65	21.82	3.05	5.40	
Less: Fixed overheads	3.00	2.50	1.50	0.84	
	28.65	19.32	1.55	4.56	
Setting	0.05	0.03	0.02	–	
Variable cost	28.70	19.35	1.57	4.56	54.18

The lowest possible price could be (200 × 54.18) = £10,836 per batch of 200 which would cover the whole of the variable cost.

However, the above-mentioned price would not be making any contribution towards the recovery of the fixed overheads. If the company is to make a profit, it has to recover its fixed overheads.

Even in this case, the selling price cannot really be set simply by reference to the variable costs. The prices at which competitors are offering the same product, plus engaging in market research should also be considered. Of particular importance are the likely reactions of competitors eg, if the strategy starts a price war the company could lose more than it gains.

In addition, the company needs to think about what the likely outcome will be if other customers of the product concerned find out about the 'special price'!

Finally, the company must realise that this kind of strategy cannot work overnight, it does take time. It could, in fact, be a number of years before the company can charge the customer the full price.

(b)   For outputs up to 7,000 units/Sales up to 7,000 units

	£	£	£	£	£
Selling price	13.00	12.00	11.00	10.00	9.00
Less: Variable cost	6.20	6.20	6.20	6.20	6.20
	6.80	5.80	4.80	3.80	2.80

For outputs and sales over 7,000 units

	£	£	£
Selling price	11.00	10.00	9.00
Less: Bought-out finished price	7.75	7.75	7.00
	3.25	2.25	2.00

Selling price £	Volume units	Contribution per unit £	£	Total contribution £
13	5,000	6.80		34,000
12	6,000	5.80		34,800
11	7,000	4.80	33,600	
	200	3.25	650	
				34,250
10	7,000	3.80	26,600	
	4,200	2.25	9,450	
				36,050
9	7,000	2.80	19,600	
	6,400	2.00	12,800	
				32,400

The price of £10, and sales of 11,200 units would maximise the profit, as illustrated above at £36,050 provided the estimates prove to be correct.

(c)   Management can increase their company's production capacity by:

– improving product design so that the production process can be simplified and take up less time;

– improving plant lay-out, production methods and production scheduling, to reduce idle time and avoid bottlenecks;

– introducing the working of overtime and/or 'shift working', if this has not already been done, to make more production time available;

– introducing or improving an existing incentive scheme which makes use of the standard costing system, to enhance productivity.

Note

In (c), other ways of overcoming the problem which could be considered are:

– Buying certain components from outside suppliers rather than manufacturing them, which frees machines and equipment for other purposes.

– Employing sub-contracting manufacturers to produce completed products which also frees production facilities.

79   (Answer 5 of examination)

5   (a)   The company will need additional finance to fund both working and fixed capital needs.

As sales are expected to increase by 20%, and since working capital needs are expected to rise in line with sales, the predicted working capital needs will be 20% above the existing working capital level. Ignoring tax liability, this is:

$$1.2 \times [\text{Stock} + \text{Debtors} + \text{Cash} - \text{Trade creditors}]$$
$$= 1.2 \times [£16m + £23m + £6m - £18m]$$
$$= £32.4m, \text{ an increase of } £5.4m$$

Together with the additional capital expenditures of £20m, the total funding requirement:

$$= [£5.4m + £20m]$$
$$= £25.4m$$

This funding requirement can be met partly by internal finance and partly by new external capital. The internal finance available will derive from depreciation provisions and retained earnings, after accounting for anticipated liabilities, such as taxation, that is, from cash flow.

Note that the profit margin on sales of £100m (£10 × 10m units) before interest and tax was 16% in 1994/95. If depreciation of £5m for 1994/95 is added back, this yields a cash flow cost of sales of £79m (ignoring movements in current assets/liabilities). No further adjustment for depreciation is required.

Using the same margin, and making a simple operating cash flow projection based on the accounts and other information provided:

Inflows	£m	£m
Sales in 1995/96: (£10 × 10m units) + 20%	120.00	
Cost of sales before depreciation: (£79m + 20%)	(94.80)	
Operating cash flow		25.20
Outflows		
Tax liability for 1994/95	(5.00)	
Interest payments: 12% × £20m	(2.40)	
Dividends: 1.1 × £5m	(5.50)	
		(12.90)
Net internal finance generated		12.30
Funding requirements		(25.40)
Net additional external finance required		(13.10)

(b)   A wide variety of financing options is open to Burnsall including the following:

(i)   Some new equipment could be leased via a long-term capital lease. Tax relief is available on rental payments, lowering the effective cost of using the equipment. Lessors may 'tailor' a leasing package to suit Burnsall's specific needs regarding timing of payments and provision of ancillary services. Alternatively, good quality property assets at present owned by Burnsall could be sold to a financial institution and their continued use secured via a leaseback arrangement, although this arrangement usually involves losing any capital appreciation of the assets.

(ii)   If Burnsall's assets are of sufficient quality ie, easily saleable, it may be possible to raise a mortgage secured on them. This enables retention of ownership.

(iii)   Burnsall could make a debenture issue, interest on which would be tax-allowable. The present level of gearing (long-term debt to equity) is relatively low at £20m/£122m = 16%, Burnsall has no short-term debt apart from trade creditors and the Inland Revenue, and its interest cover is healthy at profit before tax and interest divided by interest charges = [16% × £100m]/[12% × £20m] = 6.7 times (even higher on a cashflow basis). It is likely that Burnsall could make a sizeable debt issue without unnerving the market. Any new debenture would be subordinate to the existing long-term debt and probably carry a higher interest rate.

(iv)   An alternative to a debt issue is a rights issue of ordinary shares. Because rights issues are made at a discount to the existing market price, they result in lower EPS and thus market price, although if existing shareholders take up their allocations, neither their wealth nor their control is diluted. If the market approves of the intended use of funds, a capital gain may ensue, although the company and its advisers must carefully manage the issue regarding the declared reasons and its timing in order to avoid unsettling the market.

Examiner's note: only four sources are required for the answer, but other sources of finance may also be mentioned, such as:

(v)   Burnsall could approach a venture capitalist such as 3i, which specialises in extending development capital to small-to-medium-sized firms. However, 3i may require an equity stake, and possibly insist on placing an appointee on the board of directors to monitor its interests.

(vi)   Burnsall could utilise official sources of aid such as a regional development agency depending on its location, or perhaps the European Investment Bank.

---

80   (Answer 6 of examination)

6   (a)   The main function of public enterprise is to serve the public interest – in the case of a water undertaking, it would be responsible for ensuring a safe and reliable supply of water to households at an affordable price which would also require close attention to control of operating and distribution costs. Prior to privatisation, UK public enterprises were also expected to achieve a target rate of return on capital which struck a balance between the going rate in the private sector and the long-term perspective involved in such operations. The authority would also have faced political constraints on achieving its objectives in the form of pressure to keep water charges down and also periodic restrictions on capital expenditure.

One problem faced by such enterprises was their inability to generate the funds necessary to finance the levels of investment required to maintain water supplies of acceptable quality.

Once privatised, NW would be required to generate returns for shareholders at least as great as comparable enterprises of equivalent risk. Moreover, it would be expected to generate a stream of steadily rising dividends to satisfy its institutional investors with their relatively predictable stream of liabilities.

Any capital committed to fixed investment would have to achieve efficiency in the use of resources and to achieve the level of returns required by the stock market. In the UK, it is alleged that there is an over-concern with short-term results, both to satisfy existing investors and to preserve the stock market rating of the company. Although this may safeguard future supplies of capital, it has militated against infrastructure projects and activities such as R & D, which generate their greatest returns in the more distant future.

(b)   (i)   **Shareholders**

In financial theory, companies are supposed to maximise the wealth of shareholders, as measured by the stock market value of the equity. In the absence of perfect information, it is not possible to measure the relationship between achieved shareholder wealth and the outright maximum. However, good indicators of the benefits received by shareholders are the returns they obtain in the form of dividend payments and share price appreciation.

Dividends

The pro forma dividend was 7p and by 1994 the dividend per share had grown by 186% to 20p, an average annual growth of around 19%. The pro forma payout ratio was 33%, falling to 31% by 1994. The pro forma EPS was 21p rising by 210% to 65p, an average annual increase of nearly 21%. This suggests that the company wishes to align dividend increases to increases in EPS over time.

Share price

The flotation price was £1, rising to £1.60 on the first day of dealing. By 1990, the EPS had become 29p. Given a P/E ratio of 7, this implies a market price of 203p per share. By 1994, the EPS had risen to 65p, and with a P/E ratio of 7.5, this corresponds to a market price of 488p. Compared to the close of first-day's dealings, the growth rate was 205% (a little over 20% as an annual average) and over the period 1990 – 1994, the growth was 140% (an annual average of about 25%).

Although information about returns in the market in general and those enjoyed by shareholders of comparable companies are not available to act as a yardstick, these figures suggest considerable increases in shareholders' wealth, and at a rate substantially above the increase in the Retail Price Index (RPI).

(ii)   **Consumers**

Although NW's ability to raise prices is ostensibly restrained by the industry regulator, turnover has risen by 38% over the period, an annual average of 5.5%. This is above the rate of inflation over this period (about 2% pa) and also above the trend rate of increase in demand (also 2% pa). This suggests relatively weak regulation, perhaps reflecting the industry's alleged need to earn profits in order to invest, or perhaps that NW has diversified into other, unregulated activities which can sustain higher rates of product price inflation.

However, before accusing NW of exploiting the consumer, one would have to examine whether it did lay down new investment, and also how productive it had been, especially using indicators like purity and reliability of water supply.

(iii)   **Workforce**

Numbers employed have fallen from 12,000 to 10,000 ie, 17%. The average remuneration has risen from £8,333 to £8,600, a mere 1% in nominal terms *(tutorial note:* 1% is the annual average*)* but about minus 8% in real terms, after allowing for the 9% inflation in retail prices over this period. This suggests a worsening of returns to the labour force, although a shift in the skill mix away from skilled workers and/or a change in conditions of employment away from full-time towards part-time and contract working might explain the figures recorded. Certainly, the efficiency of the labour force as measured by sales per employee (up from £37,500 to £62,000 – an increase of 65%) has outstripped movements in pay. However, apparently greater labour efficiency could be due to product price inflation and/or the impact of new investment.

The directors, however, seem to have benefited greatly. It is not stated whether the number of directors has increased, but as a group, their emoluments have trebled. Arguably, this might have been necessary to bring hitherto depressed levels of public sector rewards into line with remuneration elsewhere in the private sector in order to retain competent executives. Conversely, the actual remuneration may be understated as it does not appear to include non-salary items such as share options, which would presumably be very valuable given the share price appreciation that has occurred over this period.

(iv)   **Macro-economic objectives**

There are numerous indicators whereby NW's contribution to the achievement of macro-economic policies can be assessed. Among these are the following:

(1)   *Price stability*

–   *Via its pricing policy.* As noted NW's revenues have risen by 38% in nominal terms and 29% in real terms. This questions the company's degree of responsibility in cooperating with the government's anti-inflationary policy.

– *Via its pay policy.* There is evidence that NW has held down rates of pay, but if this has not been reflected in a restrained pricing policy, then the benefits accrue to shareholders rather than to society at large. Moreover, the rapid increase in directors' emoluments is hardly anti-inflationary, providing signals to the labour force which are likely to sour industrial relations.

(2)   *Economic growth*

– *Via its capital expenditure.* Higher profitability has been implicitly condoned by the regulator in order to allow NW to generate funds for new investment. This appears to have been achieved. Capital expenditure has nearly quadrupled. As well as benefiting the industry itself, this will have provided multiplier effects on the rest of the economy to the extent that equipment has been domestically-sourced.

– *Via efficiency improvements.* It is not possible to calculate non-financial indicators of efficiency, but there are clear signs of enhanced financial performance. The sharp increase in sales per employee has been noted. In addition, the return on capital as measured by operating profit to total assets has moved steadily upward as follows:

1988	*1990*	*1992*	*1994*
26%	29%	36%	39%

JUNE 1996 QUESTIONS

Section A - This question is compulsory and MUST be attempted

---

81   (Question 1 of examination)

Behemoth plc is a steel manufacturer which operates the full range of production processes from iron-making to steel-rolling and pressing. Being highly capital-intensive, its cost structure includes a high proportion of fixed costs. It is considering means of making some of its fixed commitments more flexible and thus converting certain fixed costs into variable costs. In particular, it is proposing to overhaul its input supply systems and transfer its labour force on to more flexible contracts.

The managers of Behemoth are unsure about the overall effect of these measures, partly because they are unclear about the precise behaviour of costs as output is varied, using the existing procedures and contracts. However, they believe that, at current output levels, about 75% of its total costs are fixed.

Behemoth hires a consultancy firm to investigate the present relationship between cost and output and also to advise on the likely impact of the proposed changes on the cost structure. The consultants have studied cost-output data for the past five years, and using a linear regression model, estimate the following line of best fit:

$$TC = 1,400 + 46V$$

where

TC   =   Total operating cost in £m per annum
V   =   Volume of production per annum (millions of tonnes of steel)

The consultants estimate that the proposed changes will require an outlay of £100m to lower fixed costs to £1,300m per annum and raise variable costs to £50 per tonne, but will not affect the total capacity, reckoned to be 12m tonnes per annum. Some directors argue that these developments should be financed by borrowing at a fixed rate of 8%, interest rates having fallen during the recent recession. The expenditure can be wholly written off for tax purposes in one year. The rate of corporation tax is 33%, payable a year in arrears.

In 1995, a year of economic recovery, Behemoth produced an output of 10m tonnes of steel products at an average price of £200 per tonne. It expects to average an output of 11m tonnes per annum over the whole economic cycle. Behemoth's shareholders have instructed its managers to pursue a target rate of return of 15% on the book value of equity.

Behemoth's accounting statements for the most recent period are shown

Profit and loss account for year ended 31 December 1995

	£m
Sales	2,000
Operating costs	(1,920)
Operating profit	80
Interest charges	(8)
Earnings before tax	72
Corporation tax payable	(10)
Profit after tax	62

Balance sheet as at 31 December 1995

	£m
Fixed assets	1,800
Net current assets	300
10% Loan stock	(80)
Net assets	2,020
Issued share capital	800
Reserves	1,200
Shareholders' funds	2,020

Required

(a)   Explain the difference between operating and financial gearing.   (5 marks)

(b)   Explain why a steel producer such as Behemoth should be concerned about its levels of operating and financial gearing.   (5 marks)

(c)   Interpret the meaning of the regression equation obtained by the consultant, and discuss any reservations you would have about relying on it for decision-making.

Make use of the profit and loss account in your answer in order to check the validity of the estimated cost function.   (8 marks)

(d)   Assume that the management of Behemoth accept the validity of the consultant's computations.

Advise the board as to the desirability of the proposed measures, taking into account:

(i)   the payback period
(ii)   the effect on the break-even point
(iii)   the effect on financial gearing.

Carefully specify any assumptions you make.   (12 marks)

(e)   What volume of output should Behemoth produce in order to meet the specified rate of return?

Comment on the feasibility of this target.   (5 marks)
(Total 35 marks)

Section B - This question is compulsory and MUST be attempted

Answer FIVE of the six parts of this question

Each part carries five marks

82	**(Question 2 of examination)**

(a)   (i)   Briefly explain why 'Monetarist' economists argue against using short-term variations in the money supply to influence the economy.

(ii)   How do such variations affect company decisions?   (5 marks)

(b)   Describe briefly what a 'rights issue' is and explain why such issues are a common way of raising additional finance.   (5 marks)

(c)   Explain briefly the possible advantages of having worker representatives and junior management participating in the budget preparation process.   (5 marks)

(d)   You are provided with the following information:

	Budget	Actual
Sales (units)	72,000	64,000
Selling price	£10 per unit	£8.40 per unit
Variable cost	£6 per unit	£6.20 per unit

Using a contribution approach, calculate appropriate variances and comment briefly on the possible causes of those variances.   (5 marks)

(e)   ZXC plc operates a process costing system. Discuss briefly the issues which need to be considered in valuing materials to be included in work in progress.   (5 marks)

(f)   Discuss briefly the options available to a company to utilise its idle production capacity, and identify the associated financial benefits.   (5 marks)

(Total 25 marks)

Section C - ONE question ONLY to be attempted

83   (Question 3 of examination)

(a)   Discuss the advantages and disadvantages of using the 'full cost' (absorption costing) method for dealing with the costs of internal services. Include in your answer comments on the motivational aspects of this method of costing.   (7 marks)

(b)   Describe the factors which affect the choice of bases of apportionment by which internal services are to be apportioned.   (5 marks)

(c)   JR Co Ltd's budgeted overheads for the forthcoming period applicable to its production departments, are as follows:

	£'000
1	870
2	690

The budgeted total costs for the forthcoming period for the service departments, are as follows:

	£'000
G	160
H	82

The use made of each of the service has been estimated as follows:

	Production department		Service department	
	1	2	G	H
G (%)	60	30	-	10
H (%)	50	30	20	-

Required

Apportion the service department costs to production departments:

(i)   using the step-wise ('elimination') method, starting with G, and
(ii)   the reciprocal (simultaneous-equation) method, and
(iii)   comment briefly on your figures.

(8 marks)
(Total 20 marks)

84   (Question 4 of examination)

Sychwedd plc manufacture and sell three products R, S, and T which make use of two machine groups, 1 and 2. The budget for period 1, the first quarter of their next accounting year, includes the following information:

	Machine Group	
Fixed overhead absorption rates:	*1*	*2*
Rate per machine hour	£10	£11.20

	Product R	*Product S*	*Product T*
Sales (kilos)	12,000	25,000	40,000
	£	£	£
Sales	120,000	250,000	360,000
Variable costs	73,560	164,250	284,400
Fixed overheads	19,752	38,300	42,400
Budgeted net profit	26,688	47,450	33,200

For the second quarter (period 2), it is estimated that the budgeted machine hours and direct labour hours needed to produce 1,000 kilos of each of the products are:

	Machine Group	
Machine hours	*1*	*2*
Product		
R	75	80
S	30	110
T	50	50
Direct labour hours		
Product		
R	30	40
S	10	50
T	20	20
Budgeted fixed overheads (to be absorbed using a machine hour rate)	£40,800	£68,365
Budgeted variable labour and overheads, rate per direct labour hour	£7.50	£8.50

	Product R	*Product S*	*Product T*
Budgeted material costs per 1,000 kilos	£4,508	£5,096	£6,125
Expected sales (kilos)	10,000	25,000	50,000
Planned price changes Compared with period 1	10% increase	no change	no change

A sales commission of 4% of the sales value will be paid.

There are no budgeted opening or closing stocks ie, all production is expected to be sold.

Required

(a)   Compute the machine hour rate for each machine group for period 2.   (3 marks)

(b)   Calculate the budgeted contribution and net profit for each of the three products for period 2.

(9 marks)

(c)   Assuming that the sales trend shown over the two periods is forecast to continue, comment briefly on the figures and advise management accordingly.   (8 marks)

(Total 20 marks)

Section D - ONE question ONLY to be attempted

85   **(Question 5 of examination)**

(a)   Discuss:

(i)   the significance of trade creditors in a firm's working capital cycle, and   (4 marks)

(ii)   the dangers of over-reliance on trade credit as a source of finance.   (4 marks)

(b)   Keswick plc traditionally follows a highly aggressive working capital policy, with no long-term borrowing. Key details from its recently complied accounts appear below:

	£m
Sales (all on credit)	10.00
Earnings before interest and tax (EBIT)	2.00
Interest payments for the year	0.50
Shareholders' funds	2.00
(comprising £1m issued share capital, par value 25p, and £1m revenue reserves)	
Debtors	0.40
Stocks	0.70
Trade creditors	1.50
Bank overdraft	3.00

A major supplier which accounts for 50% of Keswick's cost of sales, is highly concerned about Keswick's policy of taking extended trade credit. The supplier offers Keswick the opportunity to pay for supplies within 15 days in return for a discount of 5% on the invoiced value.

Keswick holds no cash balances but is able to borrow on overdraft from its bank at 12%. Tax on corporate profit is paid at 33%.

Required

Determine the costs and benefits to Keswick of making this arrangement with its supplier, and recommend whether Keswick should accept the offer.

Your answer should include the effects on:

-     The working capital cycle
-     Interest cover
-     Profits after tax
-     Earnings per share
-     Return on equity
-     Capital gearing.

(12 marks)

(Total 20 marks)

86   (Question 6 of examination)

(a)   Briefly explain the main features of the following:

- Sale-and-leaseback
- Hire-purchase
- Financial leasing

(b)   Howgill Ltd is the leasing subsidiary of a major commercial bank. It is approached by Clint plc, a company entirely financed by equity, which operates in the pharmaceutical industry, with a request to arrange a lease contract to acquire new computer-controlled manufacturing equipment to further automate its production line. The outlay involved is £20m. The equipment will have only a four-year operating life due to the fast rate of technical change in this industry, and no residual worth. The basic project has a positive net present value when operating cash flows are discounted at the shareholders' required rate of return.

Howgill would finance the purchase of the machinery by borrowing at a pre-tax annual interest rate of 15%. The purchase would be completed on the final day of its accounting year, when it would also require the first of the annual rental payments. Howgill currently pays tax at 33%, 12 months after its financial year end. A writing-down allowance is available based on a 25% reducing balance.

Under the terms of the lease contract, Howgill would also provide maintenance services, valued by Clint at £750,000 pa. These would be supplied by Howgill's computer maintenance sub-division at no incremental cost as it currently has spare capacity which is expected to persist for the foreseeable future.

Clint has the same financial year as Howgill, also pays tax at 33% and its own bank will lend at 18% before tax.

Required

Calculate the minimum rental which Howgill would have to charge in order to just break-even on the lease contract.

(Note: you may assume that the rental is wholly tax-allowable as a business expense.)

(6 marks)

(c)   Assume that Howgill does proceed with the contract and charges an annual rental of £7m.

Calculate whether, on purely financial criteria, Clint should lease the asset or borrow in order to purchase it outright:

(i)   ignoring the benefit to Clint of the maintenance savings   (6 marks)
(ii)   allowing for the maintenance savings.   (2 marks)

(Total 20 marks)

EXAMINER'S COMMENTS

General comments

Results overall were disappointing, there being little evidence of improvement in the quality of answers over time. Candidates still come forward to this exam under prepared, especially in the Financial Management (FM) area. Yet again, it seems that candidates are seeing paper 8 as an exam in Management Accounting (MA) with a little FM 'tacked on', and/or are relying on knowledge gained in earlier MA studies to carry them through. On this occasion, inadequate answers to MA questions frustrated this policy.

The standard of presentation was generally poor, presenting difficulties for markers in questions 5 and 6 particularly. Candidates still fail to read the rubric properly eg, a large number did all six sections of question 2, they fail to manage their time properly eg, leaving the case study with its 35 marks until last, and fail to answer the question set, often providing answers appropriate to the preceding exam paper.

A further shortcoming was a predilection for the discursive style of answer, often totally neglecting to utilise the numerical information provided in the question. This was noticeable in question 1 (c) and question 5 (b). This strategy is unlikely to achieve many marks.

Question 1: the case study was particularly poorly done. It required candidates to examine the financing decision of a company in the context of its operating environment and its existing financial structure. As such, the question was testing knowledge and understanding from Section 7 of the syllabus. Candidates must appreciate that it is not enough simply to be able to describe different types of finance - they have to understand when to utilise them and the effect which they have on key indicators. In particular, the question required knowledge of operating gearing and cost-volume profit analysis. These should be familiar concepts and are not peculiar to financial management.

Part (a) required a distinction between operating and financial gearing.

This caused great difficulties. Remarkably few candidates were able to give a coherent explanation of financial gearing or operating gearing. Most had little idea about the latter, discussing various irrelevant issues. The better answers tried to relate to the question, and used the figures provided to illustrate the ratios.

Part (b) required an explanation of why a highly capital intensive company should worry about each type of gearing.

This invited explicit reference to the context of the question ie, the company is highly capital intensive with, therefore, a high break-even point, and thus is highly exposed to cyclical variations in volume. Since adding a layer of financial gearing worsens this exposure, it should be very wary of debt financing because it raises the break-even volume. This line of argument was missed by most candidates, although some marks were available for descriptions of general problems related to debt financing.

Part (c) required ability to interpret a linear regression equation, and to explain its limitations.

Candidates were mainly able to identify the fixed and variable components of the cost function, and to apply them in some fashion to the Profit and Loss data provided. However, such comparisons were usually let down by not comparing like with like ie, by using different volumes. The limitations of linear regression were not generally appreciated. Comments demonstrating candidates' lack of understanding and confusion with linear programming were very common.

Part (d) required an assessment of the effect of a proposed internal restructuring on break-even point and financial gearing and also calculation of a pay back period for the project.

The majority of candidates did not realise that this was a straightforward cost-saving exercise, with an initial outlay generating higher variable costs and lower fixed costs. Many answers were in the form of a projected Profit and Loss statement or a cash flow forecast over many periods instead of a one-line answer. Many candidates undertook DCF calculations, most omitted the effect of tax and many included interest charges. Many candidates confused break-even analysis with payback analysis - they are similar in concept but the former identifies a break-even volume and the latter a point in time when cash outlay is recovered. Interest charges should, however, appear in a break-even calculation - this aspect was usually omitted. Most attempts at the gearing component of this section were reasonable.

Part (e) required assessment of the required volume to achieve a specified return on equity.

The majority of candidates omitted this section, although there were easy marks obtainable. It simply required an additional break-even calculation, introducing a required return on investment ie, an additional fixed charge. Many candidates related the required return to the issued share capital rather than to equity and most also ignored the tax charge.

Section B

Question 2: Part (a) required candidates to discuss problems with monetary policy from a Monetarist perspective, and to explain the problems which short-term monetary variations present to firms.

This question was not popular and was very badly done, reflecting candidates' habitual unease with issues of economics. Few answered the question set, preferring to outline the Quantity Theory and specifying the impacts of monetary variations on prices and interest rates, neglecting to mention problem areas such as time lags and perverse longer-term effects. Some did mention the link between interest rate movements and investment and financing decisions but very few understood that greater price uncertainty hinders firms' attempts to plan production and investment.

(b)   **This section called upon candidates to describe a 'rights issue' and to explain why such issues are in common use.** On the whole, the description was very well done. However, a number of candidates often confused 'rights issues' with 'bonus issues'. The reasons why 'rights issues' are used was also very well done by a considerable number of candidates. The weaker answers were those that were very thin and lacked full explanation of the reasons why they were used.

(c)   **This open ended short scenario question concerned the benefits of worker and junior management participation in the budget preparation process.** An encouraging number of candidates received very good marks for this question. However many candidates did not answer the question set, in whole or part. For example some candidates included a lot of irrelevant detail when describing budgets or the benefits of budgeting.

(d)   **The candidates were required to demonstrate and apply their knowledge of standard costing to a simple marginal costing contribution variance analysis and discussion of the situation.** Many candidates failed to calculate the contribution variance and many did not offer any suggested reasons as to why the adverse variances may have occurred.

(e)   **This question required candidates to discuss the issues relating to the valuation of materials to be included in the work in progress by a company using a process costing system.** A considerable number of candidates focused on one aspect only and excluded various other aspects.

Some candidates merely gave a list of bullet points which limits marks available when the question specifically asks for a discussion or description.

(f)   **This question called for a discussion of how to utilise idle production capacity and the identification of the financial benefits.** Many candidates gave sensible acceptable answers for the first part of the question. Practical sensible suggestions were awarded marks. A large number of candidates did however, fail to spell out the financial benefits which could result from their suggestions. A number of candidates did not answer the question set, and offered a description of the causes of 'idle time' with a particular emphasis on labour problems.

Section C

Question 3: (a) and (b) required a discussion of the advantages and disadvantages of absorption costing for dealing with internal services, comments on motivational aspects and the factors affecting the choice of the bases by which internal services are apportioned.

Candidates who scored low marks, did so because they could not write much at all about the subject and failed to discuss the matter, as applied to internal services and/or motivational aspects.

(c) (i) AND (ii) Only a very small number of candidates were able to work out (ii) using the simultaneous equation method. If candidates used the repeated distribution method and gave good reason why, marks were awarded.

(iii)   Sensible comments were rewarded. A considerable number of candidates did not attempt this part of the question.

Question 4: (a) this part of the question required the calculation of a machine hour rate, and was generally answered well by candidates.

(b)   This part required a lot of workings, and many candidates obtained good marks for this part.

(c)   Candidates should have noted that eight marks had been allocated to this part of the question. The performance for part (c) was very disappointing particularly in the light of pleasing answers to parts (a) and (b); some did not even bother to attempt this part of the question at all, thus throwing away the 8 marks that it carried.

Section D

Question 5: part (a) required a discussion of the significance of trade creditors in the working capital cycle, and of the dangers of over-reliance on trade credit.

This was generally quite well done, offering relatively easy marks for the well-prepared candidate. There was some confusion between debtors and creditors and a pronounced tendency not to fully explain the points made, especially with regard to short and long-term liquidity implications.

Part (b) required analysis of selected accounts data to assess the effects of a new credit arrangement with suppliers on key financial indicators.

This was not well done. Many candidates opted for a discursive approach, often preferring to ignore totally the information provided, thus disqualifying themselves from the higher marks. It appeared that some might have been puzzled by the absence of a separate figure for purchases, although the question clearly stated that the supplier accounted for 50% of the cost of sales. Assuming no stock movements, it follows that purchases from this supplier are 50% of the difference between sales and the EBIT, ie, 50% × [£10m - £2m] = £4m. Using sales as a proxy was acceptable although not for full marks. Candidates have to read the question carefully and utilise the information provided, specifying any assumptions.

Even if candidates did fail to proceed along the expected lines, there were opportunities for easy marks obtainable from calculating accounting indicators. However, presentation was particularly poor, with relatively few systematic attempts to answer the question in a structured way. Although the question clearly required a 'before and after' approach, remarkably few candidates could supply the correct starting figures. There were many basic errors in calculation of PAT (eg, failure to allow for tax-deductibility of interest). EPS (eg, using profit before tax, incorrect calculation of the number of shares), and ROI (eg, using only issued share capital as the denominator). Calculations of profit and interest cover also tended to neglect the beneficial effect of the discount offered, which applied to a full year's supplies rather than to outstanding balances.

Question 6: part (a) required explanations of sale and leaseback (SAL), HP and financial leasing.

This was generally quite well done. However, there were recurrent errors. For example, the impression that with a SAL, the asset is purchased then immediately resold for cash (in which case, why bother?), confusion between operating and financial leasing, and statements to the effect that a financial lease is off-balance sheet and 'normally' involves an option to buy.

Part (b) and (c) required a lease evaluation from both lessor's (b) and lessee's (c) perspectives.

There was much confusion here, leaving the impression that too few candidates understood the distinction between the two parties and their roles. Answers were poorly presented, and rarely offered an actual solution, indicating a poor understanding of the significance of the numerical data derived. The analysis required a standard DCF lease evaluation, although many answers were given in undiscounted form. Many candidates threw in the maintenance charge for the lessor, ignoring its non incremental nature, many candidates who did do a DCF analysis included interest in the cash flows and most omitted the lessor's liability to tax on rentals. In calculating the lessee's break-even rental, most candidates failed to appreciate that an annuity application was required, simply dividing by the number of years. The bright spot was in calculating the WDAs and subsequent tax savings (yet often with insufficient years and often ignoring the balancing allowance). Astute candidates realised that this operation could be utilised again in evaluating the lessee's lease-or-buy decision. The few who offered coherently structured answers, appreciating the different positions of the two parties, scored high marks.

ANSWERS TO JUNE 1996 EXAMINATION

It should be noted that the following answers are probably fuller than would be expected from the average candidate under exam conditions. Answers are provided in this degree of detail on the principle of offering guidance on the approach required, and on the range and depth of knowledge that would be expected from an excellent candidate.

81 (Answer 1 of examination)

(a) Most businesses operate with a mixture of variable and fixed factors of production, giving rise to variable and fixed production costs, respectively. Operating gearing refers to the relative importance of fixed costs in the firm's cost structure, costs which have to be met regardless of the firm's level of output and sales revenue. In general, the higher the proportion of fixed-to-variable costs, the higher is the firm's break-even volume of output. As sales expand beyond the break-even point, profits before interest and tax, and shareholder earnings, will rise by a greater proportion.

Financial gearing refers to the proportion of debt finance in the firm's capital structure (capital gearing) and also to the proportion of earnings which are pre-empted by prior interest charges (income gearing). It is obligatory to meet interest payments, irrespective of the level of sales revenue and operating profits. Generally, introducing financial gearing into the capital structure will raise earnings per ordinary share and generate a multiplier effect on shareholder earnings as sales increase. However, since this effect also operates in a downward direction, a geared capital structure increases the likely variability in shareholder earnings. It also raises the probability of financial failure should the company be unable to meet interest charges in a poor trading year.

(b) Behemoth operates in a highly cyclical industry, producing a basic product whose demand tends to fluctuate to a greater degree than the overall economy. Steel usually leads the economy into recession and is one of the last sectors to recover.

Capital-intensive firms like Behemoth have a high level of operating gearing. As a result, they are especially prone to the impact of oscillations in the business cycle. As their output volume decreases, their earnings before interest and tax decline sharply and vice versa. Therefore, such companies are regarded as relatively risky and the stock market attaches a low price-earnings ratio to their earnings. In other words, investors tend to seek a relatively higher return from holding their shares to compensate for the greater variability in earnings and the potential loss. The addition of a second tier of risk in the form of financial gearing serves to accentuate the risk of inability to meet prior charges. Given the need to meet these interest charges, the effect of financial gearing is to raise the firm's break-even point. Generally speaking, companies with high operating gearing should not over-rely on debt finance.

(c) The regression equation suggests that total production cost comprises a fixed element (the intercept of the line, £1,400m) and a variable element, as given by the slope of the line fitted. It appears that for every unit produced, variable cost increases by £46 ie, the average variable (or unit variable) cost is £46.

However, there are many drawbacks with this method of modelling which may undermine its usefulness as a decision guide.

(i) We are not told the correlation coefficient and thus do not know how close a fit the line is to the observations. If the correlation is low, then the fitted line may be unreliable.

(ii) Even though we may obtain a good correlation for a linear relationship, it is possible that the true relationship contains elements of curvature.

(iii) The relationship derived, even if correctly-shaped, is only valid over the observed ranges of output. In other words, when extended to higher or lower output ranges, the shape of the relationship may be different. For example, it is likely that at very low outputs, operating costs fall sharply due to the exploitation of indivisibilies, while at high outputs, they may rise sharply due to pressures on capacity leading to more breakdowns and idle time, etc.

(iv)   The relationship is based on past data. One imagines that the analyst would have corrected for inflation over the study period, but it is possible that his results are still contaminated by structural changes like the coming on-stream of new equipment, changes in product quality and changes in working practices. His results are only an average relationship over a lengthy period. However, to take a shorter period could expose the model to the undue influence of random events.

(v)   The underlying data may be biased by the inclusion in fixed costs of allocated cots, such as head office expenses. The focus should be solely on costs incurred at this particular operating unit.

Notwithstanding these reservations, it is possible to obtain a rough cross-check on the validity of the regression line by inspection of the accounts. The total cost of operation is reckoned to split into 75% fixed and 25% variable. Of the operating costs of £1,920m, this would correspond to £1,440m fixed and £480m variable. Given an output volume of 10m tonnes, this yields a per unit variable cost of £48, similar to the estimate obtained by the consultants.

(d)   **Payback**

1995 was a year of economic recovery, during which Behemoth produced 10m tonnes against a capacity of 12m tonnes. Accepting the consultants' estimate and assuming an average output over the cycle of 11m tonnes, the project will generate annual savings of:

[reduction in fixed cost of £1,400m - £1,300m]
    - [increase in variable cost of 11m × £4 per unit]
        = [£100m - £44m] = £56m

Assuming Behemoth's profitability recovers sufficiently to absorb the tax relief on the expenditure, the annual cash flows associated with the new expenditure are:

Item (£m)/Year	0	1	2	3	etc
Outlay	(100)				
Tax saving		33			
Net cash saving		56	56	56	etc
Tax at 33%			(18)	(18)	etc
Net cash flows	(100)	89	38	38	etc

Clearly, on these assumptions, the outlay generates a very rapid payback of just over one year. Inability to claim the tax relief immediately would slow down the payback, while a lower output figure could improve it, since variable costs are now higher.

Break-even

The break-even volume at present can be deducted by inspection of the accounts*. Fixed costs are £1,440m and variable costs per unit are £48. With a product price of £200 per tonne, and allowing for interest charges, this gives break-even at:

$$\frac{£1,440m + £8m}{£200 - £48} = \frac{£1,448m}{£152} = 9.53m \text{ units}$$

This corresponds to 79% of the full capacity of 12m units.

With the new production arrangements, and assuming debt financing, generating additional interest charges of (£100m × 8%) = £8m, the new break-even volume would be:

$$\frac{£1,300m + £8m + £8m}{£200 - £50} = \frac{£1,316m}{£150} = 8.77m \text{ units}$$

This corresponds to 73% of the full capacity of 12m units.

However, these calculations assume a given product price of £200. In reality, steel prices vary substantially over the trade cycle. In addition, variations in the product mix would influence the average price.

*   Alternatively, the answer may incorporate cost data from the regression equation.

Financial gearing

(i)   Capital gearing. Behemoth already has £80m/£2,020m = 4%. Financing the project with debt would raise the long-term debt by £100m to £180m, and ignoring the eventual beneficial impact of the project's returns on retained earnings and equity, the capital gearing would rise to £180m/£2,020m = 9%.

(ii)   Interest cover. Initially, the interest cover is high at £80m/£8m = 10 times. The additional interest charges of £8m would lower this to £80m/£16m = 5 times, again ignoring the cash flow and profit benefit of the new expenditure.

Despite the high operating gearing, the additional risks posed by financial gearing do not look excessive. The directors will have to take a view on this, bearing in mind the stage of the economic cycle and the likelihood of keeping operating profits above £16m, the minimum level required to cover the new total interest charges.

(e)   Shareholders require a return of 15% on the book value of their equity. Behemoth currently achieves profits after tax of just £62m on an equity base of £2,020m ie, ROE = £62m/£2,020m = 3.1%. The target profit after tax is (15% × £2,020m) = £303m. This is equivalent to approximately [£303m/1 - 33%] = £452m pre tax. This can be treated as tantamount to an additional fixed charge. In all, fixed charges become:

$$\text{Fixed production costs} + \text{Interest charges} + \text{Profit target}$$
$$= £1,300m + £16m + £452m = £1,768m$$

With an average product price of £200 and the new unit variable cost of £50, this suggests a required volume of:

$$\frac{£1,768m}{£200 - £50} = 11.8m \text{ tonnes}$$

This output corresponds to virtually full production capacity, seemingly a formidable target.

---

82   (Answer 2 of examination)

(a)   (i)   'Monetarist' economists are very sceptical about the ability of governments to successfully fine-tune the economy using either fiscal or monetary means. Two major problems in using short-term variations in the money supply are:

1.   **Forecasting difficulties**

When using any policy instrument to control economic fluctuations, policy-makers need information about the present state of the economy and in which direction it is tending. This requires timely collection of economic data and accurate forecasting for the need to act to be recognised. Monetarists emphasise problems of data-gathering and forecasting, inevitably based on past data, suggesting that delays in these areas are likely to have a perverse impact. Instead of short-term monetary manipulation, they stress the need to allow the money stock to grow in line with the overall economy.

2.   **Measurement difficulties**

To control any economic magnitude, it is useful to be able to measure it. Over time, new, widely-acceptable methods of payment have become available, and until they are built into definitions of money, they have the capacity to distort measurement of the 'true' stock of spending power. Experience has shown that when economic authorities attempt to restrict monetary growth, new forms of money emerge at a quicker rate.

(ii)   Company decision-makers value stable economic conditions because stability aids forward planning. If the rate of monetary expansion is broadly known, they will accommodate their economic actions to suit the expected rate of inflation. If the government begins to increase monetary growth, people cannot predict the upward movement in the rate of inflation. Such an increase in uncertainty is likely to dislocate their decision-making in important ways. For example, they may apply price increases above the current rate of inflation, thus exacerbating the inflationary process. In addition, they may postpone replacement investments or forgo new capital expenditure, thus reducing their ability to respond to future increases in demand.

(b)   A rights issue can be made at the discretion of the directors and does not have to be approved by the company in general meeting. It can be made by a company whose shares are listed on the Stock Exchange and provides existing shareholders with an invitation to subscribe for shares usually at a price which is below the current market price. This allows the existing shareholders to maintain their current level, of control eg, in respect of voting rights. The ex-rights share price, will however depend on the market's reaction and expectations.

The reasons why such issues are very common are:

-     They provide the shareholders with some flexibility. They can either sell their rights in the market or keep them and pay for them in full. This means that such issues usually succeed as they in effect force shareholders to go one way or the other, ie, keep the shares or assign some/all of them.

-     The costs of a rights issue, for example when compared with a new issue of equity finance tends to be much cheaper with lower administrative costs and lower under-writing fees. The company making the issue will have to produce a brochure eg, with details, terms, capital structure data, future prospects, and dividend prospects etc, but, provided that the issue is for less than 10% of the class of shares concerned, the company does not have the expense of having to produce and issue a prospectus.

-     Companies may use a rights issue to reduce their gearing in book value terms by increasing the ordinary share capital, and may also use some of the cash received to pay off some/all of their long-term debt which could reduce the gearing, in market value terms, all other things remaining equal.

(c)   The possible benefits of involving worker representatives and junior management in the budget preparation process are:

-     They know their area and being able to draw upon their knowledge and experience could save their organisation a lot of money. For example, they could point out that if their organisation was to invest in a new machine which was being proposed by senior management, that it would also be necessary to buy certain additional equipment, in order to be able to carry out all of the functions for which it is being acquired.

-     They are in regular contact with the workers and know what can and cannot be done eg, if a target is set too high this may cause a reduction in motivation and lead to poor industrial relations. Thus, they can make a valuable input which should help ensure that targets set are fair, reasonable and attainable.

-     Those junior managers who have to put the plans into practice, will be more committed to doing so if they were actively involved in the budget preparation process. For example it is difficult for them to be 'fully accountable' if they were not a party to the discussion which helped to formulate the plans.

-     Being involved in various budget committee meetings by such personnel could also help improve communications. For example, if the organisation does not spell out its objectives and plans clearly, those not involved in the meetings will either tend to follow their own personal objectives or formulate their own perceived objectives for their organisation.

-     Participation by worker representatives and junior management should enable them to make their views known and prompt them to make constructive comments/recommendations and propose realistic plans.

(d)   The variance between the budgeted contribution (for the actual level of activity) and the actual contribution is:

	Selling price £	Variable cost £	Contribution £	Contribution for 64,000 units £
	←	**Per Unit**	→	Contribution for
Budget	10.00	6.00	4.00	256,000
Actual	8.40	6.20	2.20	140,800
Variance	(1.60)	(0.20)	(1.80)	(115,200)

The contribution variance is made up of

		£
Sales price variance	£1.60 × 64,000	(102,400)
Variable cost variance	£0.20 × 64,000	(12,800)
Contribution variance		(115,200)

The sales variances are:

			£
Total variance:	Budget (£10 × 72,000)		720,000
	Actual (£8.40 × 64,000)	537,600	
			(182,400)

This is made up of:

	£
Sales volume variance	
(Budget 72,000 units - Actual 64,000 units × £10	(80,000)
Sales price variance (as above)	(102,400)
	(182,400)

or the sales volume variance could be calculated as:

	£
Actual quantity at standard contribution 64,000 × (£10 − £6) =	256,000
Budgeted quantity at standard contribution 72,000 × (£10 - £6) =	288,000
Sales quantity variance	£32,000 A

and the total sales variance is:

	£
Actual sales at actual price and standard variable cost 64,000 × (£8.40 − £6)	153,600
Budgeted sales at standard contribution 72,000 × (£10 − £6)	288,000
Total sales variance	134,400 A

The reasons for the adverse variances could have been caused by a combination of factors such as:

-    Competition at home and overseas forcing selling prices down and/or accepting a number of large bulk orders, but still necessitating a reduction in demand/market share.

-    Changes in technology/life-styles etc. This could also reduce demand for the product.

- The adverse variance in the variable costs could have been caused by using a different labour-mix in terms of skill levels and/or using materials of a higher quality than that which was planned.

- Additionally, the assumptions on which the budget was based, could have changed during the budget period and the budget not revised.

(e)   The work in progress will be 100% complete for the input received into the process from the immediately preceding process for materials, layout and overheads.

The value of the material content of work in progress will depend on:

The method of valuation used

The method used to price the materials issued to the process eg, FIFO (first in, first out), LIFO (last in, first out), AVECO (average cost), or standard cost could have a significant impact on the valuation.

Estimating the degree of completion

Unlike labour and overheads which can be semi-complete, the work in progress will be 100% complete for all material which has been used in the process up to the date of valuation.

For example, if the work in progress is estimated to be 70% complete, all the material from the preceding process will be included and so will:

- any material added at the start of the processing, and

- any material added to the processing before it reaches the 70% degree of completion stage, but

material which would be added after the 70% completion stage or at the end of processing would be excluded.

The treatment of losses

In the above example if a loss happens before the 70% completion stage then it should be accounted for and will have an impact on the value of work in progress, and vice versa.

Other considerations

Materials returned and not used in the processing should be adjusted for in the valuation. Also, the value of work in progress could be reduced by a proportion of the sales of scrap which could be credited to the process account.

Note: in addition to the above, answers could have also included a paragraph about the problems of dealing with *normal and abnormal losses.*

(f)   If idle production capacity such as idle plant and machinery can be utilised it could help to improve the profitability of the capital employed in the following ways:

- increasing the marketing effort to bring about an increase in demand for existing products eg, via pricing policies, special promotions, advertising etc.

- accepting special orders which make a contribution towards the recovery of fixed overheads by making use of the idle capacity, however, the contribution generated must be greater than any reduction in fixed overheads which may have taken place if the idle capacity was not used, or greater than any increase in the fixed overheads if the idle capacity is used.

- moving idle plant and machinery to another department or another factory could reduce the amount which has to be expended on new plant and machinery and the associated interest charges etc on the financing of such assets.

- better labour and material utilisation eg, materials which are already in stock could be used on one of the special orders which brings about savings in holding costs

- identifying surplus assets which could either be sold off to improve cash flow and create space or sub-let to a third-party.

---

83   (Answer 3 of examination)

(a)   The advantages and disadvantages (including the motivational aspects) of using the 'full cost' method for dealing with internal service department costs are:

The full cost method is worthy of consideration because it does attempt to ensure that all/most of our internal services costs are recovered in product costs. It also encourages managers to consider the support costs which affect their area of activity and that production is charged with a 'fair share' of the costs.

However, problems can arise from the adoption of such a system particularly where the costs for which managers are responsible are outside their control.

The system can help to motivate managers by making them aware of what such support costs consist of and encourages them to assist services departments in controlling their costs.

However, the motivation of managers could suffer as a result of using such a system where:

- their department/cost centre is revenue earning and their profits distorted because of the subjective nature of the cost apportionments

- they are held responsible for costs over which they have no control

- competition between departments/costs centres could produce conflict as a direct result of 'unfair' allocations/apportionments of expenditure.

Note: (not part of the answer). This 'open-ended' question could include other factors eg, the link with SSAP 9.

(b)   The factors which affect the selection of the bases of apportionment for the costs of internal services, are as follows:

- The service which each service department provides to each other and to each production department.

- Selecting an appropriate base of apportionment eg, number of employees, value of purchase orders, number of stores issue notes, direct labour hours etc.

- The number of departments which have to be serviced and the amount of the overhead expenditure involved.

- Being able to produce realistic technical estimates about the usage of the service.

- The cost/benefit, in terms of the amount of work involved in implementing the system.

It must be noted that certain methods of apportioning internal services do ignore the services provided to other services eg, the 'elimination' (or 'two step') method. Even if the ranking used in these methods is done very carefully the effect on the costs which are apportioned could be quite significant.

(c)   (i)   The 'step-wise' ('elimination') method

	Production depts		Internal services	
	1	*2*	*G*	*H*
	£'000	£'000	£'000	£'000
Overheads	870	690	160	82
G apportioned	96	48	-160	16
				98
H apportioned	61	37		-98
	1,027	775		

(ii)   The reciprocal (simultaneous equation) method
let x = costs of department G
and y = costs of department H
x = 160 + 0.2y
y =   82 + 0.1x
multiply by 10, to eliminate decimals, gives:

$$\begin{array}{rl} & \text{£'000} \\ 10x - 2y = & 1{,}600 \ (1) \\ -x + 10y = & 820 \ (2) \end{array}$$

multiply equation (1) by 5, and add to equation (2), will give:

$$\begin{array}{rll} & & \text{£'000} \\ 50x - 10y & = & 8{,}000 \\ -x + 10y & = & 820 \\ \hline 49x & = & 8{,}820 \end{array}$$

$$\therefore x = \frac{8{,}820}{49} = \qquad 180$$

$$\text{and } y = \frac{820 + 180}{10} = \qquad 100$$

		Production depts	
	Total	*1*	*2*
Internal Services	£'000	£'000	£'000
G (180 × 90%)	162	($\frac{6}{9}$) 108	($\frac{3}{9}$) 54
H (100 × 80%)	80	($\frac{5}{8}$) 50	($\frac{3}{8}$) 30
	242	158	84
Overheads (given)		870	690
		1,028	774

(iii)   The step-wise method is simple to compute. Given that the figures are budgeted figures ie, estimates. The degree of accuracy is questionable, whichever method is used. However, the 'step-wise' method ignores the services provided to other services which have been cleared ie, the service provided by G to H is taken into account but, the service provided by H to G is ignored.

The calculations in this computation are only £1,000 different but, there could be much wider differences. The reciprocal method, does take into account the services provided by internal services to each other and could therefore be considered the more equitable of the two methods.

84   (Answer 4 of examination)

(a)

		Machine group	
Period 2		*1*	*2*
Product			
R (10 × machine hours per 1,000)		750	800
S (25 × machine hours per 1,000)		750	2,750
T (50 × machine hours per 1,000)		2,500	2,500
Budgeted machine hours		4,000	6,050
Overheads (given)		£40,800	£68,365
Machine hour rate		£10.20	£11.30

(b)

		Product Profitability Analysis		
Period 2		*Product R*	*Product S*	*Product T*
	Kilos	10,000	25,000	50,000
		£	£	£
Sales	(A)	110,000	250,000	450,000
Direct materials		45,080	127,400	306,250
Variable labour and overheads		5,650	12,500	16,000
	(see W1)			
Sales commission at 4%		4,400	10,000	18,000
Variable cost	(B)	55,130	149,900	340,250
Contribution	(A)-(B)	54,870	100,100	109,750
Fixed overheads	(W2)	16,690	38,725	53,750
Budgeted net profit		38,180	61,375	56,000

WORKINGS

(W1)

Variable labour and overheads

Machine Group				*Labour and Overhead rate per*		*Products*	
	Direct labour				*R*	*S*	*T*
hours:	*R*	*S*	*T*	*hour*	*£*	*£*	*£*
1	30 :	10 :	20	£7.50	225	75	150
2	40 :	50 :	20	£8.50	340	425	170
					565	500	320
Number of batches				10	25	50	
					5,650	12,500	16,000

(W2)

Fixed overheads

Machine Group	Machine hours			Machine hour rate	Products		
	R	S	T		R £	S £	T £
1	75 :	30 :	50	£10.20	765	306	510
2	80 :	110 :	50	£11.30	904	1,243	565
					1,669	1,549	1,075
Number of batches				10	25	50	
					16,690	38,725	53,750

The net profit figures have been calculated using absorption costing ie, absorbing fixed overheads into the product costs via arbitrary bases such as floor area, number of employees etc, in addition to the variable costs.

The fixed overhead recovery rate uses machine hours ie, an output based measure, when in fact a lot of the fixed overheads will tend to vary more with time than output. Absorption costing is an attempt to ensure that costs are recovered. It does not attempt to provide accurate and realistic product costs. The marginal costing contribution approach, only includes those costs which vary with output ie, the variable costs, and by indicating the amount which each product contributes towards the recovery of the fixed overheads and profit, is considered to be the more appropriate method for decision-making purposes.

(c)   At the outset it should be noted that the budgets are only estimates and that the assumptions on which they were based could change. They provide targets against which the actual performance can be compared as and when the information becomes available.

For decision-making purposes management need to use a contribution approach and also assess where the product is in its life cycle.

The sales of product R are expected to fall. If this continues in the future, the product will be in the decline stage of its *life cycle* and a time could come when its contribution would not cover the fixed overheads assigned to it, meaning that they would have to be recovered out of the contributions generated by the other products.

Product S, if it continues to remain static in terms of the sales demand would appear to have reached its peak. However, there should be a significant increase in period two in its contribution, possibly resulting from increased efficiency, improved productivity and cost reductions.

Product T could well be into its growth stage with an anticipated 25% increase in volume planned for period two. Here also the selling price is expected to remain unchanged and increases in efficiency etc should help to increase the contribution per kilo from £1.89 to around £2.20.

The management need to consider what action they can take to reverse the trends in products S and T and search for new products.

Management also needs to be made aware of the very high proportion of material costs eg, material cost for all products as a percentage of the total cost is over 73%. This high level of investment in materials should make inventory management a very high priority. In order to reduce material costs and expensive holding costs, management will need to monitor and review the situation at frequent intervals. They could consider actions which would reduce waste eg, better design/production methods, or reduce the cost eg, by using substitutes.

Note: it is not necessary to mention and use the keywords relating to the product life cycle in the answer.

85   (Answer 5 of examination)

(a)   (i)   For many firms, trade creditors - suppliers of goods and services - represent the major component of current liabilities, the amounts owed by the company which have to be repaid within the next accounting period.   Together with current assets - cash, stock and debtors - current liabilities determine the firm's net working capital position ie, the net sum it invests in working capital.

Different suppliers will operate different credit periods, but the average trade credit period in days can be calculated as follows:

$$\text{Trade creditors/Credit purchases} \times 365$$

Sometimes, it is expressed in terms of total purchases and sometimes in terms of overall cost of sales. The length of the trade credit period depends partly on competitive relationships among suppliers and partly on the firm's own working capital policy.

The trade credit period is an important element in a company's cash conversion cycle - the length of time between a firm making payment for its purchases of materials and labour and receiving payment for its sales.   The time period over which net current assets have to be financed depends not only on policy towards suppliers but also on debtor management and stock control policy:

Cash conversion cycle =
[Debtor days + stock period] − [trade credit period]

(ii)   In effect, because trade credit represents temporary borrowing from suppliers until invoices are paid, it becomes an important method of financing the firm's investment in current assets.   Firms may be tempted to view trade creditors as a cheap source of finance, especially as in the UK at least, it is currently interest-free.   Having a debtors collection period shorter than the trade collection period may be taken as a sign of efficient working capital management.   However, trade credit is not free.

First, by delaying payment of accounts due, the company may be passing up valuable discounts, thus effectively increasing the cost of goods sold.

Second, excessive delay in the settlement of invoices can undermine the existence of the business in a number of ways.   Existing suppliers may be unwilling to extend more credit until existing accounts are settled, they may begin to attach a lower priority to future orders placed, they may raise prices in the future or simply not supply at all.   In addition, if the firm acquires a reputation among the business community as a bad payer, its relationships with other suppliers may be soured.

(b)   Working capital cycle

At present the working capital cycle is:

Debtor days:	£0.4m/£10m	×	365	=	15 days
Stock days:	£0.7m/£8m	×	365	=	32 days (cost of sales = £10m - £2m)
Creditor days:	£1.5m/£8m	×	365	=	(68 days)
		Total			(21 days)

Clearly, Keswick is exceptionally efficient in its use of working capital.

The proposed arrangement would shorten creditor days in relation to half of cost of sales to 15 days.   The effect is to lower the average to:

$$(\tfrac{1}{2} \times 68 \text{ days}) + (\tfrac{1}{2} \times 15 \text{ days}) = 41.5 \text{ days}$$

Overall, this will increase cycle time to:

$$[15 + 32 − 41.5 \text{ days}] \text{ ie, to } 5.5 \text{ days}$$

Interest cover

At present, interest cover (earnings before interest and tax divided by interest) is:
= £2m/£0.5m = 4.0 times, which is not unduly low.

The advanced payment will raise interest costs but will generate savings via the discount. The discount applies to half of cost of sales, ie, $\frac{1}{2}$ × £8m × 5% = £0.2m. The EBIT will increase accordingly.

The net advanced payment of (£4m − £0.2m) = £3.8m will have to be financed for an extra (68 − 15) days, generating interest costs of:

$$[£3.8m \times 12\% \times {}^{53}\!/_{365}] = £66,214$$

The interest cover slightly declines to:

$$[£2.0m + £0.2m]/[£0.50m + £0.066m] = 3.89 \text{ times}$$

Profit after tax, ROE and EPS

The 'before' and 'after' profit and loss accounts appear thus:

	£m *No discount*	£m *With discount*
Sales	10.000	10.000
Cost of sales	(8.000)	(7.800)
Earnings before interest and tax	2.000	2.200
Interest	(0.500)	(0.566)
Taxable profit	1.500	1.634
Tax at 33%	(0.495)	(0.539)
Profit after tax	1.005	1.095

$$\text{ROE} = \frac{£1.005m}{£2m} = 50.3\% \qquad \frac{£1.095m}{£2m} = 54.8\%$$

$$\text{EPS} = \frac{£1.005m}{£1m \times 4} = 25.1p \qquad \frac{£1.095m}{4m} = 27.4p$$

The proposal appears beneficial to Keswick in terms of the effect on profitability measures ie, EBIT, PAT, EPS, and ROE. However, it does have a marginally harmful effect on its interest cover. It also lengthens its working capital cycle and turns it into a net demander of working capital. This suggests an increase in its capital gearing.

Before the adjustment, gearing at book values (overdraft/shareholder's funds) was:

$$£3.0m/£2m = 150\%$$

The overdraft will increase by:

$$[£3.8m \times {}^{53}\!/_{365}] = £0.55m$$

Ignoring the beneficial effect on equity, gearing after the adjustment becomes:

$$£3.55m/£2m = 178\%$$

This looks rather perilous, considering the short-term nature of much of the debt, and Keswick's low liquidity. Perhaps Keswick should reconsider its policy regarding long-term borrowing, although whether prospective lenders would oblige is probably doubtful.

86   (Answer 6 of examination)

(a)   Sale and leaseback (SAL)

SAL is an arrangement whereby a firm sells an asset, usually land or a building, to a financial institution and simultaneously enters an agreement to lease the property back form the purchaser. The seller receives the purchase price almost at once, but is committed to a series of rental payments over an agreed period, long enough for the purchaser to recoup his initial outlay plus an element of profit. The main advantage to the vendor is the rapidity with which otherwise illiquid assets can be converted into cash. SAL is therefore suitable for capital-rationed companies who are eager to finance expansion programmes before perceived market opportunities evaporate.

The main disadvantage for the vendor of the asset is the loss of participation in any capital appreciation. A further disadvantage is the reduction in the balance sheet value of *owned* assets and hence possible reduction in the company's future capacity to borrow.

Hire purchase (HP)

In an HP contract, equipment is purchased on behalf of the intended user by a finance house, usually a subsidiary of a bank. The user pays a periodic hire charge, commonly monthly. This includes both an interest element on the initial outlay plus recovery of capital. The ownership of the asset passes to the user at the end of the contract period, unless the user defaults on the payment schedule, in which case, the owner can re-possess the asset. To ensure that the asset is worth re-possessing, the hire period is always set at less than the expected useful life of the asset. A feature of an HP contract is that the user, ie, future owner, can claim capital allowances on the initial cost of the asset.

Financial leasing

A finance lease is a contract where equipment is purchased by a leasing company, often a subsidiary of a bank, for long-term hire. The hire period corresponds to the expected lifetime of the asset, and, in most cases, the ownership of the asset does not pass to the user. In the UK, capital allowances are available to the purchaser, and may be passed on to the user in the form of a reduced rental charge. If the owner does relinquish ownership, these capital allowances are clawed back by the tax authorities. In the UK, both the leased asset and the corresponding stream of rental liabilities have to appear on the user's balance sheet. As a result, finance leasing cannot be used to disguise gearing but it is helpful to the capital-rationed firm, and also considerably cheaper than HP.

(b)   For Howgill to break-even, the present value of its after-tax rental receipts must equal the present value of its costs. The cost incurred is the initial outlay on the asset, net of the present value of capital allowances. Given spare capacity in the computer maintenance division, the opportunity cost of using these facilities is zero.

Consider the present value of the tax savings. It is assumed that Howgill can begin to set off the available allowances against profits immediately, ie, beginning in 1996, the financial year in which the acquisition takes place.

				(£m)		
Year	*0*	*1*	*2*	*3*	*4*	*5*
Written-down value	15.00	11.25	8.44	6.33	0	
Allowance claimed	5.00	3.75	2.81	2.11	6.33	
Tax saving at 33%		1.65	1.24	0.93	0.70	2.09
Discount factor at 10%*		0.909	0.826	0.751	0.683	0.621
Present value		1.50	1.02	0.70	0.48	1.30

Present Value of tax savings = 5.00 ie, £5.00m

* Note: This discount rate is found as follows:

15% [1 − 33%] = 10%

(Strictly speaking, the tax delay should also be allowed for. This reduces the effective tax rate to 28.7%, thus yielding a discount rate of about 10.5%.

This effect is not incorporated in this solution but either approach is acceptable.)

The tax savings have a total value of £5m, reducing the effective cost of the equipment to £15m. The present value of the after-tax rentals must therefore at least cover this amount. The rentals are payable from year 0 to year 3 inclusive, while the tax payable on this income will become due at the end of year 1 - 4 inclusive.

Denoting the rental payment as R, we need to solve the following expression (denominated in £m):

15 = R + [3-year annuity at 10% of R] less [4-year annuity at 10% of R times 33%]

ie,

$$15 = R + R [2.487] - R (33\%) [3.170]$$
$$15 = R [1 + 2.487 - 1.046]$$
$$15 = 2.441R$$

whence   R = 6.15 ie, £6.15m is the required annual rental.

(c)   To evaluate the lease decision from Clint's viewpoint, it is necessary to compare the cashflows associated with leasing with those connected with borrowing-in-order-to-buy, using Clint's borrowing cost of 18% adjusted for tax. In incremental terms:

(all figs in £m)

Year	0	1	2	3	4	5
Lease						
Rentals	(7.00)	(7.00)	(7.00)	(7.00)		
Tax savings		2.31	2.31	2.31	2.31	
Net (L)	(7.00)	(4.69)	(4.69)	(4.69)	2.31	
Borrow-to-buy						
Outlay	(20.00)					
Tax savings		1.65	1.24	0.93	0.70	2.09
Net (B)	(20.00)	1.65	1.24	0.93	0.70	2.09
Incremental cash flows [L-B]:						
	13.00	(6.34)	(5.93)	(5.62)	1.61	(2.09)
Discount factor						
at 12%*	1.000	0.893	0.797	0.712	0.636	0.567
PV	13.000	(5.66)	(4.73)	(4.00)	1.02	(1.19)

Net present value = (£1.56m) which argues against leasing.

Note: this discount rate is found as follows:
$$18\% [1 - 33\%] = 12\%.$$

(If the tax delay is incorporated, the discount rate, becomes around 12.8%. Either approach is acceptable).

However, this result overlooks the value of the maintenance costs, which lessees often have to bear themselves. The savings comprise a four-year annuity of £0.75m less a four year annuity of tax payments, but delayed by a year. These have a present value of:

PV of cost savings (£m) at 12%:
$$= 0.75 [3.037] - 0.75 [(33\%) (3.037)]/1.12$$
$$= (2.28 - 0.67) = 1.61 \text{ (ie) £1.61m}$$

These cost savings have the effect of reversing the decision ie, they make the lease worthwhile, viz:

PV of cost savings	=	£1.61m
NPV of lease decision	=	£(1.56m)
Revised value of lease	=	+ £0.05m

However, the decision to lease is highly marginal.

DECEMBER 1996 QUESTIONS

Section A - This question is compulsory and MUST be attempted

87   (Question 1 of examination)

LKL plc is a manufacturer of sports equipment and is proposing to start project VZ, a new product line. This project would be for the four years from the start of year 19X1 to the end of 19X4. There would be no production of the new product after 19X4.

You have recently joined the company's accounting and finance team and have been provided with the following information relating to the project:

Capital expenditure

A feasibility study costing £45,000 was completed and paid for last year. This study recommended that the company buy new plant and machinery costing £1,640,000 to be paid for at the start of the project. The machinery and plant would be depreciated at 20% of cost per annum and sold during year 19X5 for £242,000 receivable at the end of 19X5.

As a result of the proposed project it was also recommended that an old machine be sold for cash at the start of the project for its book value of £16,000. This machine had been scheduled to be sold for cash at the end of 19X2 for its book value of £12,000.

Other data relating to the new product line:

	19X1 £'000	19X2 £'000	19X3 £'000	19X4 £'000
Sales	1,000	1,300	1,500	1,800
Debtors (at the year end)	84	115	140	160
Lost contribution				
on existing products	30	40	40	36
Purchases	400	500	580	620
Creditors (at the year end)	80	100	110	120
Payments to sub-contractors,	60	90	80	80
including prepayments of	5	10	8	8
Net tax payable				
associated with this project	96	142	174	275
Fixed overheads and advertising:				
With new line	1,330	1,100	990	900
Without new line	1,200	1,000	900	800

Notes

-       The year-end debtors and creditors are received and paid in the following year.

-       The net tax payable has taken into account the effect of any capital allowances. There is a one year time-lag in the payment of tax.

-       The company's cost of capital is a constant 10% per annum.

-       It can be assumed that operating cash flows occur at the year end.

-       Apart from the data and information supplied there are no other financial implications after 19X4.

Labour costs

From the start of the project, three employees currently working in another department and earning £12,000 each would be transferred to work on the new product line, and an employee currently earning £20,000 would be promoted to work on the new line at a salary of £30,000 per annum. The effect of the transfer of employees from the other department to the project is included in the lost contribution figures given above.

As a direct result of introducing the new product line, four employees in another department currently earning £10,000 each would have to be made redundant at the end of 19X1 and paid redundancy pay of £15,500 each at the end of 19X2.

Agreement had been reached with the trade unions for wages and salaries to be increased by 5% each year from the start of 19X2.

Material costs

Material XNT which is already in stock, and for which the company has no other use, cost the company £6,400 last year, and can be used in the manufacture of the new product. If it is not used the company would have to dispose of it at a cost to the company of £2,000 in 19X1.

Material XPZ is also in stock and will be used on the new line. It cost the company £11,500 some years ago. The company has no other use for it, but could sell it on the open market for £3,000 in 19X1.

Required

(a)   Prepare and present a cash flow budget for project VZ, for the period 19X1 to 19X5 and calculate the net present value of the project.

(14 marks)

(b)   Write a short report for the board of directors which:

    (i)   explains why certain figures which were provided in (a) were excluded from your cash flow budget, and

    (ii)   advises them on whether or not the project should be undertaken, and lists other factors which would also need to be considered.

(7 marks)

(c)   LKL needs to raise £5 million to finance project VZ, and other new projects. The proposed investment of the £5 million is expected to yield pre-tax profits of £2 million per annum. Earnings on existing investments are expected to remain at their current level. From the data supplied below:

Balance Sheet (extract from last year):

	£'000
Authorised share capital Ordinary shares of 50p each	20,000
Issued ordinary share capital, Shares of 50p each	2,500
Reserves	4,000
10% Debentures (20X4)	2,000
Bank Overdraft (secured)	2,000
	10,500

Other Information: £'000

	£'000
Turnover	55,000
Net profit after interest and tax	3,000
Interest paid	200
Dividends paid and proposed	800

The 50p ordinary shares are currently quoted at £2.25 per share. The company's tax rate is 33%. The average gearing percentage for the industry in which the company operates is 35% (computed as debt as a percentage of debt plus equity, based on book values, and excluding bank overdrafts).

(i)   Calculate and comment briefly on the company's current capital gearing.

Discuss briefly the effect on gearing and EPS at the end of the first full year following the new investment if the £5 million new finance is raised in each of the following ways;

(ii)   By issuing ordinary shares at £2 each.

(iii)   By issuing 5% convertible loan stock, convertible in 20X4. The conversion ratio is 40 shares per £100 of loan stock.

(iv)   By issuing 7.5% undated debentures.

(You should ignore issue costs in your answers to parts ii - iv)

(14 marks)
(Total: 35 marks)

Section B. - This question is compulsory and MUST be attempted

Answer FIVE of the six parts of this question

88	**(Question 2 of examination)**

(a)   Explain the purpose of cartels such as OPEC, and why they are inherently unstable arrangements.

(5 marks)

(b)   Briefly explain why companies issue share warrants and why they may be attractive to investors.

(5 marks)

(c)   For what reasons may a small but rapidly growing company prefer to borrow via a term loan rather than an overdraft?

(5 marks)

(d)   Identify the effects on private sector businesses of a significant public sector budget deficit.

(5 marks)

(e)   Briefly explain the relationship which you would normally expect to find in an information-efficient capital market between relative yields on the following types of security:

-      preference shares
-      corporate bonds
-      equities
-      government stock

(5 marks)

(f)   Briefly explain the relevance of three measures which may be used to assess performance in public sector services which provide education.

(5 marks)
(Total: 25 marks)

Section C - ONE question ONLY to be attempted

89   (Question 3 of examination)

A manufacturing company has provided you with the following data which relates to component RYX, for the period which has just ended:

	Budget	Actual
Number of labour hours	8,400	7,980
Production units	1,200	1,100
Overhead cost (all fixed)	£22,260	£25,536

Overheads are absorbed at a rate per standard labour hour.

Required:

(a)   (i)   Calculate the fixed production overhead cost variance and the following subsidiary variances:

-    expenditure
-    efficiency
-    capacity

(ii)   Provide a summary statement of these four variances.

(7 marks)

(b)   Briefly discuss the possible reasons why adverse fixed production overhead expenditure, efficiency and capacity variances occur.

(10 marks)

(c)   Briefly discuss two examples of inter-relationships between the fixed production overhead efficiency variances and the material and labour variances.

(3 marks)
(Total: 20 marks)

90   (Question 4 of examination)

The following information relates to product J, for quarter three, which has just ended:

	Production (units)	Sales (units)	Fixed Overheads £'000	Variable costs £'000
Budget	40,000	38,000	300	1,800
Actual	46,000	42,000	318	2,070

The selling price of product J was £72 per unit.
The fixed overheads were absorbed at a predetermined rate per unit. At the beginning of quarter three, there was an opening stock of product J of 2,000 units valued at £25 per unit variable costs and £5 per unit fixed overheads.

Required:

(a) (i) Calculate the fixed overhead absorption rate per unit for the last quarter, and

Present profit statements using FIFO (first in, first out) using:

(ii) absorption costing, and

(iii) marginal costing, and

(iv) reconcile and explain the difference between the profits or losses.

(12 marks)

(b) Using the same data present similar statements to those required in part (a), using the AVECO (average cost) method of valuation, reconcile the profit or loss figures, and comment briefly on the variations between the profits or losses in (a) and (b).

(8 marks)
(Total: 20 marks)

Section D - ONE question ONLY to be attempted.

91	**(Question 5 of examination)**

(a) The Treasurer of Ripley plc is contemplating a change in financial policy. At present, Ripley's balance sheet shows that fixed assets are of equal magnitude to the amount of long-term debt and equity financing. It is proposed to take advantage of a recent fall in interest rates by replacing the long-term debt capital with an overdraft. In addition, the Treasurer wants to speed up debtor collection by offering early payment discounts to customers and to slow down the rate of payment to creditors.

As his assistant, you are required to write a brief memorandum to other Board members explaining the rationales of the old and new policies and pin-pointing the factors to be considered in making such a switch of policy.

(6 marks)

(b) Bramham plc, which currently has negligible cash holdings, expects to have to make a series of cash payments (P) of £1.5m over the forthcoming year. These will become due at a steady rate. It has two alternative ways of meeting this liability.

Firstly, it can make periodic sales from existing holdings of short-term securities. According to Bramham's financial advisers, the most likely average percentage rate of return (i) on these securities is 12% over the forthcoming year, although this estimate is highly uncertain. Whenever Bramham sells securities, it incurs a transaction fee (T) of £25, and places the proceeds on short-term deposit at 5% per annum interest until needed. The following formula specifies the optimal amount of cash raised (Q) for each sale of securities:

$$Q = \sqrt{\frac{2 \times P \times T}{i}}$$

The second policy involves taking a secured loan for the full £1.5m over one year at an interest rate of 14% based on the initial balance of the loan. The lender also imposes a flat arrangement fee of £5,000, which could be met out of existing balances. The sum borrowed would be placed in a notice deposit at 9% and drawn down at no cost as and when required.

Bramham's Treasurer believes that cash balances will be run down at an even rate throughout the year.

Required:

Advise Bramham as to the most beneficial cash management policy.

Note: ignore tax and the time value of money in your answer.

(9 marks)

(c)   Discuss the limitations of the model of cash management used in part (b).

(5 marks)

(Total: 20 marks)

---

92   (Question 6 of examination)

(a)   Burley plc, a manufacturer of building products, mainly supplies the wholesale trade. It has recently suffered falling demand due to economic recession, and thus has spare capacity. It now perceives an opportunity to produce designer ceramic tiles for the home improvement market. It has already paid £0.5m for development expenditure, market research and a feasibility study.

The initial analysis reveals scope for selling 150,000 boxes per annum over a five-year period at a price of £20 per box. Estimated operating costs, largely based on experience, are as follows:

Cost per box of tiles (£) (at today's prices):

Material cost	8.00
Direct labour	2.00
Variable overhead	1.50
Fixed overhead (allocated)	1.50
Distribution, etc.	2.00

Production can take place in existing facilities although initial re-design and set-up costs would be £2m after allowing for all relevant tax reliefs. Returns from the project would be taxed at 33%.

Burley's shareholders require a nominal return of 14% per annum after tax, which includes allowance for generally-expected inflation of 5.5% per annum. It can be assumed that all operating cash flows occur at year ends.

Required:

Assess the financial desirability of this venture in *real* terms, finding both the Net Present Value and the Internal Rate of Return (to the nearest 1%) offered by the project.

Note: Assume no tax delay.

(7 marks)

(b)   Briefly explain the purpose of sensitivity analysis in relation to project appraisal, indicating the drawbacks with this procedure.

(6 marks)

(c)   Determine the values of

(i)   price
(ii)   volume

at which the project's NPV becomes zero.

Discuss your results, suggesting appropriate management action.

(7 marks)

(Total: 20 marks)

ANSWERS TO DECEMBER 1996 EXAMINATION

It should be noted that the following answers are probably fuller than would be expected from the average candidate under exam conditions. Answers are provided in this degree of detail on the principle of offering guidance on the approach required, and on the range and depth of knowledge that would be expected from an excellent candidate.

87   (Answer 1 of examination)

Project VZ

(a)   Budgeted Incremental Cash Flows

Inflows:	19X1 £'000	19X2 £'000	19X3 £'000	19X4 £'000	19X5 £'000
Sales (W1)	916	1,269	1,475	1,780	160
Savings, employees made redundant		42	44.1	46.3	
Residual value new machine					242
Material XNT, saving on cost of disposal	2				
(A)	918	1,311	1,519.1	1,826.3	402
Outflows:					
Purchases (W2)	320	480	570	610	120
Sale of old machine not received		12			
Labour:					
Employee promoted	10	10.5	11.03	11.58	
Redundancy pay		62			
Materials:					
Material XPZ, lost residual value	3				
Sub-contractors	60	90	80	80	
Lost contribution from Existing product	30	40	40	36	
Overheads and Advertising	130	100	90	100	
Taxation		96	142	174	275
(B)	553	890.5	933.03	1,011.58	395
Incremental Cash flow (A - B)	365	420.5	586.07	814.72	7

Workings

(W1)

	19X1 £'000	19X2 £'000	19X3 £'000	19X4 £'000	19X5 £'000
Opening debtors	-	84	115	140	160
Add sales	1,000	1,300	1,500	1,800	-
	1,000	1,384	1,615	1,940	160
Less closing debtors	84	115	140	160	-
Cash from sales	916	1,269	1,475	1,780	160

(W2)

	19X1	19X2	19X3	19X4	19X5
Opening creditors	-	80	100	110	120
Add purchases	400	500	580	620	-
	400	580	680	730	120
Less closing creditors	80	100	110	120	-
Cash from purchases	320	480	570	610	120

The net present value of Project VZ

Year	Cash Flow £'000	PV at 10%	P.V. £'000
19X1	365.0	.909	331.8
19X2	420.5	.826	347.3
19X3	586.0	.751	440.1
19X4	814.7	.683	556.5
19X5	7.0	.621	4.3
			1,680.0
Less Initial investment (1,640 - 16)			1,624.0
Net present value			56.0

(b)

3rd October, 19X0

To The Board of Directors of LKL plc
From R.U. Tre-Vere, Accounting and Finance team

Preliminary Report Re-The New Product Line
I have now prepared the cash flow budget enclosed herewith, and computed the net present value of the project.

The cash flows

The principal reason why certain figures were not included in the cash flows is that they are **incremental cash flows** and only include the income and expenditure which will arise **only if the project goes ahead.**

The Following Figures were not included in the incremental cash flows:

-        the feasibility study which cost £45,000 had to be paid out whether or not the project went ahead.

-     the depreciation is a non-cash movement item. The cash expended on the asset moves when it is paid over to the vendor.

-     the three employees paid £12,000 each would continue to receive that amount whether or not the project goes ahead.

-     the cost of the materials XNT and XPZ was paid out some time ago and is not therefore a relevant cash flow.

-     the prepayments were already included in the amounts paid to the sub-contractors and did not require any adjustment to the cash flows. The relevant figures are the actual cash to be paid to them each year, e.g. 19X1 £60,000, and so on.

The net present value (NPV)

The NPV of the project is a positive £56,000. This indicates, that using our cost of capital 10% as our discount rate, the project is wealth creating. However, if the project is considered to be high risk, then the cash flows will need to be discounted at a higher rate to take this into account.

In addition to looking at the cash flows and net present value, other factors will also need to be considered such as: servicing and maintenance, reliability of the plant and machinery, availability of spare parts, retraining of operatives, importing and foreign exchange problems if it is being supplied from another country etc.

Please do not hesitate to contact me should you require further information.

R. U. Tre-Vere ACCA

(c)   (i)   The company's current gearing *(£'000s)*

$$\frac{£2,000}{£8,500} \times 100 = 23.53\%$$

The current gearing position is on the low side, particularly when compared with the industry average of 35%. This provides an indication that the company still has the scope and capacity to attract more debt.

There is however, a large secured bank overdraft, and it is quite likely that quite a high proportion of it represents hard-core debt. It is also most unlikely that the bankers would call in such a large overdraft at short notice. If the overdraft were included in the gearing calculation, and treated as debt, the gearing ratio 38.1% is a little above the industry average.

Current earning per share (£'000)

$$\text{EPS} \quad \frac{£3,000}{5,000} = 60\text{p per share}$$

(ii)   *An issue of ordinary shares*

$$\text{Number of new shares} = \frac{£5,000,000}{£2} = 2,500,000 \text{ shares}$$

		£'000
Earnings Current net profit after interest and tax		3,000

	£'000	
Additional earnings	2,000	
Less tax at 33%	660	1,340
		4,340

EPS $\dfrac{£4,340}{7,500} = 58\text{p per share}$

Gearing $\dfrac{2,000}{13,500} \times 100 = 14.81\%$

More equity would reduce the gearing further. The gearing in the future would also tend to fall due to increases in reserves via retained earnings.

The scheme would reduce the EPS by 2p per share when compared with current earnings. Other considerations which should be looked at are:

-   the control factor i.e. those shareholders who currently control the company could lose control unless they buy some of the shares being offered.

(iii)   *5% convertible loan stock earnings*

		£'000
Current (as above)		3,000

	£'000	
Plus Additional earnings	2,000	
Less Loan stock interest at 5%	250	
	1,750	
Less tax at 33%	578	1,172
		£4,172

Undiluted EPS $\dfrac{£4,172}{5,000} = 83\text{p per share}$

The gearing at the time of issuing the convertible loan stock would be:

$$\frac{£7,000}{13,500} \times 100 = 51.85\%$$

This figure would be expected to decrease in future years as a result of 'ploughing back' profits by way of retained earnings i.e. increasing the equity. On conversion the gearing percentage should fall quite significantly. This would be affected by the retained earnings, new loans taken out and old loans paid off.

The fully diluted earnings per share i.e. where all the holders convert, would be:

Earnings £4,340 as per scheme (i)

$$\text{EPS} \quad \frac{£4,340}{7,000 \text{ shares}} = 62\text{p per share}$$

For the period in which the holders cannot or do not convert the undiluted EPS, (provided earnings remain at this level and tax rates do not change), is much greater, at 83p per share as indicated above.

If and when the holders convert a dilution of earnings will take place and the control of the company may be affected. If the interest rate is fixed, the company would appear to have locked in to quite a low rate compared with the 7½% debentures i.e. the convertibles have a low service cost. The gearing would be well above the current industry average, but on conversion would fall well below it.

(iv)   *7½% debentures*

Earnings	£'000	£'000
Current		3,000
Add Additional	2,000	
Less Interest at 7½%	375	
	1,625	
Less tax at 33%	536	1,089
		£4,089

$$\text{EPS} = \frac{£4,089}{5,000} = 82\text{p per share}$$

The EPS again illustrates that using more debt i.e. becoming more highly geared, can increase the earnings of the Ordinary Shareholders i.e. EPS 82p per share compared with current earnings of 60p per share. However, the increase in gearing, which would be higher than the industry average, does place the increased risk of insolvency on the company. If trading conditions are bad, the company still has to pay the interest on the debentures.

Note (not part of the answer)

Marks would be awarded to those candidates who comment on and/or provide gearing calculations which increase the equity via the estimated retained earnings resulting from investing the £5 million.

---

88   (Answer 2 of examination)

(a)   Cartels are formal agreements among producers, usually of commodities and other homogeneous goods, which are designed to restrict competition in order to yield sustained super-normal profits. Cartels can take various forms, for example, agreements to set a common price and agreements to share out a given market, often on a regional basis. The more comprehensive the agreement, the more closely the behaviour of the industry resembles that of monopoly. Because prices are generally higher and output volumes generally lower than under outright competition, cartels are regarded as potentially contrary to the interests of consumers, if not totally illegal, and thus liable to scrutiny by the competition authorities. The recent investigation of the steel price-fixing cartel by the European competition authorities resulted in heavy fines for several major producers.

In order to operate effectively, a cartel should involve a clearly-specified contract between all suppliers of the product(s) which specifies mutually advantageous prices and volumes. However, lack of information, often deliberately withheld by members, may prevent the cartel arrangement from perfectly replicating the monopolist. In addition to a formal agreement, the cartel needs a policing mechanism to ensure that members adhere to these arrangements. If a member firm believes that it can increase sales volume without fear of discovery, it may hope to increase profits if the market price holds. Generally, however, in markets for homogeneous goods, greater supply will exert downward pressure on the market price and fracture the cohesion of the cartel. The inability to enforce agreed output quotas of member firms plus increased supply from non-OPEC producers, explains why OPEC has been unable to control the world price of oil in recent years.

The experience of OPEC suggests that unless a cartel arrangement is tightly specified and vigorously policed, it is unlikely to offer member firms persistently higher profits than under outright competition.

(b)   A share warrant is an option to purchase ordinary shares, usually attached to issues of fixed interest loan stock. The warrant holder has the right to buy a specific number of shares at a specified price at, or leading up to, a specific date (apart from perpetual warrants which have no time limit).

Warrants have attractions to both companies and investors. They offer investors an opportunity to share in the future prosperity of the company and perhaps make a capital gain should the market price exceed the conversion price at the relevant date. For this reason, the loan stock to which they are attached can often be issued at a coupon rate lower than the going rate for bonds of the appropriate risk. When warrants are exercised by investors other than existing ordinary shareholders, this dilutes the control and earnings of the existing owners. Hence, apart from any interest savings, warrants may not be popular with existing shareholders.

Warrants can be traded separately from the securities to which they are originally attached. They are sometimes called 'geared plays', because variations in market share prices cause more than proportional variations in the market price of warrants. For example, assume that the ordinary shares of ABC plc are trading at £2 each, and that existing warrants entitle the holders to exercise at a price of £1.50. The value of each warrant should thus be £0.50. If the market price per ordinary share rises by 10% to £2.20, the market value of each warrant should rise by (£0.20/£0.50) = 40% to £0.70, the prospective gain on conversion.

(c)   Small firms are often unable to provide suitable security to satisfy lenders' requirements for long-term lending. Consequently, they are forced into using overdraft facilities to a greater degree than larger, more established firms. Overdraft finance has the advantage of incurring interest on a daily basis on the overdrawn balance only, but suffers from certain inherent disadvantages. The attractions of a term loan may best be appreciated by considering these drawbacks.

First, overdrafts are granted for relatively short periods, perhaps six months to a year, and although they may be extended, renewal is not guaranteed. Second, the advance is repayable at very short notice, technically on demand. Demands by the bank to repay at short notice or to accelerate the repayment schedule, may exert intolerable strains on a company's cash flow. Third, they carry variable rates of interest, thereby exposing the company to economic risks outside its control.

By contrast, a loan can be arranged over a term to suit the borrower's needs. So long as the borrower meets the agreed repayment profile (and, in practice, certain other restrictions imposed by the lender), it enjoys unhindered access to the finance for the agreed term, without fear of sudden recall. In addition, the repayment profile may be negotiable to suit the expected cash flow profile of the company. For example, the growing company may be unable to exploit tax reliefs on interest payments in its early years, thus raising the effective cost of finance. In such cases, the bank may consent to an interest holiday, whereby interest is 'rolled up' into the debt. Similar arrangements can be made regarding repayment of capital, ranging from an equal periodic profile to repayment mainly or wholly at the termination of the loan.

Finally, the interest rate can often be fixed, although banks may apply a premium over the overdraft rate for this facility. This has significant advantages for cash flow forecasting. Conversely, if the company is quite well-established and can offer attractive security, the rate of interest may be lower than on an overdraft.

In summary, the advantages of a term loan hinge on its reliability and its versatility regarding initial arrangements.

(d)   Many businesses benefit directly from higher public sector deficits. If these are caused by higher public spending (rather than lower tax revenues), then the sectors where this expenditure is targeted will benefit. Eventually, firms in most sectors of the economy will achieve higher sales, as the multiplier effects spread out across the economy. However, when public sector tax revenue falls short of public expenditure, this creates a need to borrow, termed in the UK, the Public Sector Borrowing Requirement (PSBR).

Among the ways in which the government can finance a PSBR are borrowing from the central bank ('printing money'), borrowing directly from the banking system, or by issuing government securities. These are usually sold by the nation's central bank acting on behalf of the government.

In the UK, Government stock has traditionally been issued on the open market, although since 1995, more reliance has been placed on a system of auctions. In order to pay for stock, individuals and institutions write cheques payable to the Bank of England (BOE), drawn on their own bank accounts, thus establishing a liability for their banks to the BOE. These liabilities are normally settled by the BOE reducing the bankers' operational balances of cash and liquid assets which it holds. As these are not allowed to fall below a defined level, a sufficiently large sale of government stock can exert such pressure on banks' liquidity as to force them to rein back their lending and/or sell securities in the money market to raise cash. An increase in the supply of securities offered to the market will lower their prices and thus increase their yields (assuming they carry a fixed nominal interest rate). These adjustments will cause chain reactions throughout the various sectors of the short-term money market exerting upward pressure on short-term interest rates, and normally, on long-term interest rates as well. Hence, 'the term structure of interest rates' or 'yield curve', will be shifted upwards.

Thus, an increase in public expenditure financed by borrowing raises interest rates generally, thus raising the cost of debt for business borrowers, the higher interest payments eventually worsening their cash flow. It may also cause a fall in share prices which will reduce the ability of companies to raise new equity capital. If, as monetarists believe, the important components of national expenditure are interest-elastic, the increase in interest rates will dampen consumer and business expenditure, thus reducing business turnover and profits. Monetarists also argue that if the additional demand created by the government worsens inflationary expectations, this could cause people to contract economic activity e.g. lower investment expenditure.

In addition, a higher interest rate is likely to strengthen the exchange rate making exports more expensive for overseas buyers and imports cheaper on the domestic market. Hence, exporters will suffer but importers will gain.

(e)   Generally, risk and return are positively related via 'the risk-return trade off' - to encourage rational investors to incur greater risks, they have to be offered the inducement of higher potential returns. In an information-efficient capital market, securities will be priced so as to reflect their relative risks. The current market value of a security is found by discounting the future expected stream of returns at a rate suitably adjusted for risk. Put alternatively, the market price at any time will reflect the required return or yield on that security. It is important to recognise that the yield has two components, the flat yield (the annual payment divided by the present market price), and the potential capital gain. In the case of fixed interest securities, the former tends to be more important, but as the overall risk of the security increases, the potential capital gain tends to assume greater significance. However, there are exceptions e.g. in the case of 'junk bonds' where capital gains are not often expected but the return has to be high to compensate for lack of security.

The securities cited in the question are listed below in descending order of safety i.e. going down the list, the risk, and therefore the required return, increases.

-    Government stock - these are virtually free of default risk as few governments renege on their debt obligations, although the risk of interest rate changes, with the resulting impact on capital values, increases with time. Thus the yield on long-dated government stock is usually greater than on short-dated stock. Given the low degree of risk, the yield on government stock tends to set the benchmark for other yields in the market.

-    Corporate bonds - these do carry default risk, but are usually secured on specific corporate assets (or carry a floating charge).

-    Preference shares - these come in various forms, but generally offer a fixed percentage dividend based on the par value of the share. Sometimes, the holders can participate further in profits if earnings exceed a certain level, and sometimes, the dividend can be passed if company earnings are exceptionally depressed. The precise yield will depend on the type of preference share, but generally they are regarded as more risky than corporate bonds - they have an inferior claim over both company earnings and distribution of the proceeds of a liquidation.

-    Equities - the most risky of all securities, since dividends are a payment out of residual earnings, which are subject to greatest fluctuation. This is due to the effect of inherent business fluctuations and financial gearing (although many companies attempt to 'smooth' dividend payments).

(f)   To ensure that the scarce resources which have been placed at their disposal are used efficiently and effectively, public sector services such as education need to place a high priority on their financial control and performance. There has always been a quest for 'yard sticks' in such organisations i.e. ways in which performance can be measured, compared and evaluated.

One of the measures which tends to be used in education is the amount spent on each pupil/student, i.e. the cost per pupil/student, for each school or college etc. It should be noted however, that the amount spent per head is no indication that the amount involved has been spent wisely and is not necessarily a measure of efficiency. It can be used in two ways:

1.   To support the view that it is possible to provide a similar service at a lower cost, or

2.   By political parties who point to the fact that in their areas of influence, more is spent per pupil/student on education.

Where the educational establishment provides a meals service, comparisons can be made using the cost of each meal served or on a cost per pupil/student basis. Such comparisons would only be valid if the meals mix and volume of meals served were similar. Where the meals service was revenue earning performance could also be evaluated using ratios for profitability etc.

In cases where the educational establishment provides a library, cost comparisons could be made with similar sized libraries using the cost per book, or cost per pupil or cost of new books.

Note (not part of the answer)

Other appropriate measures/cost units could be used e.g. the cost per successful student.

89   (Answer 3 of examination)

(a)   Budgeted fixed Overhead Rate

$$\frac{£22,260}{8,400 \text{ hours}} = £2.65 \text{ per hour}$$

Standard labour hours per unit of production

$$\frac{8,400}{1,200} = 7 \text{ hours per unit}$$

Production fixed overhead cost variance:

Standard labour hours for actual production $1,100 \times 7 = \underline{7,700}$ standard hours

	£
Actual cost	25,536
Less Standard cost $(7,700 \times £2.65)$	20,405
	5,131 (A)*

Fixed production overhead expenditure variance:

	£
Actual cost	25,536
Less Standard cost as per budget	22,260
	3,276 (A)

Fixed production overhead efficiency variance:

Actual hours	7,980
Less Standard hours	7,700
	$280 \times £2.65 = \underline{742}$ (A)

Fixed production overhead capacity variance:

Actual hours	7,980
Less Budgeted standard hours	8,400
	$420 \times £2.65 = £\underline{1,113}$ (A)

    * (A) = Adverse
      (F) = Favourable

Proof   *Production fixed overhead variances:*

	£
Expenditure variance	3,276 (A)
Efficiency variance	742 (A)
Capacity variance	1,113 (A)
Cost variance	£5,131 (A)

(b)   *The production fixed overhead expenditure variance.* This is the difference between the budgeted and actual overhead for the period and provides an indication of the efficiency in keeping to the spending targets which are set.

An adverse variance is an indication of over-spending in one or more of the component parts which make up the overhead cost e.g. rent of premises, light and heat, insurance of buildings etc. The causes of such variances could have been a higher than planned inflation rate, an unexpected outcome to a rent review, colder weather, the area in which the firm is situated becoming a higher risk area for insurance purposes etc.

However, it should be noted that under-spending is not always an indication of efficiency and should be investigated.

The production fixed overhead efficiency variance compares standard and actual efficiency in terms of hours, multiplied by the standard rate applicable to the actual production. An adverse variance means that more hours than planned were taken because of, for example: using different skill levels of labour, poor quality materials which take longer to work on or result in more spoilt work, poor training, poor motivation/morale, poor working conditions, poor supervision etc.

The production fixed overhead capacity variance compares the actual and planned capacity and is the difference between the budgeted and actual levels of activity, valued at the standard overhead rate. Adverse variances could be caused by a failure to attract orders e.g. because of a poor assessment of demand and/or not monitoring competitors. It could have also been caused by machines breaking down e.g. as a result of poor servicing and maintenance, or using defective or poor quality materials, power failures, or labour disputes etc.

(c)   Two examples of the inter-relationships between the overhead efficiency variances and the labour and material variances are as follows:

Using an unskilled or semi-skilled worker to do the work usually performed by a skilled worker will tend to lead to a favourable labour rate variance, an adverse labour efficiency variance and an adverse material usage variance and an adverse overhead efficiency variance.

Using defective or poor quality materials could lead to an adverse material usage variance, an adverse labour efficiency variance and an adverse overhead efficiency variance, and in some cases a favourable material price variance.

---

90   (Answer 4 of examination)

(a)   (i)   Fixed overhead absorption rate per unit

$$\frac{\text{Budgeted FOH}}{\text{Budgeted Production}} \qquad\qquad \frac{£300,000}{40,000} = £\underline{7.5}$$

(ii) *Absorption Costing (FIFO) Profit Statement*

	£'000	£'000
Sales 42,000 × £72		3,024
Less cost of sales:		
Opening stock 2,000 × £30	60	
Add Production 46,000 × £52.5 (W1)	2,415	
	2,475	
Less Closing Stock 6,000 × £52.5	315	2,160
		864
Add Over-absorption (W2)		27
	Profit	891

Workings

		Per unit £
W1	Variable Cost	$45\left(\text{ie, } \dfrac{£1,800,000}{40,000}\right)$
	Fixed O.H. (as above)	7.5
		52.5

W2	Fixed Overhead absorbed	46,000 × £7.5	= 345,000
	Less Actual		318,000
			£27,000

(iii) *Marginal Costing (FIFO) Profit Statement*

	£'000	£'000
Sales (as above)		3,024
Less cost of sales		
Opening stock 2,000 × £25	50	
Add Production 46,000 × £45 (W1)	2,070	
	2,120	
Less Closing Stock 6,000 × £45	270	
		1,850
Contribution		1,174
Less fixed overheads (actual)		318
	Profit	856

(iv)   *Reconciliation*   *Profit*

      Absorption   891
      Marginal   856

                                                            35

      Fixed overheads in Closing Stock
          6,000 × £7.50   45
      Less Opening stock 2,000 × £7.50   10

                                                            35

The difference is explained by the Fixed Overheads being carried forward in stock valuations.

The figures presented using absorption costing (FIFO) give a higher profit because more of the fixed overheads are carried forward into the next accounting period than were brought forward from the last accounting period. The fixed overhead absorption rate is dependent on the estimation of both the production units and the fixed overheads, and as illustrated both may vary when the actual figures are known. Thus, it can be seen that in the absorption costing statement the over-absorption of the fixed overheads have to be adjusted for at the end of the period. In the marginal cost statements the fixed overheads are treated as 'period costs' and not carried forward in stock valuations to the next accounting period. The question of under- or over-absorption does not arise in marginal costing. Marginal costing by using only the variable costs shows how much contribution is being made, and is regarded as giving a more useful set of figures for decision making purposes.

(b)   *Absorption Costing (AVECO) Profit Statement*

	£'000	£'000
Sales		3,024
Less cost of sales		
Opening stock plus production (48,000 × £51.56)	2,475	
Less Closing Stock (6,000 × £51.56)	309	2,166
		858
Plus Over-absorption		27
Profit		885

Marginal Costing (AVECO) Profit Statement

	£'000	£'000
Sales		3,024
Less cost of sales		
Opening stock plus production (48,000 at £44.17)	2,120	
Less Closing Stock 6,000 × £44.17	265	1,855
Contribution		1,169
Less fixed Overheads		318
Profit		851

Reconciliation Difference in profits		34

Absorption closing stock =	309	
Less Marginal closing stock =	265	44

Less Fixed costs in absorption opening stock		10
		34

The variations in the profits in (a) and (b) of £6,000 and £5,000 respectively are caused by using the two different methods of valuation (FIFO and AVECO). The method of valuation can affect the profit and losses for both the absorption and the marginal approaches, and could lead to much wider variations than those illustrated.

---

91 (Answer 5 of examination)

(a)
Memo to:	Ripley plc Main Board
From:	An(n) Accountant
Subject:	Alternative Financial Strategies

The present policy is termed a 'matching' financial policy. This attempts to match the maturity of financial liabilities to the lifetime of the assets acquired with this finance. It involves financing long-term assets with long-term finance such as equity or loan stock and financing short-term assets with short-term finance such as trade credit or bank overdrafts. This avoids the potential wastefulness of over-capitalisation whereby short-term assets are purchased with long-term finance i.e. the company having to service finance not continuously invested in income-earning assets. It also avoids the dangers of under-capitalisation which entails exposure to finance being withdrawn when the company is not easily able to liquidate its assets. In practice, some short-term assets may be regarded as permanent and it may be thought sensible to finance these by long-term finance and the fluctuating remainder by short-term finance.

The proposed policy is an 'aggressive policy' which involves far heavier reliance on short-term finance, thus attempting to minimise long-term financing costs. This requires very careful manipulation of the relationship between creditors and debtors (maximising trade creditors and minimising debtors), and highly efficient stock control and cash management. While it may offer financial savings, it exposes the company to the risk of illiquidity and hence possible failure to meet financial obligations. In addition, it involves greater exposure to interest rate risk. The company should be mindful of the inverse relationship between interest rate changes and the value of its assets and liabilities.

Before embarking on such an aggressive policy, the Board should consider the following factors:

- How good are we at forecasting cash inflows and outflows? How volatile is our net cash flow? Is there any seasonal pattern evident?

- How efficiently do we manage our cash balances? Do we ever have excessive cash holdings which can be reduced by careful and active management?

- Do we have suitable information systems to provide early warnings of illiquidity?

- Do we have any holdings of marketable securities that can be realised if we run into unexpected liquidity problems?

- How liquid are our fixed assets? Can any of these be converted into cash without unduly disrupting productive operations?

-       Do we have any unused long- or short-term credit lines? These may have to be utilised if we meet liquidity problems.

-       How will the stock market perceive our switch towards a more aggressive and less liquid financial policy?

(b)   To determine the net benefits of each policy, both cash costs and opportunity costs have to be considered.

First, consider the cash management costs expected from each policy over the course of the forthcoming year.

Policy 1 Selling securities

The cash transaction costs are partly offset by small interest earnings on the average cash balance held. Transactions costs:

Optimal proceeds per sale:	$Q = \sqrt{\dfrac{2 \times £1.5m \times £25}{0.12}}$ = £25,000	
No of sales	= £1.5m/£25,000 = 60	
Transaction costs	= 60 × £25 =	£1,500
Average cash balances:	= £25,000/2 = £12,500	

Interest on short-term deposits:
Av cash balance × 5%   = £12,500 × 5%   =   (£625)

Total management costs   £875

Policy 2 Secured loan facility

Assuming an even run-down in cash balances:

Interest charges   = £1.5m × 14%   =   £210,000

Offsetting interest receipts:

(= average balance × 9%) $= \dfrac{£1.5m}{2} \times 9\%$ =   (£67,500)

Arrangement fee: =   £5,000

Total management costs   £147,500

Hence, the policy of periodic security sales appears greatly superior in cost terms by [£147,500 - £875] = £146,625. However, this simple comparison ignores the income likely to be received from the portfolio of securities under each policy. By taking the secured loan, the company preserves intact its expected returns of [12% × £1.5m = £180,000] from the portfolio. Conversely, making periodic sales from the portfolio during the year lowers the returns to: [average holding of securities × 12%] = £1.5m/2 × 12% = £90,000.

The net benefits from the two policies can be shown thus:

Security sales
Income from portfolio	£90,000		
Net management costs	(£875)	Net income	£89,125

Loan alternative
Income from portfolio	£180,000		
Net management costs	(£147,500)	Net income	£32,500
		Difference	£56,625

The policy of periodic security sales thus offers greater benefits. However, it is necessary to consider also the company's net worth position at the end of the year ahead. By relying on security sales, the company would avoid the need to repay a loan at the end of the year, but, against this, will have no holdings of securities to fall back on. Moreover, the capital value of this portfolio is uncertain, due to exposure to variation in the return from the portfolio. For example, if money market rates rose over the year, the capital value of the portfolio would probably fall, although the extent of the decrease in value would depend on the nearness to maturity of the securities.

(c)   Some limitations of the simple inventory model are:

-       It assumes a steady run-down in cash holdings between successive security sales. In reality, the pattern of cash holdings is likely to be far more erratic, with exceptional demands for cash punctuated by periods of excessive liquidity. However, the period between sales is short enough and the transaction cost low enough to allow flexibility in cash management.

-       It allows for no buffer stock of cash. In reality, security sales are unlikely to be made when cash balances drop to zero, but when they fall to a level deemed to be the safe minimum.

-       It uses a 'highly uncertain' estimate of the return from the portfolio. Bramham should investigate the implications of assuming alternative (higher and lower) rates, and perhaps determine a 'break-even rate' at which the two policies are equally attractive. In this example, the actual rate would have to be well above 12% to achieve this result.

-       There may be economies in bulk-selling of securities, although exploiting these would increase the holding cost.

92   (Answer 6 of examination)

(a)   In a real-terms analysis, the real rate of return required by shareholders has to be used. This is found as follows:

$$\frac{1 + \text{nominal rate}}{1 + \text{inflation rate}} - 1 = (1.14/1.055) - 1 = 8\%$$

The relevant operating costs per box, after removing the allocated overhead are $(8.00 + 2.00 + 1.50 + 2.00) =$ £13.50. The costs of the initial research etc are not relevant as they are sunk. The set-up cost has already been adjusted for tax reliefs but the annual cash flows will be taxed at 33%.

The NPV of the project is given by:

$$
\begin{aligned}
\text{NPV(£)} \quad &= \quad [\text{PV of after-tax cash inflows}] - [\text{set-up costs}] \\
&= \quad 0.15m\ [20 - 13.50]\ (1 - 33\%)\ \text{PVIFA}_{8.5} - 2m \\
&= \quad 0.65m\ (3.993) - 2m \\
&= \quad +2.6m - 2m \\
&= \quad +0.6m\ \text{ie},\ +£0.6m
\end{aligned}
$$

Hence, the project is attractive according to the NPV criterion.

The IRR is simply the discount rate, R, which generates a zero NPV ie, the solution to the expression:

$$\text{NPV} = 0 = 0.65m\ (\text{PVIFA}_{R.5}) - 2m$$
whence $\text{PVIFA}_{R.5} = 2m/0.65 = 3.077$

To the nearest 1%, IRR = 19%. Since this exceeds the required return of 8% in real terms, the project is acceptable.

(b)   A sensitivity analysis examines the impact of specified variations in key factors on the initially-calculated NPV. The starting point for a sensitivity analysis is the NPV using the 'most likely' value or 'best estimate' for each key variable. Taking the resulting 'base case' NPV as a reference point, the aim is to identify those factors which have the greatest impact on the profitability of the project if their realised values deviate from expectations. This intelligence signals to managers where they should arrange to focus resources in order to secure favourable outcomes.

Problems with sensitivity analysis include the following:

-        It deals with changes in isolation, and tends to ignore interactions between variables. For example, advertising may alter the volume of output as well as influencing price, and price and volume are usually related.

-        It assumes that specified changes persist throughout the project lifetime - e.g. a postulated 10% change in volume may be projected for each year of operation. In reality, variations in key factors tend to fluctuate randomly.

-        It may reveal as critical, factors over which managers have no control, thus offering no guide to action. Nonetheless, it may still help to clarify the risks to which the project is exposed.

-        It does not provide a decision rule e.g. it does not indicate the maximum acceptable levels of sensitivity.

-        It gives no indication of the likelihood of the variations under consideration. Variations in a factor which are potentially devastating but have a minimal chance of occurring provide little cause for concern.

(c)   The values for which NPV becomes zero are found by calculating the break-even values for the selected variables. Once determined, these give an indication of the sensitivity of the NPV to changes in these factors

(i)   Price (P)

$$NPV = 0 = 0.15m [P - 13.50] (1 - 33\%) (PVIFA_{8,5}) - 2m$$
$$whence = 0 = [0.15mP - 2.025] (2.675) - 2m$$
$$0 = 0.4P - 5.42m - 2m$$
$$0.4P = 7.42m$$
$$P = £18.55$$

This means price can drop by [£20 - £18.55]/£20 = 7% from the level assumed in the initial evaluation without making the NPV negative.

needs only 7% to Break case.

(ii)   Volume (V)

Using a similar procedure:

$$NPV = 0 = V[20 - 13.50] (1 - 33\%) (PVIFA_{8,5}) - 2m$$
$$0 = V [17.39m] - 2m$$
$$V = 2m/17.39m$$
$$= 115,000$$

This means volume can drop by [150,000 - 115,000]/150,000 = 23% from the level assumed in the initial evaluation without making the NPV negative.

The results suggest that the NPV of the project is more sensitive to price variations than to changes in volume. Since price seems to be the more critical factor, management might plan to engage in price support measures like advertising and promotional expenditure. It might also attempt to obtain exclusive supply contracts with retailers, although these could violate competition regulations. Measures such as these are likely to be costly, in turn reducing the NPV of the project. It is possible that by making such adjustments, other variables become more critical, necessitating further analysis. At this stage, we might infer that, given the project has a positive NPV of £0.6m, Burley could afford to engage in promotional activity with a present value marginally below this amount over the lifetime of the project.

Certificate Examination - Paper 8   **Marking Scheme**
Managerial Finance

Question 1   *Marks*

(a)   Workings, cash from sales and cash for purchases   3
       Computing/tabulating the cash inflows   2½
       Computing/tabulating the cash outflows   6
       Computing/tabulating the net present value   2½
                                                                 —
                                                            14 marks

(b)   The report - the heading, introduction and concluding statement etc   1½
       Making the point about the incremental cash flows arising
          only if the project goes ahead   1
       Items which were excluded - feasibility study, depreciation, the three
          employees, materials XNT and XPZ, and the prepayments (½ mark each,
          but to include very brief comment on each)   2½
       Comments on NPV e.g. wealth creating, risk etc.   1
       Brief description of other factors which will have to be taken into account   1
                                                                 —
                                                             7 marks

(c)   (i)   Gearing calculation/s and comments   2
       (ii)   Earnings per share calculation   1½
              Gearing calculation and comment   1
              Effect of scheme on EPS and the control factor   1
       (iii) Calculation of undiluted EPS and comments   3
              Calculation of fully diluted EPS and comments   3
       (iv)   Calculation/comments re the EPS   2½
                                                                 —
                                                            14 marks
                                                                 —
                                        Total marks 35
                                                                 —
Question 2

(a)   Explanation of purpose of cartels:
          i.e. to increase joint profits e.g. by supply restriction   2
       Reasons for instability:
          inadequately specified and policed agreement   1
          clandestine output increases   1
          inability to control entry   1
                                                                 —
                                                             5 marks

(b)   Explanation of features and purpose of warrants   2
       Attraction to investors:
          separately tradable   1
          prospect of capital gain   1
          mention of gearing effect   1
                                                                 —
                                                             5 marks

(c)   Problems with overdrafts:
          easily recalled by bank   1
          possible inability to renew facility   ½
          variable interest rate   1
       Advantages of loans:
          fixed term and conditions/easier cash flow planning   1½
          can be 'tailor-made'   1
                                                                 —
                                                             5 marks

		Marks
(d)	Appeal of deficits:	
	higher spending/profits in directly-benefiting sectors	½
	multiplier effects on rest of economy	½
	Problems:	
	effect on interest rates with explanation	2
	effect on exchange rate/impact on exporters and importers	1
	impact on expenditure generally	1
		——
		5 marks
(e)	Concept of risk-return trade off	½
	Components of overall returns	½
	Explanation of risk-return characteristics of each security	4
		——
		5 marks
(f)	1 mark per point explained:	
	The use of scarce resources; measures/cost units in education;	
	how the measures can be used e.g. services at a lower cost/	
	for political purposes; meals service example; library example	
		——
		5 marks
		——
		Total marks 25
		——

Question 3

		Marks
(a)	Calculations	
	Budgeted FOH rate and standard labour hours per unit	1½
	Standard labour hours	½
	Production FOH cost variance	1
	FOH expenditure variance	1
	FOH efficiency variance	1
	FOH capacity variance	1
	Proof	1
		——
		7 marks
(b)	Production FOH expenditure variance ½ to 1 mark per point	
	explained e.g. definition; what an adverse variance indicates;	
	causes of adverse variances; etc.	4
	Production FOH efficiency variance ½ to 1 mark per point	
	explained e.g. what it compares; what an adverse variance indicates	
	plus examples.	3
	Production FOH capacity variance ½ to 1 mark per point	
	explained e.g. what it compares; Causes and examples of	
	adverse variances	3
		——
		10 marks
(c)	1½ points per example of the inter-relationships between the	
	FOH efficiency and labour and material variances.	3
		——
		3 marks
		——
		Total marks 20
		——

Marks

Question 4

(a)
	(i)	Calculation of FOH absorption rate	1
	(ii)	Absorption costing (FIFO) profit statement including the workings	5
	(iii)	Marginal costing (FIFO) profit statement	2½
	(iv)	Reconciliation	1

Explanations:
½ mark per point explained e.g. why the higher profit with
absorption FIFO? rate depends on estimates of production units
and FOH; adjustment needed for over-absorption; treatment of
FOH in marginal costing; etc.   2½
                                                                 ———
                                                              12 marks

(b) Absorption profit statement (AVECO)   3
Marginal costing profit statement (AVECO)   2½
Reconciliation   1½
Brief comment re the causes of variations in profits using the
two valuation methods (FIFO and AVECO)   1
                                                                 ———
                                                               8 marks
                                                                 ———
                                                    Total marks 20
                                                                 ———

Question 5

(a) Explanation of matching strategy   2
Explanation of aggressive policy   2
For each valid issue raised, ½ mark up to max of   2
                                                                 ———
                                                               6 marks

(b) Policy 1:
Use of square root formula   2
Calculation of transaction costs   1
Calculation of interest income   1
Policy 2:
Calculation of net interest costs   1

Comparison of policies with discussions and recommendations:
Simple comparison of cash management costs   1
Recognition of overall net benefits   3
                                                                 ———
                                                               9 marks

(c) For each valid difficulty raised, up to one mark
(but each requires an element of explanation)   (max 5 marks)
                                                                 ———
                                                    Total marks 20
                                                                 ———

Question 6

(a) Specification of discount rate   1
Specification of relevant operating cost   1
Reconciliation of sunk cost   1
Calculation of (after-tax) NPV   2
Calculation of IRR   2
                                                                 ———
                                                               7 marks

(b)   Explanation of role of sensitivity analysis   2
             For each valid difficulty raised, up to one mark,
                (but each requires an element of explanation)   max 4

                                                                     6 marks

(c)   Calculation of break-even values at 1.5 marks each   3
             Recognition of critical factor   1
             Discussion of implications for management action   3

                                                                      7 marks

                                                       Total marks 20

Present value table

Present value of £1 ie, $\dfrac{1}{(1+r)^n}$

where   r   =   discount rate
          n   =   number of periods until payment

Discount rates (r)

Periods (n)	1%	2%	3%	4%	5%	6%	7%	8%	9%	10%	
1	0.990	0.980	0.971	0.962	0.952	0.943	0.935	0.926	0.917	0.909	1
2	0.980	0.961	0.943	0.925	0.907	0.890	0.873	0.857	0.842	0.826	2
3	0.971	0.942	0.915	0.889	0.864	0.840	0.816	0.794	0.772	0.751	3
4	0.961	0.924	0.888	0.855	0.823	0.792	0.763	0.735	0.708	0.683	4
5	0.951	0.906	0.863	0.822	0.784	0.747	0.713	0.681	0.650	0.621	5
6	0.942	0.888	0.837	0.790	0.746	0.705	0.666	0.630	0.596	0.564	6
7	0.933	0.871	0.813	0.760	0.711	0.665	0.623	0.583	0.547	0.513	7
8	0.923	0.853	0.789	0.731	0.677	0.627	0.582	0.540	0.502	0.467	8
9	0.914	0.837	0.766	0.703	0.645	0.592	0.544	0.500	0.460	0.424	9
10	0.905	0.820	0.744	0.676	0.614	0.558	0.508	0.463	0.422	0.386	10
11	0.896	0.804	0.722	0.650	0.585	0.527	0.475	0.429	0.388	0.350	11
12	0.887	0.788	0.701	0.625	0.557	0.497	0.444	0.397	0.356	0.319	12
13	0.879	0.773	0.681	0.601	0.530	0.469	0.415	0.368	0.326	0.290	13
14	0.870	0.758	0.661	0.577	0.505	0.442	0.388	0.340	0.299	0.263	14
15	0.861	0.743	0.642	0.555	0.481	0.417	0.362	0.315	0.275	0.239	15

	11%	12%	13%	14%	15%	16%	17%	18%	19%	20%	
1	0.901	0.893	0.885	0.877	0.870	0.862	0.855	0.847	0.840	0.833	1
2	0.812	0.797	0.783	0.769	0.756	0.743	0.731	0.718	0.706	0.694	2
3	0.731	0.712	0.693	0.675	0.658	0.641	0.624	0.609	0.593	0.579	3
4	0.659	0.636	0.613	0.592	0.572	0.552	0.534	0.516	0.499	0.482	4
5	0.593	0.567	0.543	0.519	0.497	0.476	0.456	0.437	0.419	0.402	5
6	0.535	0.507	0.480	0.456	0.432	0.410	0.390	0.370	0.352	0.335	6
7	0.482	0.452	0.425	0.400	0.376	0.354	0.333	0.314	0.296	0.279	7
8	0.434	0.404	0.376	0.351	0.327	0.305	0.285	0.266	0.249	0.233	8
9	0.391	0.361	0.333	0.308	0.284	0.263	0.243	0.225	0.209	0.194	9
10	0.352	0.322	0.295	0.270	0.247	0.227	0.208	0.191	0.176	0.162	10
11	0.317	0.287	0.261	0.237	0.215	0.195	0.178	0.162	0.148	0.135	11
12	0.286	0.257	0.231	0.208	0.187	0.168	0.152	0.137	0.124	0.112	12
13	0.258	0.229	0.204	0.182	0.163	0.145	0.130	0.116	0.104	0.093	13
14	0.232	0.205	0.181	0.160	0.141	0.125	0.111	0.099	0.088	0.078	14
15	0.209	0.183	0.160	0.140	0.123	0.108	0.095	0.084	0.074	0.065	15

Annuity Table

Present value of an annuity of 1 ie, $\dfrac{1-(1+r)^{-n}}{r}$

where   r   =   discount rate

          n   =   number of periods

Discount rates (r)

Periods (n)	1%	2%	3%	4%	5%	6%	7%	8%	9%	10%	
1	0.990	0.980	0.971	0.962	0.952	0.943	0.935	0.926	0.917	0.909	1
2	1.970	1.942	1.913	1.886	1.859	1.833	1.808	1.783	1.759	1.736	2
3	2.941	2.884	2.829	2.775	2.723	2.673	2.624	2.577	2.531	2.487	3
4	3.902	3.808	3.717	3.630	3.546	3.465	3.387	3.312	3.240	3.170	4
5	4.853	4.713	4.580	4.452	4.329	4.212	4.100	3.993	3.890	3.791	5
6	5.795	5.601	5.417	5.242	5.076	4.917	4.767	4.623	4.486	4.355	6
7	6.728	6.472	6.230	6.002	5.786	5.582	5.389	5.206	5.033	4.868	7
8	7.652	7.325	7.020	6.733	6.463	6.210	5.971	5.747	5.535	5.335	8
9	8.566	8.162	7.786	7.435	7.108	6.802	6.515	6.247	5.995	5.759	9
10	9.471	8.983	8.530	8.111	7.722	7.360	7.024	6.710	6.418	6.145	10
11	10.37	9.787	9.253	8.760	8.306	7.887	7.499	7.139	6.805	6.495	11
12	11.26	10.58	9.954	9.385	8.863	8.384	7.943	7.536	7.161	6.814	12
13	12.13	11.35	10.63	9.986	9.394	8.853	8.358	7.904	7.487	7.103	13
14	13.00	12.11	11.30	10.56	9.899	9.295	8.745	8.244	7.786	7.367	14
15	13.87	12.85	11.94	11.12	10.38	9.712	9.108	8.559	8.061	7.606	15

	11%	12%	13%	14%	15%	16%	17%	18%	19%	20%	
1	0.901	0.893	0.885	0.877	0.870	0.862	0.855	0.847	0.840	0.833	1
2	1.713	1.690	1.668	1.647	1.626	1.605	1.585	1.566	1.547	1.528	2
3	2.444	2.402	2.361	2.322	2.283	2.246	2.210	2.174	2.140	2.106	3
4	3.102	3.037	2.974	2.914	2.855	2.798	2.743	2.690	2.639	2.589	4
5	3.696	3.605	3.517	3.433	3.352	3.274	3.199	3.127	3.058	2.991	5
6	4.231	4.111	3.998	3.889	3.784	3.685	3.589	3.498	3.410	3.326	6
7	4.712	4.564	4.423	4.288	4.160	4.039	3.922	3.812	3.706	3.605	7
8	5.146	4.968	4.799	4.639	4.487	4.344	4.207	4.078	3.954	3.837	8
9	5.537	5.328	5.132	4.946	4.772	4.607	4.451	4.303	4.163	4.031	9
10	5.889	5.650	5.426	5.216	5.019	4.833	4.659	4.494	4.339	4.192	10
11	6.207	5.938	5.687	5.453	5.234	5.029	4.836	4.656	4.486	4.327	11
12	6.492	6.194	5.918	5.660	5.421	5.197	4.988	4.793	4.611	4.439	12
13	6.750	6.424	6.122	5.842	5.583	5.342	5.118	4.910	4.715	4.533	13
14	6.982	6.628	6.302	6.002	5.724	5.468	5.229	5.008	4.802	4.611	14
15	7.191	6.811	6.462	6.142	5.847	5.575	5.324	5.092	4.876	4.675	15

Student Questionnaire

Because we believe in listening to our customers, this questionnaire has been designed to discover exactly what you think about us and our materials. We want to know how we can continue improving our customer support and how to make our top class books even better - how do you use our books, what do you like about them and what else would you like to see us do to make them better?

1 Where did you hear about the ACCA Official Series?

☐ Colleague or friend   ☐ Employer recommendation   ☐ Lecturer recommendation
☐ AT Foulks Lynch mailshot   ☐ Conference   ☐ ACCA literature
☐ Students' Newsletter   ☐ Internet   ☐ Other ....

2 Do you think the ACCA Official Series is:

☐ Excellent   ☐ Good   ☐ Average   ☐ Poor   ☐ No opinion

3 Please evaluate AT Foulks Lynch service using the following criteria:

	Excellent	Good	Average	Poor	No opinion
Professional	☐	☐	☐	☐	☐
Polite	☐	☐	☐	☐	☐
Informed	☐	☐	☐	☐	☐
Helpful	☐	☐	☐	☐	☐

4 How did you obtain this book?

☐ From a bookshop   ☐ From your college   ☐ From us by mail order
☐ From us by telephone   ☐ Internet   ☐ Other ....

5 How long did it take to receive your materials? .... days.

☐ Very fast   ☐ Fast   ☐ Satisfactory   ☐ Slow   ☐ No opinion

6 How do you rate the value of the sections of the Managerial Finance Revision Series?

		Excellent	Good	Average	Poor	No opinion
1	Syllabus and examination format	☐	☐	☐	☐	☐
2	Analysis of past papers	☐	☐	☐	☐	☐
3	General revision guidance	☐	☐	☐	☐	☐
4	Examination techniques	☐	☐	☐	☐	☐
5	Key revision topics	☐	☐	☐	☐	☐
6	Updates	☐	☐	☐	☐	☐
7	Practice questions and answers	☐	☐	☐	☐	☐
9	The New Syllabus Examinations with the examiners' own answers	☐	☐	☐	☐	☐

Continued/...

7 Have you purchased any other ACCA Official Series' titles?
If so, please specify title(s) and your rating of each below:

Title	Excellent	Good	Average	Poor	No opinion
....	☐	☐	☐	☐	☐
....	☐	☐	☐	☐	☐
....	☐	☐	☐	☐	☐
....	☐	☐	☐	☐	☐

8 Have you used publications other than the ACCA Official Series?
If so, please specify title(s) and your rating of each below:

Title and Publisher	Excellent	Good	Average	Poor	No opinion
....	☐	☐	☐	☐	☐
....	☐	☐	☐	☐	☐
....	☐	☐	☐	☐	☐
....	☐	☐	☐	☐	☐

9 Will you buy the ACCA Official Series material again?

☐ Yes   ☐ No   ☐ Not sure

Why? ....

10 Please write here any additional comments you might have on any of the above areas or tell us what you would like us to do to make the books even better:

....

....

....

....

11 Your details: these are for the internal use of the ACCA and AT Foulks Lynch Ltd only and will not be supplied to any outside organisations.

Name
....

Address
....

....

Telephone
....

Do you have your own e-mail address?   ☐ Yes   ☐ No
Do you have access to the World Wide Web?   ☐ Yes   ☐ No
Do you have access to a CD Rom Drive?   ☐ Yes   ☐ No

Please send to:

Quality Feedback Department
FREEPOST 2254
AT Foulks Lynch Ltd, 4 The Griffin Centre, Staines Road, Feltham, Middlesex, TW14 0BR.

Thank you for your time.

ACCA
AT FOULKS LYNCH

HOTLINES	AT FOULKS LYNCH LTD
Telephone: 0181 844 0667	Number 4, The Griffin Centre
Enquiries: 0181 831 9990	Staines Road, Feltham
Fax: 0181 831 9991	Middlesex TW14 0HS

Examination Date: June 97 ☐ December 97* ☐ *Please note that the FA97 Revision Series for taxation papers will be published in June.	Publications			Distance Learning Includes all materials, helpline & marking	Open Learning	
	Textbooks	Revision Series	Lynchpins		Materials	Helpline & Marking
Module A - Foundation Stage						
1 Accounting Framework	£17 ☐	£9.95 ☐	£5 ☐	£79 ☐	£99 ☐	£20 ☐
2 Legal Framework	£17 ☐	£9.95 ☐	£5 ☐	£79 ☐	£99 ☐	£20 ☐
Module B						
3 Management Information	£17 ☐	£9.95 ☐	£5 ☐	£79 ☐	£99 ☐	£20 ☐
4 Organisational Framework	£17 ☐	£9.95 ☐	£5 ☐	£79 ☐	£99 ☐	£20 ☐
Module C - Certificate Stage						
5 Information Analysis	£17 ☐	£9.95 ☐	£5 ☐	£79 ☐	£99 ☐	£20 ☐
6 Audit Framework	£17 ☐	£9.95 ☐	£5 ☐	£79 ☐	£99 ☐	£20 ☐
Module D						
7 Tax Framework (FA96)	£17 ☐	£9.00 ☐	£5 ☐	£79 ☐	£99 ☐	£20 ☐
8 Managerial Finance	£17 ☐	£9.95 ☐	£5 ☐	£79 ☐	£99 ☐	£20 ☐
Module E - Professional Stage						
9 ICDM	£18 ☐	£9.95 ☐	£5 ☐	£79 ☐	£99 ☐	£20 ☐
10 Accounting & Audit Practice	£20 ☐	£9.95 ☐	£5 ☐	£79 ☐	£99 ☐	£20 ☐
11 Tax Planning (FA96)	£18 ☐	£9.00 ☐	£5 ☐	£79 ☐	£99 ☐	£20 ☐
Module F						
12 Management & Strategy	£18 ☐	£9.95 ☐	£5 ☐	£79 ☐	£99 ☐	£20 ☐
13 Financial Rep Environment	£18 ☐	£9.95 ☐	£5 ☐	£79 ☐	£99 ☐	£20 ☐
14 Financial Strategy	£18 ☐	£9.95 ☐	£5 ☐	£79 ☐	£99 ☐	£20 ☐
POSTAGE UK Mainland	£2.00/book	£1.00/book	£1.00/book	£5.00/subject	£5.00/subject	Postage free
NI, ROI & EU Countries	£5.00/book	£3.00/book	£3.00/book	£15.00/subject	£15.00/subject	
Rest of world standard air service	£10.00/book	£8.00/book	£8.00/book	£25.00/subject	£25.00/subject	
Rest of world courier service	£22.00/book	£20.00/book	£14.00/book	£47.00/subject	£47.00/subject	

SINGLE ITEM SUPPLEMENT: If you only order 1 item, INCREASE postage costs by £2.50 for UK, NI & EU Countries or by £10.00 for Rest of World Services

TOTAL	Sub Total £	
	Postage £	
	Total £	

All details correct at time of printing.

Order Total £	

DELIVERY DETAILS

Student's name (print)

Address

Postcode

Telephone   Deliver to home ☐

Company name

Address

Postcode

Telephone   Fax

Monthly report to go to employer ☐   Deliver to work ☐

Please Allow:	UK mainland	- 5-10 workdays
	NI, ROI & EU Countries	- 1-3 weeks
	Rest of world standard air service	- up to 6 weeks
	Rest of world courier service	- 10 workdays

PAYMENT OPTIONS

1. I enclose Cheque/PO/Bankers Draft for £_____
   Please make cheques payable to AT Foulks Lynch Ltd.

2. Charge Access/Visa Acc No: Expiry Date |___|___|___|

   |___|___|___|___|___|___|___|___|___|___|___|___|

Signature   Date

DECLARATION

I agree to pay as indicated on this form and understand that AT Foulks Lynch Terms and Conditions apply (available on request). I understand that AT Foulks Lynch Ltd are not liable for non-delivery if the rest of world standard air service is used.

Signature   Date

Notes: All delivery times subject to stock availability. Signature required on receipt (except rest of world standard air service). Please give both addresses for Distance Learning students where possible.

Source: ACRSF7